George William Cox

Tales of ancient Greece

George William Cox

Tales of ancient Greece

ISBN/EAN: 9783337073688

Printed in Europe, USA, Canada, Australia, Japan

Cover: Foto ©ninafisch / pixelio.de

More available books at **www.hansebooks.com**

TALES

OF

ANCIENT GREECE.

TALES

OF

ANCIENT GREECE.

BY THE REV.

SIR GEORGE W. COX, M.A., BART.

AUTHOR OF "A HISTORY OF GREECE," ETC.

𝔑𝔢𝔴 𝔈𝔡𝔦𝔱𝔦𝔬𝔫.

LONDON:

C. KEGAN PAUL & CO., 1 PATERNOSTER SQUARE.

1879.

𝔅𝔞𝔩𝔩𝔞𝔫𝔱𝔶𝔫𝔢 𝔓𝔯𝔢𝔰𝔰
BALLANTYNE, HANSON AND CO.
EDINBURGH AND LONDON

PREFACE.

———o———

THE Tales collected in this volume have, with
one exception, appeared in the 'Tales from
Greek Mythology,' 'The Gods and Heroes,'
and 'Tales of Thebes and Argos.'

The 'Tales from Greek Mythology' were written for
the use of young children. It has been found necessary
to modify a few of these stories, to bring them nearer to
the level of the rest. The story of the 'Vengeance of
Odysseus' has been added to complete the series of
legends from the Odyssey, so as to give some idea of
that poem as a whole.

In place of the longer introductions prefixed to the
'Gods and Heroes' and to the 'Tales of Thebes and
Argos,' a new introduction is given, tracing each story to
its earliest form, and resolving it into its original elements.
I have here placed before the reader results rather than
proofs. Recent discussions on the subject seem to justify
the conviction that the foundations of the science of
Comparative Mythology have been firmly laid, and that
its method is unassailable. That the story of the Trojan

War is almost wholly mythical, has been conceded even by the stoutest champions of Homeric unity. That it contains some few grains of actual history, is all that they venture to urge ; and to this plea the answer is, that while such possibilities cannot be denied, there is no warrant for a more positive conclusion.

But the very process which has stripped these legends of all value as a chronicle of actual events has invested them with a new and infinitely deeper interest. Less than ever are they mere idle tales to please the fancy or while away a weary hour ; less than ever are they worthless fictions which the historian or philosopher may afford to despise. These legends, taken as a whole, present to us a form of society and a condition of thought through which all mankind had to pass long before the dawn of history. Yet that state of things was as real as the time in which we live. They who spoke the language of these early tales were men and women with joys and sorrows and interests here and hereafter not unlike our own. To turn aside from what they have to tell us is a cold and irrational selfishness; to examine their utterances carefully and patiently is nothing less than our bounden duty. Something they have to tell us of what men thought in times which could not be very far removed from the birth of the human race, of the aspects under which the outward world was presented to their eyes, of the rela- tion which they felt to exist between themselves and the things or beings which they saw and felt on the earth and in the heavens. It is possible that such an examination may impart to us a knowledge which may bring with it both comfort and encouragement : it is idle to check it by uttering set phrases which may convey no meaning even to those who use them.

I gladly acknowledge myself indebted for many valuable suggestions and remarks to M. Baudry, who, with M. Délerot, has translated this series of Tales into French.[1] I may also be permitted to take this opportunity of expressing my thanks for a translation which shows throughout that the task has been a labour of love.

[1] Les Dieux et les Héros : Hachette et Cie.

CONTENTS.

——o——

		PAGE
INTRODUCTION	. . . .	xiii

THE GODS AND HEROES.

		PAGE
I.	THE DELIAN APOLLO	3
II.	THE PYTHIAN APOLLO	4
III.	NIOBÊ AND LÊTÔ	9
IV.	DAPHNÊ	12
V.	KYRÊNÊ	13
VI.	HERMES	15
VII.	THE SORROW OF DÊMÊTÊR	26
VIII.	THE SLEEP OF ENDYMIÔN	30
IX.	PHAETHON	33
X.	BRIAREÔS	35
XI.	SEMELÊ	37
XII.	DIONYSOS	39
XIII.	PENTHEUS	42
XIV.	ASKLEPIOS	44
XV.	IXION	47
XVI.	TANTALOS	53
XVII.	THE TOILS OF HERAKLES	55
XVIII.	ADMÊTOS	62
XIX.	EPIMÊTHEUS AND PANDÔRA	64
XX.	IÔ AND PROMÊTHEUS	67
XXI.	DEUKALION	72
XXII.	POSEIDON AND ATHÊNÊ	75
XXIII.	MEDUSA	79
XXIV.	DANAÊ	82
XXV.	PERSEUS	85
XXVI.	ANDROMEDA	91
XXVII.	AKRISIOS	99
XXVIII.	KEPHALOS AND PROKRIS	103
XXIX.	SKYLLA	112
XXX.	PHRIXOS AND HELLÊ	115
XXXI.	MEDEIA	122
XXXII.	THESEUS	126
XXXIII.	ARIADNÊ	132

PAGE

XXXIV. ARETHUSA 136
XXXV. TYRO 138
XXXVI. NARKISSOS 140
XXXVII. ORPHEUS AND EURYDIKÊ 141
XXXVIII. KADMOS AND EUROPA 146
XXXIX. BELLEROPHÔN 153
XL. ALTHAIA AND THE BURNING BRAND . . . 157
XLI. IAMOS 162

TALES OF THE TROJAN WAR.

XLII. ŒNÔNÊ 167
XLIII. IPHIGENEIA 177
XLIV. ACHILLEUS 181
XLV. SARPÊDON 188
XLVI. MEMNÔN 192
XLVII. HEKTOR AND ANDROMACHÊ . . . 193
XLVIII. THE LOTOS-EATERS 199
XLIX. ODYSSEUS AND POLYPHEMOS . . . 204
L. ODYSSEUS AND KIRKÊ 213
LI. ODYSSEUS AND THE SEIRENS . . . 219
LII. THE CATTLE OF HÊLIOS 222
LIII. ODYSSEUS AND KALYPSO 230
LIV. ODYSSEUS AND NAUSIKAÂ . . . 237
LV. THE VENGEANCE OF ODYSSEUS . . . 241

TALES OF THEBES.

LVI. LAÏOS 263
LXVII. ŒDIPUS 268
LVIII. POLYNEIKES 274
LIX. ANTIGONÊ 277
LX. ERIPHYLÊ 279

MISCELLANEOUS TALES.

LXI. ATYS AND ADRASTOS 285
LXII. THE VENGEANCE OF APOLLO . . . 292
LXIII. THE STORY OF ARÎON 298
LXIV. THE BATTLE OF THE FROGS AND THE MICE . 303
LXV. THE TREASURES OF RHAMPSINITOS . . 309

PRONUNCIATION

OF

PROPER NAMES OCCURRING IN THIS WORK.

———o———

In the present Edition an effort has been made to assimilate the spelling of proper names as nearly as possible to the Greek. An exception has been made in the case of some names, of which the Latin forms are to us familiar sounds, or even household words. Thus it has been thought better not to substitute Kyklôps for Cyclops, or Phoibos Apollôn for Phœbus Apollo. But in general it will be admitted that much is lost by departing from the Greek forms; and the change will have been made to some purpose if it leads even to the partial abandonment of our insular pronunciation of the vowels in Greek or Latin names. We should thus see that in many cases the Latin forms involved no change of sound. The Greek Moirai and the Latin Mœræ were pronounced precisely alike; and the difficulty is at once in great part surmounted if we bear in mind that the Greek *ai* and the Latin *æ* should be pronounced like *ai* in *fail*, the Greek *oi* and *ei* and the Latin *œ* like *ee* in *sheen*.

The following List of Names and Words occurring in this volume is confined to those of which the quantity may possibly appear doubtful to readers not acquainted with Greek.

Achĕlŏŏs	Agāvē	Alkmēnē	Antĭgŏnē
Achĕrōn	Agĕlāŏs	Amāzōn	Aphrŏdītē
Admētos	Aipўtŏs	Andrŏgĕōs	Amphĭārāŏs
Aiăkos	Agŏra	Andrŏmĕda	Amphĭmĕdōn
Aēthlĭŏs	Akrĭsĭos	Amphīōn	Amphĭnŏmŏs
Aiētēs	Alkĭdĭkē	Apătē	Amythāōn
Agamēdēs	Alkĭnŏŏs	Antĭŏpē	Antĭnŏŏs

Arēnē
Arĕtē (Virtue, p. 72)
Arētē, mother of Nausĭkăā
Argŭphĕa
Arīon
Artĕmĭs
Asklēpĭos
Astўănax
Athămas
Athēnē
Autŏlўkŏs
Autŏmĕdōn
Autŏnŏŏs
Axўlos
Bĕrŏē
Bŏrĕas
Boibēĭs
Bălĭŏs
Brĭărĕōs
Chărĭtĕs
Cyclōpĕs
Dănăē
Deĭpўlē
Deĭăneira
Dēmētēr
Deukălĭōn
Dĭŏnўsos
Doulĭchíon
Dĭŏmēdēs
Dōdōna
Eĕtĭōn
Endўmĭōn
Enīpeus
Enkēlădŏs
Epăphŏs
Epĭgŏnoi
Epĭmētheus
Erĭphўlē
Etĕŏklēs
Ergīnŏs
Eumĕnĭdĕs
Eurīpŏs

Erīnўs
Erīnўĕs
Eurōpa
Eurōtas
Eurўălē
Eurўlŏchŏs
Eurўmăchŏs
Eurўtŏs
Eurўdīkē
Eurўnŏmē
Harmŏnĭa
Hĕkăbē
Hĕkătē
Hĕlĕnŏs
Hespĕrŏs
Hespĕrĭdĕs
Hēlĭos
Hērăklēs
Hēsĭŏneus
Hўpĕrīon
Ilĭon
Iphĭtŏs
Iăsīon
Iămŏs
Idŏmĕneus
Ithăka
Ixīon
Ismēnē
Iŏlē
Kăpăneus
Kălўdōn
Klĕŏbis
Klўmĕnē
Kourētēs
Kĕlĕŏs
Kĕphălŏs
Kēphīsos
Kerbĕros
Kolōnos
Kўbēbē
Kўrēnē
Kyllēnē
Kŏrōnis
Krommўōn

Lampĕtĭē
Lăŏdămeia
Lăŏdīkē
Lăŏmĕdōn
Lāĭŏs
Labdăkŏs
Leiōdēs
Lykāōn
Lўkŏsoura
Mărăthōn
Melanthĭos
Medūsa
Malĕa
Mænălos
Mykēnæ
Mĕgără
Mĕrŏpē
Nausĭkăā
Nĭobē
Nĕphĕlē
Nērĭtos
Œchălĭā
Œdĭpūs
Okălĕa
Œnōnē
Ogўgĭa
Okĕănos
Omphălē
Orchŏmĕnŏs
Orīōn
Ortўgĭa
Ourănos
Paiēōn
Pandīōn
Pandōra
Pandărĕōs
Pătăra
Peirĭthŏŏs
Pēgăsos
Pĕlĭas
Pēnĕlŏpē
Persĕphŏnē
Phăĕthōn
Phaĕthoūsa

Philoktētēs
Phlĕgўas
Phlĕgўĕs
Phўlăkŏs
Polyphēmos
Pīĕrĭa
Phaisăna
Pēlĭōn
Phĕræ
Phĕrēs
Perĭphētēs
Pŏlўbos
Promētheus
Prŏdĭkos
Salmōneus
Sarpēdōn
Sĕlēnē
Sĕmĕlē
Sĕrīphos
Sĭdērō
Sĭmŏeĭs
Sĭpўlos
Stymphālos
Symplēgădĕs
Tænăron
Tantălos
Tēlĕmos
Tēlĕmăchos
Teutămĭdas
Teirĕsĭas
Tēlĕphassa
Telphūsa
Thănătŏs
Thĕŏdōros
Thēra
Thersītēs
Thrinăkĭa
Tithōnos
Tlēpŏlĕmos
Trāchis
Trŏphōnĭos
Tўphāōn
Typhōeūs
Theoklўmĕnos

INTRODUCTION.

———o———

THE results obtained from the examination of **Language in its several** forms leave no room for doubt **that the great** stream of mythology has been traced **to its fountain-head.** We can no longer shut our **eyes** to the **fact** that there **was a** stage in **the** history of human speech, during which **all the abstract** words **in** constant use among ourselves were **utterly unknown,** when **men** had formed no notions **of virtue or prudence, of** thought **and** intellect, of slavery **or freedom,** but spoke only of **the man who** was strong, **who could point the** way to others **and** choose one thing out of many, of the man **who was bound to any other or able to do as he** pleased.

That **even** this **stage** was **not the earliest in the** history of language is now **a** growing opinion among philologists ; but for **the** comparison of legends current **in** different countries **it is** not necessary **to** carry the search further back. Language without words denoting abstract qualities implies a condition of thought in which men were only awakening to a sense of the objects which surrounded them, and points **to** a time when **the world** was to them full of strange **sights** and sounds, some beautiful, some bewildering, some terrific, when, in short, **they knew** little of themselves **beyond** the vague consciousness **of** their existen**ce, and nothing of** the **phenomena of the** world without. **In** such **a** state they could **but** attribute to all that they **saw or** touched or heard **a life which was like** their own in its consciousness, its joys, and its sufferings. That power of sympathising with nature which we are apt to regard as the peculiar gift of the poet was then shared alike by all. This sympathy was not the result of any effort. It was inseparably bound up with the words which rose to their lips. It implied no special purity of heart or mind; it pointed to no Arcadian paradise where shepherds knew not how to wrong or oppress or torment each other. We say that the morning light rests on the mountains; they said that the sun was greeting his bride, as naturally as our own poet would speak of the sunlight clasping the earth, or the moonbeams as kissing the sea.

We have then before us a stage of language corresponding to a stage in the history of the human mind, in which all sensible objects were regarded as instinct with a conscious life. The varying phases of that life were therefore described as truthfully as they described their own feelings or sufferings; and hence every phrase became a picture. But so long as the conditions of their life remained unchanged, they knew perfectly what the picture meant, and ran no risk of confusing one with another. Thus they had but to describe the things which they saw, felt, or heard, in order to heap up an inexhaustible store of phrases faithfully describing the facts of the world from their point of view. This language was indeed the result of an observation not less keen than that by which the inductive philosopher extorts the secrets of the natural world. Nor was its range much narrower. Each object received its own measure of attention, and no one phenomenon was so treated as to leave no room for others in their turn. They could not fail to note the changes of days and years, of growth and decay, of calm and storm; but the objects which so changed were to them living things, and the rising and setting of the sun, the return of winter and summer, became a drama in which the actors were their enemies or their friends.

That this is a strict statement of facts in the history of the human mind, philology alone would abundantly prove; but not a few of these phrases have come down to us in their earliest form, and point to the long-buried stratum of language of which they are the fragments. These relics exhibit in their germs the myths which afterwards became the legends of gods and heroes with human forms, and furnished the groundwork of the epic poems, whether of the Eastern or the Western world.

So **long** as we do not suppose that this great fabric **was reared** by system, it matters little how we **arrange** the legends of which it is made up. We may take the daily alternation of light and darkness, or the yearly changes of summer and winter, so long as we do not fancy that these old phrases spoke only of the sun in his daily course, or only of vapours and storms. The mythical or myth-making language of mankind had no partialities ; and if the career of the sun occupies a large extent of the horizon, **we** cannot fairly simulate ignorance of the cause.

Men **so placed** would not fail to put into words the thoughts or emotions roused in **them** by the varying phases **of that** mighty world **on** which we, not less than they, feel **that our** life depends, although we may know something **more** of its nature.

Thus grew up a multitude of expressions which described the sun as the child of the night, as the destroyer of the darkness, as the lover of the dawn and the dew—of phrases which would go on to speak of **him** as killing the dew with his spears, and of forsaking the dawn as he rose in the heaven. The feeling **that** the fruits of the earth were called forth by his warmth would find utterance in words which spoke of him as the friend and the benefactor of man ; while the constant recurrence of his work would lead them to describe him as a being constrained to toil for others, as doomed to travel over many lands, and as finding everywhere things on which he could bestow his love or which he might destroy by his power. His journey, again, might be across cloudless skies, or amid alternations **of** storm and calm ; his light might break fitfully through the clouds, or be hidden for many a weary hour, to burst forth at last with dazzling splendour as he sank down in the western sky.

He would thus be described as facing many dangers and many enemies, none of whom, however, may arrest his course ; as sullen, or capricious, or resentful; as grieving for the loss of the dawn whom he had loved, or as nursing his great wrath and vowing a pitiless vengeance. Then as the veil was rent at eventide, they would speak of the chief, who had long remained still, girding on his armour ; or of the wanderer throwing off his disguise, and seizing his bow or spear to smite his enemies ; of the invincible warrior whose face gleams with the flush of victory when the fight is over, as he greets the fair-haired Dawn who closes as she had begun the day. To the wealth of images thus lavished on the daily life and death of the sun there would be no limit. He was the child of the morning, or her husband, or her destroyer ; he forsook her and he returned to her, either in calm serenity or only to sink presently in deeper gloom.

So with other sights and sounds. The darkness of night brought with it a feeling of vague horror and dread ; the return of daylight cheered them with a sense of unspeakable gladness ; and thus the sun who scattered the black shades of night would be the mighty champion doing battle with the biting snake which lurked in its dreary hiding-place. But as the sun accomplishes his journey day by day through the heaven, the character of the seasons is changed. The buds and blossoms of spring-time expand in the flowers and fruits of summer, and the leaves fall and wither on the approach of winter. Thus the daughter of the earth would be spoken of as dying or as dead, as severed from her mother for five or six weary months, to be restored to her again until the time for her return to the dark land should once more arrive. But as no other power than that of the sun can recall vegetation to life, this child of the earth would be represented as buried in a sleep from which the touch of the sun alone could rouse her, when he slays the frost and cold which lie like snakes around her motionless form.

It is unnecessary to multiply instances for the sake of showing that this language was the perfectly natural and even involuntary utterance of thoughts awakened, not by

one or another, but by all the phenomena of the outward
world. Winds and storms, thunder and lightning, drought,
famine and pestilence, mists and vapours, were all endowed
with the same life in a language which could adapt itself
with a boundless elasticity to all physical conditions whatsoever. The thunder became the dark speech of the cloud
which brought sickness and death. The eye of light which
glares down through the dense storm vapours was the eye
of the monstrous child sprung from the union of the earth
and the sea. If drought scorched the crops, it was because
the chariot of the sun approached too near to the earth.
If the storm kindled the forests into flame, it was because
the wind was hungry ; and if the fire alone devoured that
which came in its way, it was because the wind, though
able to kindle fire, could not satisfy with food the cravings
of its hunger.

It would therefore be a grave error to suppose that the
form of thought which laid the foundations of the most
complicated mythology found utterance in phrases applicable
only to one particular set of phenomena, instead of embrac-
ing all alike in proportion to the impression made by them
on their imaginations, their hopes, and their fears. That
these phrases would furnish the germs of myths or legends
teeming with human feeling, as soon as the meaning of the
phrases was in part or wholly forgotten, was as inevitable as
that in the infancy of our race men should attribute to all
sensible objects the same kind of life which they were conscious of possessing themselves. To trace back the theft
of the Golden Fleece or the fair-haired Helen to the theft
of the light from the sky by the dark night, to refer the
wrath of the great chieftain of Phthia to the grief of the sun
for the loss of the morning, may appear like the reduction
of a complicated tale to a form too simple to be consistent
with facts. But the objection applies with neither more nor
less force to the phenomena of speech, in which it seems
impossible to resist the conclusion that ' the final perfection
of the noblest languages has been **the result** of a slow and
gradual development, under the impulse of tendencies and

through the instrumentality of processes, which are even yet active in every living tongue ; that all this wealth has grown by long accumulation out of an original poverty ; and that the actual germs of language were a scanty list of formless roots, representing a few of the most obvious sensible acts and phenomena appearing in ourselves, our fellow-creatures, and the nature by which we are surrounded.' [1]

The mythology of the Greeks exhibits the impressions made by a vast range of phenomena, although the climatic conditions of the Hellenic land would necessarily bring into prominence the career of the sun in his daily journey through the heaven rather than the interchange of summer and winter. That nothing more would be needed for the growth of legends capable of being expanded into any number of epic poems, the history of Greek epical literature abundantly proves ; and we have only to see now that the most intricate myths have earlier forms in which the physical meaning of the phrases employed is no longer a matter of doubt.

Of the two legends narrated in the poems afterwards combined in the Hymn to Apollo, the former (I.) relates the birth of the sun from the darkness, which is called his mother. The wanderings of Lêtô, which represent the weary march of the night before the day breaks, come to an end, as they could find an end, only in Delos, the bright land. Why the myth should be localised especially in the barren island of the Egean sea, is a question with which we are not much concerned, although the meaning of local names is a subject of no little interest. It may be enough to say that a multitude of names are but translations of that of Delos, that Sarpêdon and Glaukos are alike born in the Lykian land of light, that Zeus is nursed in the cave of Dictê, that the Hellenes themselves are the children of the Sun, and that the same idea is set forth in the names of Athens, Arkadia, Lykosoura, Argos, Europa. At length the child is born, and a halo of serene light encircles his cradle where the nymphs bathe him in pure water and gird a broad golden

---

[1] Whitney, On Language and the Study of Language, p. 398.

band around his form. Here, then, in Delos, is for a while the place of his rest; and to Delos, after all his wanderings, he returns with undiminished gladness, just as each day the sun reappears in the east with undiminished splendour.

But as the minutes go by, the sun rising in the heavens is invested with a more dazzling majesty, and he becomes Chrysâôr, the lord of the golden sword, the invincible weapon which never misses its mark. Now begins (II.) his westward journey to Pytho, so named, the story went, because the sun-god there slew the great dragon which meets its doom at the hand of every solar hero, as Vritra, the biting snake, who lurks in the dark cloud, is smitten by the club of Indra, the rain-giver. The rest of the legend accounts for the greatness of the Delphian temple, and the pre-eminence of the oracle which was inspired with the wisdom of Apollo.

In the tale of Niobê (III.) Phœbus is seen armed with his irresistible arrows, dealing death to all at whom he aims them. The beauty of the children of Niobê is the beauty of clouds flushed with the light of morning, which are scattered presently from before the face of the morning sun. Her tears are the rain-drops which turn to ice on the mountain-summits, where men fancy that they see her form hardened into stone.

The story of Daphnê (IV.) is but one of a large class of legends which relate the love of the Sun for the Dawn, who flies at his approach, and at length, as he draws nearer to her, vanishes away. Still, although his first love is gone, other brides await him in other lands; but in the tale of Kyrênê (V.) we have an instance of mythological language applied to an event to which we may assign something of an historical character in its bare outline. The myth, which spoke of the maiden whom Apollo loved and carried to Libya, thus represents the fact that 'the town of Kyrênê in Thessaly sent a colony to Libya under the auspices of Apollo.'[1]

1 Max Müller, Comparative Mythology, Chips from a German Workshop, ii. 68.

The legend of Hermes (VI.) is so transparent, that the clue being once furnished, we trace with ease the old mythical phrases even in the minutest details. Hermes, the being who *moves*, is simply air in motion, which in one hour may breathe as softly as a child in its cradle, and in the next may tear up forests in its rage. If his fury may appal, in his gentler moments he soothes and charms us, for the gift of music is his birthright, just as an incommunicable wisdom is the heritage of the sun, who can pry into the depths of the sea which no winds can ever stir. The child drives before him the cattle of Phœbus, as the bright clouds are driven across the heaven by the breeze of an hour old. But Hermes, with his tamarisk sandals, makes strange marks on the sands of the plain ; as we should say, the wind strengthens, and tosses the leaves and branches across the road tracks. And still the wind moves until the branches which it has rubbed together burst into a blaze and consume the flesh with which the hungry Hermes may not appease his hunger. Onward yet it goes, but more slowly, until with a faint sigh it sinks to rest once more like a child in its cradle. But the mischief which it has done remains, and Phœbus, the lord of the bright clouds which the wind drove across the sky, comes to search for them. From this old phrase sprang up the legend of the rivalry of Hermes and Apollo, for the sun envied to Hermes his gift of song, whether it be sweet and soft, stirring or sublime, while the wind would have from the Sun-god his power of piercing the hidden depths into which the wind cannot find its way. The exchange can be made only in part : the Sun will place his bright cattle in charge of the wind, who shall drive them to their pastures, and the wind will waken the softer music of his harp when Phœbus journeys across the blue skies of summer. Throughout, even in its minutest touches, the myth is faithful to its leading idea. The capriciousness of the wind, shown in the sudden gust which makes Phœbus loose his hold of the child, his prying search into every nook and cranny, his mocking laugh at the folk who come to see the mischief wrought by him, his twistings and turnings, his shifty evasions, his downright lies, his gentleness and his rage, the gigantic strength which he can put forth **at** will, the sweet repose to which he can return at pleasure, all stand out with life-like fidelity as characteristics of the wind in contrast to the absolute truthfulness, the searching glance, and the boundless knowledge of the lord of light.

The myth of the Sorrow of Dêmêtêr (VII.) brings us to the great subject of the mythology of Northern Europe. The absence of Persephonê in the dark land of Hades is the sleep of Brynhild within the coils of the dragon on the Glistening Heath. Her departure is the death of the summer, when the earth seeks in vain for the fruits and flowers which had gladdened her since the days of spring. Here, as in the myth of Hermes, Hêlios alone can tell Dêmêtêr whither her child is gone. The sun alone can see where the summer has been hidden away. The key once given, the legend explains itself. As Sigurd wakens Brynhild, so Hermes brings Persephonê to Dêmêtêr, and the six or seven months of summer begin again, when the grief **of the** mourning mother has passed away.

The myth **of** Endymiôn (VIII.) is even more transparent. Indeed, it has scarcely reached that crystallised state in which alone a myth strictly deserves the name. The rays of the setting sun rest on the peaceful valley which glistens with its radiance; the moon comes forth to gaze on the setting sun; she asks him to journey with her **to** other **lands, but he** cannot do so, and **as** her eyes still remain fixed upon him, he plunges suddenly into the dreamless sleep of the Latmian land.

'One who cannot guide the fiery horses sits in the chariot of the sun.' So ran the phrase which, scarcely disguised in the brief myth of Phaethon (IX.), rose naturally to the lips of men when all herbage was scorched and withered in times of drought. In his brightness Phaethon resembles Hêlios, but he is not the same being; he lacks either his wisdom or his strength. The story is repeated in the legends of Patroklos and Telemachos, who faintly reflect the power and majesty of Achilleus and Odysseus. The

thunderbolt which smites Phaethon in the chariot is the
lightning ushering in the storm which brings rain to the
parched earth.

The monstrous forms assumed by clouds and vapours
are seen in their most terrific aspect in Briareôs (X.), the
giant with the hundred arms, while the majesty of the
heaven when clothed in its robe of storms finds expression
in the myth of Semelê (XI.), the daughter of the king who
came to his home in the West from the purple land of
morning. But the rain-storms quicken the vine plants;
and the child of Semelê is born amid the din of the thunder
and the blaze of the lightnings. Thus the lord of the vine
and of the teeming fruits of earth grows up, like Hermes, a
being of mighty strength, capable of doing wondrous things
at will—soothing, irritating, or maddening the minds of
men, whether as the Hellenic Dionysos (XII.) or as the
Soma of the Hindoo. The strange rites of the women who
follow him are the frantic revels of worshippers excited by
wine; but the story of his return to Thebes, of the resistance which he encounters at the hands of the Thrakian
Lykourgos or the Kadmeian Pentheus (XIII.), points to a
change in the religious system of the Hellenic tribes, and
would thus denote an historical fact. The myth would
seem further to show that the change came from the East,
and that in it we have a point of affinity to Syrian systems
like that which is furnished by the myths of Tammuz and
Adonis.

The desertion of Korônis (XIV.) by Phœbus is precisely
parallel to the desertion of Prokris (XXVIII.) by Kephalos.
In both it is the crystallisation of the mythical phrase, ' The
sun kisses the dew, and the dew is faithless.' Each dew-
drop reflects its peculiar image, yet it is the image of the
same object. Hence in the story of Prokris the new lover
is Kephalos himself in disguise; in that of Asklepios,
Korônis gives her love to Ischys, a name which simply
denotes the sun in his strength as contrasted with his
gentler aspect on his rising. The doom which lies on
Daphnê (IV.), Arethusa (XXXIV.), and Prokris, lies also

on Korônis ; but her child Asklepios represents the
wisdom and beneficence of the bright being who brings
light and life to men. The sun wakens the earth to life
when the winter is done ; and thus Asklepios was the
raiser of the dead, until, like Semelê, he was smitten by the
thunderbolts of Zeus. The wrath of Apollo on his death is
but another form of the sorrow of Dêmêtêr, while the bondage to which he is doomed in the house of Admêtos is the
subjection of Herakles to Eurystheus, of Achilleus to
Agamemnon, the toil of the mighty sun for weak and
mortal man.

Whatever be the origin of the name, Ixion (XV.) is the
sun of noonday, whose four-spoked wheel, in the words of
Pindar, is seen whirling in the highest heaven. His wife
Dia (the pure air of morning) is the child of the darkness
which will gaze on the treasures of the sun, although warned
that he cannot do so and live. But the doom which requites
his rashness brings on Ixion the guilt of his death, and Ixion
ascends to the throne of Zeus in the highest æther to receive
purification, as the sun leaves beneath him the vapours
which soil his brightness. In this abode of unsullied purity
he sees the face of Hêrê (the cloudless air), and seeks to
win her love. But Zeus cheats him with a phantom and
binds him to the blazing wheel which revolves eternally in
the heaven.

The punishment of the Sun comes before us again in the
story of the Phrygian Tantalos (XVI.), whose palace is like
the house of Hêlios in its dazzling splendour. In Tantalos
also we have the wisdom of Hêlios, of Phœbus, and of the
wise man Sisyphos ; the wisdom which Hêlios gives to
Medeia, but which Phœbus cannot give to Hermes. At
first his action is purely beneficent, like that of the sun in
the genial spring ; but the heat becomes more fierce, and as
the phrase went, 'The Sun slays the fruits which he wakened
into life,' so it was said that Tantalos had slain his son and
spread his scorched limbs in the face of Zeus, the high
heaven, and that he had met his doom. The more that
the blazing Sun looks down on fruits and flowers or spark-

ling waters, the more do they droop and die, and the stream-beds are turned into slime, while over his head beetles the frowning mass of cloud like that which hangs over Thebes, while the Sphinx (the demon of the thunder) utters her dark sayings.

The bondage of Apollo, which concludes the myth of Asklepios, is the leading idea of the almost endless series of legends which, without any fixed order or system, relate the toils of Herakles (XVII.) Throughout, Herakles is the toiling sun, labouring for the benefit of others, not his own, and doing hard service for a mean and cruel taskmaster. Almost at his birth **he** strangles the serpents of darkness, and goes upon his way full of strength and beauty. Temptations to sloth and luxury are offered to him in vain. He has his work to do, and nothing can stay him from doing it, as nothing can arrest the sun in his journey through the heaven. Like all the other solar heroes, he has his early love, and Iolê here plays the part of Daphnê. Of his toils it is scarcely necessary to speak in detail. They are but a thousand variations on the story of the great conflict which Indra wages against Vritra, the demon of darkness. He has his brides in all lands, as the fruits of the earth ripen everywhere under the genial rays of the sun. But although he wins Dêianeira, he may not tarry in Kalydon. He yet must reach the goal, and there, when he offers up his great sacrifice, he puts on the robe by which Dêianeira hoped to win back his love for herself, the coat, in Professor Max Müller's words, ' which in the Veda the mothers weave for their bright son ; the clouds which rise from the waters and surround the sun like a dark raiment. Herakles tries to tear it off ; his fierce splendour breaks through the thickening gloom, but fiery mists embrace him and are mingled with the parting rays of the sun, and the dying hero is seen through the scattered clouds of the sky, tearing his own body to pieces, till at last his bright form is consumed in a general conflagration.'[1] But Iolê stands by his

---

[1] Chips from a German Workshop, ii. 89.

side, cheering him to the last, and thus the fair-haired Dawn closes, as it had begun, the day.[1]

In the myth of Admêtos (XVIII.) Herakles reappears as the kindly benefactor, who goes down into the dark land and there wrests from the grasp of death the fair twilight, which dies away at sundown, to be brought back again in the morning.

The myth of Epimêtheus (XIX.) is in part a mere institutional legend to account for the assignment of the bones and fat as the portion of the gods in burnt sacrifices, just as the story of Poseidon and Athênê (XXII.) is devised to explain the name of Athens, the city of the dawn-goddess. The story of Pandôra points to the same train of thought, which in the Hesiodic ages made men start from a state of absolute happiness, in contrast with other myths, which represented them as beginning their existence in utter helplessness and misery, and slowly learning the commonest things by the aid of Promêtheus or Phorôneus. These two, then, with Hermes, are the **givers of** fire to men; but the progress made by the sons of men in knowledge and power wakens the jealousy of Zeus, and Promêtheus (XX.), the deliverer, is chained on the desolate crags of Caucasus, until Herakles, the descendant of the Argive Iô (a name akin to that of Iolê, Iokastê (LVI.), Iamos (XLI.), and Iolâos, with many others), comes to set him free.

The resemblance of the myth of Deukalion (XXI.) to the narrative of the Noachian deluge it is unnecessary to **point out.**[2] It may be enough to remark here, that the legend of Deukalion is interwoven with other legends, as with those of Endymiôn and of Minos, in which old mythical phrases are again and again reproduced with a marvellous variety of combination.

The story of Medusa (XXIII.) belongs to the great series of myths which, having Perseus for their centre, were localised in the Peloponnesian Argos. The myths

[1] Odyssey, v. 390; x. 144.
[2] For the points of difference, see Notes [51], [52].

had existed in a simpler form during the ages in which the name Argos had carried with it no geographical meaning, but, like Lykia and Delos, Athens and Arkadia, denoted simply the bright land of the Dawn and the Sun. These dynastic legends are in all cases genuine subjects for epic poetry ; and the myth of Perseus, which certainly cannot be assigned to the latest class of such narratives, furnishes a theme not less magnificent than that of the Trojan war. Whether it was treated at any length in epic poems now lost, we cannot say ; but the existence of this great series of mythical tales, scarcely noticed in the poems to which we give the name 'Homeric,' is at once proof of the slender value of arguments drawn from the silence of the authors of the Iliad or the Odyssey. In these dynastic legends, again, the tendency of myths to reproduce themselves, with differences only of names and of local colouring, becomes especially manifest. The mythical history of Perseus is, in all its essential features, the history of the Attic hero Theseus, and of the Theban Œdipus ; and they all reappear with heightened colours in the myths of Herakles. But neither Thebans nor Athenians could penetrate through the thin veil which scarcely concealed the substantial identity of all these legends ; and thus the Argives of Peloponnesus, having already one solar hero in Perseus, repeated his career in the legend of his alleged descendant Herakles.

The life of Perseus, like that of Theseus, Herakles, Œdipus, and Odysseus, is one of toil. His adversaries are dragons and Gorgons, the beings who dwell on the confines of light and darkness, or in the deep abysses of night. The doubtful gloaming is the home of the Graiai, and the mortal Medusa is the night which comes to an end on the rising of the sun, while her deathless sisters are the powers of the eternal darkness which no sun ever penetrates. The mysterious beauty of the former would naturally be expressed by phrases suggestive of a rivalry between the goddess of the night and the goddess of the dawn, and this would lead to the idea of the curse which imparted to the face of Medusa its deadly power.

But the sun which scatters the darkness is also the child of the **darkness; and** so the phrase went that the child was **to be** the destroyer of his parents ; and oracles, it was said, warned the latter **of** the doom **which** would **overtake** them. This is followed in all **cases** by the exposure and the rescue of the babe ; and Danaê (XXIV.), a name which carries us to other names of the morning, plays the part of Iokastê in the story of Œdipus, of Augê in that of Telephos, and of Ilia and Mandanê in the **myths** of Romulus and Cyrus. **In Diktys and** Polydektes we have faint reflexions, again, of the powers of light and of darkness. Polydektes is, in fact, Polydegmon, or Hades, the darkness which swallows all that comes within its grasp; Diktys is the genial light which is born **in** the cave of Dikte; but the light is the brother of the darkness **as the sun is** the child of the night, and **so** Diktys **and Polydektes** are **brethren.** So, again, **the** night is the lover of the twilight **or the** dawn, and thus Polydektes **woos** Danaê as Paris wooed the Argive Helen. On her **refusal** to grant his prayer, Polydektes sends Perseus away **on a** toilsome errand ; but this errand is only **a** reproduction of the conflict of Apollo with Python, and **of** Indra with Vritra. Beginning his western journey, Perseus (XXV.) reaches first the bright Argive land, and there **during the** still hours of night he receives **the** invincible weapons which are to carry him scathless through all his battles. It **is** scarcely necessary to say that these weapons are the heritage of all the solar heroes, that they are found in the hands of Phœbus **and** Herakles, of Œdipus, Achilleus, Philoktetes, of Sigurd, Rustem, Indra, Isfendiyar, of Telephos, Meleagros, Theseus, Kadmos, Bellerophôn, **and all** other slayers of noxious and fearful things. **With the** death of Medusa **the** first part of his labours **comes** to an end. The night is slain, and the sun rises into the serene regions of the upper air, the beautiful Hyperborean gardens, while the dark sisters hasten after him to avenge the death

of Medusa. Their chase is vain. Perseus has reached
the bright land where there is no storm or tumult, the
peaceful home where Penelopê weaves her web of evening
clouds, to be undone again until their fairy forms are
seen once more in the morning (XXVI.) Here, however,
he may not tarry; but, as with the Teutonic Sigurd, his
toil is now to bring with it its own reward. The good
sword Gram slays the dragon Fafnir, and Sigurd wins
Brynhild ; the sword of Hermes smites the Libyan monster,
and Andromeda becomes the bride of Perseus. But here,
too, the imagery of other tales is repeated, and Phineus is
only another form of Polydektes, and, like him, is turned
to stone by the deadly countenance which Perseus holds up
before them. His work is done, and with his mother and
his bride he re-enters Argos in triumph ; but the fate must
be accomplished, and Perseus unwittingly becomes the
slayer of Akrisios (XXVII.), as Œdipus slays Laios, and
as Theseus unknowingly causes the death of his father
Aigeus.

In the myth of Kephalos (XXVIII.) the invincible
weapons of Perseus reappear in the hands of Artemis, and
slay the beautiful and guileless Prokris. Even in the most
complicated versions of the tale, the mythical phrases
which lie at its root may be traced with the utmost clearness. The very name Prokris denotes dew, and, true to
the old saying, the Athenian who had forgotten the meaning of the name, stilled called her the child of Hersê (the
dew). In its simplest form the myth brings before us a
series of phrases, each of which furnishes an incident in
the story. The dew sparkles on the hill-side (Prokris lies
on the slopes of Hymettos). The sun (Kephalos denotes
the head of the orb as it rises slowly from the sea) loves
the dew (Kephalos loves Prokris). But the dawn loves the
sun (Eôs loves Kephalos). The dawn is jealous of the
dew (Eôs is jealous of Prokris) ; and the dew takes delight
in more than one lover, who yet is one and the same ; in
other words, the dewdrops exhibit a thousand images of
the same sun (Kephalos in disguise wins the love of

Prokris). The dew flashes for a time with dazzling brightness (Prokris is armed with the spear of Artemis). The
sun takes this brightness to himself, while he looks down
on the dew (Prokris yields up the spear for the love of
Kephalos). The dew lingers latest in the thicket (Prokris
watches Kephalos from her secret bower). The dew is
dried up and dies as the sun rises in the sky (Prokris is
smitten by the spear of Kephalos).

The rest of the tale reproduces the legends of Herakles
and Bellerophôn. Like them, Kephalos must journey to
the west, doing great deeds, and sink as the sun goes down
into the waters of the western sea.

But the rays of the sun, which are sometimes called his
spears or his sword, are sometimes the golden locks which
no razor has ever touched. These locks of Phœbus Aker-
sekomês (the unshorn) are endowed with a mysterious
power to ward off all harm from their possessors, and they
reappear in the purple lock which Skylla (XXIX.), like
another Delilah, takes from the head of Nisos while he
sleeps, and thus delivers him and his people into the power
of Minos.

In the myth of Phrixos and Hellê (XXX.) the sunlight
becomes a golden fleece, just as in the legend of Herakles,
and again in that of Medeia, it becomes a robe which
devours the flesh of those who put it on. This fleece is
borne from the Western land far away to the East; and
the Argonautic expedition sets forth to recover and to bring
back the lost treasure. The chieftains of all the tribes,
afterwards known collectively as the Hellenês, are carried
in the speaking ship to the Kolchian land, whence after a
long and perilous voyage they reach once more their own
country. The whole narrative is in substance a close
parallel to that of the Trojan war. In both cases a treasure is lost; in both an allied army goes from the West to
the East in order to recover it; in both there is a long and
hard conflict before the prize is won, while the returning
chieftains undergo many dangers and losses on their homeward voyage. There are thus two struggles, one to recover

the robbed treasures, the other to reach their home and establish their title to their old inheritance, a title which Odysseus establishes only when he has bathed his hall in the blood of the suitors of Penelopê. The two legends, of the Golden Fleece and of the Trojan War, are thus a third time repeated in the myths which relate the departure of the Herakleids from Argos and their reconquest of the Peloponnesos after the lapse of generations. The journey of Phrixos and Hellê on the back of the golden-fleeced ram thus answers to the departure of Helen from Sparta to Ilion. The name Hellê, like that of Hellên, itself denotes the bright light, whether of the morning, or of the evening when it fades away from the sky after sundown. But Phrixos and Hellê are both the children of the mist, the illumined atmosphere, not the light-giving sun. Hence Hellê dies on the journey, while Phrixos (the cold air) still lives on, until the light is again kindled in the East. In the voyage of the Argo we have the journey of the children of the Sun, who seek for the light on which their life depends, and which again vanishes from the west soon after the dangers of the return have been successfully surmounted.

Not a few of the phrases which originally denoted only the phenomena of the day are exhibited in the myth of Medeia (XXXI.) The wisdom of the Sun is bestowed on his daughter the Morning (Hêlios has filled the heart of Medeia with wisdom). The dawn puts on the glory of the sun (Medeia is clothed with the robe of Hêlios). The dawn wakens the sleepers to a new life (Medeia renews the limbs of the aged to youth). The sun deserts the dawn (Iason cares no more for the Kolchian Medeia). The sun's rays bear onward the chariot of the morning (the dragons draw the chariot of Medeia).

In Theseus (XXXII.) we see a reflexion at once of Perseus and of Herakles; but the myth is instructive chiefly as carrying us to the Teutonic legend of the Volsunga Saga. The weapons of the Sun can be handled effectively only by the Sun himself; and thus Theseus becomes master of his father's sword, as Sigmund draws out the blade from the tree-trunk into which Odin had thrust it to the hilt. He is the son of Aithra (the pure air), as Œdipus is the son of Iokastê (the violet light of morning); and as Œdipus must overcome the Sphinx, so must Theseus do battle with the Minotaur (XXXIII.), who devoured the children of the dawn goddess Athênê, as Vritra hides the cattle of Indra in the dark lurking places which answer to the labyrinth of Knossos. The abandonment of Ariadnê by Theseus is, again, the desertion of Medeia by Iason, or of Brynhild by Sigurd. The Sun may not tarry with his first love, whether it be that he leaves her, or that she vanishes away as he strives to reach her.

The chase of the huntsman Alpheios after Arethusa (XXXIV.) is the pursuit of Daphnê by Apollo. As Daphnê plunges into the Peneian stream, so Arethusa plunges into the sea and reappears on the Ortygian shore of the twilight or quail land. The dawn, which has fled from Phœbus in the morning, comes back again at eventide, and is united with him just when the journey of both has well-nigh come to an end.

The chief incidents in the myth of Tyro (XXXV.) are found in the legends of Perseus, of Hellê, and of Romulus, whose mother, Ilia, fills precisely the part of Tyro. In Narkissos, again (XXXVI.), we look on Endymiôn, the tired Sun hurrying to his rest, and dead to the love which is lavished on him ; and as the name Endymiôn denotes the sudden plunge of the sun into the sea, so Narkissos means the deadly lethargy which makes him deaf to the pleadings of Echo, as Endymiôn had been deaf to the entreaties of Selênê.

In the myth of Orpheus (XXXVII.) the beautiful Eurydikê, whose name in its thcusand modifications belongs to the dawn, is bitten by the serpent of night, and Orpheus resolves to seek her out in Hades, as Herakles vowed to rescue Alkestis from the grasp of Thanatos (Death). The marvellous power of song which Phœbus had received from Hermes (VI.) disarms the fierce guardians of the shadowy kingdom, and Eurydikê is suffered to follow Orpheus, on

the one condition that he is not to look back until he has
reached the earth.   But the course of his love may not run
more smoothly than that of Phœbus for Daphnê, of Alpheios
for Arethusa, of Kephalos for Prokris.   The Sun loves the
dew and the dawn ; and dew and dawn alike are smitten
by the splendour of his countenance.   But the Sun grieves
for their death, and Orpheus mourns until the women of
the land take vengeance on him for a coldness akin to that
of Narkissos and Endymiôn.   He is torn limb from limb ;
and in this catastrophe we see the blood-red sunset which
closes the career of Heraklês.

   In the story of Europa (XXXVIII.) we have a myth substantially identical with that of Kephalos or Bellerophôn
employed as a legend to explain the founding of the Bœotian
Thebes.   Europa, whose name suggests a comparison with
those of Euryganeia, Eurydikê, Euryphassa, Eurytos, and
many others, is the morning with its broad-spreading light,
born in the Phœnician or purple land of the dawn.   She is
the child of Telephassa, the being who shines from far.   But
she is soon taken from her beautiful home.   In Hindoo
myths the bull Indra shatters the car of Daphnê : in the
Greek tale he carries Europa over seas and mountains, journeying always, like the sun, from east to west, until he gives
her a home in the Hesperian Delphi.   The Dawn has been
taken from the sky ; but her mother follows her, until at
length she sinks to sleep in the Thessalian plain in the evening, just as the pale and tender light which precedes the
sun-rising reappears again only to die out in the western
heavens at eventide.

   The myth of Bellerophôn (XXXIX.) is but another version
of the servitude of Apollo in the house of Admêtos, of Herakles to Eurystheus and Laomedon.   The love and jealousy
of Anteia for the beautiful Hipponoös are a reflexion of the
love and jealousy of Eôs in the legend of Kephalos ; and on
Bellerophôn, as on Kephalos, they entail a long and weary
pilgrimage.   Like Herakles, Hipponoös is sent forth to do
battle with terrific foes ; but he is pre-eminently Bellerophontes, the slayer of the monster Belleros, the demon of

the cloud who appears in the Veda as a ram, in other words, as a shaggy and hairy animal, according to the meaning of the name. Thus the shaggy she-goat slain **by** Hipponoös carries us at once to the monster slain by Indra, and Bellerophontes becomes a mere reflexion of the Vedic Indra Vritrahan, the slayer of Vritra.[1] But the afternoon of the life of Bellerophôn is gloomy as an autumn day when the sun sinks slowly through the pale-coloured sky which is seen beneath the dark cloud-canopy of the upper heavens. This rift of light, when the sun seems to rest without motion, is the Aleian plain through which Bellerophôn wanders until, like Kephalos, he reaches the Western sea.

In the story of Althàia and the Burning Brand (XL.), Meleagros, in his irresistible strength, in his love, his unselfish toil for others, his caprice and his early doom, is so completely the prototype of Achilleus, that the aged Phoinix uses his story in the Iliad as a warning to the son of Peleus that he should conquer his unreasonable anger. Achilleus and Meleagros represent alike the short-lived sun, whose course is one of toil for others, ending in an early death after a series of wonderful victories alternating with periods of darkness and gloom. But the life of Meleagros, like that of Olger the Dane, is connected directly with that of the torch which the Moirai threw on the hearth at his birth. The day must die when the torch of the sun is extinguished in the sea, but it cannot die sooner ; and thus the storing away of the rescued brand is the rescuing of the sun from **his** doom of death during the hours which pass between morning and eventide. The episode of the Kalydonian boar is only one of the thousand versions in which the battle of the Sun with the noxious powers of darkness is related with a marvellous wealth of varied colouring. But while the poets of the Iliad leave Achilleus in the hour of his triumph over Hektor, the myth of Meleagros carries on the story to the fatal moment when the brand saved from the burning is once again cast upon the fire.

[1] Max Müller, Chips from a German Workshop, ii. 185.

The tale of Iamos (XLI.) is professedly a legend to account for the honour and influence of the soothsayers known as the Iamidai ; but the name connects itself with those of Iolê, Iokastê, Iasion, Iolâos, Ion, words significant of the violet hues seen in the sky whether of the morning or the evening ; and thus the story of Iamos is the story of the birth of the morning, which is here cherished by the serpents of the night, for the Drakontes, or keen-eyed beings, may represent the penetrating light of the dawn not less than the hateful and terrifying darkness. We may note further that the wisdom of Iamos comes from the sun-god Phœbus, just as Hêlios gives to Medeia her marvellous wisdom and power.

The siege of Troy is, in Professor Max Müller's words, 'a repetition of the daily siege of the East by the solar powers that every evening are robbed of their brightest treasures in the West.' It is thus reduced to the mythical phrases which said, '.The light, or the Dawn, is stolen from the heaven. The dark beings have carried her far away. The children of the Sun are gone to bring her back ; but the journey is long and weary. They do battle with the robbers who will not yield up their prize. For ten long hours the fight lasts on. Then the Sun bursts out in his splendour ; the dark dwelling of the thieves falls down, and the light which they had hidden away comes forth in all its former beauty.' The story of Helen is thus a counterpart of the story of Phrixos and Hellê. In either case a treasure is stolen ; and the chieftains gather together to go in search of it. In both there is the long and perilous voyage, the protracted conflict, the recovery of the treasure, and the return of the chieftains to their home in the West. In the earliest form assumed by the myth, Agamemnon and his allies are the children of the Sun, who arm themselves to rescue the Dawn from the grasp of the thief who has taken her away ; and Paris (XLII.) with his allies represents the dark power of night which blots out the light from the sky. The phrases into which the myth thus resolves itself are found in the oldest Vedic hymns. The Panis (Paris) steal the cows of Indra, who sends Saramâ (Helen) to find them and bring them back. The Panis seek to seduce Saramâ from her allegiance to Indra, and to retain her in their dark lurking place. For a while she yields to the temptation ; but afterwards she returns to tell Indra where his cattle (the tinted clouds of morning) are hidden away. Here then we have the germ which was expanded into the story of the seduction of Helen by Paris, of the long search of her kinsfolk, **and of** her return to her glowing Western home, 'pardoned **and** glorified.' But the expanded myth shows also the blending of several ideas. The great conflict of the Iliad **is** the battle of the powers of light and darkness, and Paris represents the night fighting with the children of the day. ·**But** the great storehouse of mythical speech furnished a thousand phrases applicable to any of the fated actors who play their part in the great drama ; and Paris is thus invested with not a few of the characteristics of Achilleus and other solar heroes. Like Perseus, Œdipus, Romulus, and Cyrus, he is doomed to bring ruin on his parents ; like them he is exposed in his infancy on the hill-side, and rescued by **a** shepherd. As Sigurd gives up Brynhild, and Achilleus is parted from Brisêis, so Paris forsakes Œnônê for one who dwells nearer to the Western sea. Then follows a time of capricious inaction, which answers to the sullenness and anger of Achilleus and Meleagros. But Paris is the slayer of Achilleus at the Skaian or Western gates of the evening, and **here** he appears as the Pani, or dark power, who blots out the light of the sun from the heaven, while in the sequel of the story, which describes Œnôné as returning to him when he is smitten by the arrow of Philoktetes, we have the myth of the Dawn light, ever fair and ever young, looking on the death of the Sun, whom she cannot save from the doom which is on him.

The legend of Iphigeneia (XLIII.) is found in many forms ; but the most important is the version of Æschylus, who has given to it a deep moral significance as the event for which the avenging Atê brooded heavily on the house of Agamemnon. The same moral element entered even more deeply into the myth of Œdipus ; but the sacrifice of

Iphigeneia during the long voyage to Ilion, and in order to bring it to a successful issue, points to phrases which had said once that the child of the light, the daughter of the Sun, must die during the lagging hours of darkness in order that the Dawn may come back with all its glory in the morning.

Whether there may or may not have been some Phthiotic chieftain bearing the name of Achilleus (XLIV.), is a question with which we are scarcely concerned, when even writers who contend most strenuously for the historical character of the Trojan war allow that there may have been no Helen to provoke the struggle, and that Achilleus and Agamemnon may perhaps have never met at all. The Achilleus of Homer is one whose story is interwoven inextricably with that of Agamemnon and Menelaos; and the chief features in the narrative are these. He comes to fight, as he emphatically says, in a quarrel which is not his own, and to win wealth and glory for others, not for himself. He is deprived of Brisêis by command of a chief whom he regards as in every way his inferior He has an invincible spear, and his chariot is drawn by undying horses who have the gift of articulate speech. In his friend Patroklos we have the reflexion of his beauty and splendour without his strength. He is doomed to a terrible struggle with a formidable enemy, and his victory is to be followed by his own early death. These are features which he shares with Kephalos, Bellerophôn, Theseus, Meleagros, Perseus, Œdipus, Sigurd. What Eurystheus is to Herakles, that Agamemnon is to Achilleus; and the final conflict in the Iliad is the counterpart of the slaughter of the suitors in the Odyssey. Thus the story of the mythical Achilleus may be traced to its germ in phrases which, as in the myth of Herakles, spoke of the Sun as doomed to toil for man, as being parted from the Dawn in the morning, as grieving for her loss and nursing his wrath behind a thick veil of clouds, as sending forth a reflexion of himself in the light which breaks the surrounding gloom only to be swallowed up again in the darkness, as vowing vengeance for the death of his friend, as coming forth at last in intolerable splendour, and bathing the heavens in the blood-red hues which light up the torn vapours that crowd around him, as offering a terrible sacrifice on the funeral pyre of his friend, and then revealing a countenance from which all wrath and sullenness has passed away, as he sinks to rest ' in one unclouded blaze of living light.'

The legend of Sarpêdon (XLV.) is a transparent solar myth interwoven with the story of Paris, the dark being who steals the evening light from the West. His name denotes the golden splendour which stretches across the morning sky. He is the chieftain of Lykia, the land of light; his friend and avenger is Glaukos, the glistering. His mother is the daughter of Bellerophôn, the slayer of the demon of darkness. But the morning light must die, and Sarpêdon is smitten down in the prime of his manhood. Then the powers of sleep and death bear him during the night to his Eastern home, which they reach just as the day dawns. It is the journey of the Sun from the Latmian cave to the home of the Morning; and another version of the same myth would speak of Sarpêdon rising again from his couch, like Adonis and Osiris, in all the radiance of his former beauty.

Memnôn also (XLVI.) is the sun in his short career and his early death. He is the child of Eôs, the morning, and her tears fall on his body like rain at sundown. But more particularly Memnôn rises again, and thus the myth takes us a step beyond the legend of Sarpêdon, which stops at the end of the eastward journey, when the night is done.

The parting of Hektor and Andromachê (XLVII.) is an incident of touching human interest, for which it is unnecessary to seek any mythical origin. It marks that stage in the conflict between the powers of light and darkness, in which Athênê, the dawn goddess, opposes herself inexorably to the latter.

With the story of the Lotos-eaters (XLVIII.) we begin the tale of the weary trials and wanderings of Odysseus before he can see again the wife whom he had left to go to the war at Ilion. He belongs to the great company of chiefs who bring back Helen from Troy, and his homeward voyage is the counterpart of the voyage of Iason and his comrades as they return in the Argo with the Golden Fleece. The whole series of legends of which the myth is composed had its origin in phrases which described the general phenomena of daytime from the rising of the sun to its setting. The Sun leaves his bride, the twilight, in the sky when he sinks beneath the sea, to journey in silence and darkness to the scene of the great fight with the powers of darkness. The ten weary years of the war are the weary hours of the night ; in the tenth the fortress falls, as the dark shades are scattered at break of day. The victory is won ; but the Sun still longs to see again the fair and beautiful bride from whom he was parted yestereve. Dangers may await him, but these cannot arrest his steps ; things lovely may lavish their beauty upon him, but they cannot make him forget her. His long journey must begin—a strange chequered course, alternating between gloom and splendour, between joy and utter hopelessness. But do what he will, he cannot reach his home until another series of ten long years has come to an end—the sun cannot see the twilight until another day is done. He is first carried to the land of the Lotos-eaters, the fair fields of the deep blue heaven where the bright cirri float lazily as if they could linger there for ever. In the legend of Polyphemos (XLIX.) he encounters the one-eyed monster, the child of the sea and the storm-cloud. The shapeless vapours which rise from the waters, and through which the sun, like a huge eye, sheds a sickly light, assume strange and gigantic forms, which appear as the Sphinx in the story of Œdipus, as Cacus in that of Herakles, as Vritra in the primitive mythical phrases that tell of the exploits of Indra. Like all gigantic forms in Aryan tradition, the Cyclops is outwitted, and falls a victim to the being who is endowed with the higher wisdom which is the inheritance of Phœbus, the lord of light. This idea of an encounter between the keen-eyed sun and the huge unwieldy storm-cloud furnished the germ of the story which relates the victory of Odysseus over the stupid and brutal son of Poseidon.

In the myth of Kirkê (L.) we see before us a being whose wisdom and craft marks her affinity to Medeia, while in the food which turns the companions of Odysseus into swine we have only another version of the story of the Lotos-eaters. In either case they who partake of the food forget their homes, their wives, and their children, and cease to live the life of thinking men. In the Seirens (LI.) we have another of the many foes which the solar heroes have to encounter in their westward journey—the soft and treacherous calms which tempt the mariner to his ruin. But the myth of the Cattle of Hêlios (LII.) carries us again to phrases familiar to the writers of the Vedic hymns. Every morning the bright and glistering daughters of the Dawn drive the fleecy clouds to their bright pastures in the broad heaven, and each reappearance marks the lapse of another day. Hence the story ran that the whole herd consisted of three hundred and fifty cattle, whose number was never increased nor lessened. But in the Vedic hymns these cattle are still the clouds, and the phrases still remain transparent in their meaning. In the Greek myth this earlier meaning has been in part forgotten, and the children of the early morning (Neaira) feed the cattle of Hêlios in the local home of Thrinakia. But they are still sacred. None may harm them with impunity ; and by laying hands upon them the comrades of Odysseus insure their own destruction. They had killed the days (the cattle) of the sun, they had wasted their time, and thus they should never **reach** their journey's end.

The cave of the beautiful Kalypso, the veiling goddess (LIII.), brings before us again the cave of the Latmian hill, where Endymiôn plunges into his deep and dreamless slumber, and Narkissos hides his beauty and his grief. What Selênê is to Endymiôn, what Lêtô is to Zeus, what Echo **is to** Narkissos, that is Kalypso to Odysseus. It is the bright and beautiful night which veils the sun from mortal eyes in her chamber flashing with a thousand stars,

and lulls the wayfarer to sleep with an irresistible spell.
But once again the morning comes, and Hermes delivers
him from the soft dominion of Kalypso. From her odorous
home he is carried, after grievous buffetings on the stormy
sea, to the fair Phæakian land (LIV.), where he rests as
Perseus rested in the delicious Hyperborean gardens. He
has reached the region of the bright clouds unsullied by
grosser vapours, and bathed in undying splendour. But
here, though fair forms cluster round him, he yet may not
tarry, and so at last he stands on the rugged soil of his
island home (LV.) The dark mists have again gathered
round him; his body is bent, his beauty is marred, his eye
has lost its brightness. But there is yet one who can restore him to his ancient strength and glory, though he
stands a beggar in his own hall. Athênê, the dawn, who
filled him with irresistible might in the conflict at Ilion,
will restore him to the freshness of youth before he is
restored to Penelopê, the weaver of the bright web of
morning clouds which have many times faded away, while
the sun struggled wearily through the dark and angry sky.
A few phrases which spoke of the disguised chief seizing
his bow, as the hidden sun darts his ray through the cloud-
rift, of the scattering of the heavy vapours which had
gathered round the dawn light, of the awful slaughter as
they fall beneath his irresistible arrows, of the consumma-
tion of his vengeance, and the serene peace which follows
the hard battle as Penelopê stands once more by his side,
supply all the incidents of a tale which is precisely parallel
to the legends of Achilleus and Sigurd, and is in the closest
agreement with those of Perseus, Œdipus, Theseus, Herakles, and many others. In truth, the tale is found in all
lands peopled by Aryan races; and the forms which it has
assumed attest by their very differences their independent
growth from one and the same fertile stem. The popular
tales of Southern India dwell frequently on a chief who is
separated from his newly-married bride, to be restored to
her only when a long series of years, generally eighteen,
has come to an end. This chief, like Achilleus, Odysseus,

and Herakles, sets off to do great exploits in other lands;
but in some of the stories he falls among vagabonds, who
induce him to take some food which makes him forget his
home, his people, and himself, and who disguise him as a
beggar. Thus the long years are spent, until his forsaken
wife spies him out from among the ignoble crowd, and at
once recognises him in spite of his squalid raiment and
wasted features. In this instance Odysseus yields to the
seduction of the Lotos-eaters, and his wife acts the part of
Athênê in discerning the bright hero even while the shadows
close thickest around his form.[1]

The dynastic legend of Thebes has, like those of Argos
and Athens, localised a number of phrases which described
originally some phenomena of the outer world. The Sun
is the child of darkness, and he is doomed to slay his
father. He is the child also of the dawn, whose soft violet
hues tint the clouds of early morning. But while the
morning is his mother, so also is the dawn his bride.
From her he is parted at the beginning of his course; to
her he is reunited at its close. But he has other foes beside the darkness, and he must encounter danger for the
benefit of others, not for his own. The demon of drought
vexes the land; the dark thunder-clouds brood on the
mountain summit. Who can understand its dark sayings?
Who can read aright its bewildering riddle? He only on
whom rests the wisdom of Phœbus; he only whose glance
is like the dazzling glare of the great eye of day. But the
sun has slain the darkness of the night, and now he solves
the riddle of the monster, who leaps from the rock and is
slain. The storm-cloud is pierced by the irresistible rays,
and the prisoned waters refresh the thirsting earth. There
remains yet the reward of victory. The evening has come,
and the violet hues of morning reappear. So is Œdipus
wedded to Iokastê (LVI.) Thus far the story followed
strictly the old solar phrases; but at this point it received

---

[1] Old Deccan Days, Hindoo Fairy Tales current in Southern
India. By M. Frere.

at the hands of the Greek poets an ethical turn, which supplied the germ for its dark and gloomy sequel. The marriage of the mother with her child was an unnatural crime for which a stern recompense must be exacted, even when the actors are wholly unconscious of the evil which they have done. But even here the poets write with a singular fidelity to the old mythical speech. The tender light of evening is suddenly blotted out by the dark vapours ; the light of the sun is quenched in gloom. In other words, Iokastê dies in her bridal chamber, and Œdipus tears out his eyes (LVII.) The woful time at length draws to an end, and amidst the crash of the thunder he sinks into his grave, unseen by mortal eye ; but this grave is in the sacred land of the gentle beings whose name (Erînys, Saranyû) carries us again to the dawn light which steals across the sky at the break and the close of day.

Laïos, then, is to Œdipus what Akrisios is to Perseus, or Aleos to Telephos—the dark night from which the day is born, the enemy[1] whom the sun will slay. The fate of Perseus and of Telephos is also the lot of Œdipus. The babe is exposed on a bare hill-side, as the sun seems to rest on the earth (Ida) at its rising. But he has yet a long course before him. Like Theseus, Romulus, Cyrus, and the rest, he grows up both wise and strong, and the Sphinx is discomfited by him as Vritra is smitten by the spear of Indra. The word tells its own tale. The Sphinx is the being who shuts up the waters in the dark thunder-cloud.

The rest of the story is a necessary sequel to the un-natural marriage of Œdipus and Iokastê. A grievous doom must rest on the children of such a union ; and the sons of Œdipus, by their hateful strife, bring ruin on themselves and on their country (LVIII.) One child alone remains faithful to her father. It is Antigonê (LIX.), the light which looks forth from the east when the sun sinks down in the west, as Selênê comes to gaze upon

[1] Max Müller, Chips from a German Workshop, ii. 168.

Endymiôn. The remainder of the legend belongs rather to the region of ethics, and turns on the violation of positive human enactment for the sake of discharging a natural duty of prior obligation.

The legend of Eriphylê (LX.) must be classed with the sequel of the story of Œdipus. In both we can trace mythical phrases; but the tale, as a whole, is the development of moral ideas. This ethical character marks especially the myths which have grown up round persons who are undoubtedly historical, and more especially round Crœsus, king of Lydia. The existence of a Lydian monarchy and its overthrow by Cyrus are not to be doubted. But the story of Crœsus, as related by Herodotos, is, like the Book of Job, the expression of the thought of the time on the great problem of human life. It illustrates, in part, the irresistible accomplishment of doom, as in the death of the beautiful Atys (LXI.), and partly the conviction that the spiritual condition of men is not to be measured by their outward fortunes.

The story of the vengeance of Apollo (LXII.) may be a local legend possibly founded on historical fact; it marks in Herodotos the culminating point in the pride and arrogance of Xerxes, and the beginning of his ruin. How far it may relate to some real incident in the Persian invasion, is a question with which we are not here concerned.[1] Like that of Arîon (LXIII.), it may contain a substratum of fact embellished by the introduction of the marvellous.

The 'Battle of the Frogs and Mice' (LXIV.) is remarkable chiefly as the earliest satire on the great epics of the Homeric poets, and as showing that a sharp line of distinction must be drawn between the mythology of the Greeks and their religion. The story of Rhampsinitos (LXV.), which Herodotos heard in Egypt, is included in this series, not only for its wit and cleverness, but as showing the existence of a common popular mythology relating

---

[1] Such evidence as we have on this subject I have given in the 'History of Greece,' vol. i. p. 527.

neither to gods nor heroes.   The leading idea of the tale, which in the Teutonic versions becomes the story of the Master Thief, is found in the Arabian story of the Forty Thieves, a narrative which exhibits points of contact with the popular tales of Northern Europe,[1] just as features in the story of Aristomenes of Eira appear also in the voyages of Sindbad.

[1] For example, with the ' Wonderful Quern :' Dasent's ' Popular Tales from the Norse.'   Powell and Magnusson's Icelandic Legends.

THE GODS AND HEROES.

A

FROM land to land the lady Lêtô wandered in fear and sorrow, for no city or country would give her a home where she might abide in peace. From Crete to Athens, from Athens to Ægina, from Ægina to the heights of Pelion and Athos, through all the islands of the wide Ægæan Sea, Skyros and Imbros and Lemnos, and Chios the fairest of all, she passed, seeking a home. But in vain she prayed each land to receive her, until she came to the island of Delos, and promised to raise it to great glory if only there she might rest in peace. And she lifted up her voice and said, 'Listen to me, O island of the dark sea. If thou wilt grant me a home, all nations shall come unto thee, and great wealth shall flow in upon thee; for here shall Phœbus Apollo, the lord of light and life, be born, and men shall come hither to know his will and win his favour.' Then answered Delos, and said, 'Lady, thou promisest great things; but they say that the power of Phœbus Apollo will be such as nothing on the wide earth may withstand; and mine is but a poor and stony soil, where there is little to please the eye of those who look upon me. Wherefore I fear that he will despise my hard and barren land, and go to some other country where he will build a more glorious temple, and grant richer gifts to the people who come to worship him.' But Lêtô sware by the dark water of Styx, and the wide heaven above, and the broad earth around her, that in Delos should be the shrine of Phœbus, and that there should the rich offerings burn on his altar the whole year round.

So Lêtô rested in the island of Delos, and there was Phœbus Apollo born. And there was joy among the undying gods who dwell in Olympos, and the earth laughed beneath the smile of heaven. Then was his temple built in Delos, and men came to it from all lands to learn his will and offer rich sacrifices on his altar.[1]

---o---

THE PYTHIAN APOLLO.

LONG time Apollo abode in Delos; and every year all the children of Iôn were gathered to the feast which was held before his temple. But at length it came to pass that Apollo went through many lands, journeying towards Pytho. With harp in hand he drew nigh to the gates of Olympos, where Zeus and the gods dwell in their glory; and straightway all rejoiced for the sweetness of his harping. The Muses sang the undying gifts of the gods, and the griefs and woes of mortal men who cannot flee from old age and death. The bright Horai joined hands together with Hêbê and Harmonia; and Ares stood by the side of Aphroditê with Hermes the slayer of Argos, gazing on the face of Phœbus Apollo, which glistened as with the light of the new-risen sun. Then from Olympos he went down into the Pierian land, to Iolkos and the Le-lantian plain; but it pleased him not there to build himself a home. Thence he wandered on to Mykalessos, and, traversing the grassy plains of Teumessos, came to the sacred Thebes; but neither would he dwell there, for no man had yet come thither, neither was there road or path, but only wild forest in all the land.

Further and further he roamed, across the stream of Kephîsos and beyond Okalea and Haliartos, until he came to Telphûsa. There he thought to build himself a temple, for the land was rich and fair; so he said, 'Beautiful Telphûsa,[2] here would I rest in thy happy vale, and here shall men come to ask my will and seek for aid in the hour of fear; and great glory shall come to thee while I abide in thy land.' But Telphûsa was moved with anger as she saw Phœbus marking out the place for his shrine and laying its foundations; and she spake craftily to him and said, 'Listen to me, Phœbus Apollo. Thou seekest here to have a home, but here thou canst never rest in peace; for my broad plain will tempt men to the strife of battle, and the tramp of war-horses shall vex the stillness of thy holy temple. Nay, even in time of peace, the lowing cattle shall come in crowds to my fountain, and the tumult will grieve thine heart. But go thou to Krisa, and make for thyself a home in the hidden clefts of Parnassos, and thither shall men hasten with their gifts from the utmost bounds of the earth.' So Apollo believed her words, and he went on through the land of the Phlegyes until he came to Krisa. There he laid the foundations of his shrine in the deep cleft of Parnassos; and Trophonios and Agamedes, the children of Ergînos, raised the walls. There also he found the mighty dragon who nursed Typhâon, the child of Hêrê, and he smote him, and said, 'Rot there upon the ground, and vex not more the children of men. The days of thy life are ended, neither can Typhöeus himself aid thee now, or Chimæra of the evil name. But the earth and the burning sun shall consume and scorch·thy body.' So the dragon died, and his body rotted on the ground;

wherefore the name of that place is called Pytho, and
they worship Phœbus Apollo as the great Pythian
king.

But Phœbus knew now that Telphûsa had deceived
him, because she said nothing of the great dragon of
Krisa, or of the roughness of the land. So he hastened
back in his anger and said, 'Thou hast beguiled me,
Telphûsa, with thy crafty words ; but no more shall thy
fountain send forth its sweet water, and the glory shall be
mine alone.' Then Apollo hurled great crags down and
choked the stream near the beautiful fountain, and the
glory departed from Telphûsa.

Then he thought within himself what men he should
choose to be his priests at Pytho ; and far away, as he
stood on a high hill, he saw a ship sailing on the wine-
faced sea, and the men who were in it were Cretans,
sailing from the land of King Minos to barter their goods
with the men of Pylos. So Phœbus leaped into the sea,
and changed his form to the form of a dolphin, and
hastened to meet the ship. None knew whence the
great fish came which smote the side of their vessel with
its mighty fins ; but all marvelled at the sight, as the
dolphin guided the ship through the dark waters, and
they sat trembling with fear, as they sped on without a
sail by the force of the strong south wind. From the
headland of Malea and the land of the Lakonians they
passed to Helos and to Tænaron where Helios dwells in
whom the sons of men take delight, and where his cattle
feed in the rich pastures.[3] There the sailors would have
ended their wanderings ; but they sought in vain to land,
for the **ship** would not obey **its** helm. Onward it went
along the coast of the island of Pelops, for the mighty
dolphin guided it. So from Arênê and Arguphea it came
to the sandy Pylos, by Chalkis and Dymê to the land of

the Epeians, to Pheræ and to Ithaka. There the men saw spread out before them the waters which wash the shores of Krisa ; and the strong west wind came with its fierce breath, and drove them on to the east and towards the sunrising until they came to Krisa.

Then Phœbus Apollo came forth from the sea like a star, and the brightness of his glory reached up to the high heaven. Into his shrine he hastened, and on the altar he kindled the undying fire, and his bright arrows were hurled abroad, till all Krisa was filled with the blaze of his lightnings, so that fear came upon all, and the cries of the women rose shrill on the sultry air. Then, swift as a thought of the heart, he hastened back to the ship ; but his form was now the form of a man in his beauty, and his golden locks flowed down over his broad shoulders. From the shore he called out to the men in the Cretan ship, and said, ' Who are ye, strangers ? and do ye come as thieves and robbers, bringing terror and sorrow whithersoever ye may go ? Why stay ye thus, tarrying in your ship, and seek not to come out upon the land ? Surely ye must know that all who sail on the wide sea rejoice when their ship comes to the shore, that so they may come forth and feast with the people of the land.' So spake Phœbus Apollo ; and the leader of the Cretans took courage and said, ' Stranger, sure I am that thou art no mortal man, but one of the bright heroes or the undying gods. Wherefore tell us now the name of this land and of the people who dwell in it. Hither we never sought to come, for we were sailing from the land of Minos to barter our wares at Pylos ; but some one of the gods hath brought us hither against our will.' Then spake the mighty Apollo and said to them, ' O strangers, who have dwelt in Knossos of the Cretan land, think not to return to your ancient home, to your wives or to your

children.   Here ye must guard and keep my shrine,
and ye shall be honoured of all the children of men.
For I am the son of Zeus, and my name is Phœbus
Apollo.   It was I who brought you hither across the
wide sea, not in guile or anger, but that in all time to
come ye may have great power and glory, that ye may
learn the counsels of the undying gods and make known
their will to men.   Hasten then to do my bidding; let
down your sails, and bring your ship to the shore.   Then
bring out your goods and build an altar on the beach,
and kindle a fire, and offer white barley as an offering;
and because I led you hither under the form of a dolphin,
so worship me as the Delphian god.   Then eat bread
and drink wine, as much as your soul may lust after;
and after that come with me to the holy place, where ye
shall guard my temple.'

So they obeyed the words of Phœbus; and when they
had offered the white barley and feasted richly on the
sea-shore, they rose up to go, and Apollo led them on
their way.   His harp was in his hand, and he made
sweet music, such as no mortal ear had heard before;
and they raised the chant Io Pæan, for a new power was
breathed into their hearts, as they went along.   They
thought not now of toil or sorrow; but with feet un-
wearied they went up the hill until they reached the clefts
of Parnassos, where Phœbus would have them dwell.

Then out spake the leader of the Cretans and said
boldly, 'O king, thou hast brought us far away from our
homes to a strange land; whence are we to get food
here?   No harvest will grow on these bare rocks, no
meadows are spread out before our eyes.   The whole
and is bare and desolate.'   But the son of Zeus smiled
and said, 'O foolish men, and easy to be cast down, if
ye had your wish ye would gain nothing but care and toil.

But listen to me and ponder well my words. Stretch forth your hands, and slay each day the rich offerings, for they shall come to you without stint and sparing, seeing that the sons of men shall hasten hither from all lands, to learn my will and ask for aid in the hour of fear. Only guard ye my temple well, and keep your hands clean and your heart pure; for if ye deal rightly, no man shall take away your glory; but if ye speak lies and do iniquity, if ye hurt the people who come to my altar, and make them to go astray, then shall other men rise up in your place, and ye yourselves shall be thrust out for ever, because ye would not obey my words.' 4

—*o*—

NIOBÊ AND LÊTÔ.

IN the little island of Delos there lived a long time ago a lady who was called Niobê. She had many sons and many daughters, and she was very proud of them, for she thought that in all the island of Delos, and even in all the world, there were no children so beautiful as her own. And as they walked, and leaped, and ran amongst the hills and valleys of that rocky island, all the people looked at them and said, 'Surely there are no other children like the children of the lady Niobê.' And Niobê was so pleased at hearing this, that she began to boast to every one how strong and beautiful her sons and daughters were.

Now in this island of Delos there lived also the lady Lêtô. She had only two children, and their names were Artemis and Phœbus Apollo; but they were very strong and fair indeed. And whenever the lady Niobê saw them, she tried to think that her own children were still more beautiful, although **she** could hardly help feeling that she had never seen any so glorious as Artemis and Apollo. So one day the lady Lêtô and the lady Niobê were together, and their children were playing before them; and Phœbus Apollo played on his golden harp, and then he shot from **his** golden bow the arrows which never missed their mark. But Niobê never thought of Apollo's bow, and **the** arrows **which** he had in his quiver; and she began **to** boast to the lady Lêtô of the beauty of her children, **and** she said, 'See, Lêtô; look at my seven sons and my seven daughters, and see how strong and fair they are. Apollo and Artemis are beautiful, I know, but my children are fairer still; and **you have** only two children, while **I have** seven sons **and seven** daughters.' So Niobê went on boasting, **and never** thought whether she should make Lêtô angry. But Lêtô said nothing until Niobê and her children were gone, and then she called Apollo, and said to him, 'I do not love the lady Niobê. She is always boasting that her sons and daughters are more beautiful than you **and** your sister; and I wish you to show her that no one else is so strong as my children, or so beautiful.' Then Phœbus Apollo was angry, and a dark frown came upon his fair young face, and his eyes were like the flaming fire.[5] But he said nothing; and he took his golden bow in his hand, and put his quiver with his terrible arrows across his shoulder, and went away to the hills where he knew that the lady Niobê and her children were. And **when he saw them he** went and **stood on a** bare high **rock, an**d stretched the string of his golden bow, and **took** an arrow from his quiver.[6] Then he held out the **bow,** and drew the string to his breast, until the point of the arrow touched the bow; and then he let the arrow fly. Straight to its mark it went, and one of the lady

Niobê's sons fell dead. Then another arrow flew swiftly from the bow, and another, and another, and another, till all the sons and all the daughters of Niobê lay dead on the hill-side. Then Apollo **called** out to Niobê and said, 'Go and boast now of your beautiful **children.**'

It had all passed so quickly that Niobê scarcely **knew whether it** was not a dream. She could not believe **that her** children were really gone—all her sons and **all** her daughters, whóm she had just now seen so happy and strong around her. But there they lay still and cold upon the ground. Their eyes were closed as if they were asleep, and their faces had still a happy smile, which made them look more beautiful than ever. And Niobê went to them all one by one, and touched their cold hands, and kissed their pale cheeks; and then she knew that the arrows of Phœbus Apollo had killed them. Then she sat down on a stone which was close to them, and the tears flowed from her eyes, and they streamed down her face, as she sat there as still as her children who lay dead before her. She never raised her head to look at the blue sky—she never moved hand or foot, but she sat weeping on the cold rock till she became as cold as the rock herself. And still her tears flowed on, and still her body grew colder and colder, until her heart beat **no** more, and the lady Niobê was dead. But there she still seemed to sit and weep, for her great grief had turned her into a stone; and all the people, whenever they came near that place, said, 'See, there sits the lady Niobê, who was turned into stone, when Phœbus Apollo killed all her children, because she boasted that no one was so beautiful as they were.' And long after, when the stone was grown old and covered with moss, the people still thought they could see the form of the lady Niobê; for the stone, which did not look much like the form of a woman when they came near to it, seemed at a distance just as though Niobê still sat there, weeping for her beautiful children whom Phœbus Apollo slew.[7]

———o———

DAPHNÊ.

IN the vale of Tempê, where the stream of Peneios flows beneath the heights of Olympus towards the sea, the beautiful Daphnê passed the days of her happy childhood. Fresh as the earliest morning, she climbed the crags to greet the first rays of the rising sun ; and when he had driven his fiery horses over the sky, she watched his chariot sink behind the western mountains. Over hill and dale she roamed, free and light as the breeze of spring. Other maidens round her spoke each of her love, but Daphnê cared not to listen to the voice of man, though many a one sought her to be his wife.

One day, as she stood on the slopes of Ossa in the glow of early morning, she saw before her a glorious form. The light of the new-risen sun fell on his face with a golden splendour, and she knew that it was Phœbus Apollo. Hastily he ran towards her, and said, 'I have found thee, Child of the Morning. Others thou hast cast aside, but from me thou canst not escape. I have sought thee long, and now will I make thee mine.' But the heart of Daphnê was bold and strong ; and her cheek flushed and her eye sparkled with anger, as she said, 'I know neither love nor bondage. I live free among the streams and hills ; and to none will I yield my freedom.' Then the face of Apollo grew dark with anger, and he drew near to seize the maiden ; but swift as the wind she fled away. Over hill and dale, over crag and river, the feet of Daphnê fell lightly as falling leaves in autumn; but nearer yet **came** Phœbus Apollo, till **at last** the strength of the maiden began to fail. Then she stretched out her hands, and cried for help to the lady Dêmêtêr; but she came not to her aid. Her head was dizzy, and her limbs trembled in utter feebleness as she drew near to the broad river which gladdens the plains of Thessaly, till she almost felt the breath of Phœbus, and her robe was almost in his grasp. Then, with a wild cry, **she** said, 'Father Peneios, receive thy child,' and she rushed into the stream, whose waters closed gently over her.

She was gone; and Apollo mourned for his madness in chasing thus the free maiden. And he said, 'I have punished myself by my folly; the light of the morning is taken out of the day. I must go on alone till **my** journey shall draw towards its end.'[8] Then he spake the word, and a laurel came up on the bank where Daphnê had plunged into the stream; and the green bush with its thick clustering leaves keeps her name for ever.

—— o ——

KYRÊNÊ.

AMONG the valleys and hills of Thessaly, Kyrênê, the fair-armed daughter of Hypseus, wandered free **as** the deer upon the mountain side. Of all the maidens of the land, there was none to vie with her in beauty; neither was there any that could be matched with her for strength **of arm** and speed of **foot.** She touched not the loom or the spindle; she cared not for banquets with those who revel under houses. Her feasts were spread on the green grass, beneath the branching tree ; and with her spear and dagger she went fearless among the beasts of the field, or sought them out in their dens.

One day she was roaming along the winding banks of Peneios, when a lion sprang from a thicket across her path. Neither spear nor dagger was in her hand, but the heart of Kyrênê knew no fear, and she grappled with him until the beast sank wearied at her feet. She had conquered, but not unseen, for Phœbus Apollo had watched the maiden as she battled with the angry lion ; and straightway he called the wise centaur Cheiron, who had taught him in the days of his youth. ' Come forth,' he said, ' from thy dark cave, and teach me once again, for I have a question to ask thee. Look at yonder maiden, and the beast which lies beaten at her feet ; and tell me (for thou art wise) whence she comes, and what name she bears. Who is she, that thus she wanders in these lonely valleys without fear and without hurt? Tell me if she may be wooed and won.' Then Cheiron looked steadfastly at the face of Phœbus, and a smile passed over his countenance as he answered, ' There are hidden keys to unlock the prison-house of love ; but why askest thou me of the maiden's name and race,—thou who knowest the end of all things, and all the paths along which the sons of men are journeying? Thou has counted the leaves which burst forth in the spring-time, and the grains of sand which the wind tosses on the river-bank, or by the sea-shore. But if I must needs match thee in subtle wisdom, then listen to my words. The maiden is wooed and won already ; ard thou art going to bear her as thy bride over the dark sea, and place her in golden halls on the far-off Libyan land. There she shall have a home rich in every fruit that may grow up from the earth ; and there shall thy son Aristaios be born, on whose lips the bright Horai shall shed nectar and ambrosia, so that he may not come under the doom of mortal men.'[9]

Then Phœbus Apollo smiled as he answered, 'Of a truth, Cheiron, thou deservest thy fame, for there are none to match with thee in wisdom; and now I go to bear Kyrênê to the land which shall be called by her name, and where, in time to come, her children shall build great and mighty cities, and their name shall be spread abroad throughout all the earth for strength and wisdom.'

So the maiden Kyrênê came to the Libyan land, and there Aristaios her child was born. And Hermes carried the babe to the bright Horai, who granted him an endless life; and he dwelt in the broad Libyan plains, tending his flocks, and bringing forth rich harvests from the earth. For him the bees wrought their sweetest honey; for him the sheep gave their softest wool; for him the cornfields waved with the fullest grain. No blight touched the grapes which his hand had tended; no sickness vexed the herds which fed in his pastures. And they who dwelt in the land said, 'Strife and war bring no such gifts as these to the sons of men; therefore let us live in peace.'[10]

———o———

HERMES.[11]

EARLY in the morning, long ago, in a cave of the great Kyllenian hill, lay the new-born Hermes, the son of Zeus and Maia. The cradle-clothes were scarcely stirred by his soft breathing, while he slept as peacefully as the children of mortal mothers. But the sun had not driven his fiery

chariot over half the heaven, when the babe arose from
his sacred cradle and stepped forth from the dark cavern.
Before the threshold a tortoise fed lazily on the grass ;
and when the child saw it, he laughed merrily. 'Ah !
this is luck indeed,' he said ; 'whence hast thou come,
pretty creature, with thy bright speckled shell ? Thou
art mine now, and I must take thee into my cave. It is
better to be under shelter than out of doors ; and though
there may be some use in thee while thou livest, it will
comfort thee to think that thou wilt sing sweetly when
thou art dead.'

So the child Hermes took up his treasure in both
arms, and carried it into the cavern. There he took an
iron probe, and pierced out the life of the tortoise ; and
quick as thought, he drilled holes in its shell, and fixed
in them reed-canes. Then across the shell he fastened
a piece of ox-hide, and with seven sheep-gut cords he
finished the making of his lyre. Presently he struck it
with the bow, and a wave of sweet music swelled out
upon the air. Like the merry songs of youths and
maidens, as they sport in village feasts, rose the song of
the child Hermes ; and his eyes laughed slily as he sang
of the loves of Zeus and Maia, and how he himself was
born of the mighty race of the gods. Still he sang on,
telling of all that he saw around him in the glittering
home of the nymph, his mother. But all the while, as
he sang, his mind was pondering on other things ; and
when the song was ended, he went forth from the cave,
like a thief in the night, on his wily errand.

The sun was hastening down the slope of heaven with
his chariot and horses to the slow-rolling stream of
Ocean, as Hermes came to the shadowy hills of Pieria,
where the cattle of the gods feed in their large pastures.
There he took fifty from the herd, and made ready to

drive them to the Kyllenian hill.[12]   But before him
lay vast plains of sand; and, therefore, lest the track
of the cattle should tell the **tale of** his thieving, he
drove the beasts round about by crooked paths, until
it seemed as though they had gone to the place from
which he had stolen them.[13]   He had taken good
care that his own footsteps should not betray him, for
with branches of tamarisk and myrtle, well twisted with
their leaves, he hastily made himself sandals, and sped
away from Pieria.   One man alone saw him, a very old
man, who was working in his vineyard on the sunny
plain of Onchêstos.   To him Hermes went quickly,
and said, 'Old man, thou wilt have plenty of wine
when these roots come all into bearing trim.   Meanwhile, keep **a** wise head on thy crumpled shoulders,
and take heed not to remember more **than** may be convenient.'

Onwards, over dark hills, and through sounding dells,
and across flowery plains, hastened the child Hermes,
driving his flock before him.   The night waxed and
waned, and the moon had climbed **to** her watchtower
in the heaven, when, in the flush of early morning,
Hermes reached the banks of the great Alpheian
stream.   There he turned his herd to feed on the
grassy **plain,** while he gathered logs of wood, and,
rubbing two sticks together, kindled the first flame
that burned upon the earth where dwell the sons of
men.[14]   The smoke went up to the heaven, and the
flame crackled fiercely beneath it, as Hermes brought
forth two of the herd, and, tumbling them **on** their
back, pierced out the life of both.   **Their** hides he
placed on the hard rock; their flesh he cut up into
twelve portions; and so Hermes hath the right of
ordering all sacrifices [15] which the children of men

B

offer to the undying gods.   But he ate not of the flesh
or fat, although hunger sorely pressed him;[16] and he
burnt the bones in the fire, and tossed his tamarisk
sandals into the swift stream of Alpheios.   Then he
quenched the fire, and with all his might trampled
down the ashes, until the pale moon rose up again in
the sky.   So he sped on his way to Kyllênê.   Neither
god nor man saw him as he went, nor did the dogs
bark.   Early in the morning he reached his mother's
cave, and darted through the keyhole of the door,
softly as a summer breeze.   Without a sound his little
feet paced the stony floor, till he reached his cradle
and lay down, playing like a babe among the clothes
with his left hand, while his right held the tortoise-lyre
hidden underneath them.

But, wily though he was, he could not cheat his
mother.   To his cradle she came and said, 'Whither
hast thou wandered in the dark night?   Crafty rogue,
mischief will be thy ruin.   The Son of Lêtô will soon
be here, and bear thee away bound in chains not easily
shaken off.   Out of my sight, little wretch, born to
worry the blessed gods and plague the race of men!'
'Mother,' said Hermes gently, 'why talk thus to me,
as though I were like mortal babes, a poor cowering
thing, to cry for a little scolding?   I know thy interest
and mine : why should we stay here in this wretched
cave, with never a gift nor a feast to cheer our hearts?
I shall not stay.   It is pleasanter to banquet with the
gods than to dwell in a cavern in draughts of whistling
wind.   I shall try my luck against Apollo, for I mean
to be his peer; and if he will not suffer me, and if
Zeus my father takes not up my cause, I will see what
I can do for myself, by going to the shrine of Pytho
and stealing thence the tripods and cauldrons, the

iron vessels and glittering robes. If I may not have honour in Olympos, I can at least be the prince of thieves.'

Meanwhile, as they talked together, Eôs rose up from the deep ocean stream, and her tender light flushed across the sky, while Apollo hastened to Onchêstos and the holy grove of Poseidon. There the old man was at work in his vineyard, and to him Phœbus went quickly and said, 'Friend hedger, I am come from Pieria looking for my cows. Fifty of them have been driven away, and the bull has been left behind with the four dogs who guarded them. Tell me, old man, hast thou seen any one with these cows, on the road?' But the old man said that it would be a hard matter to tell of all that he might chance to see. 'Many travellers journey on this road, some with evil thoughts, some with good; I cannot well remember all. This only I know, that yesterday, from the rising up of the sun to its setting, I was digging in my vineyard; and I think, but I am not sure, that I saw a child with a herd of cattle. A babe he was, and he held a staff in his hand, and, as he went, he wandered strangely from the path on either side.'

Then Phœbus stayed not to hear more, for now he knew of a surety that the new-born son of Zeus had done him the mischief. Wrapped in a purple mist, he hastened to beautiful Pylos, and came on the track of the cattle. 'O Zeus!' he cried, 'this is indeed a marvel. I see the footprints of cattle, but they are marked as though the cattle were going to the asphodel meadow, not away from it. Of man or woman, of wolf, bear, or lion, I spy not a single trace. Only here and there I behold the footprint of some strange monster, who has left his mark at random on either side of the road.' So

on he sped to the woody heights of Kyllênê, and stood
on the doorstep of Maia's cave. Straightway the child
Hermes nestled under the cradle-clothes in fear, like a
new-born babe asleep. But, seeing through all his craft,
Phœbus looked steadily through all the cave and opened
three secret places full of the food and drink of the gods,
and full also of gold and silver and raiment ; but not a
cow was in any of them. At last he fixed his eyes
sternly on the child and said, 'Wily babe, where are my
cows ? If thou wilt not tell me, there will be strife
between us ; and then I shall hurl thee down to the
gloomy Tartaros, to the land of darkness whence neither
thy father nor thy mother can bring thee back, and
where thy kingdom shall be only over the ghosts of
men.' 'Ah !' said Hermes, 'these are dreadful words
indeed ; but why dost thou chide me thus, or come here
to look for cows ? I have not seen or heard of them,
nor has any one told me of them. I cannot tell where
they are, or get the reward, if any were promised, for
discovering them. This is no work of mine ; what do
I care for but for sleeping and sucking, and playing
with my cradle-clothes, and being washed in warm
water ? My friend, it will be much better that no one
should hear of such a silly quarrel. The undying gods
would laugh at the very thought of a little babe leaving
its cradle to run after cows. I was born but yesterday.
My feet are soft, and the ground is hard. But if it be
any comfort to thee, I will swear by my father's head
(and that is a very great oath) that I have not done this
deed, nor seen any one else steal your cows, and that I
do not know what cows are.'

As he spoke he looked stealthily from one side to the
other, while his eyes winked slily, and he made a long
soft whistling sound, as if the words of Phœbus had

amused him mightily. 'Well, friend,' said Apollo, with a smile, 'thou wilt break into many a house, I see, and thy followers after thee; and thy fancy for beef will set many a herdsman grieving. But come down from the cradle, or this sleep will be thy last. Only this honour can I promise thee, to be called the prince of thieves for ever.' So without more ado Phœbus caught up the babe in his arms; but Hermes gave so mighty a sneeze that he quickly let him fall, and Phœbus said to him gravely, 'This is the sign that I shall find my cows: show me, then, the way.' In great fear Hermes started up and pulled the cradle-clothes over both his ears, as he said, 'Cruel god, what dost thou seek to do with me? Why worry me thus about cows? I would there were not a cow in all the earth. I stole them not, nor have I seen any one steal the cows, whatever things cows may be. I know nothing but their name. But come; Zeus must decide the quarrel between us.'

Thus each with his own purpose spake to the other, and their minds grew all the darker, for Phœbus sought only to know where his cows might be, while Hermes strove only to cheat him. So they went quickly and sulkily on, the babe first, and Phœbus following after him, till they came to the heights of Olympos and the home of the mighty Zeus. There Zeus sat on the throne of judgement, and all the undying gods stood around him. Before them in the midst stood Phœbus and the child Hermes, and Zeus said, 'Thou hast brought a fine booty after thy hunt to-day, Phœbus—a child of a day old. A fine matter is this to put before the gods.'

'My father,' said Apollo quickly, 'I have a tale to tell which will show that I am not the only plunderer. After a weary search, I found this babe in the cave of Kyllênê;

and a thief he is such as I have never seen whether
among gods or men.   Yester eve he stole my cattle from
the meadow, and drove them straight towards Pylos to
the shore of the sounding sea.   The tracks left were such
that gods and men might well marvel at them.   The
footprints of the cows on the sand were as though they
were going to my meadows, not away from them ; his
own footmarks beggar all words, as if he had gone neither
on his feet nor on his hands, and as if the oak tops had
suddenly taken to walking.   So was it on the sandy soil ;
and after this was passed, there remained no marks at
all.   But an old man saw him driving them on the road
to Pylos.   There he shut up the cattle at his leisure, and,
going to his mother's cave, lay down in his cradle like a
spark in a mass of cinders, which an eagle could scarcely
spy out.   When I taxed him with the theft, he boldly
denied it, and told me that he had not seen the cows or
heard aught of them, and could not get the reward if one
were offered for restoring them.'

So the words of Phœbus were ended, and the child
Hermes made obeisance to Zeus, the lord of all the gods,
and said, 'Father Zeus, I shall tell thee the truth, for I
am a very truthful being, and I know not how to tell a
lie.   This morning, when the sun was but newly risen,
Phœbus came to my mother's cave, looking for cows.
He brought no witnesses ; he urged me by force to confess ; he threatened to hurl me into the abyss of Tartaros.[17]   Yet he has all the strength of early manhood,
while I, as he knows, was born but yesterday, and am
not in the least like a cattle-reiver.   Believe me (by thy
love for me, thy child) that I have not brought these
cows home, or passed beyond my mother's threshold.
This is strict truth.   Nay, by Hêlios and the other gods,
I swear that I love thee and have respect for Phœbus.

Thou knowest that I am **guiltless,** and, if thou wilt, I will also swear it. **But, spite** of all his strength, **I** will avenge myself some day on Phœbus for his unkindness; and then help **thou** the weaker.'

So spake Hermes, winking his eyes and holding the clothes to his shoulders; and **Zeus** laughed aloud at the wiliness of the babe, and bade Phœbus and **the** child be friends. Then he bowed his head and charged Hermes to show the spot where he had hidden the cattle, and **the child obeyed,** for none may despise that sign and **live.** To Pylos they hastened and **to the** broad stream of Alpheios, and from the fold Hermes drove forth the cattle. But as he stood apart, Apollo beheld the hides flung on the rock, and he asked Hermes, 'How wast thou able, cunning rogue, to flay two cows, thou a child but one day old? I fear thy might in time to come, and I cannot let thee live.' Again he seized the child, and bound him fast with willow bands; but the child tore them from his body like flax, so that Phœbus marvelled greatly. In vain Hermes sought a place wherein to hide **him-**self, and great fear came upon him till he **thought of** his tortoise-lyre. With his bow he touched the strings, and the wave of song swelled out upon the air **more** full and sweet than ever. He sang of the undying gods and the dark earth, how it was made at the first, and how to each **of** the gods his own appointed portion was given, till the heart of Apollo was filled with a mighty longing, and he spake to Hermes, and said, 'Cattle-reiver, wily rogue, thy song is worth fifty head of cattle. We will settle our strife by and by. Meanwhile, tell me, was this wondrous gift of song born with thee, or hast thou it as **a gift from** any god or mortal man? Never on Olympos, from those who cannot die, have I heard such strains as these. **They** who hear thee may have what they will, be it mirth,

or love, or sleep.   Great is thy power, and great shall be
thy renown, and by my cornel staff I swear that I will
not stand in the way of thy honour or deceive thee in
anywise.'

Then said **Hermes,** 'I grudge thee not my skill, son
of Lêtô, for I seek but thy friendship.   Yet thy gifts
from Zeus are great.   Thou knowest his mind, thou
canst declare his will, and reveal what is stored up in
time to come for undying gods or mortal men.   This
knowledge I fain would have.   But my power of song
shall this day be thine.   Take my lyre, the soother of
the wearied, the sweet companion in hours of sorrow or
of feasting.   To those who come skilled in its language,
it can discourse sweetly of all things, and drive away all
thoughts that annoy and cares that vex the soul.   To
those who touch it, not knowing how to draw forth its
speech, it will babble strange nonsense, and rave with
uncertain moanings.   But thy knowledge is born with
thee, and so my lyre is thine.   Wherefore now let us
feed the herds together, and with our care they shall
thrive and multiply.   There is no more cause for anger.'

So saying, the babe held out the lyre, and Phœbus
Apollo took it.   In his turn he gave to the child Hermes
a glittering scourge, with charge over his flocks and herds.
Then, touching the chords of the lyre, he filled the air
with sweet music, and they both took their way to
Olympos, and Zeus was glad at heart to see that the
wrath of Apollo had passed away.   But Phœbus dreaded
yet the wiles of Hermes, and said, ' I fear me much, child
of Maia, that in time to come thou mayest steal both my
harp and my bow, and take away my honour among
men.   Come now, and swear to me by the dark water of
Styx that thou wilt never do me wrong.'   Then Hermes
bowed his head, and sware never to steal anything from

Apollo, and never to lay hands on his holy shrine ; and
Phœbus sware that of all the undying gods there should
be none so dear to him as Hermes. ' And of this love,'
he said, ' I will give thee a pledge. My golden rod shall
guard thee, and teach thee all that Zeus may say to me
for the well or ill doing of gods or men. But the higher
knowledge for which thou didst pray may not be thine ;
for that is hidden in the mind of Zeus, and I have sworn
a great oath that none shall learn it from me. But the
man who comes to me with true signs, I will never
deceive ; and he who puts trust in false omens and then
comes to inquire at my shrine,[18] shall be answered according to his folly, but his offering shall go into my
treasure-house. Yet further, son of Maia, in the clefts of
Parnassos far away dwell the winged Thriai,[19] who taught
me long ago the secret things of times to come. Go
thou then to the three sisters, and thus shalt thou test
them. If they have eaten of the honeycomb before they
speak, they will answer thee truly ; but if they lack the
sweet food of the gods, they will seek to lead astray those
who come to them. These I give thee for thy counsel-
lors ; only follow them warily ; and have thou dominion
over all flocks and herds, and over all living things that
feed on the wide earth ; and be thou the guide to lead
the souls of mortal men to the dark kingdom of Hades.'

So was the love of Apollo for Hermes made sure; and
Hermes hath his place amongst all the deathless gods
and dying men. Nevertheless, the sons of men have
from him no great gain, for all night long he vexes them
with his treacherous wiles.[20]

N the fields of Enna, in the happy island of Sicily, the beautiful Persephonê was playing with the girls who lived there with her. She was the daughter of the lady Dêmêtêr, and every one loved them both; for Dêmêtêr was good and kind to all, and no one could be more gentle and merry than Persephonê. She and her companions were gathering flowers from the field, to make crowns for their long flowing hair. They had picked many roses and lilies and hyacinths which grew in clusters around them, when Persephonê thought she saw a splendid flower far off; and away she ran, as fast as she could, to get it. It was a beautiful narcissus,²² with a hundred heads springing from one stem; and the perfume which came from its flowers gladdened the broad heaven above, and the earth and sea around it. Eagerly Persephonê stretched out her hand to take this splendid prize, when the earth opened, and a chariot stood before her drawn by four coal-black horses; and in the chariot there was a man with a dark and solemn face, which looked as though he could never smile, and as though he had never been happy. In a moment he got out of his chariot, seized Persephonê round the waist, and put her on the seat by his side. Then he touched the horses with his whip, and they drew the chariot down into the great gulf, and the earth closed over them again.

Presently the girls who had been playing with Persephonê came up to the place where the beautiful narcissus was growing; but they could not see her anywhere. And they said, 'Here is the very flower which

she ran to pick, and **there** is no place **here where** she
can be hiding.' Still for a long time they searched for
her through the fields of Enna; and when the evening
was come, they went home to tell the lady **Dêmêtêr that**
they could not tell what had become of Persephonê.

Very terrible was the sorrow of Dêmêtêr when she was
told that her child was lost. She put a dark robe on her
shoulders, and took a flaming torch in her hand, and
went over land and sea to look for Persephonê. **But no**
one could tell her where she was gone. When ten days
were passed she met Hekatê, and asked her about her
child; but Hekatê said, 'I heard her voice, as she cried
out when some one seized her; but I did not see it
with my eyes, and so I know not where she is gone.'
Then she went to Hêlios, and said to him, 'O Hêlios,
tell me about my child. Thou seest everything on the
earth, sitting **in the** bright sun.' Then Hêlios said to
Dêmêtêr, 'I pity thee for thy great sorrow, and I will tell
thee the truth. It is Hades who has taken away Persephonê to be his wife in the dark **and gloomy land**
which lies beneath in the earth.'

Then the rage of Dêmêtêr was more **terrible than her**
sorrow had been; and she would not stay in the palace
of Zeus, on the great Thessalian hill, because it was Zeus
who had allowed Hades to take away Persephonê. So
she went down from Olympos, and wandered on a long
way until she came to Eleusis, just as the sun was
going down into his golden cup [23] behind the dark blue
hills. There Dêmêtêr sat down close to a fountain,
where the water bubbled out from the green turf and fell
into a clear basin, over which some dark olive-trees
spread their branches. Just then **the** daughters of Keleos,
the king of Eleusis, came to the fountain with pitchers on
their heads to draw water; and when they saw Dêmêtêr,

they knew from her face that she must have some great grief; and they spoke kindly to her, and asked if they could do anything to help her. Then she told them how she had lost and was searching for her child; and they said, 'Come home and live with us: and our father and mother will give you everything that you can want, and do all that they can to soothe your sorrow. 'So Dêmêtêr went down to the house of Keleos, and she stayed there for a whole year. And all this time, although the daughters of Keleos were very gentle and kind to her, she went on mourning and weeping for Persephonê. She never laughed or smiled, and scarcely ever did she speak to any one, because of her great grief. And even the earth, and the things which grow on the earth, mourned for the sorrow which had come upon Dêmêtêr. There was no fruit upon the trees, no corn came up in the fields, and no flowers blossomed in the gardens. And Zeus looked down from his high Thessalian hill, and saw that everything must die unless he could soothe the grief and anger of Dêmêtêr. So he sent Hermes down to Hades, the dark and stern king, to bid him send Persephonê to see her mother Dêmêtêr. But before Hades let her go, he gave her a pomegranate to eat, because he did not wish her to stay away from him always, and he knew that she must come back if she tasted but one of his pomegranate seeds. Then the great chariot was brought before the door of the palace, and Hermes touched with his whip the coal-black horses, and away they went as swiftly as the wind, until they came close to Eleusis. Then Hermes left Persephonê, and the coal-black horses drew the chariot away again to the dark home of King Hades.

The sun was sinking down in the sky when Hermes left Persephonê, and as she came near to the fountain she saw some one sitting near it in a long black robe, and she knew that it must be her mother who still wept and mourned for her child. And as Dêmêtêr heard the rustling of her dress, she lifted up her face, and Persephonê stood before her.

Then the joy of Dêmêtêr was greater, as she clasped her daughter to her breast, than her grief and her sorrow had been. Again and again she held Persephonê in her arms, and asked her about all that had happened to her. And she said, 'Now that you are come back to me, I shall never let you go away again; Hades shall not have my child to live with him in his dreary kingdom.' But Persephonê said, 'It may not be so, my mother; I cannot stay with you always; for before Hermes brought me away to see you, Hades gave me a pomegranate, and I have eaten some of the seeds; and after tasting the seed I must go back to him again when six months have passed by. And indeed, I am not afraid to go; for although Hades never smiles or laughs, and everything in his palace is dark and gloomy, still he is very kind to me; and I think that he feels almost happy since I have been his wife. But do not be sorry, my mother, for he has promised to let me come up and stay with you for six months in every year, and the other six months I must spend with him in the land which lies beneath the earth.'

So Dêmêtêr was comforted for her daughter Persephonê, and the earth and all the things that grew in it felt that her anger and sorrow had passed away. Once more the trees bore their fruits, the flowers spread out their sweet blossoms in the garden, and the golden corn waved like the sea under the soft summer breeze. So the six months passed happily away, and then Hermes came with his coal-black horses to take Persephonê to the dark land. And she said to her mother, 'Do not

weep much ; the gloomy king whose wife I am is so kind
to me that I cannot be really unhappy ; and in six months
more he will let me come to you again.' But still, whenever the time came round for Persephonê to go back to
Hades, Dêmêtêr thought of the happy days when her
child was a merry girl playing with her companions and
gathering the bright flowers in the beautiful plains of
Enna.

——o——

THE SLEEP OF ENDYMIÔN.[24]

ONE beautiful evening, when the sun was sinking
down in the west, Selênê was wandering on the
banks of the river Meander ; and she thought
that of all the places which she had ever
seen there was none more lovely than the quiet valley
through which that gentle river was flowing. On her
right hand rose a hill, whose sides were covered with
trees and flowers ; where the vine clambered over the
elm, and the purple grapes shone out from amongst the
dark leaves. Then Selênê asked some people who were
passing by to tell her the name of the hill, and they told
her that it was called the hill of Latmos. On she went,
under the tall trees, whose branches waved over her in
the clear evening light, till at last she reached the top,
and looking down on the valley which lay beneath her.
Then Selênê was indeed astonished, for she had never
seen anything so beautiful before, even in a dream.
She had fancied that nothing could be more lovely than
the vale of the Meander, and now she saw something
far more beautiful than the rocks and stones and clear
bright water of that winding river. It was a small valley,
at the bottom of which a lake shone like silver in the

light of the setting sun. All around it beautiful trees covered the sloping banks; and their long branches drooped down over the water. Not a breath of wind was stirring the dark leaves—not a bird was flying in the air. Only the large green dragon-fly floated lazily on the lake, while the swan lay half asleep on the silvery waters. On one side, in the loveliest corner of the valley, there was a marble temple, whose pillars shone like the white snow; and, leading down to the lake, there were steps of marble, over which the palm-trees spread their branches; and everywhere were clusters of all beautiful flowers, amongst which mosses, and ferns, and the green ivy were tangled. There was the white narcissus and the purple tulip—the dark hyacinth and the soft red rose. But more beautiful than all the trees and flowers, a man lay sleeping on the marble steps of the temple. It was Endymiôn, who lived in this quiet valley, where the storms never came, and where the dark rain-clouds never covered the sides of the mountain. There he lay in the still evening hour; and at first Selênê thought that it could scarcely be a living man whom she saw, for he lay as still as if he were made of marble himself. And as she looked upon him, Selênê drew in her breath for wonder; and she went gently down the valley till she came to the steps where Endymiôn lay asleep. Presently the sun sank behind the hill, and the rich glow of the evening made the silvery lake gleam like gold; and Endymiôn awoke and saw Selênê standing near him. Then Selênê said, 'I am wandering over the earth; and I may not stay here. Come away, and I will show you larger lakes and more glorious valleys than these.' But Endymiôn said, 'Lady, I cannot go. There may be lakes which are larger, and valleys more splendid than this; but I love this still and quiet place, where the storms never come, and the sky is never black with clouds. You must not ask me to leave the cool shade of these sleeping trees, and the myrtles and roses which twine under the tall elms, and these waters, where the swans rest in the hot hours of the day and the dragon-fly spreads his green and golden wings to the sun.'

Many times did Selênê ask him, but Endymiôn would not leave his pleasant home; and at last she said, 'I can stay no more; but if you will not come with me, then you shall sleep on these marble steps and never wake up again.' So Selênê left him; and presently a deep sleep came over Endymiôn, and his hands dropped down by his side, and he lay without moving on the steps of the temple, while the evening breeze began to stir gently the broad leaves of the palm-trees, and the lilies which bowed their heads over the calm water. There he lay all through the still and happy[25] night; and there he lay when the sun rose up from the sea, and mounted up with his fiery horses into the sky. There was a charm now on this beautiful valley, which made the breeze more gentle and the lake more still than ever. The green dragon-flies came floating lazily in the air near Endymiôn, but he never opened his eyes; and the swans looked up from the lake, to see if he was coming to feed them : but he stirred not in his deep and dreamless sleep. There he lay day and night, for weeks, and months, and years; and many times, when the sun went down into the sea, Selênê came and stood on the Lat-mian hill, and watched Endymiôn as he lay asleep on the marble steps beneath the drooping palm-trees; and she said, 'I have punished him because he would not leave his home; and Endymiôn sleeps for ever in the land of Latmos.'

IN the golden house which Hephaistos had wrought for him with his wondrous skill, Hêlios saw nothing fairer than his son Phaethon; and he said to his mother Klymenê that no mortal child might be matched with him for beauty. And Phaethon heard the words, and his heart was filled with an evil pride. . So he stood before the throne of Hêlios and said, 'O father, who dwellest in the dazzling light, they say that I am thy child; but how shall I know it while I live in thy house without name and glory? Give me a token, that men may know me to be thy son.' Then Hêlios bade him speak, and sware to grant his prayer; and Phaethon said, 'I will guide thy chariot for one day through the high heaven; bid the Horai make ready the horses for me, when Eôs spreads her quivering light in the sky.' But the· heart of Hêlios was filled with fear, and he besought his son with many tears to call back his words. 'O Phaethon, bright child of Klymenê, for all thy beauty thou art mortal still; and the horses of Hêlios obey no earthly master.' But Phaethon hearkened not to his words, and hastened away to the dwelling of the Horai who guard the fiery horses. 'Make ready for me,' he said, 'the chariot of Hêlios, for this day I go through the high heaven in the stead of my father.'

The fair-haired Eôs spread her faint light in the pale sky, and Lampetiê was driving the cattle of Hêlios to their bright pastures,[26] when the Horai brought forth his horses and harnessed them to the fiery chariot. With eager hand Phaethon seized the reins, and the horses sped upon their way up the heights of the blue heaven, until the heart of Phaethon was full of fear and the reins quivered in his grasp. Wildly and more madly sped the steeds, till at last they hurried from the track which led to the Hesperian land. Down from their path they plunged, and drew near to the broad plains of earth. Fiercer and fiercer flashed the scorching flames; the trees bowed down their withered heads; the green grass shrivelled on the hillsides; the rivers vanished from their slimy beds, and the black vapours rose with smoke and fire from the hidden depths of the mighty hills. Then in every land the sons of men lay dying on the scorched and gaping ground. They looked up to the yellow sky, but the clouds came not; they sought the rivers and fountains, but no water glistened on their seething beds; and young and old, all lay down in madness of heart to sleep the sleep of death.

So sped the horses of Hêlios on their fiery wanderings, and Zeus looked down from his Thessalian hill and saw that all living things on the earth must die unless Phaethon should be smitten down from his father's chariot. Then the mighty thunders woke in the hot sky which mourned for the clouds that were dead; and the streams of lightning rushed forth upon Phaethon, and bore him from the blazing heaven far down beneath the waters of the green sea.

But his sisters wept sore for the death of the bright Phaethon, and the daughters of Hesperos built his tomb on the sea-shore, that all men might remember the name of the son of Hêlios and say, 'Phaethon fell from his father's chariot, but he lost not his glory, for his heart was set upon great things.' [27]

BRIAREÔS.

HERE was strife in the halls of Olympos, for Zeus had conquered the ancient gods, and sat on the throne of his father Kronos. In his hand he held the thunderbolts; the lightning slumbered at his feet; and around him all the gods trembled for the greatness of his power. For he laid hard tasks on all, and spake hard words; and he thought to rule harshly over the gods who dwell on the earth and in the broad sea. All the day long Hermes toiled on weary errands to do his will; for Zeus sought to crush all alike, and remembered not the time when he too was weak and powerless.

Then were there secret whisperings, as the gods of earth and sea took counsel together; and Poseidon, the lord of the dark waters, spake in fierce anger and said, 'Hearken to me, Hêrê and Athênê, and let us rise up against Zeus, and teach him that he has not power over all. See how he bears himself in his new majesty,—how he thinks not of the aid which we gave him in the war with his father Kronos,—how he has smitten down even the mightiest of his friends. For Promêtheus, who gave fire to mortal men and saved them from biting cold and gnawing hunger, lies chained on the crags of Caucasus; and if he shrink not to bind the Titan, see that he smite not thee also in his wrath, O lady Hêrê.' And Athênê said, 'The wisdom of Zeus is departed from him, and all his deeds are done now in craft and falsehood; let us bind him fast, lest all the heaven and earth be filled with strife and war.' So they vowed a vow that they would no more bear the tyranny of Zeus; and Hephaistos forged strong chains at their bidding **to cast around him** when sleep lay heavy on his eyelids.

But Thetis heard the words of Poseidon and Athênê, as she sat beneath the waters in her coral cave; and she rose up like a white mist from the sea, and knelt before the throne of Zeus. Then she clasped her arms round his knees and said, 'O Zeus, the gods tremble at thy might, but they love not thy hard words; and they say that thy wisdom hath departed from thee, and that thou doest all things in craft and falsehood. Hearken to me, O Zeus; for Hephaistos hath forged the chain, and the lady Hêrê, and Poseidon the lord of the sea, and the pure Athênê have vowed a vow to bind thee fast when sleep lies heavy on thine eyes. Let me therefore go, that I may bring Briareôs to aid thee with his hundred **hands; and** when he **sits** by thy side, then shalt thou need no more to fear the wrath of Hêrê and Poseidon. And when the peril is past, then, O Zeus, remember that thou must rule gently and justly, for that power shall not stand which fights with truth and love; and forget **not** those who aid thee, nor reward them as thou hast rewarded Promêtheus on the crags of Caucasus; for it may be that, in time to come, I may ask a boon from thee for Achilleus my child, who dwells now in the house of his father Peleus; and when that hour shall come, then call to mind how in time past I saved thee from the chains of Hephaistos.'

Then Zeus spake gently, and said, 'Hasten, Thetis, and bring hither the mighty Briareôs that he may guard me with his hundred hands; and fear not for the words that thou hast spoken, for Zeus will not cast aside good counsel, and the gods shall hate me no more for hard and unkindly words.'

So from the depths of the inmost earth Thetis summoned Briareôs **to** the aid of **Zeus ;** and presently his giant form was **seen in the hall of** Olympos, and **the** gods trembled as he sat down by the side of Zeus, exulting **in** the greatness of his strength. And Zeus spake and said, ' Hearken to me, O lady Hêrê, and Poseidon, and Athênê. I know your counsels, and how ye purposed to bind me for my evil deeds ; but fear not. Only do **my** bidding in time to come, and ye shall no more have **cause to** say that Zeus is a hard and cruel master.' [28]

---o---

SEMELÊ.

THROUGH all the Bœotian **land, Semelê, the** daughter of King Kadmos, **was** known **for** her great beauty ; and when Zeus looked **on** her in her father's **house at** Thebes, he loved the maiden, and it wakened the wrath of Hêrê, **so that** she sought how she might slay her. And **when she** knew that Zeus went many **times down from Olympos to** see the daughter of Kadmos, **she bade Beroê, her nurse, go** to Semelê and cheat her **into her ruin.** So **Beroê went** and spake crafty words to Semelê, and told **her** of the glories of Olympos. **'There** Zeus dwells,' she said, ' high **above** the dark **clouds ; and the** thunder roars and the lightning flashes about his throne. There his fiery horses bear him in terrible majesty when he goes to visit Hêrê the queen, and the sun is blotted out from the sky in the thick darkness which **he** spreads **around** him.' Then **Beroê** hastened away, for her work was done ; and Semelê pondered on the words which she had heard, and when Zeus came again, she said to him, ' Why comest thou to me **always so calmly** and gently ? **I love** to see thee kind and tender to me, but I seek also to behold thy majesty. Come to me once as thou art when thou goest to see Hêrê the queen.' Then Zeus said, 'Ah, Semelê, thou knowest not what thou wouldest have. Hêrê, the queen, is of the race of the bright gods, and immortal blood flows in her veins; but thou art the child of mortal man, and thine eyes will fail before the blinding glare of my lightnings, and thy form be scorched by the searing flame.' But Semelê answered gaily, 'O Zeus, it cannot be so fearful as thou sayest; else even the race of the bright gods would quail before thy splendour. But thou hast promised long ago to grant me whatsoever I shall ask of thee, and I would that thou shouldst come to me in all thy great glory.' So Zeus promised to come as she wished, although he knew that then Semelê must die. Not long after, as she sat alone, there came a deep stillness over the air. She heard no sound, but a great horror fell on her, and she felt as if she were taken away far from all help of men; and suddenly from the dead stillness burst the angry lightnings, and the blazing flame scorched up her body, as Zeus drew near to meet her. So amidst the blaze of the lightning and the crashing of the thunderbolts her child Dionysos was born.

Long time Semelê wandered in the land of shadows beneath the earth, until Dionysos had grown up into manhood and become the god of the feast and wine-cup. Then he went down to the kingdom of Hades, and led his mother away from her dark home,[29] and Zeus and all the gods welcomed her by the name of Thyônê as she entered the halls of Olympos.

IN the dark land beneath the earth, where wander the ghosts of men, lay Semelê, the daughter of Kadmos, while her child **Dionysos grew up** full of strength and beauty **on the flowery** plain of Orchomenos. But the wrath of the lady **Hêrê** still burned alike against the mother and the child. **No** pity felt she for the hapless maiden whom the fiery lightning of Zeus had slain; and so in the prison-house of Hades Semelê mourned for the love which she had lost, waiting till her child should lead her forth to the banquet of the gods. **But for him the** wiles of Hêrê boded long toil and grievous peril. On the land and on the sea strange things befel him; but from all dangers **his own** strong **arm** and the love of Zeus, his father, rescued him. Thus throughout the land men spake of his beauty and his strength, and said that he was worthy to be the child of the maiden who had dared to look **on the majesty of** Zeus. At length the days of his youth were ended, **and** a great yearning filled his **heart to wander through** the earth and behold the cities and the ways of **men. So** from Orchomenos Dionysos journeyed to the sea-shore, and he stood on a jutting rock to **gaze** on the tumbling waters. The glad music of the waves fell upon his ear and filled his soul with a wild joy. His dark locks streamed gloriously over his shoulders, and his purple robe rustled in the soft summer breeze. **Before** him on the blue waters the ships danced merrily in the sparkling sunlight, as they hastened from shore to shore on the **errands** of war or peace. Presently a ship drew near to the beach. Her white sail **was lowered** hastily to the

deck, and five of her crew leaped out and plunged
through the sea-foam to the shore, near the rock on
which stood Dionysos. 'Come with us,' they said, with
rough voices, as they seized him in their brawny arms;
'it is not every day that Tyrrhenian mariners fall in
with youths like thee.' With rude jests they dragged
him to the ship, and there made ready to bind him.
' A brave youth and fair he is,' they said; ' we shall not
lack bidders when we put forth our goods for sale.' So
round his limbs they fastened stout withy bands, but
they fell from off him as withered leaves fall from trees
in autumn, and a careless smile played on his face as he
sat down and looked calmly on the robbers who stood
before him. Then on a sudden the voice of the helmsman was heard as he shouted, ' Fools, what do ye?
The wrath of Zeus is hurrying you to your doom. This
youth is not of mortal race; and who can tell which of
the undying gods has put on this beautiful form? Send
him straightway from the ship in peace, if ye fear not a
deadly storm as we cross the open sea.' Loud laughed
the crew, as their chief answered jeeringly, ' Look out
for the breeze, wise helmsman, and draw up the sail to
the wind. That is more thy task than to busy thyself
with our doings. Fear not for the boy. The withy
bands were but weak; it is no great marvel that he
shook them off. He shall go with us, and before we
reach Egypt or Cyprus or the land of the Hyperboreans,
doubtless he will tell us his name and the name of his
father and his mother. Fear not; we have found a god-
send.'

So the sail was drawn up to the mast, and it swelled
proudly before the breeze as the ship dashed through
the crested waves. And still the sun shone brightly
down on the water, and the soft white clouds floated

lazily in the heavens, as the mighty Dionysos began to
show signs and wonders before the robbers who had
seized him. **Over the deck ran** a stream of purple wine,
and a fragrance as of a heavenly banquet filled **the** air.
Over mast and sailyard clambered the clustering vine,
and dark masses of grapes hung glistening **from** the
branches. The ivy twined in tangled masses round the
tackling, and bright garlands shone, like jewelled crowns,
on every oar-pin. Then a great terror fell on all, as
they cried to the old helmsman, 'Quick, turn the ship to
the shore; there is no hope **for us** here.' But there
followed a mightier wonder still. A loud roar broke
upon the air, and a tawny lion stood before them, with
a grim and grisly bear by his side.[30] Cowering like
pitiful slaves, the Tyrrhenians crowded to the stern, and
crouched round the good helmsman. Then the lion
sprang and seized the chief, **and** the men leaped in their
agony over the ship's side. But the power of **Dionysos**
followed them **still; and a** change came **over their**
bodies as they heard a voice which said, '**In the form of**
dolphins shall **ye** wander through the sea for many
generations. No rest shall ye have by night or by day,
while ye fly from the ravenous sharks that **shall** chase
you through the seas.'

But before the old helmsman again stood Dionysos,
the young and fair, in all the glory of undying beauty.
Again his dark locks flowed gently over his shoulders,
and the purple robe rustled softly in the breeze. 'Fear
not,' he said, 'good friend and true, because thou hast
aided one who is sprung from the deathless race of the
gods. I am Dionysos, the child of Zeus, the lord of the
wine-cup and the revel. Thou hast stood by me in the
hour of peril; wherefore my power shall shield thee
from the violence of evil men and soothe thee in a green

old age, till thine eyes close in the sleep of death and thou goest forth to dwell among brave heroes and good men in the asphodel meadows of Elysium.'

Then at the bidding of Dionysos, the north wind came and wafted the ship to the land of Egypt, where Proteus was king.   And so began the long wanderings of the son of Semelê, through the regions of the Ethiopians and the Indians, towards the rising of the sun.   Whithersoever he went, the women of the land gathered round him with wild cries and songs, and he showed them of his secret things, punishing grievously all who set at nought the new laws which he ordained.   So, at his word, Lykurgos, the Edonian chieftain, was slain by his people, and none dared any more to speak against Dionysos, until he came back to the city where Semelê, his mother, had been smitten by the lightnings of Zeus.

—o—

PENTHEUS.

FOR many years Dionysos wandered far away from the land of his birth ; and wherever he went, he taught the people of the country to worship him as a god, and showed them strange rites.   Far away he roamed, to the regions where the Ganges rolls his mighty stream into the Indian sea, and where the Nile brings every year rich gifts from the southern mountains.   And in all the lands to which he came, he made the women gather round him and honour him with wild cries and screams and marvellous customs such as they had never known before.   As he went onwards, the face of the land was changed.   The women grouped themselves in companies far away from the sight of men, and, high up on the barren hills or down in the narrow valleys, with wild movements and fierce shoutings, paid honour to Dionysos, the lord of the wine-cup and the feast. At length, through the Thracian highlands and the soft plains of Thessaly, Dionysos came back to Thebes, where he had been born amid the roar of the thunder and the blaze of the fiery lightning. Kadmos the king, who had built the city, was now old and weak, and he had made Pentheus, the child of his daughter Agâvê, king in his stead. So Pentheus sought to rule the people well, as his father Kadmos had done, and to train them in the old laws, that they might be quiet in the days of peace, and orderly and brave in war.

Thus it came to pass that when Dionysos came near to Thebes, and commanded all the people to receive the new rites which he sought to teach them, it grieved Pentheus at the heart; and when he saw how the women seemed smitten with madness, and that they wandered away in groups to desert places, where they lurked for many days and nights far from the sight of men, he mourned for the evils which his kinsman Dionysos was bringing upon the land. So King Pentheus made a law that none should follow these new customs, and that the women should stay quietly doing their own work in their homes. But when they heard this, they were all full of fury, for Dionysos had deceived them by his treacherous words, and even Kadmos himself, in his weakness and his old age, had been led astray by them. In crowds they thronged around the house of Pentheus, raising loud shouts in honour of Dionysos, and besought him to follow the new way; but he would not hearken to them.

Thus it was for many days; and when all the city was

shaken by the madness of the new worship, Pentheus
thought that he would see with his own eyes the strange
rites by which the women in their lurking-places did
honour to Dionysos. So he went secretly to some
hidden dells whither he knew that the women had
gone; but Dionysos saw him and laid his hands upon
him, and straightway the mind of King Pentheus himself was darkened, and the madness of the worshippers
was upon him also. Then in his folly he climbed a tall
pine-tree, to see what the women did in their revelry;
but on a sudden one of them saw him, and they shrieked
wildly and rooted up the tree in their fury. With one
accord they seized Pentheus and tore him in pieces;
and his own mother Agâvê was among the first to lay
hands on her son. So Dionysos the wine god triumphed;
and this was the way in which the new worship was set
up in the Hellenic land.[31]

———o———

ASKLEPIOS.

N the shores of the lake Boibêis, the golden-
haired Apollo saw and loved Korônis, the
beautiful daughter of Phlegyas.[32] Many a
time they wandered beneath the branching
elms while the dewdrops glistened like jewels on the
leaves, or sat beneath the ivy bowers as the light of
evening faded from the sky and the blue veil of mist fell
upon the sleeping hills. But at length the day came
when Apollo must journey to the western land, and as
he held Korônis in his arms, his voice fell softly and
sadly on her ear. 'I go,' he said, 'to a land that is very

far off, but surely I will return. More precious to me than aught else on **the wide earth** is thy love, Korônis. Let not its flower fade, but keep it fresh and pure as now, till I come to thee again. The dancing Horai trip quickly by, Korônis, and when they bring the day on which I may clasp thee in mine arms once more, it may be that I shall find thee watching proudly over the child **of our love.'**

He was gone; and for Korônis it seemed as though **the sun had** ceased to shine **in the** heaven. For many a day she cared not to wander **by** the winding shore in **the** light of early morning, **or to** rest in the myrtle bowers as the flush of evening faded from the sky. Her thoughts went back to the days that were passed, when Apollo the golden-haired made her glad with the music of his voice. But at length a stranger came to the Boibêan land, and dwelt **in the house** of Phlegyas, and the spell of his glorious beauty fell upon Korônis, and dimmed the love which she had borne for Apollo who **was** far away. Again for her the sun shone **brightly in** the heaven, and the birds filled the air with a joyous music; but the tale went swiftly through the land, and Apollo heard the evil tidings as he journeyed **back** with his sister Artemis to the house of Phlegyas. A look of sorrow that may not be told passed over **his** fair face; but Artemis stretched forth her hand towards the flashing sun and sware that the maiden should rue her fickleness. Soon, on the shore of the lake Boibêis, Korônis lay smitten by the spear which may never miss its mark, and her child Asklepios lay a helpless babe by her side. Then the voice of Apollo was heard saying, '**Slay** not **the** child with the mother;[33] he is born to do great things; but bear him to the wise centaur Cheiron, and bid him train the boy in all his wisdom and teach him

to do brave deeds, that men may praise his name in the
generations that shall be hereafter.'

So in the deep glens of Pelion the child Asklepios
grew up to manhood under the teaching of Cheiron the
wise and good.   In all the land there was none that
might vie with him in strength of body; but the people
marvelled yet more at his wisdom, which passed the
wisdom of the sons of men, for he had learned the
power of every herb and leaf to stay the pangs of sickness and bring back health to the wasted form.   Day by
day the fame of his doings was spread abroad more
widely through the land, so that all who were sick
hastened to Asklepios and besought his help.   But soon
there went forth a rumour that the strength of death had
been conquered by him, and that Athênê, the mighty
daughter of Zeus, had taught Asklepios how to bring
back the dead from the dark kingdom of Hades.   Then,
as the number of those whom he brought from the
gloomy Stygian land increased more and more, Hades
went in hot anger to Olympos, and spake bitter words
against the son of Korônis, so that the heart of Zeus
was stirred with a great fear lest the children of men
should be delivered from death and defy the power of
the gods.   Then Zeus bowed his head, and the lightnings flashed from heaven, and Asklepios was smitten
down by the scathing thunderbolt.

Mighty and terrible was the grief that stirred the soul
of the golden-haired Apollo, when his son was slain.
The sun shone dimly from the heaven; the birds were
silent in the darkened groves; the trees bowed down
their heads in sorrow; and the hearts of all the sons of
men fainted within them, because the healer of their
pains and sickness lived no more upon the earth.   But
the wrath of Apollo was mightier than his grief, and he

smote the giant Cyclôpes who shaped the fiery lightnings far down in the depths of the burning mountain.[34] Then the anger of Zeus was kindled against his own child, the golden-haired Apollo, and he spake the word that he should be banished from the home of the gods to the dark Stygian land. But the lady Lêtô fell at his knees and besought him for her child, and the doom was given that a whole year long he should serve as a bondman in the house of Admêtos, who ruled in Pherai.

---o---

IXION.

AIR as the blushing clouds which float in early morning across the blue heaven, the beautiful Dia gladdened the hearts of all who dwelt in the house of her father Hesioneus. There was no guile in her soft clear eye, for the light of Eôs was not more pure than the light of the maiden's countenance. There was no craft in her smile, for on her rested the love and the wisdom of Athênê. Many a chieftain sought to win her for his bride; but her heart beat with love only for Ixion the beautiful and mighty, who came to the halls of Hesioneus with horses which cannot grow old or die.[35] The golden hair flashed a glory from his head dazzling as the rays which stream from Hêlios when he drives his chariot up the heights of heaven; and his flowing robe glistened as he moved, like the vesture which the sun-god gave to the wise maiden Medeia, who dwelt in Kolchis.

Long time Ixion abode in the house of Hesioneus, for Hesioneus was loth to part with his child. But at the last Ixion sware to give for her a ransom precious as the

golden fruits which Hêlios wins from the teeming earth.
So the word was spoken, and Dia the fair became the
wife of the son of Amythaon, and the undying horses
bare her away in his gleaming chariot.   Many a day and
month and year the fiery steeds of Hêlios sped on their
burning path, and sank down hot and wearied in the
western sea; but no gifts came from Ixion,[36] and Hesioneus waited in vain for the wealth which had tempted
him to barter away his child.   Messenger after messenger
went and **came**, and always the tidings were that Ixion
had better things to do than to waste his wealth **on** the
mean and greedy.   'Tell him,' he said, 'that every **day**
I journey across the wide earth, gladdening the hearts **of**
the children of men, and that his child has now a **more**
glorious home than that of the mighty gods who dwell on
the high Olympos.   What would he have more?'   Then
day by day Hesioneus held converse with himself, and
his people heard the words which came sadly from his
lips.   'What would I more?' he said; 'I would
have the love of my child.   I let her depart, when
not the wealth of Phœbus himself could recompense me
for her loss.   I bartered her for gifts, and Ixion withholds
the wealth which he sware to give.   Yet were all the
riches of his treasure-house lying now before me, one
loving glance from the eyes of Dia would be more than
worth them all.'

But when his messengers went yet again to plead with
Ixion, and their words were all spoken in vain, Hesioneus
resolved to deal craftily, and he sent his servants by night
and stole the undying horses which bare his gleaming
chariot.   Then **the heart of** Ixion **was** humbled within
him, for he said, 'My people look for me daily throughout the wide earth.   If they see not my face, their souls
will faint with fear; they will not care to sow their fields,

and the golden harvests of Dêmêtêr will wave no more in the summer breeze.' So there came messengers from Ixion, who said, ' If thou wouldest have the wealth which thou seekest, come to the house of Ixion, and the gifts shall be thine, and thine eyes shall once more look upon thy child.' In haste Hesioneus went forth from his home. like a dark and lonely cloud stealing across the broad heaven. All night long he sped upon his way, and, as the light of Eôs flushed the eastern sky, he saw afar off the form of a fair woman who beckoned to him with her long white arms. Then the heart of the old man revived, and he said, ' It is Dia, my child. It is enough if I can but hear her voice and clasp her in mine arms and die.' But his limbs trembled for joy, and he waited until presently his daughter came and stood beside him. On her face there rested a softer beauty than in the former days, and the sound of her voice was more tender and loving, as she said, ' My father, Zeus has made clear to me many dark things, for he has given me power to search out the secret treasures of the earth, and to learn from the wise beings who lurk in its hidden places the things that shall be hereafter. And now I see that thy life is wellnigh done, if thou seekest to look upon the treasures of Ixion, for no man may gaze upon them and live. Go back then to thy home, if thou wouldest not die. I would that I might come with thee, but so it may not be. Each day I must welcome Ixion when his fiery horses come back from their long journey, and every morning I must harness them to his gleaming chariot before he speeds upon his way. Yet thou hast seen my face, and thou knowest that I love thee now even as in the days of my childhood.' But the old greed filled again the heart of Hesioneus, and he said, ' The faith of Ixion is pledged. If he withhold still the treasures which he

D

sware to give, he shall never more see the deathless horses.
I will go myself into his treasure-house, and see whether
in very truth he has the wealth of which he makes such
proud boasting.'   Then Dia clasped her arms once again
around her father, and she kissed his face, and said sadly,
' Farewell, then, **my** father ; I go to my home, for even
the eyes of Dia may not gaze on the secret treasures of
Ixion.'   So Dia left him, and when the old man turned
to look on her departing form, it faded from his sight as
the clouds melt away before the sun at noonday.   Yet
once again he toiled on his way, until before his glorious
home he saw Ixion, radiant as Phœbus Apollo in his
beauty ; but there was anger in his kindling eye, for **he**
was wroth for the theft of his undying horses.   Then the
voicé of Ixion smote the ear of Hesioneus, harsh as the
flapping of the wings of Erìnys when she wanders through
the air.   ' So thou wilt see my secret treasures.   Take
heed that thy sight be strong.'   But Hesioneus spake in
haste and said, ' Thy faith is pledged, not only to let me
see them, but to bestow them on me as my own, for
therefore didst thou win Dia my child to be thy wife.'
Then Ixion opened the door of his treasure-house and
thrust in Hesioneus, and the everlasting fire devoured
him.

But far above, in the pure heaven, Zeus beheld the
deed of Ixion, and the tidings were sent abroad to all the
gods of Olympos, and to all the sons of men, that Ixion
had slain Hesioneus by craft and guile.   A horror of
great blackness fell on the heaven above and the earth
beneath for the sin of which Zeus alone can purge away
the guilt.   Once more Dia made ready her husband's
chariot, and once more he sped on his fiery journey ; but
all men turned away their faces, and the trees bowed
their scorched and withered heads to the ground.   The

flowers drooped sick on their stalks and died, the corn was kindled like dried stubble on the earth, and Ixion said within himself, 'My sin is great; men will not look upon my face as in the old time, and the gods of Olympos will not cleanse my hands from the guilt of my treacherous deed.' So he went straightway and fell down humbled before the throne of Zeus, and said, 'O thou that dwellest in the pure æther far above the dark cloud, my hands are foul with blood, and thou alone canst cleanse them: therefore purge mine iniquity, lest all living things die throughout the wide earth.'

Then the undying gods were summoned to the judgement-seat of Zeus. By the side of the son of Kronos stood Hermes, ever bright and fair, the messenger who flies on his golden sandals more swiftly than a dream; but fairer and more glorious than all who stood near his throne was the lady Hêrê, the queen of the blue heaven. On her brow rested the majesty of Zeus and the glory of a boundless love which sheds gladness on the teeming earth and the broad sea. And even as he stood before the judgement-seat, the eyes of Ixion rested with a strange yearning on her undying beauty, and he scarce heard the words which cleansed him from bloodguiltiness.

So Ixion tarried in the house of Zeus, far above in the pure æther, where only the light clouds weave a fairy network at the rising and setting of the sun. Day by day his glance rested more warm and loving on the countenance of the lady Hêrê, and Zeus saw that her heart too was kindled by a strange love, so that a fierce wrath was stirred within him.

Presently he called **Hermes** the messenger **and said,** 'Bring up from among the children of Nephelê one who shall wear the semblance of the lady Hêrê, and place **her in** the path of Ixion when he wanders forth on the morrow.' So Hermes sped away on his errand, and on that day Ixion spake secretly with Hêrê, and tempted her to fly from the house of Zeus. 'Come with me,' he said; 'the winds of heaven cannot vie in speed with my deathless horses; and the palace of Zeus is but as the house of the dead by the side of my glorious home.' Then the heart of Ixion bounded with a mighty delight as he heard the words of Hêrê. 'To-morrow I will meet thee in the land of the children of Nephelê.' So on the morrow, when the light clouds had spread their fairy net-work over the heaven, Ixion stole away from the house of Zeus to meet the lady Hêrê. As he went, the fairy web faded from the sky, and it seemed to him that the lady Hêrê stood before him in all her beauty. 'Hêrê, great queen of the unstained heaven,' he said, 'come with me, for I am worthy of thy love, and I quail not for all the majesty of Zeus.' But even as he stretched forth his arms, the bright form vanished away. The crashing thunder rolled through the sky, and he heard the voice of Zeus saying, 'I cleansed thee from thy guilt; I shel-tered thee in my home; and thou hast dealt with me treacherously as thou didst before with Hesioneus. Thou hast sought the love of Hêrê; but the maiden which stood before thee was but a child of Nephelê, whom Hermes brought hither to cheat thee with the semblance of the wife of Zeus. Wherefore hear thy doom. No more shall thy deathless horses speed with thy glistening chariot over the earth, but high in the heaven a blazing wheel shall bear thee through the roll-ing years; and the doom shall be on thee for ever and ever.'

So was Ixion bound on the fiery-wheel, and the sons of men see the flashing spokes [37] day by day as it whirls in the high heaven.

ENEATH the mighty rocks of Sipylos stood the palace of Tantalos the Phrygian king, gleaming with the blaze of gold and jewels. Its burnished roofs glistened from afar like the rays which dance on ruffled waters. Its marble columns flashed with hues rich as the hues of purple clouds which gather round the sun as he sinks down in the sky. And far and wide was known the name of the mighty chieftain, who was wiser than all the sons of mortal men; for his wife Euryanassa,[38] they said, came of the race of the undying gods, and to Tantalos Zeus had given the power of Hêlios, that he might know his secret counsels and see into the hidden things of earth and air and sea. Many a time, so the people said, he held converse with Zeus himself in his home on the high Olympos; and day by day his wealth increased, his flocks and herds multiplied exceedingly, and in his fields the golden corn waved like a sunlit sea.

But, as the years rolled round, there were dark sayings spread abroad, that the wisdom of Tantalos was turned to craft, and that his wealth and power were used for evil ends. Men said that he had sinned like Promêtheus the Titan, and had stolen from the banquet-hall of Zeus the food and drink of the gods, and given them to mortal men. And tales yet more strange were told, how that Pandareôs brought to him the hound which Rhea placed in the cave of Diktê to guard the child Zeus, and how, when Hermes bade him yield up the dog, Tantalos laughed him to scorn, and said, 'Dost thou ask me for the hound which guarded Zeus in the days of his childhood? It were as well to ask me for the unseen breeze which sighs through the groves of Sipylos.'

Then, last of all, men spake in whispers of a sin yet more fearful which Tantalos had sinned, and the tale was told that Zeus and all the gods came down from Olympos to feast in his banquet-hall, and how, when the red wine sparkled in the golden goblets, Tantalos placed savoury meat before Zeus, and bade him eat of a costly food, and, when the feast was ended, told him that in the dish had lain the limbs of the child Pelops, whose sunny smile had gladdened the hearts of mortal men. Then came the day of vengeance, for Zeus bade Hermes bring back Pelops again from the kingdom of Hades to the land of living men, and on Tantalos was passed a doom which should torment him for ever and ever. In the shadowy region where wander the ghosts of men, Tantalos, they said, lay prisoned in a beautiful garden, gazing on bright flowers and glistening fruits and laughing waters ; but for all that his tongue was parched, and his limbs were faint with hunger. No drop of water might cool his lips, no luscious fruit might soothe his agony. If he bowed his head to drink, the water fled away ; if he stretched forth his hand to pluck the golden apples, the branches vanished like mists before the face of the rising sun ; and in place of ripe fruits glistening among green leaves, a mighty rock beetled above his head, as though it must fall and grind him to powder. Wherefore men say, when the cup of pleasure is dashed from the lips of those who would drink of it, that on them has fallen the doom of the Phrygian Tantalos.[39]

THE TOILS OF HERAKLES.

Y the doom of his father Zeus, Herakles served in Argos the false and cruel Eurystheus. For so it was that Zeus spake of the birth of Herakles to Hêrê, the queen, and said, 'This day shall a child be born of the race of Perseus, who shall be the mightiest of the sons of men.' Even so he spake, because Atê had deceived him by her evil counsel. And Hêrê asked whether this should be so in very deed; and Zeus bowed his head, and the word went forth which could not be recalled. Then Hêrê went to the mighty Eileithyiai, and by their aid she brought it about that Eurystheus was born before Herakles the son of Zeus.

So the lot was fixed that all his life long Herakles should toil at the will of a weak and crafty master. Brave in heart and stout of body, so that no man might be matched with him for strength or beauty, yet was he to have no profit of all his labour till he should come to the land of the undying gods. But it grieved Zeus that the craft of Hêrê, the queen, had brought grievous wrong on his child, and he cast forth Atê from the halls of Olympos, that she might no more dwell among the gods.[40] Then he spake the word that Herakles should dwell with the gods in Olympos, as soon as the days of his toil on earth should be ended.

Thus the child grew in the house of Amphitryon, full of beauty and might, so that men marvelled at his great strength; for as he lay one day sleeping, there came two serpents into the chamber, and twisted their long coils round the cradle, and peered upon him with their cold glassy eyes, till the sound of their hissing woke him from his slumber. But Herakles trembled not for fear, but he stretched forth his arms and placed his hands on the serpents' necks, and tightened his grasp more and more till they fell dead on the ground. Then all knew by this sign that Herakles must do great things and suffer many sorrows, but that in the end he should win the victory. So the child waxed great and strong, and none could be matched with him for strength of arm and swiftness of foot and in taming of horses and in wrestling. The best men in Argos were his teachers, and the wise centaur Cheiron was his friend, and taught him ever to help the weak and take their part against any who oppressed them. So, for all his great strength, none were more gentle than Herakles, none more full of pity for those who were bowed down by pain and labour.

But it was a sore grief to Herakles that all his life long he must toil for Eurystheus, while others were full of joy and pleasure and feasted at tables laden with good things. And so it came to pass that one day, as he thought of these things, he sat down by the wayside, where two paths met, in a lonely valley far away from the dwellings of men.[41] Suddenly, as he lifted up his eyes, he saw two women coming towards him, each from a different road. They were both fair to look upon ; but the one had a soft and gentle face, and she was clad in a seemly robe of pure white. The other looked boldly at Herakles, and her face was more ruddy, and her eyes shone with a hot and restless glare. From her shoulders streamed the long folds of her soft embroidered robe, which scantily hid the beauty of her form beneath. With a quick and eager step she hastened to Herakles, that so she might be the first to speak. And she said, ' I know, O man of much toil and sorrow, that thy heart is sad within thee, and that thou knowest not which way thou shalt turn. Come then with me, and I will lead thee on a soft and pleasant road, where no storms shall vex thee and no sorrows shall trouble thee. Thou shalt never hear of wars and battles, and sickness and pain shall not come nigh to thee; but all day long shalt thou feast at rich banquets and listen to the songs of minstrels. Thou shalt not want for sparkling wine, and soft robes, and pleasant couches; thou shalt not lack the delights of love, for the bright eyes of maidens shall look gently upon thee, and their song shall lull thee to sleep in the soft evening hour, when the stars come out in the sky.' And Herakles said, 'Thou promisest to me pleasant things, lady, and I am sorely pressed down by a hard master. What is thy name?' 'My friends,' said she, ' call me the happy and joyous one; and they who look not upon me with love have given me an evil name, but they speak falsely.'

Then the other spake and said, 'O Herakles, I too know whence thou art, and the doom that is laid upon thee, and how thou hast lived and toiled even from the days of thy childhood; and therefore I think that thou wilt give me thy love, and if thou dost, then men shall speak of thy good deeds in time to come, and my name shall be yet more exalted. But I have no fair words wherewith to cheat thee. Nothing good is ever reached without labour; nothing great is ever won without toil. If thou seek for fruit from the earth, thou must tend and till it; if thou wouldst have the favour of the undying gods, thou must come before them with prayers and offerings; if thou longest for the love of men, thou must do them good.' Then the other brake in upon her words and said, 'Thou seest, Herakles, that Aretê seeks to lead thee on a long and weary path, but my broad and easy road leads thee quickly to happiness.' Then Aretê answered her (and her eye flashed with anger), 'O wretched one, what good thing hast thou to give, and what pleasure canst thou feel, who knowest not what it is to toil? Thy lusts are pampered, thy taste is dull. Thou quaffest the rich wine before thou art thirsty, and fillest thyself with dainties before thou art hungry. Though thou art numbered amongst the undying ones, the gods have cast thee forth out of heaven, and good men scorn thee. The sweetest of all sounds, when a man's heart praises him, thou hast never heard; the sweetest of all sights, when a man looks on his good deeds, thou hast never seen. They who bow down to thee are weak and feeble in youth, and wretched and loathsome in old age. But I dwell with the gods in heaven, and with good men on the earth; and without me nothing good and pure may be thought and done. More than all others am I honoured by the gods, more than all others am I cherished by the men who love me. In peace and in war, in health and in sickness, I am the aid of all who seek me; and my help never fails. My children know the purest of all pleasures, when the hour of rest comes after the toil of day. In youth they are strong, and their limbs are quick with health; in old age they look back upon a happy life; and when they lie down to the sleep of death, their name is cherished among men for their brave and good deeds. Love me, therefore, Herakles, and obey my words, and thou shalt dwell with me, when thy toil is ended, in the home of the undying gods.'

Then Herakles bowed down his head and sware to follow her counsels; and when the two maidens passed away from his sight, he went forth with a good courage to his labour and suffering. In many a land he sojourned and toiled to do the will of the false Eurystheus. Good deeds he did for the sons of men : but he had no profit of all his labour, save the love of the gentle Iolê. Far away in Œchalia, where the sun rises from the eastern sea, he saw the maiden in the halls of Eurytos, and sought to win her **love.** But the word which Zeus spake to Hêrê the queen gave him no rest ; and Eurystheus sent him forth to other lands, and he saw the maiden no more.

But Herakles toiled on with a good heart, and soon the **glory** of his great deeds were spread abroad throughout **all** the earth. Minstrels sang how he slew the monsters and savage beasts who vexed the sons of men, how he smote the Hydra in the land of Lernai, and the wild boar which haunted the groves of Erymanthos, and the Harpies who lurked in the swamps of Stymphalos. They told how he wandered far away to the land of the setting sun, when Eurystheus bade him pluck the golden apples from the garden of the Hesperides,—how over hill and dale, across marsh and river, through thicket and forest, he came to the western sea, and crossed to the African land where Atlas lifts up his white head to the high heaven,— how he smote the dragon which guarded the brazen gates, and brought the apples to King Eurystheus. They sang of his weary journey when he roamed through the land of the Ethiopians and came to the wild and desolate heights of Caucasus,—how he saw a giant form high on the naked rock, and the vulture which gnawed the Titan's heart with its beak. They told how he slew the bird, and smote off the cruel chains, and set Promêtheus free. They sang how Eurystheus laid on him a fruitless task, and sent him down to the dark land of King Hades to bring up the monster Kerberos, how upon the **shore of** the gloomy Acheron he found the mighty hound **who** guards the home of Hades and Persephonê, how he seized him in his strong right hand and bare him to King Eurys-

theus.[42] They sang of the days when he toiled in the
land of Queen Omphalê beneath the Libyan sun, how he
destroyed the walls of Ilion when Laomedon was king,
and how he went to Kalydon and wooed and won Dêianeira, the daughter of the chieftain Oineus.

Long time he abode in Kalydon, and the people of the
land loved him for his kindly deeds. But one day his
spear smote the boy Eunomos ; and his father was not
angry, because he knew that Herakles sought not to slay
him. Yet Herakles would go forth from the land, for
his heart was grieved for the death of the child. So he
journeyed to the banks of the Evênos, where he smote
the centaur Nessos because he sought to lay hands on
Dêianeira. Swiftly the poison from the barb of the spear
ran through the centaur's veins ; but Nessos knew how to
avenge himself on Herakles, and with a faint voice he
besought Dêianeira to fill a shell with his blood, so that,
if ever she lost the love of Herakles, she might win it
again by spreading it on a robe for him to wear.

So Nessos died ; and Herakles went to the land of
Trachis, and there Dêianeira abode while he journeyed
to the eastern sea. Many times the moon waxed and
waned in the heaven, and the corn sprang up from the
ground and gave its golden harvest ; but Herakles came
not back. At last the tidings came how he had done great
deeds in distant lands, how Eurytos the king of Œchalia
was slain, and how among the captives was the daughter
of the king, the fairest of all the maidens of the land.

Then the words of Nessos came back to Dêianeira, and
she hastened to anoint a broidered robe ; for she thought
only that the love of Herakles had passed away from her,
and that she must win it to herself again. So with words
of love and honour, she sent the gift for Herakles to
put on ; and the messenger found him on the Keneian

shore, where he was offering rich sacrifice to Zeus his
father, and gave **him** the broidered robe in token of the
love of Dêianeira. Then Herakles wrapt it closely round
him, and he stood by the altar while the dark smoke went
up in a thick cloud to the heaven. Presently the vengeance of Nessos was accomplished. Through the veins
of Herakles the poison **spread** like devouring fire.
Fiercer and fiercer grew the burning pain, and Herakles
vainly strove to tear the robe and cast it **from** him. It
ate into his flesh ; and as he struggled in his agony, **the**
dark blood gushed from **his** body in streams. **Then**
came the maiden Iolê to his side. With her gentle hands
she sought to soothe his pain, and with pitying words to
cheer him in his woe. Then once more the face of Herakles flushed with a deep joy, and his eye glanced with a
pure light, as in the days of his might and strength ; and
he said, ' Ah, Iolê, brightest of maidens, thy voice shall
cheer me as I sink down in the sleep of death. **I loved**
thee in the bright morning time, when my hand was strong
and my foot swift ; but Zeus willed not that thou shouldst
be with me in my long wanderings. Yet I grieve not now,
for again thou hast come, fair as the soft clouds which
gather round the dying sun.' Then Herakles bade them
bear him to the high crest of Oita and gather wood.
So when all was ready, he lay down to rest, and they
kindled the great pile. The black mists were spreading
over the sky, but still Herakles sought to gaze on the fair
face of Iolê and to comfort her in her sorrow. 'Weep
not, Iolê,' he said ; 'my toil is done, and now is the time
for rest. I shall see thee again in the bright land which
is never trodden by the feet of night.'

Blacker and blacker grew the evening shades ; and
only the long line of light broke the darkness which
gathered round the blazing pile. Then from the high

heaven came down the thick cloud, and the din of its thunder crashed through the air. So Zeus carried his child home, and the halls of Olympos were opened to welcome the bright hero who rested from his mighty toil. There the fair maiden Aretê placed **a crown upon** his head, and Hêbê clothed him in a white robe for the banquet of the gods.[43]

----o----

ADMÉTOS.

HERE was high feasting in the halls of Pheres, because Admêtos, his son, had brought home Alkêstis, the fairest of all the daughters of Pelias,[44] to be his bride. The minstrels sang **of the** glories of the house of Pherai, and **of** the brave deeds of Admêtos—how, by the aid of the golden-haired Apollo, he had **yoked the lion and the** boar, and made them drag his chariot to Iolkos, for Pelias had **said that** only to one who came thus would **he give** his daughter Alkêstis to be his wife. So the sound **of** mirth and revelry echoed through the hall, and the red wine was poured forth in honour of Zeus and all the gods, each by his name; but the name of Artemis was forgotten, and her wrath burned sore against the house of Admêtos.

But one, mightier yet than Artemis, was nigh at hand to aid him, for Apollo, the son of Lêtô, served as a bondman in the house of Pheres, because he had slain the Cyclôpes who forged the thunderbolts of Zeus. No mortal blood flowed in his veins; but, though he could neither grow **old nor die, nor could any** of the sons of men do him hurt, yet all loved him for his gentle dealing, for **all** things had prospered in the land from the day when he came to the house of Admêtos. And so it came to pass that, when the sacrifice of the marriage feast was ended, he spake to Admêtos and said, 'The anger of Artemis my sister is **kindled** against thee, and it may be that she will smite thee with her spear which can never miss its mark. But thou hast been to me a kind task-master; and though I am here as thy bond-servant, yet have I power still with my father Zeus, and I have obtained for thee this boon, that, if thou art smitten by the spear of Artemis, thou shalt not die, if thou canst find one who in thy stead will go down to the dark kingdom of Hades.'

Many a time the sun rose up into the heaven and sank **down** to sleep beneath the western waters; and still the hours went by full of deep joy to Admêtos and his wife Alkêstis, for their hearts were knit together in a pure love, and no cloud of strife spread its dark shadow over their souls. Once only Admêtos spake to her of the words of Apollo, and Alkêstis answered with a smile, 'Where is the pain of death, my husband, for those who love truly? Without thee I care not to live; wherefore, to die for thee will be a boon.'

Once again there was high feasting in the house of Admêtos, for Herakles, the mighty son of Alkmênê, had come thither as he journeyed through many lands doing **the will of** the false Eurystheus. But, even as the min-strels sang the praises of the chieftains of Pherai, the flush of life faded from the face of Admêtos, and he felt that the hour of which Apollo had warned him was come. But soon the blood came back tingling through his veins, when he thought of the sacrifice which alone could save him from the sleep of death. Yet what will not a man do for his life? and how shall he withstand when the voice of love pleads on his side? So once again **the fair** Alkêstis looked lovingly upon him as she said, '**There is** no darkness for me in the land of Hades, if only I die

for thee;' and even as she spake, the spell passed from
Admêtos, and the strength of the daughter of Pelias
ebbed slowly away.

The sound of mirth and feasting was hushed. The harps
of the minstrels hung silent on the wall, and men spake
in whispering voices, for the awful Moirai were at hand
to bear Alkêstis to the shadowy kingdom.   On the couch
lay her fair form, pale as the white lily which floats on
the blue water, and beautiful as Eôs when her light dies
out of the sky in the evening.[45]   Yet a little while, and
the strife was ended, and Admêtos mourned in bitterness
and shame for the love which he had lost.

Then the soul of the brave Herakles was stirred within him, and he sware that the Moirai should not win the
victory.   So he departed in haste, and far away in the
unseen land he did battle with the powers of death, and
rescued Alkêstis from Hades, the stern and rugged king.

So once more she stood before Admêtos, more radiant
in her beauty than in the former days, and once more in
the halls of Pherai echoed the sound of high rejoicing,
and the minstrels sang of the mighty deed of the good
and brave Herakles, as he went on his way from the
home of Admêtos to do in other lands the bidding of the
mean Eurystheus.

EPIMÊTHEUS AND PANDÔRA.

HERE was strife between Zeus and men; for
Promêtheus stood forth on their side and
taught them how they might withstand the new
god who sat on the throne of Kronos; and he
said, 'O men, Zeus is greedy of riches and honour; and
your flocks and herds will be wasted with burnt-offerings,

if ye offer up to Zeus the whole victim.   Come and let us
make a covenant with him, that there may be a fair portion
for him and for men.'   So Promêtheus chose out a large
ox, and slew him, and divided the body.   Under the
skin he placed the entrails and the flesh, and under the
fat he placed the bones.   Then he said, 'Choose thy
portion, O Zeus, and let that on which thou layest thine
hands be thy share for ever.'   So Zeus stretched forth
his hand in haste, and placed it upon the fat ; and fierce
was his wrath when he found only the bare bones underneath it.   Wherefore men offer up to the undying gods
only the bones and fat of the victims that are slain.

Then in his anger Zeus sought how he might avenge
himself on the race of men ; and he took away from them
the gift of fire,[46] so that they were vexed by cold and
darkness and hunger, until Promêtheus brought them
down fire which he had stolen from heaven.   Then was
the rage of Zeus still more cruel, and he smote Promêtheus with his thunderbolts ; and at his bidding Hermes
bare him to the crags of Caucasus, and bound him with
iron chains to the hard rock, where the vulture gnawed
his heart with its beak.

But the wrath of Zeus was not appeased, and he sought
how he might yet more vex the race of men ; and he remembered how the Titan Promêtheus had warned then
to accept no gift from the gods, and how he left his brothe
Epimêtheus to guard them against the wiles of the son of
Kronos.   And he said within himself, 'The race of men
knows neither sickness nor pain, strife or war, theft or
falsehood ; for all these evil things are sealed up in the
great cask which is guarded by Epimêtheus.   I will let
loose these evils, and the whole earth shall be filled with
woe and misery.'

So he called Hephaistos, the lord of fire, and he said,

E

' Make ready a gift which all the undying gods shall give
to the race of man.   Take earth, and fashion it into the
shape of woman.   Very fair let it be to look upon, but
give her an evil nature, that the race of men may suffer
for all the deeds that they have done me.'   Then Hephaistos took the clay and moulded from it the image of a fair
woman, and Athênê clothed her in a beautiful robe, and
placed a crown upon her head, from which a veil fell
over her snowy shoulders.   And Hermes, the messenger
of Zeus, gave her the power of words, and a greedy mind,
to cheat and deceive the race of men.   Then Hephaistos
brought her before the assembly of the gods, and they
marvelled at the greatness of her beauty ; and Zeus took
her by the hand and gave her to Epimêtheus, and said,
' Ye toil hard, ye children of men : behold one who shall
soothe and cheer you when the hours of toil are ended.
The undying gods have taken pity on you, because ye
have none to comfort you ; and woman is their gift to
men, therefore is her name called Pandôra.' [47]

Then Epimêtheus forgot the warning of his brother,
and the race of men did obeisance to Zeus, and received
Pandôra at his hands ; for the greatness of her beauty
enslaved the hearts of all who looked upon her.   But
they rejoiced not long in the gift of the gods ; for Pandôra
saw a great cask on the threshold of the house of Epimêtheus, and she lifted the lid ; and from it came strife and
war, plague and sickness, theft and violence, grief and
sorrow.   Then in her terror she set down the lid again
upon the cask, and Hope was shut up within it, so that
she could not comfort the race of men for the grievous
evil which Pandôra had brought upon them.

IÔ AND PROMÊTHEUS.

N the halls of Inachos, king of Argos, **Zeus be-** held and loved the fair maiden Iô ; but when Hêrê the queen knew it, she was very wroth and sought to slay her.　Then Zeus changed the maiden into a heifer, to save **her** from the anger of **Hêrê ; but** presently Hêrê learned that the heifer was the maiden whom she hated, and she went to Zeus and said, 'Give me that which I shall desire ;' and Zeus answered, 'Say on.'　Then Hêrê said, 'Give me the beautiful heifer which I see feeding in the pastures of King Inachos.'　So Zeus granted her prayer, for he liked not to confess what he had done to Iô to save her from the wrath of Hêrê ; and Hêrê took the heifer and bade Argos with the hundred eyes watch over it by night and by day.

Long time Zeus sought how he might deliver the maiden from the vengeance of Hêrê ; but he strove in **vain, for** Argos never slept, and his hundred eyes saw everything around him, and none could approach without being seen and slain.　At the last Zeus sent Hermes, the bright messenger of the gods, who stole gently towards Argos, playing soft music on his lute.　Soothingly the sweet sounds fell upon his ear, and a deep sleep began to weigh down his eyelids, until Argos with the hundred eyes lay powerless before Hermes.　Then Hermes drew his sharp sword, and with a single stroke he smote off his **head ;** wherefore men call him the slayer of Argos with the hundred eyes.　But the wrath of Hêrê was fiercer than ever when she learned that her watchman was slain ; and she sware that the heifer should have no rest, but wander

in terror and pain from land to land.   So she sent a gadfly to goad the heifer with its fiery sting over hill and
valley, across sea and river, to torment her if she lay down
to rest, and madden her with pain when she sought to
sleep.   In grief and madness she fled from the pastures
of Inachos, past the city of Erechtheus into the land of
Kadmos the Theban.   On and on still she went, resting
not by night or day, through the Dorian and Thessalian
plains, until at last she came to the wild Thrakian land.
Her feet bled on the sharp stones ; her body was torn by
the thorns and brambles, and tortured by the stings of the
fearful gadfly.   Still she fled on and on, while the tears
streamed often down her cheeks, and her moaning showed
the greatness of her agony.   'O Zeus,' she said, 'dost
thou not see me in my misery ?   Thou didst tell me once
of thy love ; and dost thou suffer me now to be driven
thus wildly from land to land, without hope of comfort or
rest ?   Slay me at once, I pray thee, or suffer me to sink
into the deep sea, that so I may put off the sore burden
of my woe.'

But Iô knew not that, while she spake, one heard her
who had suffered even harder things from Zeus.   Far
above her head, towards the desolate crags of Caucasus,
the wild eagle soared shrieking in the sky, and the
vulture hovered near, as though waiting close to some
dying man till death should leave him for its prey.   Dark
snow-clouds brooded heavily on the mountain, the icy
wind crept lazily through the frozen air ; and Iô thought
that the hour of her death was come.   Then, as she
raised her head, she saw far off a giant form, which
seemed fastened by nails to the naked rock ; and a low
groan reached her ear, as of one in mortal pain, and she
heard a voice which said, 'Whence comest thou, daughter
of Inachos, into this savage wilderness ?   Hath the love of

Zeus driven thee thus to the icy corners of the earth ?'
Then Iô gazed at him in wonder and awe, and said, 'How
dost thou know my name and my sorrows ? and what is
thine own wrong ? Tell me (if it is given to thee to know)
what awaits thee and me in the time to come ; for sure
I am that thou art no mortal man. Thy giant form is as
the form of gods or heroes, who come down sometimes
to mingle with the sons of men ; and great must be the
wrath of Zeus, that thou shouldst be thus tormented here.'
Then he said, ' Maiden, thou seest the Titan Promêtheus,
who brought down fire for the children of men, and
taught them how to build themselves houses and till the
earth, and how to win for themselves food and clothing.[43]
I gave them wise thoughts and good laws and prudent
counsel, and raised them from the life of beasts to a life
which was fit for speaking men. But the son of Kronos
was afraid at my doings, lest, with the aid of men, I might
hurl him from his place and set up new gods upon his
throne. So he forgot all my good deeds in times past,
how I had aided him when the earth-born giants sought
to destroy his power and heaped rock on rock and crag
on crag to smite him on his throne ; and he caught me
by craft, telling me in smooth words how that he was my
friend, and that my honour should not fail in the halls of
Olympos. So he took me unawares and bound me with
iron chains, and bade Hephaistos take and fasten me to
this mountain-side, where the frost and wind and heat
scorch and torment me by day and night, and the vulture
gnaws my heart with its merciless beak. But my spirit
is not wholly cast down ; for I know that I have done
good to the sons of men, and that they honour the Titan
Promêtheus, who has saved them from **cold and** hunger
and sickness. And well I know, also, that the reign of
Zeus shall one day come to an end, and that another

shall sit at length upon his throne, even as now he sits
on the throne of his father Kronos.   Hither come, also,
those who seek to comfort me ; and thou seest before
thee the daughters of Okeanos, who have but now left the
green halls of their father to talk with me.   Listen then
to me, daughter of Inachos, and I will tell thee what shall
befall thee in time to come.   Hence from the ice-bound
chain of Caucasus thou shalt roam into the Scythian
land and the regions of the Chalybes.   Thence thou
shalt come to the dwelling-place of the Amâzons on the
banks of the river Thermôdon ; these shall guide thee on
thy way, until at length thou shalt come to a strait, which
thou wilt cross, and which shall tell by its name for ever
where the heifer passed from Europe into Asia.   But the
end of thy wanderings is not yet.'

Then Iô could no longer repress her grief, and her
tears burst forth afresh ; and Promêtheus said, 'Daughter
of Inachos, if thou sorrowest thus at what I have told
thee, how wilt thou bear to hear what beyond these
things there remains for thee to do?'   But Iô said, 'Of
what use is it, O Titan, to tell me of these woful
wanderings?   Better were it now to die and be at rest
from all this misery and sorrow.'   'Nay, not so, O maiden
of Argos,' said Promêtheus, 'for if thou livest, the days
will come when Zeus shall be cast down from his throne ;
and the end of his reign shall also be the end of my
sufferings.   For when thou hast passed by the Thrakian
Bosporos into the land of Asia, thou wilt wander on
through many regions, where the Gorgons dwell, and the
Arimaspians and Ethiopians, until at last thou shalt come
to the three-cornered land where the mighty Nile goes
out by its many arms into the sea.   There shall be thy
resting-place, and there shall Epaphos, thy son, be born,
from whom, in times yet far away, shall spring the great

Heracles, who shall break **my chain** and **set me free from my** long torments. And **if in this thou** doubtest **my** words, I can **tell** thee of every land through which thou **hast** passed **on** thy journey hither; but it is enough if **I** tell thee how the speaking oaks of Dodona hailed thee as one day to be the wife of Zeus and the mother of the mighty Epaphos. Hasten, then, on thy way, daughter of Inachos. Long years of pain and sorrow await thee still; but my griefs shall endure for many generations It avails not now to weep; but this comfort thou hast, that thy lot is happier than mine; and for both of us remains the surety that the right shall at last conquer, and the power of Zeus shall be brought low, even as the power of Kronos, whom he hurled from his ancient throne. Depart hence quickly, for I see Hermes the messenger drawing nigh, and perchance he comes with fresh torments for thee and me.'

So Iô went on her weary road, and Hermes drew nigh **to** Promêtheus, and bade him once again yield himself **to** the will of the mighty Zeus. But Promêtheus laughed him to scorn; and as Hermes turned to go away, the icy wind **came** shrieking through the air, and the **dark** cloud sank lower and lower down the hillside, until it covered the rock on which the body of the Titan was nailed; and the **great** mountain heaved with the earthquake, and the blazing thunderbolts darted fearfully through the sky. Brighter and brighter flashed the lightning, and louder pealed the thunder in the ears of Promêtheus; but he quailed not for all the fiery majesty of Zeus; and still, as the storm grew fiercer and the curls of fire were wreathed around his form, his voice was heard amid the din and roar, and it spake of the day when the good shall triumph, and unjust power shall be crushed and destroyed for ever.

FROM his throne on the high Olympos, Zeus looked down on the children of men, and saw that everywhere they followed only their lusts, and cared nothing for right or for law. And ever, as their hearts waxed grosser in their wickedness, they devised for themselves new rites to appease the anger of the gods, till the whole earth was filled with blood. Far away in the hidden glens of the Arcadian hills the sons of Lykaon feasted and spake proud words against the majesty of Zeus, and Zeus himself came down from his throne to see their way and their doings.

The sun was sinking down in the sky when an old man drew nigh to the gate of Lykosoura. His grey locks streamed in the breeze, and his beard fell in tangled masses over his tattered mantle. With staff in hand he plodded wearily on his way, listening to the sound of revelry which struck upon his ear. At last he came to the Agora, and the sons of Lykaon crowded round him. 'So the wise seer is come,' they said; 'what tale hast thou to tell us, old man? Canst thou sing of the days when the earth came forth from Chaos? Thou art old enough to have been there to see.' Then with rude jeering they seized him and placed him on the ground near to the place where they were feasting. 'We have done a great sacrifice to Zeus this day; and thy coming is timely, for thou shalt share the banquet.' So they placed before him a dish, and the food that was in it was the flesh of man, for with the blood of men they thought to turn aside the anger of the gods.[49] But the old man thrust aside the dish, and, as he rose up, the weariness of age passed away from his face, and the sons of Lykaon[50] were scorched by the glory of his countenance; for Zeus stood before them and scathed them all with his lightnings, and their ashes cumbered the ground.

Then **Zeus** returned to his **home** on Olympos, and he gave the word that a flood of waters should be let loose upon the earth, that the sons of men might die **for** their **great wickedness.** So the west wind rose in his might, and the dark rain-clouds veiled the whole heaven, for **the winds of** the north which drive away the mists and vapours were shut up **in their prison-house.** On hill and valley burst the merciless rain, and the rivers, loosened from their courses, rushed over the wide plains and up **the** mountain-side. From his home on the highlands of Phthia, Deukalion looked forth on the angry sky, and, when he saw the waters swelling in the valleys beneath, he called Pyrrha, his **wife, the** daughter of Epimêtheus, and said to her, ‘The time is come of which my father, the wise Promêtheus, forewarned me. Make ready, therefore, the ark which I have built, **and place in it all** that we may need for food while the flood **of waters is** out upon the earth. Far away on the crags of Caucasus the iron nails rend the flesh **of** Promêtheus, and the vulture gnaws his heart; but the words which he spake are being fulfilled, that for the wickedness of men the flood of waters would come upon the earth; for Zeus himself is but the servant of one that is mightier than he, and must do his bidding.’

Then Pyrrha hastened to make all things ready, and they waited until the waters rose up to the highlands **of** Phthia and floated away the ark of Deukalion. The fishes swam amidst the old elm-groves, **and** twined amongst the gnarled boughs oɩ the oaks, while on the face

of the waters were tossed the bodies of men; and
Deukalion looked on the dead faces of stalwart warriors,
of maidens, and of babes, as they rose and fell upon the
heaving waves. Eight days the ark was borne on the
flood, while the waters covered the hills, and all the
children of men died save a few who found a place of
shelter on the summits of the mountains. On the ninth
day the ark rested on the heights of Parnassos, and
Deukalion, with his wife Pyrrha, stepped forth upon the
desolate earth. Hour by hour the waters fled down the
valleys, and dead fishes and sea-monsters lay caught in
the tangled branches of the forest. But, far as the
eye could reach, there was no sign of living thing, save
of the vultures who wheeled in circles through the heaven
to swoop upon their prey; and Deukalion looked on
Pyrrha, and their hearts were filled with a grief which cannot be told. 'We know not,' he said, 'whether there live
any one of all the sons of men, or in what hour the sleep
of death may fall upon us. But the mighty being who
sent the flood has saved us from its waters : to him let us
build an altar and bring our thankoffering.' So the altar
was built, and Zeus had respect to the prayer of Deukalion, and presently Hermes the messenger stood before
him. 'Ask what thou wilt,' he said, 'and it shall be
granted thee, for in thee alone of all the sons of men
hath Zeus found a clean hand and a pure heart.' Then
Deukalion bowed himself before Hermes and said, 'The
whole earth lies desolate; I pray thee, let men be seen
upon it once more.' 'Even so shall it come to pass,'
said Hermes, 'if ye will cover your faces with your man-
tles and cast the bones of your mother behind you as ye
go upon your way.'

So Hermes departed to the home of Zeus, and Deukalion pondered his words, till the wisdom of his father

Promêtheus showed him that his mother was the earth, **and** that they were to cast the stones behind them as they went down from Parnassos. Then they did each as they were bidden, and the stones which Deukalion threw were turned into men, but those which were thrown by Pyrrha became women ; and the people which knew neither father nor mother went forth to their toil throughout the wide **earth.** The sun shone brightly **in** the heaven and dried up the slime beneath them ; yet was their toil but a weary labour, and so hath it been until this **day**—a struggle hard as the stones from which they have been taken.[51]

But as the years passed on, there were children born to Pyrrha and Deukalion,[52] and the old race of men still lived on the heights of Phthia.   From Hellen, their son, sprang the mighty tribes of the Hellenes ; and from Protogeneia, their daughter, was born Aëthlios, the man of toil and suffering, the father of Endymiôn the fair, who sleeps **on** the hill of Latmos.

POSEIDON AND ATHÊNÊ.[53]

NEAR the banks of the stream Kephîsos, Erechtheus had built a city in a rocky and thin-soiled land.   He was the father of a free and brave people ; and though his city was small and humble, yet Zeus by his wisdom foresaw that one day it would become the noblest of all cities throughout the wide earth.   And there was a strife between **Poseidon** the lord of the sea, and Athênê the virgin child of Zeus, to see by whose name the city of Erechtheus should be called.   So Zeus appointed a day in the which

he would judge between them in presence of the great
gods who dwell on high Olympos.

When the day was come, the gods sat each on his golden throne, on the banks of the stream Kephîsos.   High
above all was the throne of Zeus, the great father of gods
and men, and by his side sat Hêrê the queen.   This day
even the sons of men might gaze upon them, for Zeus
had laid aside his lightnings, and all the gods had come
down in peace to listen to his judgment between Poseidon and Athênê.   There sat Phœbus Apollo with his
golden harp in his hand.   His face glistened for the
brightness of his beauty; but there was no anger in his
gleaming eye, and idle by his side lay the unerring spear
with which he smites all who deal falsely and speak
lies.[54]   There beside him sat Artemis, his sister, whose
days were spent in chasing the beasts of the earth and
in sporting with the nymphs on the reedy banks of
Eurôtas.   There by the side of Zeus sat Hermes ever
bright and youthful, the spokesman of the gods, with
staff in hand to do the will of the great father.   There
sat Hephaistos the lord of fire, and Hestia who guards
the hearth.   There, too, was Arês, who delights in war;
and Dionysos, who loves the banquet and the wine-cup;
and Aphroditê, who rose from the sea-foam to fill the
earth with laughter and woe.

Before them all stood the great rivals, awaiting the
judgment of Zeus.   High in her left hand, Athênê held
the invincible spear; and on her ægis, hidden from mortal sight, was the face on which no man may gaze and
live.   Close beside her, proud in the greatness of his
power, Poseidon waited the issue of the contest.   In his
right hand gleamed the trident with which he shakes the
earth and cleaves the waters of the sea.

Then from his golden seat rose the spokesman Hermes, and his clear voice sounded over all the great council. 'Listen,' he said, 'to the will of Zeus, who judges now between Poseidon and Athênê. The city of Erechtheus shall bear the name of that god who shall bring forth out of the earth the best gift for the sons of men. If Poseidon do this, the city shall be called Poseidonia ; but if Athênê brings the higher gift, it shall be called Athens.'

Then King Poseidon rose up in the greatness of his majesty, and with his trident he smote the earth where he stood. Straightway the hill was shaken to its depths, and the earth clave asunder, and forth from the chasm leaped a horse, such as never shall be seen again for strength and beauty. His body shone white all over as the driven snow ; his mane streamed proudly in the wind as he stamped on the ground and scoured in very wantonness over hill and valley. 'Behold my gift,' said Poseidon, 'and call the city after my name. Who shall give aught better than the horse to the sons of men ? '

But Athênê looked steadfastly at the gods with her keen grey eye ; and she stooped slowly down to the ground, and planted in it a little seed which she held in her right hand. She spake no word, but still gazed calmly on that great council. Presently they saw springing from the earth a little germ, which grew up and threw out its boughs and leaves. Higher and higher it rose, with all its thick green foliage, and put forth fruit on its clustering branches. 'My gift is better, O Zeus,' she said, 'than that of King Poseidon. The horse which he has given shall bring war and strife and anguish to the children of men ; my olive-tree is the sign of peace and plenty, of health and strength, and the pledge of happiness and freedom. Shall not, then, the city of Erechtheus be called after my name ? ' [55]

Then with one accord rose the voices of the gods in the air, as they cried out, ' The gift of Athênê is the best which may be given to the sons of men ; it is the token that the city of Erechtheus shall be greater in peace than in war, and nobler in its freedom than its power.   Let the city be called Athens.'

Then Zeus, the mighty son of Kronos, bowed his head in sign of judgment that the city should be called by the name of Athênê.   From his head the immortal locks **streamed** down,[56] and the earth trembled beneath his feet as he rose from his golden throne to return to the halls of Olympos.   But still Athênê stood gazing over the land which was now her own ; and she stretched out **her** spear towards the city of Erechtheus, and said : ' I have won the victory, and here shall be my home.   Here shall my children grow up in happiness and freedom ; and hither shall the sons of men come to learn of law and order.   Here shall they see what great things may be done by mortal hands when aided by the gods who dwell on Olympos ; and when the torch of freedom has gone out at Athens, its light shall be handed on to other lands, and men shall learn that my gift is still the best, **and** they shall say that reverence for law and the freedom **of** thought and deed has come to them from the city of Erechtheus, which bears the name of Athênê.'

MEDUSA.

N the far western land, where the Hesperides guard the golden apples which Gaia gave to the lady Hêrê, dwelt the maiden Medusa, with her sisters Stheino and Euryalê, in their lonely and dismal home. Between them and the land of living men flowed the gentle stream of ocean,[57] so that only the name of the Gorgon sisters was known to the sons of men, and the heart of Medusa yearned in vain to see some face which might look on her with love and pity; for on her lay the doom of death, but her sisters could neither grow old nor die. For them there was nothing fearful in the stillness of their gloomy home, as they sat with stern unpitying faces, gazing on the silent land beyond the ocean stream. But Medusa wandered to and fro, longing to see something new in a home to which no change ever came; and her heart pined for lack of those things which gladden the souls of mortal men. For where she dwelt there was neither day nor night. She never saw the bright children of Hêlios driving his flocks to their pastures in the morning. She never beheld the stars as they look out from the sky, when the sun sinks down into his golden cup in the evening. There no clouds ever passed across the heaven, no breeze ever whispered in the air; but a pale yellow light brooded on the land everlastingly. So there rested on the face of Medusa a sadness such as the children of men may never feel; and the look of hopeless pain was the more terrible because of the greatness of her beauty. She spake not to any of her awful grief, for her sisters knew not of any such thing as gentleness

and love, and there was no comfort for her from the
fearful Graiai who were her kinsfolk. Sometimes she
sought them out in their dark caves, for it was something
to see even the faint glimmer of the light of day which
reached the dwelling of the Graiai; but they spake not
to her a word of hope when she told them of her misery,
and she wandered back to the land which the light of
Hêlios might never enter. Her brow was knit with pain,
but no tear wetted her cheek, for her grief was too great
for weeping.

But harder things yet were in store for Medusa; for
Athênê, the daughter of Zeus, came from the Libyan
land to the dwelling of the Gorgon sisters, and she
charged Medusa to go with her to the gardens where the
children of Hesperos guard the golden apples of the
lady Hêrê. Then Medusa bowed herself down at the
feet of Athênê, and besought her to have pity on her
changeless sorrow, and she said, 'Child of Zeus, thou
dwellest with thy happy kinsfolk, where Hêlios gladdens
all with his light and the Horai lead the glad dance
when Phœbus touches the strings of his golden harp.
Here there is neither night nor day, nor cloud or breeze
or storm. Let me go forth from this horrible land and
look on the face of mortal men; for I too must die, and
my heart yearns for the love which my sisters scorn.'
Then Athênê looked on her sternly, and said, 'What
hast thou to do with love? and what is the love of men
for one who is ot kin to the beings who may not die?
Tarry here till thy doom is accomplished; and then it
may be that Zeus will grant thee a place among those
who dwell in his glorious home.' But Medusa said,
'Lady, let me go forth now. I cannot tell how many
ages may pass before I die, and thou knowest not the
yearning which fills the heart of mortal things for tender-

ness and love.' Then a look of anger came over the fair
face of Athênê, and she said, ' Trouble me not. Thy
prayer is vain; and the sons of men would shrink from
thee, if thou couldst go among them, for hardly could
they look on the woful sorrow of thy countenance.' But
Medusa answered gently, ' Lady, hope has a wondrous
power to kill the deepest grief, and in the pure light of
Hêlios my face may be as fair as thine.'

Then the anger of Athênê became fiercer still, and she
said, ' Dost thou dare to vie with me?[58] I stand by the
side of Zeus, to do his will, and the splendour of his
glory rests upon me ; and what art thou, that thou
shouldst speak to me such words as these? Therefore,
hear thy doom. Henceforth, if mortal man ever look
upon thee, one glance of thy face shall turn him to
stone. Thy beauty shall still remain, but it shall be to
thee the blackness of death. The hair which streams in
golden tresses over thy fair shoulders shall be changed
into hissing snakes, which shall curl and cluster round
thy neck. On thy countenance shall be seen only fear
and dread, that so all mortal things which look on thee
may die.' So Athênê departed from her, and the blackness of great horror rested on the face of Medusa, and
the hiss of the snakes was heard as they twined around
her head and their coils were wreathed about her neck.
Yet the will of Athênê was not wholly accomplished ; for
the heart of Medusa was not changed by the doom which
gave to her face its deadly power, and she said, ' Daughter
of Zeus, there is hope yet, for thou hast left memortal still,
and, one day, I shall die.'

DANAÊ.

ROM the home of Phœbus Apollo at Delphi
came words of warning to Akrisios, the king
of Argos, when he sent to ask what should befall him in the after-days ; and the warning was
that he should be slain by the son of his daughter Danaê.
So the love of Akrisios was changed towards his child,
who was growing up fair as the flowers of spring, in her
father's house ; and he shut her up in a dungeon, caring
nothing for her wretchedness.   But the power of Zeus
was greater than the power of Akrisios, and Danaê
became the mother of Perseus ; and they called her child
the Son of the Bright Morning,[59] because Zeus had scattered the darkness of her prison-house.   Then Akrisios
feared exceedingly, and he spake the word that Danaê
and her child should die.

The first streak of day was spreading its faint light in
the eastern sky when they led Danaê to the sea-shore,
and put her in a chest, with a loaf of bread and a flask
of water.   Her child slept in her arms, and the rocking
of the waves, as they bore the chest over the heaving sea,
made him slumber yet more sweetly ; and the tears of
Danaê fell on him as she thought of the days that were
past and the death which she must die in the dark waters.
And she prayed to Zeus, and said, 'O Zeus, who hast
given me my child, canst thou hear me still and save me
from this horrible doom?'[60]   Then a deep sleep came
over Danaê, and, as she slept with the babe in her arms,
the winds carried the chest at the bidding of Poseidon,
and cast it forth on the shore of the island of Seriphos.

Now it so chanced that Diktys, the brother of Polydektes, the king of the island, was casting **a net into the** sea, when he saw something thrown up by the waves on the dry land; and he went hastily and took Danaê with her child out of the chest, and said, ' Fear not, lady; no harm shall happen to thee here, and they who have dealt hardly with thee shall not come nigh to hurt thee in this land.' So he led her to the house of King Polydektes, **who** welcomed her to his home, and Danaê had rest after all her troubles.

Thus the time went on, and the child Perseus grew up brave **and strong, and** all who saw **him** marvelled at his beauty. The light of early morning is not more pure than was the colour on his fair cheeks, and the golden locks streamed brightly over his shoulders, like the rays of the sun when they rest on the hills at midday. And Danaê said, ' My child, in the land where thou wast born, they called thee the Son of the Bright Morning. Keep thy faith, and deal justly with all men ; so shalt thou deserve the name which they gave thee.' Thus Perseus grew up, hating all things that were mean and wrong ; and all who looked on him knew that his hands were clean and his heart pure.

But there were evil days in store for Danaê—for King Polydektes sought to win her love against her will.[61] Long time he besought her to hearken to his prayer ; but her heart was far away in the land of Argos, where her child was born, and she said, ' O king, my life is sad and weary ; what is there in me that thou shouldst seek my love? There are maidens in thy kingdom fairer far than I ; leave me then **to** take care of my child while we dwell in a strange land.' Then Polydektes said hastily, ' Think not, lady, to escape me thus. If thou wilt not hearken to my words, thy child shall not remain with thee; but I will send him forth far away into the western land, that he may bring me the head of the Gorgon Medusa.

So Danaê sat weeping when Polydektes had left her, and when Perseus came he asked her why she mourned and wept; and he said, 'Tell me, my mother, if the people of this land have done thee wrong, and I will take a sword in my hand and smite them.' Then Danaê answered, 'Many toils await thee in time to come, but here thou canst do nothing. Only be of good courage, and deal truly, and one day thou shalt be able to save me from my enemies.'

Still, as the months went on, Polydektes sought to gain the love of Danaê, until at last he began to hate her because she would not listen to his prayer. And he spake the word, that Perseus must go forth to slay Medusa, and that Danaê must be shut up in a dungeon until the boy should return from the land of the Graiai and the Gorgons.

So once more Danaê lay within a prison; and the boy Perseus came to bid her farewell before he set out on his weary journey. Then Danaê folded her arms around him, and looked sadly into his eyes, and said, ' My child, whatever a mortal man can do for his mother, that, I know, thou wilt do for me; but I cannot tell whither thy long toils shall lead thee, save that the land of the Gorgons lies beyond the slow-rolling stream of Ocean. Nor can I tell how thou canst do the bidding of Polydektes, for Medusa alone of the Gorgon sisters may grow old and die, and the deadly snakes will slay those who come near, and one glance of her woful eye can turn all mortal things to stone. Once, they say, she was fair to look upon; but the lady Athênê has laid on her a dark doom, so that all who see the Gorgon's face must die. It may be, Perseus, that the heart of Medusa is full rather of grief than hatred, and that not of her own will the woful glare of her eye changes all mortal things into stone ; and, if so it be, then the deed which thou art charged to do shall set her free from a hateful life, and bring to her some of those good things for which now she yearns in vain.[62] Go then, my child, and prosper. Thou hast a great warfare before thee ; and though I know not how thou canst win the victory, yet I know that true and fair dealing gives a wondrous might to the children of men, and Zeus will strengthen the arm of those who hate treachery and lies.'

Then Perseus bade his mother take courage, and vowed a vow that he would not trust in **craft** and falsehood ; and he said, ' I know not, my mother, the dangers and the foes which await me ; but be sure that I will not meet them with any weapons which thou wouldest scorn. Only, as the days and months roll on, think not that evil has befallen me; for there is a hope within me that I shall be able to do the bidding of Polydektes and **to bear** thee hence to our Argive land.' So Perseus **went forth** with a good courage to seek **out the Gorgon Med**usa.

----*o*----

PERSEUS.

HE east wind crested with a silvery foam the waves of **the** sea of Hellê,[63] when Perseus went into the ship which was to bear **him** away from Seriphos. The white sail **was** spread to the breeze, and the **ship** sped gaily over **the** heaving waters. Soon the **blue hills rose** before **them,** and as the sun **sank** down **in the west,** Perseus trod **once** more the Argive land.

But there was **no rest** for him now in his ancient

home. On and on, through Argos and other lands, he must wander in search of the Gorgon, with nothing but his strong heart and his stout arm to help him. Yet for himself he feared not, and if his eyes filled with tears, it was only because he thought of his mother Danaê; and he said within himself, 'O my mother, I would that thou wert here. I see the towers of the fair city where Akrisios still is king; I see the home which thou longest to behold, and which now I may not enter; but one day I shall bring thee hither in triumph, when I come to win back my birthright.'

Brightly before his mind rose the vision of the time to come, as he lay down to rest beneath the blue sky; but when his eyes were closed in sleep, there stood before him a vision yet more glorious, for the lady Athênê was come from the home of Zeus, to aid the young hero as he set forth on his weary labour. Her face gleamed with a beauty such as is not given to the daughters of men. But Perseus feared not because of her majesty, for the soft spell of sleep lay on him; and he heard her words as she said, 'I am come down from Olympos where dwells thy father Zeus, to help thee in thy mighty toil. Thou art brave of heart and strong of hand, but thou knowest not the way which thou shouldest go, and thou hast no weapons with which to slay the Gorgon Medusa. Many things thou needest, but only against the freezing stare of the Gorgon's face can I guard thee now. On her countenance thou canst not look and live; and even when she is dead, one glance of that fearful face will still turn all mortal things to stone. So, when thou drawest nigh to slay her, thine eye must not rest upon her. Take good heed, then, to thyself, for while they are awake the Gorgon sisters dread no danger, for the snakes which curl around their heads warn them of every peril. Only while they sleep canst thou approach them ; and the face of Medusa, in life or in death, thou must never see. Take then this mirror, into which thou canst look, and when thou beholdest her image there, then nerve thy heart and take thine aim, and carry away with thee the head of the mortal maiden. Linger not in thy flight, for her sisters will pursue after thee, and they can neither grow old nor die.'

So Athênê departed from him ; and early in the morning he saw by his side the mirror which she had given to him ; and he said, 'Now I know that my toil is not in vain, and the help of Athênê is a pledge of yet more aid in time to come.' So he journeyed on with a good heart over hill and dale, across rivers and forests, towards the setting of the sun. Manfully he toiled on, till sleep weighed heavy on his eyes, and he lay down to rest on a broad stone in the evening. Once more before him stood a glorious form. A burnished helmet glistened on his head, a golden staff was in his hand, and on his feet were the golden sandals which bore him through the air with a flight more swift than the eagle's. And Perseus heard a voice which said, 'I am Hermes, the messenger of Zeus, and I am come to arm thee against thine ene- . mies. Take this sword, which slays all mortal things on which it may fall,[64] and go on thy way with a cheerful heart. A weary road yet lies before thee, and for many a long day must thou wander on before thou canst have other help in thy mighty toil. Far away, towards the setting of the sun, lies the Tartessian land, whence thou shalt see the white-crested mountains where Atlas holds up the pillars of the heaven. There must thou cross the dark waters, and then thou wilt find thyself in the land of the Graiai, who are of kin to the Gorgon sisters, and thou wilt see no more the glory of Hêlios, who gladdens the homes of living men. **Only a** faint light from the far-off sun comes dimly to the desolate land where, hidden in a gloomy cave, lurk the hapless Graiai.[65] These thou must seek out; and when thou hast found them, fear them not. Over their worn and wrinkled faces stream tangled masses of long grey hair; their voice comes hollow from their toothless gums, and a single **eye is** passed from one to the other when they **wish** to look forth from their dismal dwelling. **Seek** them out, for these alone can tell thee what more remaineth yet for thee to do.'

When Perseus woke in the morning, the sword of Hermes lay beside him; and he **rose** up with great joy, **and** said, 'The help of Zeus fails me not; if more is needed, will he not grant it to me? So onward he went to the Tartessian land, and thence across the dark sea towards the country of the Graiai, till he saw the pillars of Atlas rise afar off into the sky. Then as he drew nigh to the hills which lie beneath them, he came to a dark cave, and as he stooped to look into it, he fancied that he saw the grey hair which streamed over the shoulders of the Graiai. Long time he rested on the rocks without the **cave,** till he knew by their heavy breathing that the sisters **were** asleep. Then he **crept** in stealthily, and took the eye which lay beside them, and waited till they should **wake.** At last, as the faint light from the far-off sun[66] who shines on mortal men reached the cave, he saw them groping for the eye which he had taken; and presently from their toothless jaws came a hollow **voice,** which said, 'There is some one near us who is sprung from the children of men; for of old time we have known that **one** should come and leave us blind until we did his bidding.' Then Perseus came forth boldly and stood before them and said, 'Daughters of Phorkos and of

Kêtô, I know that ye are of kin to the Gorgon sisters, and to these ye must now guide me. Think not to escape by craft or guile, for in my hands is the sword of Hermes, and it slays all living things on which it may fall.' And they answered quickly, 'Slay us not, child of man, for we will deal truly by thee, and will tell thee of the things which must be done before thou canst reach the dwelling of the Gorgon sisters. Go hence along the plain which stretches before thee, then over hill and vale, and forest and desert, till thou comest to the slow-rolling Ocean stream; there call on the nymphs who dwell beneath the waters, and they shall rise at thy bidding and tell thee of many things which it is not given to us to know.'

Onwards again he went, across the plain, and over hill and vale till he came to the Ocean which flows lazily round the world of living men. No ray of the pure sunshine pierced the murky air, but the pale yellow light, which broods on the land of the Gorgons, showed to him the dark stream, as he stood on the banks and summoned the nymphs to do his bidding. Presently they stood before him, and greeted him by his name; and they said, 'O Perseus, thou art the first of living men whose feet have trodden this desolate shore. Long time have we known that the will of Zeus would bring thee hither to accomplish the doom of the mortal Medusa. We know the things of which thou art in need, and without us thy toil would in very truth be vain. Thou hast to come near to beings who can see all around them, for the snakes which twist about their heads are their eyes; and here is the helmet of Hades, which will enable thee to draw nigh to them unseen. Thou hast the sword which never falls in vain; but without this bag which we give thee, thou canst not bear away the head the sight of

which changes all mortal things to stone. And when thy
work of death is done on the mortal maiden, thou must
fly from her sisters who cannot die, and who will follow
thee more swiftly than eagles ; and here are the sandals
which shall waft thee through the air more quickly than
a dream. Hasten then, child of Danaê, for we are ready
to bear thee in our hands across the ocean stream.'

So they bear Perseus to the Gorgon land, and he
journeyed on in the pale yellow light which rests upon it
everlastingly.

On that night, in the darkness of their lonsesome
dwelling, Medusa spake to her sisters of the doom which
should one day be accomplished ; and she said, ‘ Sisters,
ye care little for the grief whose image on my face turns
all mortal things to stone. Ye who know not old age or
death, know not the awful weight of my agony, and cannot feel the signs of the change that is coming. But I
know them. The snakes which twine around my head
warn me not in vain ; but they warn me against perils
which I care not now to shun. The wrath of Athênê,
who crushed the faint hopes which lingered in my heart,
left me mortal still, and I am weary with the woe of the
ages that are past. O sisters, ye know not what it is to
pity, but something more ye know what it is to love, for
even in this living tomb we have dwelt together in peace,
and peace is of kin to love. But hearken to me now.
Mine eyes are heavy with sleep, and my heart tells me
that the doom is coming, for I am but a mortal maiden ;
and I care not if the slumber which is stealing on me be
the sleep of those whose life is done. Sisters, my lot is
happier at the least than yours ; for he who slays me is
my friend. I am weary of my woe, and it may be that
better things await me. when I am dead.'

But, even as Medusa spake, the faces of Stheino and

Euryalê remained unchanged; and it seemed as though for them the words of Medusa were but an empty sound. Presently the Gorgon sisters were all asleep. The deadly snakes lay still and quiet, and only the breath which hissed from their mouths was heard throughout the cave.

Then Perseus drew nigh, with the helmet of Hades[67] on his head, and the sandals of the nymphs on his feet. In his right hand was the sword of Hermes, and in his left the **mirror of** Athênê. Long time he gazed on the image of Medusa's face, which still showed the wreck of her ancient beauty; and he said within himself, 'Mortal maiden, well may it be that more than mortal woe should give to thy countenance its deadly power. The hour of thy doom is come; but death to thee must be a boon.' Then **the sword** of Hermes fell, and **the** great agony of Medusa was ended. So Perseus cast a veil over the dead face, and bare it away from the cave **in** the bag which the nymphs gave him on the banks of the slow-rolling Ocean.

---*0*---

ANDROMEDA.[63]

ERRIBLE was the rage of the Gorgon sisters when they woke up from their sleep and saw that the doom of Medusa had been accomplished. The snakes hissed as they rose in knotted clusters round their heads, and the Gorgons gnashed their teeth in fury, not for any love of the mortal maiden whose woes were ended, but because a child of weak and toiling men had dared to approach the daughters of Phorkos and Kêtô. Swifter than the eagles they sped from their gloomy cave; but they sought in vain to find Perseus, for the helmet of Hades was on his head, and the sandals of the nymphs were bearing him through the air like a dream. Onwards he went, not knowing whither he was borne, for he saw but dimly through the pale yellow light which brooded on the Gorgon land everlast-ingly; but presently he heard a groan as from one in mortal pain, and before him he beheld a giant form, on whose head rested the pillars of the heaven; and he heard a voice, which said, 'Hast thou slain the Gorgon Medusa, child of man, and art thou come to rid me of my long woe? Look on me, for I am Atlas, who rose up with the Titans against the power of Zeus, when Promêtheus fought on his side; and of old time have I known that for me is no hope of rest till a mortal man should bring hither the Gorgon head which can turn all living things to stone. For so was it shown to me from Zeus, when he made me bow down beneath the weight of the brazen heaven. Yet, if thou hast slain Medusa, Zeus hath been more merciful to me than to Promêtheus who was his friend, for he lies nailed on the rugged crags of Caucasus, and only thy child in the third generation shall scare away the vulture which gnaws his heart, and set the Titan free. But hasten now, Perseus, and let me look upon the Gorgon's face, for the agony of my labour is wellnigh greater than I can bear.' [69] So Perseus heark-ened to the words of Atlas, and he unveiled before him the dead face of Medusa. Eagerly he gazed for a moment on the changeless countenance, as though be-neath the blackness of great horror he yet saw the wreck of her ancient beauty and pitied her for her hopeless woe. But in an instant the straining eyes were closed, the heaving breast was still, the limbs which trembled with the weight of heaven were stiff and cold; and it seemed to Perseus, as he rose again into the pale yellow air, that the gray hairs which streamed from the giant's head were like the snow which rests on the peaks of a great mountain, and that in place of the trembling limbs he saw only the rents and clefts on a rough hill-side.

Onward yet and higher he sped, he knew not whither, on the golden sandals, till from the murky glare of the Gorgon land he passed into a soft and tender light, in which all things wore the colours of a dream.[70] It was not the light of sun or moon ; for in that land was neither day nor night. No breeze wafted the light clouds of morning through the sky, or stirred the leaves of the forest trees where the golden fruits glistened the whole year round ; but from beneath rose the echoes of sweet music, as he glided gently down to the earth. Then he took the helmet of Hades from off his head, and asked the people whom he met the name of this happy land ; and they said, 'We dwell where the icy breath of Boreas cannot chill the air or wither our fruits; therefore is our land called the garden of the Hyperboreans.' There for a while Perseus rested from his toil ; and all day long he saw the dances of happy maidens fair as Hêbê and Harmonia, and he shared the rich banquets at which the people of the land feasted with wreaths of laurel twined around their head. There he rested in a deep peace, for no sound of strife or war can ever break it ; and they know nothing of malice and hatred, of sickness or old age.

But presently Perseus remembered his mother Danaê as she lay in her prison-house at Seriphos, and he left the garden of the Hyperboreans to return to the world of toiling men ; but the people of the land knew only that it lay beyond the slow-rolling Ocean stream, and Perseus saw not whither he went as he rose on his golden sandals into the soft and dreamy air. Onwards he flew, until far beneath he beheld the Ocean river, and once more he saw the light of Hêlios as he drove his fiery chariot

through the heaven. Far **away** stretched the mighty
Libyan plain, and further yet beyond the hills which shut
it in he saw the waters of the dark sea, and the white
line of foam where the breakers were dashed upon the
shore. As he came nearer, he saw the huge rocks which
rose out of the heaving waters, and on one of them he
beheld a maiden whose limbs were fastened with chains
to a stone. The folds of her white robe fluttered in the
breeze, and her fair face was worn and wasted with the
heat by day and the cold by night. Then Perseus hastened to her and stood a long time before her, but she
saw him not, for the helmet of Hades was on his head,
and he watched her there till the tears started to his eyes
for pity. Her hands were clasped upon her breast, and
only the moving of her lips showed the greatness of her
misery. Higher and higher rose the foaming waters, till
at last the maiden said, 'O Zeus, is there none whom
thou canst send to help me?' Then Perseus took the
helmet in his hand, and stood before her in all his glorious
beauty; and the maiden knew that she had nothing to
fear when he said, 'Lady, I see that thou art in great
sorrow: tell me who it is that has wronged thee, and I
will avenge thee mightily.' And she answered, 'Stranger,
whoever thou art, I will trust thee, for thy face tells me
that thou art not one of those who deal falsely. My
name is Andromeda, and my father, Kepheus, is king of
the rich Libyan land; but there is strife between him and
the old man Nereus[71] who dwells with his daughters in
the coral caves beneath the sea; for, as I grew up in my
father's house, my mother made a vain boast of my beauty,
and said that among all the children of Nereus there was
none so fair as I. So Nereus rose from his coral caves,
and went to the king Poseidon, and said, " King of the
broad sea, Kassiopeia hath done a grievous wrong to me

and to my children. I pray thee let not her people escape for her evil words." Then Poseidon let loose the waters of the sea, and they rushed in over the Libyan plains till only the hills which shut it in remained above them, and a mighty monster came forth and devoured all the fruits of the land. In grief and terror the people fell down before my father Kepheus, and he sent to the home of Ammon[72] to ask what he should do for the plague of waters and for the savage beast who vexed them; and soon the answer came that he must chain up his daughter on a rock, till the beast came and took her for his prey. So they fastened me here to this desolate crag, and each day the monster comes nearer as the waters rise; and soon, I think, they will place me within his reach.' Then Perseus cheered her with kindly words, and said, 'Maiden, I am Perseus, to whom Zeus has given the power to do great things. I hold in my hand the sword of Hermes, which has slain the Gorgon Medusa, and I am bearing to Polydektes, who rules in Seriphos, the head which turns all who look on it into stone. Fear not, then, Andromeda. I will do battle with the monster, and, when thy foes are vanquished, I will sue for the boon of thy love.' A soft blush as of great gladness came over the pale cheek of Andromeda as she answered, 'O Perseus, why should I hide from thee my joy? Thou hast come to me like the light of morning when it breaks on a woful night.' But, even as she spake, the rage of the waves waxed greater, and the waters rose higher and higher, lashing the rocks in their fury, and the hollow roar of the monster was heard as he hastened to seize his prey. Presently by the maiden's side he saw a glorious form with the flashing sword in his hand, and he lashed the waters in fiercer anger. Then Perseus went forth to meet him, and he held aloft the sword which

Hermes gave to him, and said, 'Sword of Phœbus, let
thy stroke be sure, for thou smitest the enemy of the
helpless.' So the sword fell, and the blood of the mighty
beast reddened the waters of the green sea.

In gladness of heart Perseus led the maiden to the halls
of Kepheus, and he said, 'O king, I have slain the monster to whom thou didst give thy child for a prey: let
her go with me now to other lands, if she gainsay me not.'
But Kepheus answered, 'Tarry with us yet a while, and
the marriage feast shall be made ready, if indeed thou must
hasten away from the Libyan land.' So, at the banquet,
by the side of Perseus sate the beautiful Andromeda; but
there arose a fierce strife, for Phineus had come to the
feast, and it angered him that another should have for
his wife the maiden whom he had sought to make his
bride. Deeper and fiercer grew his rage, as he looked on
the face of Perseus, till at last he spake evil words of the
stranger who had taken away the prize which should
have been his own. But Perseus said, calmly, 'Why,
then, didst thou not slay the monster thyself and set the
maiden free?' When Phineus heard these words, his
rage almost choked him, and he charged his people to
draw their swords and slay Perseus. Wildly rose the din
in the banquet-hall, but Perseus unveiled the Gorgon's
face, and Phineus and all his people were frozen into
stone.

Then, in the still silence, Perseus bare away Andromeda from her father's home; and when they had wandered through many lands, they came at length to Seriphos.
Once more Danaê looked on the face of her son, and
said, 'My child, the months have rolled wearily since I
bade thee farewell; but sure I am that my prayer has
been heard, for thy face is as the face of one who comes
back a conqueror from battle.' Then Perseus said, 'Yes,

my mother, the help of **Zeus has never** failed me. When
the eastern breeze carried me hence to the Argive land,
my heart was full of sorrow, because I saw the city which
thou didst yearn to see, and the home which thou couldst
not enter ; and I vowed a vow to bring thee back in
triumph when I came to claim my birthright. That evening as I slept, the lady Athênê came to me from the
home of Zeus, and gave me a mirror so that I might take
the Gorgon's head without looking on the face which
turns everything into stone ; and yet another night, Hermes stood before me, and gave me the sword whose
stroke never fails, and the Graiai told me where I should
find the nymphs who gave me the helmet of Hades, and
the bag which has borne hither the Gorgon's head, and
the golden sandals which have carried me like a dream
over land and sea. O my mother, I have done wondrous
things by the aid of Zeus. By me the doom of Medusa
has been accomplished ; and I think that the words which
thou didst speak were true for the image of the **Gorgon's**
face, which I saw in Athênê's mirror, was as the countenance of one whose beauty has been marred by a woful
agony ; and whenever I have looked since on that image,
it has seemed to me as though it wore the look of one
who rested in death from a mighty pain. So, as the
giant Atlas looked on that grief-stricken brow, he felt no
more the weight of the heaven as it rested on him ; and
the grey hair which streamed from his head seemed to
me, when I left him, like the snow which clothes the
mountain-tops in winter. So, when from the happy gardens of the Hyperboreans I came to the rich Libyan
plain, and had killed the monster who sought to slay
Andromeda, the Gorgon's face turned Phineus **and** his
people into stone, when they sought to slay me because
I had won her love.' Then Danaê answered the ques-

G

tions of Perseus, and told him how Polydektes had
vexed her with his evil words, and how Diktys [73] alone
had shielded her from his brother.   And Perseus bade
Danaê be of good cheer, because the recompense of Polydektes was nigh at hand.

There was joy and feasting in Seriphos when the news
was spread abroad that Perseus had brought back for the
king the head of the Gorgon Medusa ; and Polydektes
made a great feast, and the wine sparkled in the goblets
as the minstrels sang of the great deeds of the son of
Danaê.   Then Perseus told them of all that Hermes
and Athênê had done for him.   He showed them the
helmet of Hades, and the golden sandals, and the unerring sword, and then he unveiled the face of Medusa
before Polydektes and the men who had aided him
against his mother Danaê.   So Perseus looked upon
them, as they sate at the rich banquet stiff and cold as
a stone, and he felt that his mighty work was ended.
Then, at his prayer, came Hermes, the messenger of
Zeus, and Perseus gave him back the helmet of Hades,
and the sword which had slain the Gorgon, and the
sandals which had borne him through the air like a
dream.   And Hermes gave the helmet again to Hades,
and the sandals to the Ocean nymphs ; but Athênê took
the Gorgon's head, and it was placed upon her shield.

Then Perseus spake to Danaê, and said, ' My mother,
it is time for thee to go home.   The Gorgon's face has
turned Polydektes and his people into stone, and Diktys
rules in Seriphos.'   So once more the white sails were
filled with the eastern breeze, and Danaê saw once more
the Argive land.   From city to city spread the tidings
that Perseus was come, who had slain the Gorgon, and
the youths and maidens sang ' Io Paian ' as they led the
conqueror to the halls of Akrisios.

HE shouts of 'Io Paian' reached the ear of Akrisios, as he sat in his lonely hall, marvelling at the strange things which must have happened to waken the sounds of joy and triumph; for, since the day when Danaê was cast forth with her babe on the raging waters, the glory of war had departed from Argos, and it seemed as though all the chieftains had lost their ancient strength and courage. But the wonder of Akrisios was changed to a great fear when they told him that his child Danaê was coming home, and that the hero Perseus had rescued her from Polydektes, the king of Seriphos. The memory of all the wrong which he had done to his daughter tormented him, and still in his mind dwelt the words of warning which came from Phœbus Apollo that he should one day be slain by the hands of her son; so that, as he looked forth on the sky, it seemed to him as though he should see the sun again no more.

In haste and terror Akrisios fled from his home. He tarried not to hear the voice of Danaê; he stayed not to look on the face of Perseus, nor to see that the hero who had slain the Gorgon bare him no malice for the wrongs of the former days. Quickly he sped over hill and dale, across river and forest, till he came to the house of Teutamidas, the great chieftain who ruled in Larissa.

The feast was spread in the banquet-hall, and the Thessalian minstrels sang of the brave deeds of Perseus, for even thither had his fame reached already. They told how from the land of toiling men he had passed to

the country of the Graiai and the Gorgons, how he had
slain the mortal Medusa and stiffened the giant Atlas into
stone ; and then they sang how with the sword of Hermes
he smote the mighty beast which ravaged the Libyan
land, and won Andromeda to be his bride.   Then Teutamidas spake and said, 'My friend, I envy thee for thy
happy lot, for not often in the world of men may fathers
reap such glory from their children as thou hast won from
Perseus.   In the ages to come men shall love to tell of
his great and good deeds, and from him shall spring
mighty chieftains, who shall be stirred up to a purer
courage when they remember how Perseus toiled and
triumphed before them.   And now tell me, friend, wherefore thou hast come hither.   Thy cheek is pale, and thy
hand trembles ; but I think not that it can be from the
weight of years, for thy old age is yet but green, and
thou mayest hope still to see the children of Perseus
clustering around thy knees.'

But Akrisios could scarcely answer for shame and fear ;
for he cared not to tell Teutamidas of the wrongs which
he had done to Danaê.   So he said hastily that he had
fled from a great danger, for the warning of Phœbus was
that he should be slain by his daughter's son.   And
Teutamidas said, ' Has thy daughter yet another son ? '
And then Akrisios was forced to own that he had fled
from the hero Perseus.   But the face of Teutamidas
flushed with anger as he said, ' O shame, that thou
shouldst flee from him who ought to be thy glory and
thy pride !   Everywhere men speak of the goodness and
the truth of Perseus, and I will not believe that he bears
thee a grudge for anything that thou hast done to him.
Nay, thou doest to him a more grievous wrong in
shunning him now than when thou didst cast him forth
in his mother's arms upon the angry sea.'   So he

pleaded with Akrisios for **Perseus, until he** spake the word that Danaê and her child might come to the great games which were to be held on the plain before Larissa.[74]

With shouts of 'Io Paian' the youths and maidens went out before Perseus as he passed from the city of Akrisios to go to Larissa, and everywhere as he journeyed the people came forth from town and village to greet the bright hero and the beautiful Andromeda, whom he had saved from the Libyan dragon. Onwards they went, spreading gladness everywhere, **till the** cold heart of Akrisios himself was touched with a feeling of strange joy, as he saw the band of youths and maidens who came before them to the house of Teutamidas. So once more his child Danaê stood before him, beautiful still, although the sorrows **of** twenty years had dimmed the brightness of her eye, and the merry laugh of her youth was gone. Once more he looked on the face of Perseus, and he listened to the kindly greeting of the hero whom he had wronged in the days of his helpless childhood. **But he** marvelled yet more at the beauty of Andromeda, and he thought within himself that throughout the wide earth **were** none so fair as Perseus and the wife whom he had won with the sword of Hermes.

Then, as they looked on the chiefs who strove together in the games, the shouting of the crowd told at the end of each that Perseus was the conqueror. At last they **stood forth to see** which should have most strength of **arm** in hurling **the** quoit; and, **when** Perseus aimed at **the** mark, the quoit swerved **aside and smote Akrisios on the** head; and the warning of Phœbus Apollo was accomplished.

Great was the sorrow of Teutamidas **and** his people as the chieftain of Argos lay dead **before** them; but deeper still and more bitter was the grief of Perseus for the deed which he had unwittingly done ; and he said, ' O Zeus, I have striven to keep my hands clean and to deal truly, and a hard recompense hast thou given me.'

So they went back mourning to Argos ; but although he strove heartily to rule his people well, the grief of Perseus could not be lessened while he dwelt in the house of Akrisios. So he sent a messenger to his kinsman Megapenthes [75] who ruled at Tiryns, and said, ' Come thou and rule in Argos, and I will go and dwell among thy people.' So Perseus dwelt at Tiryns, and the men of the city rejoiced that he had come to rule over them. Thus the months and years went quickly by, as Perseus strove with all his might to make his people happy and to guard them against their enemies. At his bidding, the Cyclôpes came from the far-off Lykian land, and built the mighty walls which gird the city round about ; and they helped him to build yet another city, which grew in after-times to be even greater and mightier than Tiryns. So rose the walls of Mykênæ,[76] and there too the people loved and honoured Perseus for his just dealing more than for all the deeds which he had done with the sword of Hermes. At last the time came when the hero must rest from his long toil ; but as they looked on his face, bright and beautiful even in death, the minstrels said, ' We shall hear his voice no more, but the name of Perseus shall never die.'

— *ο* —

KEPHALOS AND PROKRIS.[77]

O F all the maidens in the land of Attica none was so beautiful as Prokris, the daughter of King Erechtheus. She was the delight of her father's heart, not so much for her beauty as for her goodness and her gentleness. The sight of her fair face and the sound of her happy voice brought gladness to all who saw and heard her. Every one stopped to listen to the songs which she sang as she sat working busily at the loom ; and the maidens who dwelt with her were glad when the hour came to go with Prokris and wash their clothes[78] or draw water from the fountain.[79] Then, when all her tasks were ended, she would roam over hill and valley, into every nook and dell. There was no spot in all the land where Prokris had not been. She lay down to rest on the top of the highest hills, or by the side of the stream where it murmured among the rocks far down in the woody glen. So passed her days away ; and while all loved her and rejoiced to see her face, only Prokris knew not of her own beauty, and thought not of her own goodness. But they amongst whom she lived, the old and the young, the sorrowful and the happy, all said that Prokris, the child of Hersê,[80] was always as fair and bright as the dew of early morning.

Once in her many wanderings she had climbed the heights of Mount Hymettos, almost before the first streak of dawn was seen in the sky. Far away, as she looked over the blue sea, her eyes rested on the glittering cliffs of Eubœa, and as she looked she saw that a ship was sailing towards the shore beneath the hill of Hymettos.

Presently it reached the shore, and she could see that a man stepped out of the ship, and began to climb the hill, while the rest remained on the beach. As he came nearer to her, Prokris knew that his face was very fair, and she thought that she had never seen such beauty in mortal man before. She had heard that sometimes the gods come down from their home on Olympos to mingle among the children of men, and that sometimes the bright heroes were seen in the places where they had lived on the earth before they were taken to dwell in the halls of Zeus. As the stranger came near to her, the sun rose up brightly and without a cloud from the dark sea; and its light fell on his face, and made it gleam with more than mortal beauty. Gently he came towards her, and said, 'Lady, I am come from the far-off eastern land; and as I drew near to this shore, I saw that some one was resting here upon the hill. So I hastened to leave the ship, that I might learn the name of the country which I have reached. My name is Kephalos, and my father Hêlios lives in a beautiful home beyond the sea; but I am travelling over the earth, till I shall have gone over every land and seen all the cities which men have built. Tell me now thy name, and the name of this fair land.' Then she said, 'Stranger, my name is Prokris, and I am the daughter of King Erechtheus who dwells at Athens yonder, where thou seest the bright line of Kephîsos flowing gently towards the sea.' So Prokris guided the stranger to her father's house; and Erechtheus received him kindly, and spread a banquet before him. But as they feasted and drank the dark red wine, he thought almost that Kephalos must be one of the bright heroes come back to his own land, so fair and beautiful was he to look upon, and that none save only his own child Prokris might be compared to him for beauty.

Long time Kephalos abode in the house of Erech-theus, and, each day, he loved more and more the bright and happy Prokris: and Prokris became brighter and happier, as the eye of Kephalos rested gently and lovingly upon her. At last Kephalos told her of his love, and Erechtheus gave him his child to be his wife; and there were none in all the land who dwelt together in a love so deep and pure as that of Kephalos and Prokris.

But among the maidens of that land there was one who was named Eôs.[81] She too was fair and beautiful; but she had not the gentle spirit and the guileless heart of Prokris. Whenever Kephalos wandered forth with his young wife, then Eôs would seek to follow them stealthily; or, if she met them by chance, she would suffer her eyes to rest long on the fair face of Kephalos, till she began to envy the happiness of Prokris. And so one day, when there was a feast of the people of the land, and the maidens danced on the soft grass around the fountain, Kephalos and Eôs talked together; and Eôs suffered herself to be carried away by her evil love. From that day she sought more and more to talk with Kephalos, till at last she bowed her head before him and told him softly of her love. But Kephalos said to her gently, 'Maiden, thou art fair to look upon, and there are others who may love thee well, and thou deservest the love of any. But I may not leave Prokris, whom Erechtheus has given to me to be my wife. Forgive me, maiden, if Prokris appear to me even fairer than thou art; but I prize her gentleness more than her beauty, and Prokris with her pure love and guileless heart shall be always dearer to me than any other in all the wide earth.' Then Eôs answered him craftily, 'O Kephalos, thou hast suffered thyself to be deceived.

Prokris loves thee not as I do ; prove her love and thou shalt see that I have spoken truly.'

Thus Eôs spake to him for many days ; and the great happiness of his life was marred, for the words of Eôs would come back to his mind, as he looked on the happy and guileless Prokris. He had begun to doubt whether she were in very deed so pure and good as she seemed to be ; and at last he said to Eôs that he would prove her love. Then Eôs told him how to do so, and said that if he came before his wife as a stranger and brought to her rich gifts as from a distant land, she would forget her love for Kephalos.

With a heavy heart he went away, for he foreboded evil days from the subtle words of Eôs ; and he departed and dwelt in another land. So the time passed on, until many weeks and months had gone by ; and Prokris mourned and wept in the house of Erechtheus, until the brightness of her eye was dimmed and her voice had lost its gladness. Day after day she sought throughout all the land for Kephalos ; day after day she went up the hill of Hymettos, and as she looked towards the sea, she said, 'Surely he will come back again ; ah Kephalos, thou knowest not the love which thou hast forsaken.' Thus she pined away in her sorrow, although to all who were around her she was as gentle and as loving as ever. Her father was now old and weak, and he knew that he must soon die ; but it grieved him most of all that he must leave his child in a grief more bitter than if Kephalos had remained to comfort her. So Erechtheus died, and the people honoured him as one of the heroes of the land ; but Prokris remained in his house desolate, and all who saw her pitied her for her true love and her deep sorrow. At last she felt that Kephalos would return no more, and that she could no more be happy until she went to her father in the bright home of the heroes and the gods.

Then a look of peace and loving patience came over her fair face, and she roamed with a strange gladness through every place where Kephalos had wandered with her; and so it came to pass that one day Prokris sat resting in the early morning on the eastern slopes of Mount Hymettos, when suddenly she beheld a man coming near to her. The dress was strange, but she half thought she knew his tall form and the light step as he came up the hill. Presently he came close to her, and she felt as if she were in a strange dream. The sight of his face and the glance of his eye carried her back to the days that were past, and she started up and ran towards him, saying, 'O Kephalos, thou art come back at last; how couldst thou forsake me so long?' But the stranger answered, in a low and gentle voice (for he saw that she was in great sorrow), 'Lady, thou art deceived. I am a stranger come from a far country, and I seek to know the name of this land.' Then Prokris sat down again on the grass, and clasped her hands and said slowly, 'It is changed and I cannot tell how; yet surely it is the voice of Kephalos.' Then she turned to the stranger and said, 'O stranger, I am mourning for Kephalos whom I have loved and lost; he too came from a far land across the eastern sea. Dost thou know him, and canst thou tell me where I may find him?' And the stranger answered, 'I know him, lady; he is again in his own home far away, whither thou canst not go; yet think not of him, for he has forgotten his love.' Then the stranger spoke to her in gentle and soothing words, until her grief became less bitter. Long time he abode in the land; and it pleased Prokris to hear his voice while his eye rested kindly on

her, until she almost fancied that she was with Kephalos
once more. And she thought within herself, 'What
must that land be, from which there can come two who
are beautiful as the bright heroes?'

So at last, when with soft and gentle words he had
soothed her sorrow, the stranger spoke to her of his
love; and Prokris felt that she too could love him, for
had not Kephalos despised her love and forsaken her
long ago? So he said, 'Canst thou love me, Prokris,
instead of Kephalos?' and when she gently answered
'Yes,' then a change came over the face of the stranger,
and she saw that it was Kephalos himself who clasped
her in his arms. With a wild cry she broke from him,
and as bitter tears ran down her cheek, she said, 'O
Kephalos, Kephalos, why hast thou done thus? all my
love was thine; and *thou* hast drawn me into evil deeds.'
Then, without tarrying for his answer, with all her
strength she fled away; and she hastened to the sea-
shore and bade them make ready a ship to take her
from her father's land. Sorrowfully they did as she
besought them, and they took her to the island of Crete
far away in the eastern sea.

When Prokris was gone, the maiden Eôs came and
stood before Kephalos, and she said to him, 'My words
are true, and now must thou keep the vow by which
thou didst swear to love me, if Prokris should yield herself to a stranger.' So Kephalos dwelt with Eôs; but
for all her fond words he could not love her as still he
loved Prokris.

Meanwhile Prokris wandered, in deep and bitter
sorrow, among the hills and valleys of Crete. She cared
not to look on the fair morning as it broke on the pale
path of night; she cared not to watch the bright sun as
he rose from the dark sea, or when he sank to rest be-

hind the western waters. For her the earth had lost all its gladness, and she felt that she could die. But one day as she sat on a hill-side and looked on the broad plains which lay stretched beneath, suddenly a woman stood before her, brighter and more glorious than the daughters of men; and Prokris knew, from the spear which she held in her hand and the hound which crouched before her, that it was Artemis, the mighty child of Zeus and Lêtô. Then Prokris fell at her feet, and said, 'O lady Artemis, pity me in my great sorrow;' and Artemis answered, 'Fear not, Prokris; I know thy grief. Kephalos hath done thee a great wrong, but he shall fall by the same device wherewith he requited thy pure and trusting love.' Then **she** gave to Prokris her hound and her spear, and said, 'Hasten now to thine own land; and go stand [82] before Kephalos, and I will put a spell upon him that he may not know thee. Follow him in the chase; and at whatsoever thou mayest cast this spear, it shall fall, and from this hound no prey which thou mayest seek for shall ever escape.'

So Prokris sailed back to the land of Erechtheus with the gifts of Artemis. And when Kephalos went to the chase, Prokris followed him; and all the glory of the hunt fell to her portion, for the hound struck down whatever it seized, and her spear never missed its aim. And Kephalos marvelled greatly, and said to the maiden, 'Give me thy hound and thy spear;' and he besought the stranger many times for the gift, till at last Prokris said, 'I will not give them but for thy love; thou must forsake Eôs and come to dwell with me.' Then Kephalos said, 'I care not for Eôs; so only I have thy gifts, thou shalt have my love.' But even as he spake these words, a change came over the face of the stranger, and he saw that it was Prokris herself who stood before him.

And Prokris said, 'Ah, Kephalos, once more thou hast promised to love me ; and now may I keep thy love, and remain with thee always.   Almost I may say that I never loved any one but thee ; but thou art changed, Kephalos, although still the same ; else wouldst thou not have promised to love me for the gift of a hound and a spear.' Then Kephalos besought Prokris to forgive him, and he said, 'I am caught in the trap which I laid for thee ; but I have fallen deeper.   When thou gavest thy love to me as to a stranger, it pleased thee yet to think that I was like Kephalos ; and now my vow to thee has been given for the mere gifts which I coveted.'   But Prokris only said, 'My joy is come back to me again, and now I will leave thee no more.'

So once more in the land of Erechtheus Prokris and Kephalos dwelt together in a true and a deep love. Once more they wandered over hill and dale as in the times that were past, and looked out from the heights of Hymettos to the white shore of Euboea, as it glistened in the light of early day.   But whenever he went to the chase with the hound and the spear of Artemis, Prokris saw that Eôs still watched if haply she might talk with Kephalos alone, and win him again for herself.   Once more she was happy ; but her happiness was not what it had been when Kephalos first gave her his love, while her father Erechtheus was yet alive.   She knew that Eôs still envied her, and she sought to guard Kephalos from the danger of her treacherous look and her enticing words.   So she kept ever near him in the chase, although he saw her not ; and thus it came to pass that one day, as Prokris watched him from a thicket, the folds of her dress rustled against the branches, so that Kephalos thought it was some beast moving from its den, and hurled at her the spear of Artemis that never missed its mark. Then he heard the cry as of one who has received a deadly blow, and when he hastened into the thicket, Prokris lay smitten down to the earth before him. The coldness of death was on her face, and her bright eye was dim; but her voice was as loving as ever, while she said, 'O Kephalos, it grieves me not that thy arm hath struck me down. I have thy love; and having it, I go to the land of the bright heroes, where my father Erechtheus is waiting for his child, and where thou too shalt one day meet me, to dwell with me for ever.' One loving look she gave to Kephalos, and the smile of parting vanished in the stillness of death.

Then over the body of Prokris Kephalos wept tears of bitter sorrow; and he said, 'Ah, Eôs, Eôs, well hast thou rewarded me for doubting once a love such as thou couldst never feel.' Many days and many weeks he mourned for his lost love; and daily he sat on the slopes of Hymettos, and thought with a calm and almost happy grief how Prokris there had rested by his side. All this time the spear of Artemis was idle, and the hound went not forth to the chase, until chieftains came from other lands to ask his aid against savage beasts or men. Among them came Amphitryon, the lord of Thebes, to ask for help; and Kephalos said, 'I will do as thou wouldst have me. It is time that I should begin to journey to the bright land where Prokris dwells beyond the western sea.'

So he went with Amphitryon into the Theban land, and hunted out the savage beasts which wasted his harvests; and then he journeyed on till he came to the home of Phœbus Apollo at Delphi. There the god bade him hasten to the western sea, where he should once again find Prokris. Onward he went, across the heights and vales of Ætôlia, until at last he stood on the Leukadian cape[83] and looked out on the blue waters. The sun was sinking low down in the sky, and the golden clouds of evening were gathered round him as he hastened to his rest. And Kephalos said, ' Here must I rest also, for my journey is done, and Prokris is waiting for me in the brighter land.' [84]   There on the white cliff he stood, and just as the sun touched the waters, the strength of Kephalos failed him, and he sank gently into the sea.

So again, in the homes of the bright heroes, Kephalos found the wife whom he had loved and slain.

------*0*------

SKYLLA.

FROM the turret of her father's house, Skylla, the daughter of Nisos, watched the ships of King Minos,[85] as they drew near from the island of Crete.   Their white sails and the spears of the Cretan warriors sparkled in the sunshine, as the crested waves rose and fell, carrying the long billows to the shore. As she watched the goodly sight, Skylla thought sadly of the days that were gone, when her father had sojourned as a guest in the halls of King Minos, and she had looked on his face as on the face of a friend. But now there was strife between the chieftains of Crete and Megara, for Androgeôs, the son of Minos, had been slain by evil men as he journeyed from Megara to Athens, and Minos was come hither with his warriors to demand the price of his blood.   But when the herald came with the message of Minos, the face of Nisos the king flushed with anger, as he said, ' Go thy way to him that sent thee, and tell him that he who is guarded by the undying gods cares not for the wrath of men whose spears shall be snapped like bulrushes.' Then said the herald, 'I cannot read thy riddle, chieftain of Megara; but the blood of the gods runs in the veins of Minos, and it cannot be that the son of Europa shall fall under the hands of thee or of thy people.'

The sun went down in a flood of golden glory behind the purple heights of Geraneia; and as the mists of evening fell upon the land, the warriors of Minos made ready for the onset on the morrow. But when the light of Eôs flushed the eastern sky, and the men of Crete went forth to the battle, their strength and their brave deeds availed them nothing, for the arms of the mightiest became weak as the hands of a little child, because the secret spell, in which lay the strength of the undying gods, guarded the city of Nisos. And so it came to pass that, as day by day they fought in vain against the walls of Megara, the spirit of the men of Crete waxed feeble, and many said that they came not thither to fight against the deathless gods.

But each day as Minos led his men against the city, the daughter of Nisos had looked forth from her turret, and she saw his face, beautiful as in the days when she had sojourned in his house at Gnossos, and flushed with the pride and eagerness of war. Then the heart of Skylla was filled with a strange love, and she spake musingly within herself, 'To what end is this strife of armed men? Love is beyond all treasures, and brighter for me than love of others would be one kindly look from the bright son of Europa. I know the spell which keeps the city of the Megarians; and where is the evil of the deed, if I take the purple lock of hair which the gods have given to my father as a pledge that so long as it remains untouched, no harm shall befall his people? If I give it

H

to Minos, the struggle is ended, and it may be that I shall win his love.'

So, when the darkness of night fell again upon the earth, and all the sons of men were buried in a deep sleep, Skylla entered stealthily into her father's chamber, and shore off the purple lock in which lay his strength and the strength of his people.   Then, as the tints of early morning stole across the dark heavens, the watchmen of the Cretans beheld the form of a woman as she drew nigh to them and bade them lead her to the tent of King Minos. When she was brought before him, with downcast face she bowed herself to the earth and said, ' I have sojourned in thy halls in the days that are gone, when there was peace between thee and the house of my father Nisos.   O Minos, peace is better than war, and of all treasures the most precious is love.   Look on me then gently as in the former days, for at a great price do I seek thy kindness.   In this purple lock is the strength of my father and of his people.'   Then a strange smile passed over the face of Minos, as he said, ' The gifts of fair maidens must not be lightly cast aside ; the requital shall be made when the turmoil of strife is ended.'

With a mighty shout the Cretan warriors went forth to the onset as the fiery horses of Hêlios rose up with his chariot into the kindled heaven.   Straightway the walls of Megara fell, and the men of Crete burst into the house of Nisos.   So the city was taken, and Minos made ready to go against the men of Athens, for on them also he sought to take vengeance for the death of his son Androgeôs.   But even as he hastened to his ship, Skylla stood before him on the sea-shore.   ' Thy victory is from me,' she said ; ' where is the requital of my gift ?'   Then Minos answered, ' She who cares not for the father that has cherished her has her own reward ; and the gift

which thou didst bring me is beyond human recompense.' The light southern breeze swelled the outspread
sail, and the ship of Minos danced gaily over the rippling
waters. For a moment **the** daughter **of** Nisos stood
musing on the shore. Then she stretched forth her
arms, as with a low cry of bitter anguish she said, 'O
Love, thy sting is cruel; and my life dies poisoned by
the smile of Aphroditê !' So the waters closed over the
daughter of Nisos, as she plunged into the blue depths;
but the strife which vexes the sons of men follows her
still, when the eagle swoops down from the cloud for his
prey in the salt sea.[86]

PHRIXOS AND HELLÊ.

ANY, many years ago, there was a man called
Athamas, and he had a wife whose name was
Nephelê. They had two children—a boy and
a girl. The name of the boy was Phrixos,
and his sister was called Hellê. They were good and
happy children, and played about merrily in the fields,
and their mother Nephelê loved them dearly. But by
and by their mother was taken away from them; and
their father Athamas forgot all about her, for he had not
loved her as he ought to do. And very soon he married
another wife whose name was Ino; but she was harsh
and unkind to Phrixos and Hellê, and they began to be
very unhappy. Their cheeks were no more rosy, and
their faces no longer looked bright and cheerful, as they
used to do when they could go home to their mother
Nephelê; and so they played less and less, until none
would have thought that they were the same children who

were so happy before Nephelê was taken away.   But Ino
hated these poor children, for she was a cruel woman,
and she longed to get rid of Phrixos and Hellê, and she
thought how she might do so.   So she said that Phrixos
spoilt all the corn, and prevented it from growing, and
that they would not be able to make any bread till he was
killed.   At last she persuaded Athamas that he ought to
kill Phrixos.   But although Athamas cared nothing about
Phrixos and Hellê, still their mother Nephelê saw what
was going on, although they could not see her, because
there was a cloud between them ; and Nephelê was determined that Athamas should not hurt Phrixos.   So she
sent a ram, which had a golden fleece, to carry her children away ; and one day, when they were sitting down on
the grass (for they were too sad and unhappy to play),
they saw a beautiful ram come into the field.   And
Phrixos said to Hellê, ' Sister, look at this sheep that is
coming to us ; see, he shines all over like gold—his horns
are made of gold, and all the hair on his body is golden
too.'   So the ram came nearer and nearer, and at last he
lay down quite close to them, and looked so quiet that
Phrixos and Hellê were not at all afraid of him.   Then
they played with the sheep, and they took him by the
horns, and stroked his golden fleece, and patted him on
the head; and the ram looked so pleased that they thought
they would like to have a ride on his back.   So Phrixos
got up first, and put his arms round the ram's neck, and
little Hellê got up behind her brother and put her arms
round his waist, and then they called to the ram to stand
up and carry them about.   And the ram knew what they
wanted, and began to walk first, and then to run.   By
and by it rose up from the ground and began to fly.   And
when it first left the earth, Phrixos and Hellê became
frightened, and they begged the ram to go down again

and put them upon the ground ; but the ram turned his head round, and looked so gently at them, that they were not afraid any more. So Phrixos told Hellê to hold on tight round his waist ; and he said, 'Dear Hellê, do not be afraid, for I do not think the ram means to do us any harm, and I almost fancy that he must have been sent by our dear mother Nephelê, and that he will carry us to some better country, where the people will be kind to us as our mother used to be.'

Now it so happened that, just as the ram began to fly away with the two children on its back, Ino and Athamas came into the field, thinking how they might kill Phrixos, but they could not see him anywhere ; and when they looked up, then, high up in the air over their heads, they saw the ram flying away with the children on its back. So they cried out and made a great noise, and threw stones up into the air, thinking that the ram would get frightened and come down to the earth again ; but the ram did not care how much noise they made or how many stones they threw up. On and on he flew, higher and higher, till at last he looked only like a little yellow speck in the blue sky ; and then Ino and Athamas saw him no more.

So these wicked people sat down, very angry and unhappy. They were sorry because Phrixos and Hellê had got away all safe, when they wanted to kill them. But they were much more sorry because they had gone away on the back of a ram whose fleece was made of gold. So Ino said to Athamas, 'What a pity that we did not come into the field a little sooner, for then we might have caught this ram and killed him and stripped off his golden fleece, and we should have been rich for the rest of our days.'

All this time the ram was flying on and on, higher and

higher, with Phrixos and Hellê on its back. And Hellê began to be very tired, and she said to her brother that she could not hold on much longer; and Phrixos said, ' Dear Hellê, try and hold on as long as you possibly can : I dare say the ram will soon reach the place to which he wants to carry us, and then you shall lie down on the soft grass, and have such pleasant sleep that you will not feel tired any more.' But Hellê said, ' Dearest Phrixos, I will indeed try and hold fast as long as I can ; but my arms are becoming so weak that I am afraid that I shall not be able to hold on long.' And by and by, when she grew weaker, she said, ' Dear Phrixos, if I fall off, you will not see Hellê any more ; but you must not forget her, you must always love her as much as she loved you ; and then some day or other we shall see each other again, and live with our dear mother Nephelê.' Then Phrixos said, ' Try and hold fast a little longer still, Hellê. I can never love any one so much as I love you : but I want you to live with me on the earth, and I cannot bear to think of living without you.'

But it was of no use that he talked so kindly and tried to encourage his sister, because he was not able to make her arms and her body stronger : so by and by poor Hellê fell off, just as they were flying over a narrow part of the sea ; and she fell into it, and was drowned. And the people called the part of the sea where she fell in, the Hellespont, which means the sea of little Hellê.[87]

So Phrixos was left alone on the ram's back ; and the ram flew on and on a long way, till it came to the palace of Aiêtes, the king of Kolchis. And King Aiêtes was walking about in his garden, when he looked up into the sky, and saw something which looked very like a yellow sheep with a little boy on its back. And King Aiêtes was greatly amazed, for he had never seen so

strange a thing before; **and he called** his wife and his
children, and every one **else** that was in his house, to
come and see this wonderful sight. And they looked,
and saw the ram coming **nearer** and nearer, **and** then
they knew that it really was a boy on its back; and by
and by the ram came down **upon** the earth near their
feet, and Phrixos got off **its back.** Then King Aiêtes
went up to him, and took him **by the** hand, and asked
him who he was; and he said, 'Tell me, little boy, how
it is that you come here, **riding in** this strange way on
the back **of a ram.'** Then **Phrixos** told him how the ram
had come into the field where he and Hellê were playing,
and had carried them **away from Ino** and Athamas, who
were very unkind to **them,** and how little Hellê had
grown tired, and fallen **off** his back, and had been
drowned in the sea. **Then** King Aiêtes took Phrixos up
in his arms, and said, 'Do not be afraid, I will take care
of you and give you all **that** you want, and no one shall
hurt you here; and the ram which has carried **you**
through the air shall stay in this beautiful place, **where**
he will have as much grass to eat **as he** can possibly
want, and a stream to drink out of and **to bathe in** when-
ever he likes.'[88]

So Phrixos was taken into the palace of King Aiêtes,
and everybody loved him, because he **was** good and
kind, and never hurt any one. And he grew up healthy
and strong, and **he** learned to ride about the country
and to leap and run over the hills and valleys, and swim
about in the clear rivers. **He** had not forgotten his
sister Hellê, for **he** loved **her** still as much as ever, and
very often he wished that **she** could come and live with
him again; but he knew that she was **now** with his
mother Nephelê, in the happy land to which good people
go after they are dead. And therefore he was never un-

happy when he thought of his sister, for he said, 'One day I too shall be taken to that bright land, and live with my mother and my sister again, if I try always to do what is right.' And very often he used to go and see the beautiful ram with the golden fleece feeding in the garden, and stroke its golden locks.

But the ram was not so strong now as he was when he flew through the air with Phrixos and Hellê on his back, for he was growing old and weak; and at last the ram died, and Phrixos was very sorry. And King Aiêtes had the golden fleece taken off from his body, and they nailed it up upon the wall; and every one came to look at the fleece which was made of gold, and to hear the story of Phrixos and Hellê.

But all this while Athamas and Ino had been hunting about everywhere, to see if they could find out where the ram had gone with the children on his back; and they asked every one whom they met, if they had seen a sheep with a fleece of gold carrying away two children. But no one could tell them anything about it, till at last they came to the house of Aiêtes the king of Kolchis. And they came to the door, and asked Aiêtes if he had seen Phrixos and Hellê, and the sheep with the golden fleece. Then Aiêtes said to them, 'I have never seen little Hellê, for she fell off from the ram's back, and was drowned in the sea; but Phrixos is with me still; and as for the ram, see here is his golden fleece nailed up upon the wall.' And just then Phrixos happened to come in, and Aiêtes asked them, 'Look now, and tell me if this is the Phrixos whom you are seeking.' And when they saw him they said, 'It is indeed the same Phrixos who went away on the ram's back; but he is grown into a great man:' and they began to be afraid, because they thought they could not now ill-treat Phrixos, as they used to do when he was a little boy. So they tried to entice him away by pretending to be glad to see him ; and they said, 'Come away with us, and we shall live happily together.' But Phrixos saw from the look of their faces that they were not telling the truth, and that they hated him still ; and he said to them, 'I will not go with you ; King Aiêtes has been very good to me, and you were always unkind to me and to my sister, and therefore I will never leave King Aiêtes to go away with you.' Then they said to Aiêtes, 'Phrixos may stay here, but give us the golden fleece which came from the ram that carried away the children.' But the king said, 'I will not ;—I know that you only ask for it because you wish to sell it, and therefore you shall not have it.'

Then Ino and Athamas turned away in a rage, and went to their own country again, wretched and unhappy because they could not get the golden fleece. And they told every one that the fleece of the ram was in the palace of the king of Kolchis, and they tried to persuade every one to go in a great ship and take away the fleece by force. So a great many people came, and they all got into a large ship called the Argo, and they sailed and sailed, until at last they came to Kolchis. Then they sent some one to ask Aiêtes to give them the golden fleece, but he would not ; and they would never have found the fleece again, if the wise maiden Medeia had not shown Iason how he might do the bidding of King Aiêtes. But when Iason had won the prize and they had sailed back again to their own land, the fleece was not given to Athamas and Ino. The other people took it, for they said, 'It is quite right that we should have it, to make up for all our trouble in helping to get it.' So, with all their greediness, these wretched people remained as poor and as miserable as ever.

MEDEIA.

AR away in the Kolchian land, where her father
Aiêtes was king, the wise maiden Medeia saw
and loved Iason, who had come in the ship
Argo to search for the golden fleece.   To her
Zeus had given a wise and cunning heart, and she had
power over the hidden things of the earth, and nothing
in the broad sea could withstand her might.   She had
spells to tame the monsters which vex the children of
men, and to bring back youth to the wrinkled face and
the tottering limbs of the old.   But the spells of Eros
were mightier still, and the wise maiden forgot her
cunning as she looked on the fair countenance of Iason ;
and she said within herself that she would make him
conqueror in his struggle for the golden fleece, and go
with him to- be his wife in the far-off western land.   So
King Aiêtes brought up in vain the fire-breathing bulls
that they might scorch Iason as he ploughed the land
with the dragon's teeth ; and in vain from these teeth
sprang up the harvest of armed men ready for strife and
bloodshed.   For Medeia had anointed the body of Iason
with ointment, so that the fiery breath of the bulls hurt
him not ; and by her bidding he cast a stone among the
armed men, and they fought with one another for the
stone till all lay dead upon the ground.   Still King Aiêtes
would not give to him the golden fleece ; and the heart
of Iason was cast down till Medeia came to him and
bade him follow her.   Then she led him to a hidden
dell where the dragon guarded the fleece, and she laid
her spells on the monster and brought a heavy sleep upon
his eyes, while Iason took the fleece and hastened to
carry it on board the ship Argo.

So Medeia left her father's house, and wandered with Iason into many lands—to Iolkos, to Athens, and to Argos. And wherever she went, men marvelled at her for her wisdom and her beauty; but as they looked on her fair face and listened to her gentle voice, they knew not the power of the maiden's wrath if any one should do her wrong. So she dwelt at Iolkos in the house of Pelias, who had sent forth Iason to look for the golden fleece, that he might not be king in his stead; and the daughters of Pelias loved the beautiful Medeia, for they dreamed not that she had sworn to avenge on Pelias the wrong **which** he had done to Iason. Craftily she told the daughters of Pelias of the power of her spells, which could tame the fire-breathing bulls, and lull the dragon to sleep, and bring back the brightness of youth to the withered cheeks of the old. And the daughters of Pelias said to her, 'Our father is old, and his limbs are weak and tottering; show us how once more he can be made young.' Then Medeia took a ram and cut it up, and put its limbs into a caldron, and when she had boiled them on the hearth there came forth a lamb; and she said, 'So shall your father be brought back again to youth and strength, if ye will do to him as I have done to the ram : and when the time is come, I will speak the words of my spell, and the change shall be accomplished.' So the daughters of Pelias followed her counsel, and put the body **of** their father into the caldron ; and, as it boiled on the hearth, Medeia said, 'I must go up to the house-top and look forth on the broad heaven, that I may know the time to speak the words of my charm.' And the fire waxed fiercer and fiercer, but Medeia gazed on at the bright stars, and came not down from the house-top till the limbs of Pelias were consumed away.

Then a look of fierce hatred passed over her face, and

she said, ' Daughters of Pelias, ye have slain your father, and I go with Iason to the land of Argos.' So thither she sped with him in her dragon chariot which bore them to the house of King Kreon.

Long time she abode in Argos, rejoicing in the love of Iason and at the sight of her children who were growing up in strength and beauty. But Iason cared less and less for the wise and cunning Medeia, for she seemed not to him as one of the daughters of men ; and he loved more to look on Glaukê the daughter of the king, till at last he longed to be free from the love and the power of Medeia.

Then men talked in Argos of the love of Iason for the beautiful Glaukê ; and Medeia heard how he was going to wed another wife. Once more her face grew dark with anger, as when she left the daughters of Pelias mourning for their father; and she vowed a vow that Iason should repent of his great treachery. But she hid her anger within her heart, and her eye was bright and her voice was soft and gentle as she spake to Iason and said, ' They tell me that thou art to wed the daughter of Kreon ; I had not thought thus to lose the love for which I left my father's house and came with thee to the land of strangers. Yet do I chide thee not, for it may be thou canst not love the wise Kolchian maiden like the soft daughters of the Argive land ; and yet thou knowest not altogether how I have loved thee. Go then and dwell with Glaukê, and I will send her a bright gift, so that thou mayest not forget the days that are past.'

So Iason went away, well pleased that Medeia had spoken to him gently and upbraided him not ; and presently his children came after him to the house of Kreon, and said, ' Father, we have brought a wreath for Glaukê, and a robe which Hêlios gave to our mother Medeia

before she came away with thee from the house of her
father.' Then Glaukê came forth eagerly to take the
gifts; and she placed the glittering wreath on her head,
and wrapped the robe round her slender form. Like a
happy child, she looked into a mirror[89] to watch the
sparkling of the jewels on her fair forehead, and sat
down on the couch playing with the folds of the robe of
Hêlios. But soon a look of pain passed over her face,
and her eyes shone with a fiery light as she lifted her
hand to take the wreath away;[90] but the will of Medeia
was accomplished, for the poison had eaten into her
veins, and the robe clung with a deadly grasp to her
scorched and wasted limbs. Through the wide halls
rang the scream of her agony, as Kreon clasped his
child in his arms. Then sped the poison through his
veins also, and Kreon died with Glaukê.

Then Medeia went with her children to the house-top,
and looked up to the blue heaven; and stretching forth
her arms she said, ' O Hêlios, who didst give to me the
wise and cunning heart, I have avenged me on Iason,
even as once I avenged him on Pelias. Thou hast given
me thy power; yet, it may be, I would rather have the
lifelong love of the helpless daughters of men.'

Presently her dragon chariot rose into the sky, and
the people of Argos saw the mighty Medeia no more.[91]

THESEUS.

ANY a long year ago a little child was playing on the white sands of the bay of Troizen. His golden locks streamed in the breeze as he ran amongst the rippling waves which flung themselves lazily on the beach. Sometimes he clapped his hands in glee as the water washed over his feet, and he stopped again to look with wondering eyes at the strange things which were basking on the sunny shore, or gazed on the mighty waters which stretched away bright as a sapphire stone into the far distance. But presently some sadder thought troubled the child, for the look of gladness passed away from his face, and he went slowly to his mother, who sat among the weed-grown rocks, watching her child at play.

'Mother,' said the boy, 'I am very happy here, but may I not know to-day why I never see my father as other children do? I am not now so very young, and I think that you feel sometimes lonely, for your face looks sad and sorrowful as if you were grieving for some one who is gone away.'

Fondly and proudly the mother looked on her boy, and smoothed the golden locks on his forehead, as she said, 'My child, there is much to make us happy, and it may be that many days of gladness are in store for us both. But there is labour and toil for all, and many a hard task awaits thee, my son. Only have a brave heart, and turn away from all things mean and foul, and strength will be given thee to conquer the strongest enemy. Sit down then here by my side, and I will tell thee a tale which may make thee sad, but which must not make

thee unhappy, for none can do good to others who waste
their lives in weeping. Many summers have come and
gone since the day when a stranger drew nigh to the
house of my father Pittheus. The pale light of evening
was fading from the sky; but we could see, by his countenance and the strength of his stalwart form, that he
was come of a noble race and could do brave deeds.
When Pittheus went forth from the threshold to meet
him, the stranger grasped his hand and said, " I come
to claim the rights of our ancient friendship; for our
enemies have grown too mighty for us, and Pandion my
father rules no more in Athens. Here then let me tarry
till I can find a way to punish the men who have driven
away their king and made his children wanderers on the
earth." So Aigeus sojourned in my father's house, and
soon he won my love, and I became his wife. Swiftly
and happily the days went by, and one thing only troubled
me, and this was the thought that one day he must leave
me, to fight with his enemies and place his father again
upon his throne. But even this thought was forgotten
for a while, when Aigeus looked on thee for the first
time, and stretching forth his hands towards heaven,
said, "O Zeus, that dwellest in the dark cloud, look
down on my child, and give him strength that he may
be a better man than his father; and if thou orderest
that his life shall be one of toil, still let him have the joy
which is the lot of all who do their work with a cheerful
heart and keep their hands from all defiling things."
Then the days passed by more quickly and happily than
ever; but at last there came messengers from Athens, to
tell him that the enemies of Pandion were at strife
among themselves, and that the time was come that
Aigeus should fight for his father's house. Not many
days after this we sat here, watching thee at play among

the weeds and flowers that climb among the rocks, when thy father put his arms gently round me and said, " Aithra, **best gift of** all that the gods have ever given to me, I leave thee to go to my own land ; and I know not what things may befall me there, nor whether I may return hither to take thee to dwell with me at Athens.   But forget not the days that are gone, and faint not for lack of hope that we may meet again in the days that are coming.   Be a brave mother to our child, that so he too may grow up brave and pure ; and when he is old enough to know what he must do, tell him that he is born of a noble race, and that he must one day fight stoutly to win the heritage of his fathers."   And now, my son, thou seest yonder rock, over which the wild briars have clambered.   No hands have moved it since the day when thy father lifted it up and placed beneath it his sword and his sandals.   Then he put back the stone as it was before, and said to me, " When thou thinkest fit, tell our child that he must wait until he is able to lift this stone.   Then must he put my sandals on his feet, and gird my sword on his side, and journey to the city of his forefathers."   **From** that day, my child, I have never seen thy father's face, and the time is often weary, although the memory of the old days is sweet and my child is by my side to cheer me with his love.   So now thou knowest something of the task that lies before thee. Think of thy father's words, and make thyself ready for the toil and danger that may fall to thy lot in time to come.'[92]

The boy looked wistfully into his mother's face, and a strange feeling of love and hope and strength filled his heart, as he saw the tears start to her eyes when the tale was ended.   His arms were clasped around her neck ; but he said only, 'Mother, I will wait patiently till I am strong enough to lift the stone; but before that time comes, perhaps my father may come back from Athens.'

So for many a year more the days went by, and the boy Theseus grew up brave, truthful, and strong. None who looked upon him grudged him his beauty, for his gentleness left no room for envy; and his mother listened with a proud and glad heart to the words with which the people of the land told of his kindly deeds. At length the days of his youth were ended, but Aigeus came not back; and Theseus went to Aithra, and said, 'The time is come, my mother; I must see this day whether I am strong enough to lift the stone.' And Aithra answered gently, 'Be it as thou wilt, and as the undying gods will it, my son.' Then he went up to the rock, and nerved himself for a mighty effort, and the stone yielded slowly to his strength, and the sword and sandals lay before him. Presently he stood before Aithra, and to her it seemed that the face of Theseus was as the face of one of the bright heroes who dwell in the halls of Zeus. A flush of glorious beauty lit up his countenance, as she girt the sword to his side and said, 'The gods prosper thee, my son; and they will prosper thee, if thou livest in time to come as thou hast lived in the days that are gone.'

So Theseus bade his mother farewell, there on the white sea-shore, where long ago he had asked her first to tell him of his name and kindred. Sadly, yet with a good hope, he set out on his journey. The blue sea lay before him, and the white sails of ships glistened as they danced on the heaving waters. But Theseus had vowed a vow that he would do battle with the evil-doers who filled the land with blood, and for terror of whom the travellers walked in by-ways. So at Epidauros he fought

with the cruel Periphêtes, and smote him with his own
club ; and at the Megarian isthmus he seized the robber
Sinis, and tare him to pieces between the trunks of pines,
even as he had been wont to do with the wayfarers who
fell into his hands.   Then in the thickets of Krommyon
he slew the huge sow that ravaged the fair cornfields,
and on the borderland he fought a sore fight with Skiron,
who plundered all who came in his path, and, making
them wash his feet, hurled them, as they stooped, down
the cliffs which hung over the surging sea.   Even so did
Theseus to him, and journeying on to the banks of
Kephîsos, stretched the robber Prokroustes on the bed
on which he had twisted and tortured the limbs of his
victims till they died.

Thus amid the joyous shoutings of the people whom
he had set free, Theseus entered into the city of his
fathers ; and the rumour of him was brought to Aigeus
the king.   Then the memory of the days that were gone
came back to Aigeus, and his heart smote him as he
thought within himself that this must be the child of
Aithra, whom he had left mourning on the shore of
Troizen.   But soon there was a strife in the city, for
among the mightiest of the people were many who
mocked at Theseus and said, 'Who is this stranger that
men should exalt him thus, as though he came of the
race of heroes?   Let him show that he is the child of
Aigeus, if he would win the heritage which he claims.'
So was Theseus brought before the king, and a blush of
shame passed over the old man's face when he saw the
sword and sandals which he had left beneath the great
stone near the Troizenian shore.   Few words only he
spake of welcome, and none of love or kindness for his
child or for the wife who still yearned for the love of the
former days.   Then, at his father's bidding, Theseus

made ready to go forth once again on his path of toil, and he chafed not against the hard lot which had fallen to his portion. Only he said, 'The love of a father would sweeten my labour; but my mother's love is with me still, and the battle is for right and for law.'

So in after-times the minstrels sang of the glorious deeds of Theseus the brave and fair. They told how at the bidding of his father he went forth from the gates of Athens and smote the bull which ravaged the broad plains of Marathon, and how in the secret mazes of the labyrinth he smote the Minotauros. They sang of his exploits in the day when the Amâzons did battle with the men of Athens—how he went with Meleagros and his chieftains to the chase of the boar in Kalydon—how with the heroes in the ship Argo he brought back the golden fleece from Kolchis. They told how at the last he went down with Peirithoös his comrade into the gloomy kingdom of Hades and seized on the daughter of Dêmêtêr, to bring her to the land of living men. They sang of the fierce wrath of Hades when his lightnings burst forth and smote Peirithoös—of the dark prison-house where Theseus lay while many a rolling year went round, until at last the mighty Herakles passed the borders of the shadowy land and set the captive free.

And so it was that, when the heroes had passed to the home of Zeus and the banquet of the gods, the glory of Theseus was as the glory of the brave son of Alkmênê who toiled for the false Eurystheus; and ever, in the days of feasting, the minstrels linked together the names of Herakles and of Theseus.[93]

HE soft western breeze was bearing a ship from the Athenian land to the fair haven of Gnossos; and the waters played merrily round the ship as it sped along the paths of the sea. But on board there were mournful hearts and weeping eyes, for the youths and maidens which that ship was bearing to Crete were to be the prey of the savage Minotauros. As they came near the harbour gates, they saw the people of King Minos crowded on the shore, and they wept aloud because they should no more look on the earth and on the sun as he journeyed through the heaven.

In that throng stood Ariadnê the daughter of the king, and as she gazed on the youths and maidens who came out of the tribute ship, there passed before her one taller and fairer than all ; and she saw that his eye alone was bright and his step firm, as he moved from the shore to go to the house of Minos. Presently they all stood before the king, and he saw that one alone gazed steadfastly upon him, while the eyes of all the rest were dim with many tears. Then he said, 'What is thy name?' The young man answered, 'I am Theseus, the son of King Aigeus, and I have come as one of the tribute children ; but I part not with my life till I have battled for it with all my strength. Wherefore send me first, I pray thee, that I may fight with Minotauros ; for if I be the conqueror, then shall all these go back with me in peace to our own land.' Then Minos said, 'Thou shalt indeed go first to meet Minotauros ; but think not to conquer him in the fight, for the flame from his mouth will scorch thee, and no mortal man may withstand his strength.'

And Theseus answered, 'It is for man to do what best he may; the gods know for whom remains the victory.'

But the gentle heart of Ariadnê was moved with love and pity as she looked on his fair face and his bright and fearless eye; and she said within herself, 'I cannot kill the Minotauros or rob him of his strength, but I will guide Theseus so that he may reach the monster while sleep lies heavy upon him.'

On the next day Theseus, the Athenian, was to meet the dreadful Minotauros who dwelt in the labyrinth of Gnossos. Far within its thousand twisted alleys was his den, where he waited for his prey, as they were brought each along the winding paths. But Ariadnê talked in secret with Theseus in the still evening time, and she gave him a clue of thread, so that he might know how to come back out of the mazes of the labyrinth after he had slain the Minotauros: and when the moon looked down from heaven, she led him to a hidden gate, and bade him go forth boldly, for he should come to the monster's den while sleep lay heavy on his eyes. So when the morning came, the Minotauros lay lifeless on the ground; and there was joy and gladness in the great city of Gnossos, and Minos himself rejoiced that the youths and maidens might go back with Theseus in peace to Athens.

So once again they went into the ship, and the breeze blew softly to carry them to the homes which they had not thought to see again. But Theseus talked with Ariadnê in the house of Minos, and the maiden wept as though some great grief lay heavy upon her; and Theseus twined his arm gently round her and said, 'Fairest of maidens, thy aid hath saved me from death; but I care not now to live if I may not be with thee. Come with me, and I will lead thee to the happier land, where my father Aigeus is king. Come with me, that my people

may see and **love** the maiden who rescued the tribute
children from the savage Minotauros.'

Then Ariadnê went with him joyfully, for her own love
made her **think** that Theseus loved her not less dearly.
So she wept not as she saw the towers of Gnossos growing fainter **and fainter** while the ship sped over the
dancing waters ; and she thought only of the happy days
which she should spend in the bright Athens where
Theseus should one day be king. Gaily the ship sped upon
her way, and **there was** laughter and mirth among the
youths and maidens who were going back to their home.
And Theseus **sat by the side of** Ariadnê, speaking the
words of **a** deeper **love than in** truth he felt, and fancying
that he loved the maiden even **as** the maiden loved him.
But **while yet he** gazed on **the** beautiful Ariadnê, **the**
image of Aiglê came back to his mind, and the old love
was wakened again in his heart. **Onward** sailed the
ship, cleaving **its way** through **the** foaming waters, by the
islands of **Thêra and** Amorgos, till the high cliffs of Naxos
broke upon their sight.

The sun was sinking **down** into the sea when they
came to its winding shores, and the seamen moored the
ship to the land, and came forth to rest until the morning. There they feasted gaily on the beach, and Theseus
talked with Ariadnê until the moon was high up in the
sky. **So** they slept through **the** still hours of night ; but
when the sun was **risen,** Ariadnê was alone upon the
sea-shore. In doubt and fear, she roamed along the
beach, **but she saw no** one ; and there was no ship sailing on **the blue sea.** In many a bay **and** nook she
sought him, and she cried in bitter sorrow, '**Ah, Theseus,**
Theseus, **hast thou** forsaken me ? ' **Her feet** were
wounded by **the** sharp flints, her limbs were faint from
very weariness, and her eyes were dim with tears. Above

her rose the high cliffs like a wall, before her **was** spread
the bright and laughing sea ; and her heart **sank** within
her, for she felt that she must die. 'Ah, **Theseus,**' she
cried, 'have I done thee wrong? I pitied **thee in the**
time of thy sorrow and saved thee from thy doom ; **and**
then I listened to thy fair words, and trusted them as **a**
maiden trusts when love is first awakened within her.
Yet hast thou dealt me a hard requital. Thou art gone
to happy Athens, and it may **be thou thinkest already of**
some bright maiden who there **has crossed thy path ; and**
thou hast left me here to die for **weariness and** hunger.
So would I not requite thee for a deed of love and pity.' [94]

Wearied **and** sad **of** heart, she sank down on the rock ;
and her long hair streamed over her fair shoulders. Her
hands were clasped around her knees, and the hot tears
ran down her checks ; and she knew not that there stood
before her one fairer and brighter than the sons **of** men,
until she heard a voice which said, 'Listen to me, daughter
of Minos. I am Dionysos, the **lord** of the feast and **revel.**
I wander with light **heart and the sweet** sounds of laughter
and song **over land** and **sea ; I saw** thee **aid** Theseus
when he went into the labyrinth **to slay the Minotauros.**
I heard his fair words when **he** prayed **thee to leave** thy
home and go with him to Athens. I saw him this morning, **while yet** the stars twinkled **in the sky,** arouse his
men **and sail** away in his ship to the **land** of Aigeus ; but
I sought not to **stay** him, for, Ariadnê, thou must dwell with
me. Thy **love and** beauty are **a** gift too great for Theseus ,
but thou shalt be the bride **of** Dionysos. Thy days
shall be passed amidst feasts and banquets ; and when
thy life is ended here, thou shalt go with me to the
homes of the undying gods, and men shall see the crown
of Ariadnê in the heavens when the stars look forth at
night from the dark **sky.** Nay, weep not, Ariadnê ; thy

love for Theseus hath been but the love of a day, and I
have loved thee long before the black-sailed ship brought
him from poor and rugged Athens.' Then Ariadnê wept
no more, and in the arms of Dionysos she forgot the
false and cruel Theseus ; so that among the matrons who
thronged round the joyous wine-god the fairest and the
most joyous was Ariadnê the daughter of Minos.

ARETHUSA.[95]

N the heights of Mænalos the hunter Alpheios
saw the maiden Arethusa as she wandered
joyously with her companions over the green
swelling downs where the heather spread out
its pink blossoms to the sky. Onward she came, the
fairest of all the band, until she drew nigh to the spot
where Alpheios stood marvelling at the brightness of
her beauty. Then, as she followed the winding path on
the hill-side, she saw his eye resting upon her, and her
heart was filled with fear, for his dark face was flushed
by the toil of the long chase and his torn raiment waved
wildly in the breeze. And yet more was she afraid when
she heard the sound of his rough voice, as he prayed
her to tarry by his side. She lingered not to listen to his
words, but with light foot she sped over hill and dale and
along the bank of the river where it leaps down the
mountain cliffs and winds along the narrow valleys.

Then Alpheios vowed a vow that the maiden should
not escape him, 'I will follow thee,' he said, ' over hill
and dale, I will seek thee through rivers and seas ; and
where thou shalt rest, there will I rest also.' Onward

they sped, across the dark heights of Erymanthos and over the broad plains of Pisa, till the waters of the western sea lay spread out before them, dancing in the light of the midday sun. Then with arms outstretched, and with wearied limbs, Arethusa cried aloud and said, ' O daughters of the gentle Okeanos, I have played with you on the white shore in the days of mirth and gladness ; and now I come to your green depths. Save me from the hand of the wild huntsman.' So she plunged beneath the waves of the laughing sea, and the daughters of Okeanos bare her gently downwards till she came to the coral caves where they sat listening to the sweet song of the waters. But there they suffered her not to rest, for they said, ' Yet further must thou flee, Arethusa; for Alpheios comes behind thee.' Then in their arms they bare her gently beneath the depths of the sea, till they laid her down at last on the Ortygian shore of the Thrinakian land, as the sun was sinking down in the sky. Dimly she saw spread before her the blue hills, and she felt the soft breath of the summer breeze, as her eyes closed for weariness. Then suddenly she heard the harsh voice which scared her on the heights of Mænalos ; and she tarried not to listen to his prayer. ' Flee not away, Arethusa,' said the huntsman Alpheios ; ' I mean not to harm thee ; let me rest in thy love, and let me die for the beauty of thy fair face.' But the maiden fled with a wild cry along the winding shore, and the light step of her foot left no print on the glistening sand. ' Not thus shalt thou escape from my arms,' said the huntsman Alpheios ; and he stretched forth his hand to seize the maiden, as she drew nigh to a fountain whose waters flashed clear and bright in the light of the sinking sun. Then once again Arethusa called aloud on the daughters of Okeanos, and she said, ' O friends, once more I come

to your coral caves, for on earth there is for me no resting-
place.' So the waters closed over the maiden, and the
image of heaven came down again on the bright fountain.
Then a flush of anger passed over the face of Alpheios, as
he said, 'On earth thou hast scorned my love, O maiden;
but my form shall be fairer in thy sight when I rest beside
thee beneath the laughing waters.' So over the huntsman Alpheios flowed the Ortygian stream ; and the love
of Arethusa was given to him in the coral caves where
they dwell with the daughters of Okeanos.

—o—

T Y R O.

N the banks of the fairest stream in all the land
of Thessaly, the golden-haired Enîpeus wooed
the maiden Tyro : with her he wandered in
gladness of heart, following the path of the
winding river, and talking with her of his love. And
Tyro listened to his tender words, as day by day she
stole away from the house of her father Salmôneus, to
spend the livelong day on the banks of his beautiful
stream.

But Salmôneus was full of rage when he knew that
Tyro loved Enîpeus, and how she had become the
mother of two fair babes. There was none to plead for
Tyro and her helpless children ; for her mother Alkidikê
was dead, and Salmôneus had taken the iron-hearted
Sidêro [96] to be his wife. So he followed her evil
counsels, and he said to Tyro, 'Thy children must die,
and thou must wed Kretheus, the son of the mighty
Aiolos.'

Then Tyro hastened in bitter sorrow to the banks of

the stream, and her babes **slept in her** arms; and she stretched out her hands with **a** loud cry for aid, but Enîpeus heard her not, for he lay in his green dwelling far down beneath the happy waters. So she placed the babes amidst the thick rushes which grew along the banks, and she said, 'O Enîpeus, my father says that I may no more see thy face; but to thee I give our **children** : guard them from the anger of Salmôneus, and it may be that in time to come they will avenge my wrongs.'

There, nestled amid the tall reeds, the children slept, till a herdsman saw them as he followed his cattle along the shore. And Tyro went back in anguish of heart to the house of Salmôneus, **but** she would not have the love of Kretheus **or** listen to his words. **Then** Sidêro whispered again her **evil counsels into the ear of Salmô-**neus, **and** he shut up Tyro, so that she might not **see the** light of the **sun or** hear the voice of **man.** He cut off the golden locks that clustered on her fair cheeks; **he** clothed her in rough raiment, and bound her in fetters which gave her no rest by night **or by** day. So in her misery she pined away, and **her body was wasted** by hunger and thirst, because she would not become the wife of Kretheus. Then more and more she thought of the days when she listened to the words of Enîpeus as **she** wandered with him by the side of the sounding waters; and she said within herself, 'He heard me not when I called to him for help; but I gave him my children, and it may be that he has saved them from death; and if ever they see my face again, they shall know that I never loved any save Enîpeus, who dwells beneath the stream.'

So the years passed on, and Pelias and Neleus dwelt with the herdsman, and they grew up strong in body and

brave of soul. But Enîpeus had not forgotten the wrongs
of Tyro, and he put it into the heart of her children to
punish Sidêro for her evil counsels. So Sidêro died, and
they brought out their mother from her dreary dungeon,
and led her to the banks of the stream where she had
heard the words of Enîpeus in the former days. But
her eyes were dim with long weeping, and the words of
her children sounded strangely in her ears; and she
said, 'O my children, let me sink to sleep while I hear
your voices, which sound to me like the voice of
Enîpeus.' So she fell asleep and died, and they laid
her body in the ground by the river's bank, where
the waters of Enîpeus made their soft music near her
grave.[97]

---o---

NARKISSOS.

ON the banks of Kephîsos, Echo saw and loved
the beautiful Narkissos; but the youth cared
not for the maiden of the hills, and his heart
was cold to the words of her love, for he
mourned for his sister[98] whom Hermes had taken away
beyond the Stygian river. Day by day he sat alone by
the stream side, sorrowing for the bright maiden whose
life was bound up with his own, because they had seen
the light of the sun in the selfsame day; and thither came
Echo and sat down by his side, and sought in vain to
win his love. 'Look on me and see,' she said; 'I am
fairer than the sister for whom thou dost mourn.' But
Narkissos answered her not, for he knew that the maiden
would ever have something to say against his words. So
he sat silent and looked down into the stream, and there
he saw his own face in the clear water, and it was to

him as the face of his sister for whom he pined away in sorrow ; and his grief became less bitter as he seemed to see again her soft blue eye, and almost to hear the words which came from her lips. But the grief of Narkissos was too deep for tears, and it dried up slowly the fountain of his life. In vain the words of Echo fell upon his ears, as she prayed him to hearken to her prayer: 'Ah, Narkissos, thou mournest for one who cannot heed thy sorrow, and thou carest not for her who longs to see thy face and hear thy voice for ever.' But Narkissos saw still in the waters of Kephisos the face of his twin sister, and still gazing at it he fell asleep and died. Then the voice of Echo was heard no more, for she sat in silence by his grave ; and a beautiful flower came up close to it. Its white blossoms drooped over the banks of Kephisos where Narkissos had sat and looked down into its clear water, and the people of the land called the plant after his name.

ORPHEUS AND EURYDIKÊ.[99]

IN the pleasant valleys of a country which was called Thessaly,[100] there lived a man whose name was Orpheus. Every day he made soft music with his golden harp, and sang beautiful songs such as no one had ever heard before. And whenever Orpheus sang, then everything came to listen to him, and the trees bowed down their heads to hear ; and even the clouds sailed along more gently and brightly in the sky when he sang, and the stream which ran close to his feet made a softer noise, to show how glad his music made it.

Now Orpheus had a wife who was called Eurydikê,

whom he loved very dearly. All through the winter when the snow was on the hills, and all through the summer when the sunshine made everything beautiful, Orpheus used to sing to her; and Eurydikê sat on the grass by his side while the beasts came round to listen, and the trees bowed down their heads to hear him.

But one day when Eurydikê was playing with some children on the bank of the river, she trod upon a snake in the long grass, and the snake bit her. And by and by she began to be very sick, and Eurydikê knew that she must die. So she told the children to go to Orpheus .(for he was far away) and say how sorry she was to leave him, and that she loved him always very dearly; and then she put her head down upon the soft grass, and fell asleep and died. Sad indeed was Orpheus when the children came to tell him that Eurydikê was dead. He felt so wretched that he never played upon his golden harp, and he never opened his lips to sing; and the beasts that used to listen to him wondered why Orpheus sat all alone on the green bank where Eurydikê used to sit with him, and why it was that he never made any more of his beautiful music. All day long he sat there, and his cheeks were often wet with his tears. At last he said, 'I cannot stay here any more; I must go and look for Eurydikê. I cannot bear to be without her, and perhaps the king of the land where people go after they are dead will let her come back and live with me again.'

So he took his harp in his hand, and went to look for Eurydikê in the land which is far away, where the sun goes down into his golden cup before the night comes on. And he went on and on a very long way, till at last he came to a high and dark gateway. It was barred across with iron bars, and it was bolted and locked so that nobody could open it. It was a wretched and gloomy place, because the sunshine never came there, and it was covered with clouds and mist. In front of this great gateway there sat a monstrous dog, with three heads, and six eyes, and three tongues; and everything was dark around, except his eyes, which shone like fire, and which saw every one that dared to come near. Now when Orpheus came looking for Eurydikê, the dog raised his three heads, and opened his three mouths, and gnashed his teeth at him, and roared terribly; but when Orpheus came nearer, the dog jumped up upon his feet and got himself ready to fly at him and tear him to pieces. Then Orpheus took down his harp and began to play upon its golden strings. And the dog Kerberos (for that was his name) growled and snarled and showed the great white teeth which were in his three mouths; but he could not help hearing the sweet music, and he wondered why it was that he did not wish any more to tear Orpheus in pieces. Very soon the music made him quiet and still, and at last it lulled him to sleep; and only his heavy breathing told that there was any dog there. So when Kerberos had gone to sleep, Orpheus passed by him and came up to the gate, and he found it wide open, for it had come open of its own accord while he was singing. And he was glad when he saw this, for he thought that now he should see Eurydikê.

So he went on and on a long way, until he came to the palace of the king; and there were guards placed before the door who tried to keep him from going in; but Orpheus played upon his harp, and then they could not help letting him go.

So he went into the great hall, where he saw the king and queen sitting on a throne; and as Orpheus came near, the king called out to him with a loud and terrible

voice, 'Who are you, and how dare you to come here?
Do you not know that no one is allowed to come here
till after they are dead? I will have you chained and
placed in a dungeon, from which you will never be able
to get out.' Then Orpheus said nothing; but he took
his golden harp in his hand and began to sing more
sweetly and gently than ever, because he knew that, if he
liked to do so, the king could let him see Eurydikê again.
And as he sang, the face of the king began to look almost glad, and his anger passed away, and he began to
feel how much happier it must be to be gentle and loving than to be angry and cruel. Then the king said,
'You have made me feel happy with your sweet music,
although I have never felt happy before; and now tell
me why you have come, because you must want something or other, for, otherwise, no one would come, before
he was dead, to this sad and gloomy land of which I am
the king.' Then Orpheus said, 'O king, give me back
my dear Eurydikê, and let her go from this gloomy place
and live with me on the bright earth again.' So the king
said that she should go. And the king said to Orpheus,
'I have given you what you wanted, because you sang
so sweetly; and when you go back to the earth from this
place, your wife whom you love shall go up after you:
but remember that you must never look back until she
has reached the earth, for if you do, Eurydikê will be
brought back here, and I shall not be able to give her
to you again, even if you should sing more sweetly and
gently than ever.'

Now Orpheus was longing to see Eurydikê, and he
hoped that the king would let him see her at once; but
when the king said that he must not try to see her till
she had reached the earth, he was quite content, for he
said, 'Shall I not wait patiently a little while, that Eury-

dikê may come and live with me again?' So he promised the king that he would go up to the earth without
stopping to look behind and see whether Eurydikê was
coming after him.

Then Orpheus went away from the palace of the king,
and he passed through the dark gateway, and the dog
Kerberos did not bark or growl, for he knew that Orpheus
would not have been allowed to come back, if the king
had not wished it. So he went on and on a long way;
and he became impatient, and longed more and more to
see Eurydikê. At last he came near to the land of living
men, and he saw just a little streak of light, where the
sun was going to rise from the sea; and presently the
sky became brighter, and he saw everything before him
so clearly that he could not help turning round to look
at Eurydikê. But, ah! she had not yet quite reached
the earth, and so now he lost her again. He just saw
something pale and white, which looked like his own
dear wife; and he just heard a soft and gentle voice,
which sounded like the voice of Eurydikê, and then it
all melted away. And still he thought that he saw that
pale white face, and heard that soft and gentle voice,
which said, 'O Orpheus, Orpheus, why did you look
back? How dearly I love you, and how glad I should
have been to live with you again; but now I must go
back, because you have broken your promise to the king,
and I must not even kiss you, and say how much I love
you.'

And Orpheus sat down at the place where Eurydikê
was taken away from him; and he could not go on any
further, because he felt so miserable. There he stayed
day after day, and his cheek became more pale, and his
body weaker and weaker, till at last he knew that he
must die. And Orpheus was not sorry; for although he

K

loved the bright earth, with all its flowers and soft grass
and sunny streams, he knew that he could not be with
Eurydikê again until he had left it.   So at last he laid
his head upon the earth, and fell asleep, and died : and
then he and Eurydikê saw each other in the land which
is far away, where the sun goes down at night into his
golden cup, and were never parted again.

---o---

KADMOS AND EUROPA.[101]

IN a beautiful valley in Phœnicia, a long time
ago, two children, named Kadmos and
Europa, lived with their mother Têlephassa.
They were good and happy children, and full
of fun and merriment.   It was a very lovely place in
which they lived, where there were all sorts of beautiful
trees with fruits and flowers.   The oranges shone like
gold among the dark leaves, and great bunches of dates
hung from the tall palm-trees which bowed their heads
as if they were asleep ; and there was a delicious smell
from the lime groves, and from many fruits and flowers
which are never seen in England, but which blossom and
ripen under the hot sun in Syria.

So the years went ; and one day, as they were playing
about by the side of the river, there came into the field
a beautiful white bull.   He was quite white all over—as
white as the whitest snow ; there was not a single spot
or speck on any part of his body.   And he came and
lay down on the green grass, and remained still and
quiet.   So they went nearer and nearer to the bull ; and
the bull did not move, but looked at them with his large
eyes as if he wished to ask them to come and play with

him ; and at last they came to the place where the bull
was. Then Kadmos thought that he would be very
brave, so he put out his hand, and began to pat the bull
on his side ; and the bull only made a soft sound to
show how glad he was. Then Europa put out her hand,
and stroked him on the face, and laid hold of his white
horn, and the bull rubbed his face gently against her
dress. So by and by Kadmos thought that it would be
pleasant to have a ride on the back of the **bull**; and he
got on, and the bull rose up from the ground, and went
slowly round the field with Kadmos on his back, and
just for a minute or two Kadmos felt frightened ; but
when he saw how well and safely the bull carried him,
he was not afraid any more. So they played with the
bull until the sun sank down behind the hills, and then
they hastened home.

When they reached the house, they ran quickly to
Têlephassa, and said to her, 'Only think, we have **been**
playing in the field with a beautiful white bull.' **And**
Têlephassa was glad that they had been so happy ; but
she would not have been so glad if she had known what
the bull was going to do.

Now the next day while Europa was on its back, the
bull began to trot quickly away ; but Kadmos thought
he was only trotting away for fun. So he ran after him,
and cried out to make him stop. But the faster that
Kadmos ran, the bull ran faster still, and then Kadmos
saw that the bull was running away with his sister Europa.
Away the bull flew, all along the bank of the river, and
up the steep hill and down into the valley on the other
side ; and then he scoured along the plain beneath. And
Kadmos watched his white body, which shone like
silver as he dashed through the small bushes and the
long waving grass and the creeping plants which were

trailing about all over the ground, till at last the white body of the bull looked only like a little speck, and then Kadmos could see it no more.

Very wretched was Kadmos when his sister was taken away from him in this strange way. His eyes were full of tears so that he could scarcely see; but still he kept on looking and looking in the way that the bull had gone, and hoping that he would bring his sister back by and by. But the sun sank lower and lower in the sky, and then Kadmos saw him go down behind the hills: and he knew now that the bull would not come again; and then he began to weep bitterly. He hardly dared to go home and tell Têlephassa what had happened; and yet he knew that he ought to tell her. So he went home slowly and sadly; and Têlephassa saw him coming alone, and she began to be afraid that something had happened to Europa; and when she came up to him Kadmos could scarcely speak. At last he said, 'The bull has run away with Europa.' Then Têlephassa asked him where he had gone; and Kadmos said that he did not know. But Têlephassa said, 'Which way did he go?' and then Kadmos told her that the bull had run away towards the land of the West, where the sun goes down into his golden cup. Then Têlephassa said that they too must get up early in the morning and go towards the land of the West, and see if they could find Europa again.

That night they hardly slept at all; and their cheeks were pale and wet with their tears. And before the sun rose, and while the stars still glimmered in the pale light of the morning, they got up and went on their journey to look for Europa. Far away they went: along the valleys and over the hills, across the rivers and through the woods, and they asked every one whom they met if they had seen a white bull with a girl upon its back.

But no one had seen anything of the kind, and many people thought that Kadmos and Têlephassa were silly to ask such a question, for they said, 'Girls do not ride on the backs of bulls ; you cannot be telling us the truth.' So they went on and on, asking every one, but hearing nothing about her; and as they journeyed, sometimes they saw the great mountains rising up high into the sky, with their tops covered with snow, and shining like gold in the light of the setting sun ; sometimes they rested on the bank of a great broad river, where the large white lilies lay floating and sleeping on the water, and where the palm-trees waved their long branches above their heads. Sometimes they came to a waterfall, where the water sparkled brightly as it rushed over the great stones. And whenever they came to these beautiful places, Kadmos would say to Têlephassa, ' How we should have enjoyed staying here if Europa were with us : but we do not care to stay here now ; we must go on looking for her every-where.' So they went on and on till they came to the sea, and then they wondered how they could get across it, for it was a great deal wider than any river which they had seen. At last they found a place where the sea was narrow ; and here a boatman took them across in his boat, just where little Hellê had been drowned when she fell off the back of the ram that was carrying her and her brother away to Kolchis. So Têlephassa and Kadmos crossed over Hellespontos, which means the Sea of Hellê ; and they went on and on, over mountains and hills and rocks, and wild gloomy places, till they came to the sunny plains of Thessaly. And still they asked every one about Europa ; but they found no one who had seen her. And Kadmos saw that his mother was getting weak and thin, and that she could not walk now as far and as quickly as she had done when they had set out from home to look for his sister. So he asked her to rest for a little while. But Têlephassa said, 'We must go on, Kadmos ; for if we do, perhaps we may still find Europa.' So they went on, until at last Têlephassa felt that she could not go any further. And she said to Kadmos, 'I am very tired, and I do not think I shall be able to walk any more with you ; I must lie down and go to sleep here, and perhaps, Kadmos, I may not wake again. But if I die while I am asleep, then you must go on by yourself and look for Europa, for I am quite sure that you will find her some day, although I shall not be with you. And when you see your sister, tell her how I longed to find her again, and how much I loved her always. And now, my child, I must go to sleep ; and if I do not wake up any more, then I trust that we shall all see each other again one day, in a land which is brighter and happier than even the land in which we used to live before your sister was taken away from us.

So when she had said this, Têlephassa fell asleep, just as the daylight was going away from the sky, and when the bright round moon rose up slowly from behind the dark hill. All night long Kadmos watched by her side; and when the morning came, he saw that Têlephassa had died while she was asleep. Her face was quite still, and Kadmos knew by the happy smile which was on it, that she had gone to the bright land to which good people go when they are dead. Kadmos was very sorry to be parted from his mother ; but he was not sorry that now she could not feel tired or sorrowful any more. So Kadmos placed his mother's body in the ground; and very soon all kinds of flowers grew up upon her grave.

But Kadmos had gone on to look for his sister Europa : and presently he met a shepherd who was leading his flock of sheep. **He was very** beautiful to look **at. His** face shone as bright almost **as the** sun. He had a golden harp, and a golden bow, and arrows in a golden quiver; and his name was Phœbus Apollo. And Kadmos went up to him and said, ' Have you seen my sister Europa? a white bull ran away with her on his back. Can you tell me where I may find her?' And Phœbus Apollo said, ' I have seen your sister Europa, but I cannot tell you yet where she is: you must go on a great way further still, till you come to a town which is called Delphi, under a great mountain named Parnassus; and there perhaps you may be able to find out something about her. But when you have seen her you must not stay there; because I wish you to build a city, and become a king, and be wise and strong and good. You and Europa must follow a beautiful cow that I shall send, till it lies down upon the ground to rest; and the **place** where the cow shall lie down shall be the place where **I** wish you to build the city.'

So Kadmos went on and on till he came to the **town** of Delphi, which lay beneath the great mountain called Parnassus. And there he saw a beautiful temple with white marble pillars, which shone brightly in the light of the early morning. And Kadmos went into the temple; and there he saw his dear sister Europa. And Kadmos said, ' Europa, is it you indeed? How glad I am to find you.' Then Europa told Kadmos how the bull had brought her and left her there a long time ago, and how sorry she had been that she could not tell Têlephassa where she was. Then she said to Kadmos, ' How pale and thin and weak you look; tell me how it is you are **come** alone, and when shall I see our dear **mother?'** **Then** his eyes became full of tears, and **Kadmos said,** ' **We shall never** see our mother again in this world.

She has gone to the happy land where good people go
when they are dead. She was so tired with seeking
after you that at last she could not come any further,
and she lay down and fell asleep, and never waked up
again. But she said that when I saw you, I must tell
you how she longed to see you, and how she hoped that
we should all live together one day in the land to which
she has gone before us. And now, Europa, we must
not stay here: for I met a shepherd whose name is
Phœbus Apollo. He had a golden harp and a golden
bow, and his face shone like the sun; and he told me
that we must follow a beautiful cow which he would
send, and build a city in that place where the cow shall
lie down to rest.'

So Europa left Delphi with her brother Kadmos: and
when they had gone a little way, they saw a cow lying
down on the grass. But when they came near, the cow
got up, and began to walk in front of them: and then
they knew that this was the cow which Phœbus Apollo
had sent. So they followed the cow; and it went on
and on, a long way, and at last it lay down to rest on a
large plain; and Kadmos knew then that this was the
place where he must build the city. And there he built
a great many houses, and the city was called Thebes.
And Kadmos became the king of Thebes, and his sister
Europa lived there with him. He was a wise and good
king, and ruled his people justly and kindly. And by
and by Kadmos and Europa both fell asleep and died;
and then they saw their mother Têlephassa in the happy
land to which good people go when they are dead, and
were never parted from her any more.

———o———

HE minstrels sang of the beauty and the great deeds of Bellerophôn through all the land of Argos. His arm was strong in the battle; his feet were swift in the chase; and his heart was pure as the pure heart of Artemis and Athênê. None that were poor and weak and wretched feared the might of Bellerophôn. To them the sight of his beautiful form brought only joy and gladness; but the proud and boastful, the slanderer and the robber, dreaded the glance of his keen eye. But the hand of Zeus lay heavy upon Bellerophôn. He dwelt in the halls of King Prœtos, and served him even as Herakles servéd the mean and crafty Eurystheus. For many long years Bellerophôn knew that he must obey the bidding of a man weaker than himself; but his soul failed him not, and he went forth to his long toil with a heart strong as the sun when he rises in his strength, and pure as the heart of a little child.

But Anteia, the wife of King Prœtos, saw day by day the beauty of Bellerophôn, and she would not turn away her eye from his fair face. Every day he seemed to her to be more and more like to the bright heroes who feast with the gods in the halls of high Olympos; and her heart became filled with love, and she sought to beguile Bellerophôn by her enticing words. But he hearkened not to her evil prayer, and heeded not her tears and sighs; so her love was turned to wrath, and she vowed a vow that Bellerophôn should suffer a sore vengeance, because he would not hear her prayer. Then in her rage she went to King Prœtos and said, 'Bellerophôn,

thy slave, hath sought to do me wrong, and to lead me
astray by his crafty words. Long time he strove with
me to win my love; but I would not hearken to him.
Therefore let thine hand lie more heavy upon him than
in time past, for the evil that he hath done; and slay
him before my face.' Then was Prœtos also full of
anger; but he feared to slay Bellerophôn, lest he should
bring on himself the wrath of Zeus his father. So he
took a tablet of wood, and on it he drew grievous signs
of toil and war, of battles and death, and gave it to
Bellerophôn to carry to the far-off Lykian land, where
the father of Anteia was king; and as he bade him farewell, he said, ' Show this tablet to the king of Lykia, and
he will recompense thee for all thy good deeds which
thou hast done for me, and for the people of Argos.'

So Bellerophôn went forth on his long wandering, and
dreamed not of the evil that was to befall him by the
wicked craft of Anteia. On and on he journeyed
towards the rising of the sun, till he came to the country
of the Lykians. Then he went to the house of the
king, who welcomed him with rich banquets, and feasted
him for nine days; and on the tenth day he sought to
know wherefore Bellerophôn had come to the Lykian
land. Then Bellerophôn took the tablet of Prœtos and
gave it to the king, who saw on it grievous signs of toil
and woe, of battles and death. Presently the king spake
and said, ' There are great things which remain for thee
to do, Bellerophôn; but when thy toil is over, high
honour awaits thee here and in the homes of the bright
heroes.' So the king sent him forth to slay the terrible
Chimæra, which had the face of a lion with a goat's
body and a dragon's tail. Then Bellerophôn journeyed
yet further towards the rising of the sun, till he came to
the pastures where the winged horse Pegasos, the child

of Gorgo with the snaky hair, was feeding; and he knew that if he could tame the steed he should then be able to conquer the fierce Chimæra. Long time he sought to **seize on** Pegasos; but the 'horse snorted wildly and tore up the ground in his fury, till Bellerophôn sank wearied on the earth and a deep sleep weighed down his eyelids. Then, as he slept, Pallas Athênê came and stood by his side, and cheered him with her brave words, and gave him a philtre which should tame the wild Pegasos. When Bellerophôn awoke, the philtre was in his hand, and he knew now that he should accomplish the task which the Lykian king had given him to do. So, by the help of Athênê, he mounted the winged Pegasos and smote the Chimæra, and struck off its head; and with it he went back, and told the king of all that had befallen him. But the king was filled with rage, for he thought not to see the face of Bellerophôn again; and he charged him to go forth and do battle with the mighty Solymi and the fair Amâzons. Then Bellerophôn went forth again, for he dreamed not of guile and falsehood, and he dreaded neither man nor beast which might meet him in open battle. Long time he fought with the Solymi and the Amâzons, until all his enemies shrank from the stroke of his mighty arm, and sought for mercy. Glad of heart, Bellerophôn departed to carry his spoils to the home of the Lykian king; but as he drew nigh to it and was passing through a narrow dell where the thick brushwood covered the ground, fifty of the mightiest of the Lykians rushed upon him with fierce shoutings, and sought to slay him. At the first, Bellerophôn withheld his hands, and said, 'Lykian friends, I have feasted in the halls of your king, and eaten of his bread; surely ye are not come hither to slay me.' But they shouted the more fiercely, and hurled their spears at Bellerophôn; so he stretched forth his hand in the greatness of his strength, and did battle for his life until all the Lykians lay dead before him.

Weary in body and sad of heart, Bellerophôn entered the hall where the king was feasting with his chieftains. And the king knew that Bellerophôn could not have come thither unless he had first slain all the warriors whom he had sent forth to lie in wait for him. But he dissembled his wrath, and said, 'Welcome, Bellerophôn, bravest and mightiest of the sons of men. Thy toils are done, and the time of rest is come for thee. Thou shalt wed my daughter, and share with me my kingly power.'

Then the minstrels praised the deeds of Bellerophôn, and there was feasting for many days when he wedded the daughter of the king. But not yet was his doom accomplished; and once again the dark cloud gathered around him, laden with woe and suffering. Far away from his Lykian home, the wrath of Zeus drove him to the western land where the sun goes down into the sea. His heart was brave and guileless still, as in the days of his early youth; but the strength of his arm was weakened, and the light of his eye was now dim. Sometimes the might was given back to his limbs, and his face shone with its ancient beauty; and then, again, he wandered on in sadness and sorrow, as a man wanders in a strange path through the dark hours of night, when the moon is down. And so it was that when Bellerophôn reached the western sea, he fell asleep and died, and the last sight which he saw before his eyes were closed, was the red glare of the dying sun, as he broke through the barred clouds and plunged beneath the sea.[102]

ALTHAIA AND THE BURNING BRAND.

HERE was feasting in the halls of Oineus the chieftain of Kalydon in the Ætolian land, and all prayed for wealth and glory for the chief, and for his wife Althaia, and for the child who had on that day been born to them. And Oineus besought the king of gods and men with rich offerings, that his son Meleagros might win a name greater than his own, that he might grow up stout of heart and strong of arm, and that in time to come men might say, ‘Meleagros wrought mighty works and did good deeds to the people of the land.’

But the mighty Moirai, whose word even Zeus himself may not turn aside, had fixed the doom of Meleagros.[103] The child lay sleeping in his mother’s arms, and Althaia prayed that her son might grow up brave and gentle, and be to her a comforter in the time of age and the hour of death. Suddenly, as she yet spake, the Moirai stood before her. There was no love or pity in their cold grey eyes, and they looked down with stern unchanging faces on the mother and her child, and one of them said, ‘The brand burns on the hearth : when it is burnt wholly, thy child shall die.’ But love is swifter than thought ; and the mother snatched the burning brand from the fire, and quenched its flame in water; and she placed it in a secret place where no hand but her own might reach it.

So the child grew, brave of heart and sturdy of limb, and ever ready to hunt the wild beasts or to go against the cities of men. Many great deeds he did in the far-off Kolchian land, when the chieftains sailed with Atha-

mas and Ino to take away the golden fleece from King
Aiêtes.   But there were greater things for him to do
when he came again to Kalydon, for his father Oineus
had roused the wrath of the mighty Artemis.   There was
rich banqueting in his great hall when his harvest was
ingathered, and Zeus and all the other gods feasted on
the fat burnt-offerings ; but no gift was set apart for the
virgin child of Lêtô.   Soon she requited the wrong to
Oineus, and a savage boar was seen in the land, which
tare up the fruit-trees, and destroyed the seed in the
ground, and trampled on the green corn as it came up.
None dare to approach it, for its mighty tusks tare everything that crossed its path.   Long time the chieftains
took counsel what they should do, until Meleagros said,
'I will go forth: who will follow me?'   Then from
Kalydon and from the cities and lands round about came
mighty chieftains and brave youths, even as they had
hastened to the ship Argo when they sought to win the
golden fleece from Kolchis.   With them came the
Kourêtes who live in Pleurôn, and among them were
seen Kastor and Polydeukês the twin brethren, and
Theseus with his comrade Peirithoös, and Iason and
Admêtos.   But more beautiful than all was Atalantê, the
daughter of Schoineus, a stranger from the Arcadian land.
Much the chieftains sought to keep her from the chase,
for the maiden's arm was strong, and her feet swift, and
her aim sure ; and they liked not that she should come
from a far country to share their glory or take away their
name.   But Meleagros loved the fair and brave maiden ;
and he said, 'If she go not to the chase, neither will I
go with you.'   So they suffered her, and the chase began.
At first the boar fled, trampling down those whom he
chanced to meet, and rending them with his tusks ; but
at last he stood fiercely at bay, and fought furiously,

and many of the hunters fell, until at length the spear of Atalantê pierced his side, and then Meleagros slew him.

Then was there great gladness as they dragged the body of the boar to Kalydon, and made ready to divide the spoil. But the anger of Artemis was not yet soothed; and she roused a strife between the men of Pleurôn and the men of Kalydon. For Meleagros sought to have the head, and the Kourêtes of Pleurôn cared not to take the hide only for their portion. So the strife grew hot between them, until Meleagros slew the chieftain of the Kourêtes, who was the brother of Althaia his mother. Then he seized the head of the boar, and bare it to Atalantê, and said, 'Take, maiden, the spoils that are rightly thine. From thy spear came the first wound which smote down the boar; and well hast thou earned the prize for the fleetness of thy foot and the sureness of thy aim.'

So Atalantê took the spoils and carried them to her home in the Arcadian land; but the men of Pleurôn were full of wrath, and they made war on the men of Kalydon. Many times they fought, but in every battle the strong arm of Meleagros and his stout heart won the victory for the men of his own city; and the Kourêtes began to grow faint in spirit, so that they quailed before the spear and sword of Meleagros. But presently Meleagros was seen no more with his people, and his voice was no longer heard cheering them on to the battle. No more would he take lance in hand or lift up his shield for the strife, but he tarried in his own house by the side of the beautiful Kleopatra, whom Idas her father gave to him to be his wife.

For the heart of his mother was filled with grief and rage when she heard the story of the deadly strife, and

that Meleagros, her child, had slain her brother.   In
heavy wrath and sorrow she sat down upon the earth,
and she cast the dust from the ground into the air, and
with wild words called on Hades, the unseen king, and
Persephonê who shares his dark throne: 'Lord of the
lands beneath the earth, stretch forth thy hand against
Meleagros my child.   He has quenched the love of a
mother in my brother's blood, and I will that he should
die.'   And even as she prayed, the awful Erînys, which
wanders through the air, heard her words and sware to
accomplish the doom.   But Meleagros was yet more
wrathful when he knew that his mother had laid her curse
upon him ; and therefore he would not go forth out of
his chamber to the aid of his people in the war.

So the Kourêtes grew more and more mighty ; and
their warriors came up against the city of Kalydon, and
would no longer suffer the people to come without the
walls.   And everywhere there was faintness of heart and
grief of spirit, for the enemy had wasted their fields and
slain the bravest of the men, and little store remained to
them of food.   Day by day Oineus besought his son,
and the great men of the city fell at the knees of Meleagros and prayed him to come out to their help, but he
would not hearken.   Still he tarried in his chamber with·
his wife Kleopatra by his side, and heeded not the hunger and the wailings of the people.   Fiercer and fiercer
waxed the roar of war ; the loosened stones rolled from
the tottering wall, and the battered gates were scarce able
to keep out the enemy.   Then Kleopatra fell at her
husband's knee, and she took him by the hand, and
called him gently by his name, and said, 'O Meleagros,
if thou wilt think of thy wrath, think also of the evils
which war brings with it—how when a city is taken, the
men are slain, and the mother with her child, the old and

the young, are borne away into slavery. If the men of Pleurôn win the day, thy mother may repent her of the curse which she has laid upon thee; but thou wilt see thy children slain and me a slave.' Then Meleagros started from his couch and seized his spear and shield. He spake no word, but hastened to the walls; and soon the Kourêtes fell back **before** the spear which never missed its mark. Then he gathered the warriors of his city, and bade them open the gates, and went forth against the enemy. Long and dreadful was the battle, but at length the Kourêtes turned and fled, and the danger passed away from the men of Kalydon.

But the Moirai **still** remembered the doom of the burning brand, and the unpitying Erînys had not forgotten the curse of Althaia; and they moved the men of Kalydon to withhold the prize of his good deeds from the chieftain Meleagros. 'He came not forth,' they said, 'save at the prayer of his wife. He hearkened not when we besought him; he heeded not our misery and tears: why should we give him that which he did not win from **any** love for us?' So his people were angry with Meleagros, and his spirit grew yet more bitter within him. **Once** again he lay within his chamber, and his spear and shield hung idle on the wall; and it pleased him more **to listen the whole day** long to the soft words of Kleopatra, **than to be** doing brave and good deeds for the people of **his** land.

Then the heart of his mother Althaia was more and more turned away from him, so that she said in bitterness of spirit, 'What good shall his life now do to me?' and she brought forth the half-burnt brand from its secret place, and cast it on the hearth. Suddenly it burst into a flame, and suddenly the strength of Meleagros began to fail as he lay in the arms of Kleopatra. 'My life is

L

wasting within me,' he said; 'clasp me closer in thine arms; let others lay a curse upon me, so only I die rejoicing in thy **love.'**   Weaker and weaker grew his failing breath; but still he looked with loving eyes on the **face** of Kleopatra, and his spirit went forth with a sigh of gladness, as the **last spark of** the brand flickered out upon the hearth.

Then was there grief and sorrow in the house of Oineus and through all the city of Kalydon; but they wept **and** mourned in vain.   They thought now of his good deeds, his wise counsels, and his mighty arm; but in vain they bewailed the death of their chieftain in the glory of his age.   Yet deeper and **more bitter was the** sorrow of **Althaia,** for the love of a mother came back to her heart when the Moirai had accomplished the doom of her child.   And yet more bitterly sorrowed his wife Kleopatra, and yearned **for the love** which **had been** torn away from her.   There was no more joy **within the** halls of Oineus, for the Erînys had done **her task** well.   Soon Althaia followed her child to the unknown land, **and** Kleopatra went forth with joy to meet Meleagros in the dark kingdom of Hades and Persephonê.

------o------

IAMOS.

N the banks of Alpheios, Evadnê watched over her new-born babe, till she fled away because she feared the wrath of Aipytos, who ruled in Phaisana.   The tears streamed down her cheeks as she prayed to Phœbus Apollo who dwells at Delphi, and said, 'Lord of the bright day, look on thy child, and guard him when he lies forsaken, for I may no longer tarry near him.' So Evadnê fled away; and Phœbus sent two serpents, who fed the babe with honey as he lay amid the flowers which clustered round him. And ever more and more through all the land went forth the saying of Phœbus, that the child of Evadnê should grow up mighty in wisdom and in the power of telling the things that should happen in the time to come. Then Aipytos asked of all who dwelt in his house to tell him where he might find the son of Evadnê. But they knew not where the child lay, for the serpents had hidden him far away in a thicket, where the wild flowers sheltered him from wind and heat. Long time they searched amid the tall reeds which clothe the banks of Alpheios, until at last they found the babe lying on a bed of violets. So Aipytos took the child and called his name Iamos, and he grew up brave and wise of heart, pondering well the signs of coming grief and joy, and the tokens of hidden things which he saw in the heaven above him or on the wide earth beneath. He spake but little to the youths and maidens who dwelt in the house of Aipytos; but he wandered on the bare hills or by the stream side, musing on many things. And so it came to pass that one night, when the stars glimmered softly in the sky, Iamos plunged beneath the waters of Alpheios, and prayed to Phœbus who dwells at Delphi, and to Poseidon, the lord of the broad sea; and he besought them to open his eyes, that he might reveal to the sons of men the things which of themselves they could not see. Then they led him away to the high rocks which look down on the plain of Pisa, and they said, 'Look yonder, child of Evadnê, where the white stream of Alpheios winds its way gently to the sea. Here, in the days which are to come, Herakles, the son of the mighty Zeus, shall gather together the sons of Hellen, and give them in the solemn games the mightiest

of all bonds ; [104] hither shall they come to know the
will of Zeus, and here shall it be thy work and the work
of thy children to read to them the signs which of themselves they cannot understand.' Then Phœbus Apollo
touched his ears, and straightway the voices of the birds
spake to him clearly of the things which were to come,
and he heard their words as a man listens to the speech
of his friend. So Iamos prospered exceedingly, for the
men of all the Argive land sought aid from his wisdom,
and laid rich gifts at his feet. And he taught his children
after him to speak the truth and to deal justly, so that
none envied their great wealth, and all men spake well of
the wise children of Iamos.

TALES OF THE TROJAN WAR.

HERE was sorrow, instead of gladness, in the halls of Priam, because a son was born unto him, and because the lady Hekabê had dreamed a dream, from which the seers knew that the child should bring ruin on the Ilian land. So his mother looked with cold unloving eyes on the babe as he lay weak and helpless in his cradle; and Priam bade them take the child and leave him on rugged Ida, for the fountain of his love was closed against him.

For five days the dew fell on the babe by night, and the sun shone fiercely on him by day, as he lay on the desolate hillside; and the shepherd who placed him there to sleep the sleep of death, looked upon the child and said, 'He sleeps as babes may slumber on silken couches; the gods will it not that he should die.' So he took him to his home, and the child grew up with ruddy cheek and nimble feet, brave and hardy, so that none might be matched with him for strength and beauty. The fierce wolves came not near the flocks while Paris kept guard near the fold; the robber lurked not near the homestead when Paris sate by the hearth. So all sang of his strength and his great deeds; and they called him Alexandros, the helper of men.

Many years he tended the flocks on woody Ida; but Priam his father dwelt in Ilion, and thought not to see his face again; and he said within himself, 'Surely my child is long since dead, and no feast has been given to

the gods that Paris may dwell in peace in the dark
kingdom of Hades.' Then he charged his servants to
fetch him a bull from the herd, which might be given to
the man who should conquer in the games; and they
chose out one which Paris loved above all others that
he drove out to pasture. So he followed the servants of
Priam in grief and anger, and he stood forth and strove
with his brethren in the games; and in all of them
Paris was the conqueror. Then one of his brothers was
moved with wrath, and lifted up his sword against him;
but Paris fled to the altar of Zeus, and the voice of
Kasandra his sister was heard saying, 'O blind of eye
and heart, see ye not that this is Paris, whom ye sent to
sleep the sleep of death on woody Ida?'

But Paris would not dwell in the sacred Ilion, for he
loved not those who sought to slay him while he was
yet a helpless child; and again he tended the flocks on
the wide plains and up the rough hillsides. Strong he
was of limb and stout of heart, and his face shone with
a marvellous beauty, so that they who saw it thought
him fair as the bright heroes. There, as he wandered
in the woody dells of Ida, he saw and wooed the beautiful Œnônê, the child of the river-god Kebrên. Many a
time he sat with the maiden by the side of the stream,
and the sound of their voices was mingled with the soft
murmur of the waters. He talked to her of love, and
Œnônê looked up with a wondrous joy into his beautiful face, when the morning dew glistened white upon the
grass and when the evening star looked out upon the
pale sky.

So was Paris wedded to Œnônê, and the heart of
the maiden was full of happiness; for none was braver
or more gentle—none so stout of heart, so lithe of limb,
so tender and loving, as Paris. Thus passed the days

away in a swift dream of joy, for Œnônê thought not of the change that was coming.

There was feasting and **mirth** among gods and men, for the brave Peleus had won Thetis the maiden of the sea to be his bride; and she rose from the depths of her coral caves to go to his home in Phthia. The banquet **was** spread in his ancient hall, and the goblets sparkled **with** the dark wine, for all the gods had come down from Olympos to share the feast in the house of Peleus. Only Eris was not bidden, for she was the child of War and Hatred, and they feared to see her face in the hours of laughter and mirth; but her evil heart rested not till she found a way to avenge herself for the wrong which they had done to her.

The gods were listening to the song of Phœbus Apollo as he made sweet music on the strings of his harp, when a golden apple was cast upon the table before them. They knew not whence it came; only **they** saw that it was to be a gift for the fairest in that great throng, for so was it written on the apple. Then the joy of the feast was gone, and the music of the song ceased, for there was a strife which should have the golden prize; and Hêrê the queen said, 'The gods themselves do obeisance to me when I enter the halls of Olympos, and men sing of the glory of my majesty; therefore must the gift be mine.' But Athênê answered and said, 'Knowledge and goodness are better things than power: mine is the worthier title.' Then the fair Aphroditê lifted her white arm, and a smile of triumph passed over her face as she said, '**I am** the child of love **and** beauty, and the stars danced in the heaven for joy **as I** sprang from the sea foam; I dread not the contest, for to me alone must the golden **gift be** given.'

So the strife waxed hot in the banquet hall, till Zeus spake with a loud voice and said, 'It needs not to strive now. Amid the pine forests of Ida dwells Paris, the fairest of the sons of men ; let him be judge, and the apple shall be hers to whom he shall give it.' Then Hermes rose and led them quickly over land and sea, to go to the rough hillside where Paris wooed and won Œnônê.

Presently the messenger of Zeus stood before Paris and said, 'Fairest of the sons of men, there is strife among the undying gods, for Hêrê and Aphroditê and Athênê seek each to have the golden apple which must be given to her who is most fair.   Judge thou, therefore, between them when they come, and give peace again to the halls of Zeus.'

In a dream of joy and love Œnônê sate by the riverside, and she looked on her own fair face, which was shown to her in a still calm pool where the power of the stream came not ; and she said to herself, 'The gods are kind ; for they have given to me a better gift than that of beauty, for the love of Paris sheds for me a wondrous brightness over the heaven above and the broad earth beneath.'   Then came Paris and said, 'See, Œnônê, dearest child of the bright waters, Zeus hath called me to be judge in a weighty matter. Hither are coming Hêrê the queen and Aphroditê and Athênê, seeking each the golden apple which must be given to her alone who is the fairest.   Yet go not away, Œnônê : the broad vine-leaves have covered our summer bower ; there tarry and listen to the judgment, where none may see thee.'

So Paris sat in judgment, and Hêrê spake to him and said, 'I know that I am the fairest, for none other has beauty and majesty like mine.   Hearken then to me, and I will give thee power to do great deeds among the sons of men, and a name which the minstrels shall sing of among those who shall be born in long time to come.' But Athênê answered, 'Heed not her words, O Paris. Thy hand is strong and thy heart is pure, and the men among whom thou dwellest honour thee even now because thou hast done them good. There are better things than power and high renown : and if thou wilt hearken to me, I will give thee wisdom and strength ; and pure love shall be thine, and the memory of happy days when thou drawest near to the dark land of Hades.'

Then Paris thought that he heard the voice of Œnônê, and it seemed to whisper to him, 'Wisdom and right are better than power : give it to Athênê.' But Aphro-ditê gazed upon him with laughing eyes, as she came up closer to his side. Her dark curls fell waving over his shoulder, and he felt the breath from her rosy lips, as she laid her hand on his arm and whispered softly in his ear, 'I talk not to thee of my beauty, for it may be thou seest that I am very fair ; but hearken to me, and I will give thee for thy wife the fairest of all the daughters of men.' But Paris answered, 'I need not thy gift, O child of the bright sea foam, for fairer wife than Œnônê no mortal man may hope to have. Yet art thou the fairest of all the daughters of the undying gods ; and the gift of the fairest is thine.'

So he placed the golden apple in the palm of her snow-white hand, and the touch of her slender fingers thrilled through the heart of Paris as she parted from him with smiling lip and laughing eye. But Hêrê the queen and Athênê the virgin child of Zeus went away displeased ; and evermore their wrath lay heavy on the city and land of Ilion.

Then went Paris to Œnônê, and he twined his arms around her and said, 'Didst thou see the dark countenance of the lady Hêrê, when I gave to the fairest the gift which the fairest alone may have? Yet what care I for the wrath of Hêrê and Athênê? One smile from the lips of Aphroditê is better than their favour for a whole life long.' But Œnônê answered sadly, 'I would that thou mayest speak truly, Paris; yet in my eyes the lady Athênê is fairer far, and Aphroditê is ever false as fair.' Then Paris clasped her closer in his arms and kissed her pale cheek, and said nothing.

But the fierce wrath of Eris was not ended yet. Far away in the western land, there was sore famine in the kingdom of the mighty Menelaos; the people died by the wayside, and the warriors had no strength to go forth to the battle or the huntsmen to the chase. Many times they sought to know the will of the gods; but they heard only dark words for answers, till Phœbus Apollo said that the famine should never cease from the land until they brought from Ilion the bones of the children of Promêtheus whom Zeus bound on the desolate crags of Caucasus. So Menelaos the king departed from his home and went to the city of Priam. There he saw the beautiful Paris, and took him to the Spartan land, for he said that Paris should return home rich and wealthy. So Paris believed his words, and sailed with him over the wide sea. Long time he abode in Sparta, and day by day he saw the lady Helen in the halls of Menelaos. At the first he thought within himself, 'I would that Œnônê were here to see the wife of Menelaos, for surely she is fairer than aught else on the earth.' But soon he thought less and less of Œnônê, who was sorrowing for his long sojourn in the strange land, as she wandered amid the pine forests of woody Ida.

Quickly sped the days for Paris, for his heart was
filled with a strange love, and the will of Eris was being
accomplished within him. He thought not of Œnônê
and her lonely wanderings on heathy Ida; he cared not
for the kindly deeds of Menelaos; and so it came to pass
that, when Menelaos was far away, Paris spoke words of
evil love to Helen and beguiled her to leave her home.
Stealthily they fled away, and sailed over the sea till they
came to the Ilian land; and Helen dwelt with Paris in the
house of his father Priam.

But Œnônê mourned for the love which she had lost,
and her tears fell **into** the gentle stream of Kebrên as
she sat on its grassy banks. 'Ah me,' she said, 'my love
hath been stung by Aphroditê. O Paris, Paris! hast
thou forgotten all thy words? Here thine arms were
clasped around me, and here, as thy lips were pressed
to mine, thou didst say that the wide earth had for thee
no living thing so fair as Œnônê. Sure am I that Helen
hath brought to thee only a false joy; for her heart is
not thine as the heart of a maiden when it is given to
her first love; and sure **am I** too that Helen is not a
fairer wife than I, for my heart is all thine, and the
beauty of woman is marred when she yields herself to a
lawless love. But the cloud is gathering round thee;
and I see the evil that thou hast brought upon the land,
for **I am** sprung from the race of the gods, and mine
eyes are opened to behold the things that willingly I
would not see. I see the waters black with ships, and
the hosts of the Achaians gathered round the walls of
Ilion. I see the moons roll round, while thy people
strive in vain against the wrath of Hêrê and the might
of the son of Peleus; and far away I see the flames that
shall burn the sacred Ilion. I see thy father smitten
down in his own hall, and the spear that shall drink thy

life-blood.   Ah me ! for the doom that is coming, and for the pleasant days when we loved and wandered among the dells of Ida.'

So Paris dwelt with Helen in the house of Priam; but men said, 'This is no more the brave Alexandros,' for he lay at ease on silken couches, and his spear and shield hung idle on the wall.   For him the wine sparkled in the goblet while the sun rose high in the heavens, and he cared only to listen to the voice of Helen, or the minstrels who sang of the joys of love and the bowers of laughter-loving Aphroditê.   And Helen sat by his side in sullen mood, for she thought of the former days and of the evil which she had done to the good king Mene-laos.   Then there came into her heart a deep hatred for Paris, and she loathed him for his false words and his fond looks, as he lay quaffing the wine and taking his rest by day and by night upon the silken couches.

But throughout the streets of Ilion there was hurrying and shouting of armed men, and terror and cries of women and children ; for the hosts of the Achaians were come to take vengeance for the wrongs of Menelaos. Yet Paris heeded not the prayers of his brethren, that he should send back Helen ;[105] so she tarried by his side in his gilded chambers, and he went not forth to the battle, till all men reviled him for his evil love, because he had forsaken the fair Œnônê.

So for Paris fell the mighty Hektor ; for him died the brave Sarpêdon ; and the women of Ilion mourned for their husbands who were smitten down by the Achaian warriors.   Fiercer and fiercer grew the strife, for Hêrê and Athênê fought against the men of Troy, and no help came from the laughter-loving Aphroditê.

Many times the years went round, while yet the Achaians strove to take the city of Priam, till at last for very shame Paris took from the wall his spear and shield, and went forth to the battle; but the strength of his heart and of his arm was gone, and he trembled at the fierce war-cries, as a child trembles at the roaring of the storm. Then before the walls of Ilion there was fiercer strife, and the bodies of the slain lay in heaps upon the battle plain. Faint and weary, the people of Priam were shut up within the walls, until the Achaians burst into the gates and gave the city to sword and flame. Then the cry of men and women went up to the high heaven, and the blood ran in streams upon the ground. With a mighty blaze rose up the flames of the burning city, and the dream of Paris was ended.

Fast he fled from the wrath of Menelaos, and he cared not to look back on the Argive Helen or the slaughter of his kinsfolk and his people. But the arrow of Philoktetes came hissing through the air, and the barb was fixed in the side of Paris. Hastily he drew it from the wound; but the weapons of Herakles failed not to do their work, and the poison sped through his burning veins.[106] Onwards he hastened to the pine forests of Ida, but his limbs trembled beneath him, and he sank down as he drew nigh to the grassy bank where he had tended his flocks in the former days. 'Ah, Œnônê,' he said, 'the evil dream is over, and thy voice comes back to mine ear, soft and loving as when I wooed and won thee among the dells of Ida. Thou hearest me not, Œnônê, or else I know that, forgiving all the wrong, thou wouldst hasten to help me.'

And even as he spake, Œnônê stood before him, fair and beautiful as in the days that were past. The glory as of the pure evening time was shed upon her face, and her eye glistened with the light of an undying love. Then she laid her hand upon him, and said gently, 'Dost thou know me, Paris? I am the same Œnônê whom thou didst woo in the dells of woody Ida. My grief hath not changed me; but thou art not the same, O Paris; for thy love hath wandered far away, and thou hast yielded thyself long to an evil dream.' But Paris said, 'I have wronged thee, Œnônê, fairest and sweetest; and what may atone for the wrong? The fire burns in my veins, my head reels, and mine eye is dim; look but upon me once, that thinking on our ancient love, I may fall asleep and die.'

Then Œnônê knelt by the side of Paris, and saw the wound which the arrow of Philoktetes had made; but soon she knew that neither gods nor men could stay the poison with which Herakles had steeped his mighty weapons. There she knelt, but Paris spake not more. The coldness of death passed over him, as Œnônê looked down upon his face and thought of the days when they lived and loved amid the dells of Ida.

Long time she knelt by his side, until the stars looked forth in the sky. Then Œnônê said, 'O Eris, well hast thou worked thy will, and well hath Aphroditê done thy bidding. O Paris, we have loved and suffered, but I never did thee wrong, and now I follow thee to the dark land of Hades.'

Presently the flame shot up to heaven from the funeral pile of Paris, and Œnônê lay down to rest on the fiery couch by his side.[107]

HE ships of Agamemnon and the Achaian chieftains lay idle in Aulis on the narrow waters of
Eurîpos. In vain they longed to reach the
shores of Ilion and take vengeance on the
treacherous Paris, who had stolen away Helen from the
halls of Menelaos at Mykênai. Not a breath of wind
stirred the sails on the masts; not a ripple on the sea
moved the dark hulls of the ships. Then in his great
strait Agamemnon the king bade them bring before him
the wise seer Kalchas, and he asked him if he knew
wherefore they were made to tarry thus for weeks and
months in Aulis. Then Kalchas opened his mouth and
told them of the wrath of Artemis, how she bear hatred
to Agamemnon because once he had slain a stag in her
sacred grove, and how she withheld the winds in the
prison-house of Æolus until they should appease her
anger by a rich offering. But when the soothsayer told
them what the offering must be, then the two sons of
Atreus smote with their staves upon the ground and
lifted up their voices and wept aloud,[108] for the remedy
seemed more terrible than the evil from which they
sought to escape. Long time Agamemnon stood with
his eyes fixed upon the ground, and his chest heaved
with the greatness of his agony; but at length he spake
and said, 'A hard fate is on me, ye chiefs of the Achaians,
for it is a fearful thing to shed the blood of my child to
appease the wrath of Artemis; and yet how can I betray
the men whom I have brought hither, and leave the ships
to rot and our warriors to die for weariness and hunger?'
But the seer gave no hope that the mind of Artemis

M

would be changed ; and the word was given that Iphigeneia must die.   Presently the rumour ran through
the whole army that the virgin child of Lêtô could not
be appeased save with the blood of one as pure as
herself; and all were filled with pity for the maiden,
yet they cared not to change the judgment, because
they longed yet more to avenge the wrongs and woes
of Helen.

From the tent of Agamemnon came forth Kalchas the
seer with his servants, leading the maiden to the altar
where the great sacrifice was to be done to Artemis.
Hard by it stood the king Agamemnon and Menelaos
his brother; and the maiden sought, as she passed by
them, to meet once more her father's eye ; but his face
was turned away and buried in the folds of his robe.
He saw not his child as she looked towards him with a
beseeching glance; he knew not how she sought in vain
to speak a word, for the men who led her had laid their
hands upon her mouth, that the voice of Iphigeneia
might never be heard again.   But while the priests made
the victim ready for the sacrifice, the thoughts of Agamemnon went back to his home at Sparta, and he saw
again his child in the freshness of her beauty, as she
moved through his halls, bringing joy and gladness to
all who looked upon her.

The words of Kalchas were fulfilled, and the wrath of
Artemis passed away.   The soft western breeze rippled
the waters of Eurîpos, and in a long line the ships of
the Achaians sailed away from the shore to go to the
land of Ilion.   But the terrible Erînys, who hovers in
the air to see all the evil deeds which men may do, had
not forgotten the sacrifice of blood in Aulis.   Nine years
they fought at Troy, and in the tenth the city fell, and
the kingdom of Priam was destroyed utterly, as the sign

of the dragon had taught them long ago when they were in Aulis.[109]

Then from cliff to cliff, across sea and river, from city to city, spread the tidings that the vengeance was accomplished and Agamemnon the king was coming back in triumph and glory. From hill to hill, across plain and valley, flashed the beacon fires; and before the first grey streak of dawn broke upon the eastern sky, the old warder who kept the nightly watch in the house of Agamemnon saw the sign of victory, and hastened to bear the tidings to Klytaimnêstra the queen. Then she said, 'The gods have dealt kindly with the hosts of the Achaians; make ready to receive the king as a conqueror should be welcomed.' And when she knew that at length Agamemnon was near at hand, she made ready embroidered tapestries and spread them on the ground, that so he might not touch the earth with his foot when he alighted off his chariot. Then she stood with downcast eyes to wait the coming of the king; and when he came, she welcomed him to his home with kind and gentle words. But her look was changed when in the chariot she saw a maiden seated, and Agamemnon told her that it was Kasandra the daughter of Priam. Very fair was the maiden to look upon, but her face was worn with care and sorrow. 'She too is welcome,' said Klytaimnêstra, 'to the home of King Agamemnon.'

Then, as he stepped down from his chariot, Agamemnon said to Klytaimnêstra, 'Thy love hath carried thee too far, for thou art receiving me with honours too great for mortal man; and pride goes before a fall.' So he went on heedless to his doom. But to Kasandra the Trojan maiden Phœbus Apollo had granted the gift of prophecy; only, because she would not give him her love, he added the judgment that none should believe her words.   Presently a dark shade came over her face, and she clasped her hands as if from a sudden pain ; and she cried out, 'O Phœbus, what a sight dost thou show me !   In the blood-stained bath Agamemnon lies slain, as a wild bull in a net; and the dagger which has smitten him shall smite me also this day before the sun goes down.' But none gave heed to her wild cries until presently from within the house came a shriek loud and piercing, and then all was still again.

So the Atê of Iphigeneia came upon Agamemnon and brooded on his house, adding sin to sin and woe to woe. For the love of a child for his mother was dried up in the heart of Orestes, while he abode far away in a strange land ; and when he grew to manhood, and came back to Sparta, he slew his mother Klytaimnêstra, because she had killed his father.   Then the Erînyes of his mother fell upon him and drove him in raging madness from the land.   By day and by night they gave him no rest.   He felt their cold breath on his cheek as he lay down to sleep, and he heard the hiss of the deadly snakes which were coiled in their tangled hair.   Over hill and dale, from city to city, from land to land, they drove him with their pitiless scourge, till, faint of heart and ready to die, he fled to the sacred hill of Athênê.   There in the solemn council, when the judgment was divided whether Orestes should live or die, Athênê gave sentence that he should go free.   So the Erînyes of Klytaimnêstra fled away in grief and rage, and the Atê of Iphigeneia rested no more on the house of Agamemnon.[110]

INE years the Achaians had fought against Ilion to avenge the wrongs and the woes of Helen, and still the war went on, and only the **words** of Kalchas, which he spake long ago in Aulis,[111] cheered them with **the hope that the** day of **vengeance** was near at hand. For strife had arisen be-**tween the** king Agamemnon and the mighty son of Peleus, and it seemed **to the** men of Argos that all their toil must be **for naught.** In fierce **anger,** Achilleus vowed a **vow that he would** go forth **no more to** the battle, and **he sat in** sullen silence within his tent, **or** wandered gloomily along the sea-shore. With fresh courage the hosts of the Trojans poured out from their walls when they knew that Achilleus fought no more or the side of the Achaians, and the chieftains sought in vain for his help when the battle **went** against them. Then the face of the **war** was changed; for the **men of** Ilion came forth from their city, and shut **up the** Achaians within their camp, and fought fiercely to **take** the **ships. Many** a chief and warrior was smitten down, and **still** Achilleus sat within his tent, nursing his great **wrath, and reviling** all who **came** before him with gifts and prayers.

But dearer than all others to the child of the sea-nymph Thetis was Patroklos, the son **of** Menoitios, and the heart of Achilleus was touched with pity when he saw the tears stream down his face; and he said, ' Dear friend, tell me thy grief, and hide nothing from me. Hast **thou** evil tidings from our home at Phthia, or weepest thou for the troubles which vex us here ? ' Then

Patroklos spake out boldly, and said, 'Be not angry at my words, Achilleus. The strength of the Argives is wasted away, and the mightiest of their chieftains lie wounded or dead around their ships. They call thee the child of Peleus and of Thetis; but men will say that thou art sprung from the rugged rocks and the barren sea, if thou seest thy people undone and liftest not an arm to help them.' Then Achilleus answered, 'My friend, the vow is on me, and I cannot go ; but put thou on my armour, and go forth to the battle. Only take heed to my words, and go not in my chariot against the city of Ilion. Drive our enemies from the ships, and let them fight in the plain, and then do thou come back to my tent.'

Then the hearts of the Achaians were cheered, for next to Achilleus there was not in all the host a warrior more brave and mighty than Patroklos. At his word the Myrmidons started up from their long rest, and hastily snatched their arms to follow him to the battle. Presently Patroklos came forth. The glistening helmet of Achilleus was on his head, and his armour was girt around his body. Only he bare not his mighty spear, for no mortal man might wield that spear in battle but Achilleus. Before the tent stood the chariot, and harnessed to it were the horses Xanthos and Balios, who grow not old nor die.[112]

So Patroklos departed for the fight, and Achilleus went into his tent, and as he poured out the dark wine from a golden goblet, he prayed to Zeus, and said, 'O thou that dwellest far away in Dodona,[113] where the Selloi do thy bidding and proclaim thy will, give strength and victory to Patroklos my friend. Let him drive the men of Ilion from the ships and come back safe to me after the battle.' But Zeus heard the prayer in part only, for the doom was that Achilleus should see Patroklos alive no more.

Then the **hosts of** the Trojans trembled as Patroklos drew nigh on the chariot of Achilleus, and none dared to go forth against him. Onward sped the undying horses, and wherever they went the ground **was** red with the blood of the Trojans who were smitten down by his spear. Then Sarpêdon,[114] the great chief of **the** Lykians, spake to Glaukos, and said, 'O friend, I **must** go forth and do battle with Patroklos. The people fall beneath his sword, and it is not fit that **the** chieftains **should** be backward **in** the strife.' But the doom of Sarpêdon was sealed, and **presently his body lay** lifeless on the ground, while the men **of Argos and of** Ilion fought for his glittering **arms.**

Then the doom came on Patroklos also, for **Phœbus** Apollo fought against him **in** the battle, and in the dust was rolled the helmet which no enemy had touched **when** it rested on the head of Achilleus. Before him **flashed** the spear of Hektor, as he said, 'The hour of thy **death** is come, Patroklos, and the aid of Achilleus cannot **reach** thee now.' **But** Patroklos said **only**, 'It **is** thy time for boasting now; wait yet a little while, **and the** sword of Achilleus shall drink thy life-blood.'

So Patroklos died, and there was a fierce fight over his body, and many fell on both sides, until there was a great heap of dead around it. But away from the fight, the horses Xanthos and Balios wept for their charioteer, and they would not stir with the chariot, but stood fixed firm as pillars on **the** ground, till Zeus looked down in pity on them and said, 'Was it for this that I gave you to Peleus, **the chieftain** of Phthia—horses who cannot **grow** old **or** die, **to a** mortal man, the most wretched thing that crawls upon the earth? But fear not; no

enemy shall lay hands on the chariot of Achilleus, or on
the immortal horses which bear it. Your limbs shall be
filled with new strength, and ye shall fly like birds across
the battle-field till ye come to the tent of your master.'
Then the horses wept no more, but swift as eagles they
bare Automedon through the fight,[115] while Hektor and
his people strove fiercely to seize them. At last the
battle was over, and, while the Achaians bore the body
of Patroklos to the ships, Antilochos, the son of Nestor,
went to the tent of Achilleus, and said, 'Thy friend is
slain, and Hektor has his armour.'

Then the dark cloud of woe fell on the soul of
Achilleus. In a fierce grief he threw earth with both
hands into the air, and rent his clothes, and lay down
weeping in the dust. Far away in her coral caves beneath the sea Thetis heard the deep groans of her child,
and, like a white mist, she rose from the waters and went
to comfort him ; and she said, ' Why weepest thou, my
son ? When Agamemnon did thee wrong, thou didst pray
that the Achaians might sorely need thy aid in the battle,
and thy wish has been accomplished. So may it be
again.' But Achilleus answered, ' Of what profit is it to
me, my mother, that my prayer has been heard, since
Patroklos my friend is slain, and Hektor has my armour ?
One thing only remains to me now. I will slay Hektor
and avenge the slaughter of Patroklos.' Then the tears
ran down the cheeks of Thetis as she said, ' Then is
thine own doom accomplished, for when thou slayest
Hektor, thou hast not many days to live.' 'So then let it
be,' said Achilleus ; 'the mighty Herakles tasted of
death ; therefore let me die also, so only Hektor dies
before me.'[116]

Then Thetis sought no more to turn him from his
purpose, but she went to the house of Hephaistos to get

armour for her child in place of that which Hektor had taken from Patroklos. And Achilleus vowed a vow that twelve sons of the Trojans should be slain at the grave of his friend, and that Hektor should die before the funeral rites were done. Then Agamemnon sent him gifts, and spake kindly words,[117] so that the strife between them was ended, and Achilleus might now go forth to fight for the Achaians. So, in the armour which Hephaistos had wrought at the prayer of Thetis, he mounted his chariot, and bade his horses bring him back safe from the battle-field. Then the horse Xanthos bowed his head, and the long tresses of his **mane** flowed down to the earth as he made answer, ' We will in very truth save thee, O mighty Achilleus : but thy doom is near at hand, and the fault rests not with us now, or when we left Patroklos dead on the battle-field, for Phœbus Apollo slew him and gave the glory and the arms to Hektor.' And Achilleus said, 'Why speak to me of evil omens ? I know that I shall see my father and my mother again no more ; but if I must die in a strange land, I will first take my fill of vengeance.'[118]

Then the war-cry of Achilleus was heard again, and a mighty life was poured into the hearts of the Achaians, as they seized their arms at the sound. Thick as withering leaves in autumn fell the Trojans beneath his unerring spear. **Chief** after chief was smitten down, until their hosts fled in terror within the walls of Ilion. Only Hektor awaited his coming ; but the shadow of death was stealing over him, for Phœbus Apollo had forsaken the great champion of Troy because Zeus so willed it. So in the strife the strength **of** Hektor failed, and he sank down on the earth. The foot of Achilleus rested on his breast, **and** the spear's point was on his neck, while Hektor said, ' Slay me if thou wilt, but give back my body to my

people.   Let not the beasts of the field devour it, and
rich gifts shall be thine from my father and my mother
for this kindly deed.'   But the eyes of Achilleus flashed
with a deadly hatred as he answered, 'Were Priam to
give me thy weight in gold, it should not save thy carcass
from the birds and dogs.'   And Hektor said, 'I thought
not to persuade thee, for thy heart is made of iron ; but
see that thou pay not the penalty for thy deed, on the
day when Paris and Phœbus Apollo shall slay thee at the
Skaian gates of Ilion.'   Then the life-blood of Hektor
reddened the ground as Achilleus said, 'Die, wretch !
My fate I will meet in the hour when it may please the
undying gods to send it.'

But not yet was the vengeance of Achilleus accomplished.   At his feet lay Hektor dead, but the rage in
his heart was fierce as ever; and he tied the body to
his chariot and dragged it furiously, till none who looked
on it could say, 'This was the brave and noble Hektor.'
But things more fearful still came afterwards, for the
funeral rites were done to Patroklos, and twelve sons of
the Trojans were slain in the mighty sacrifice.   Still the
body of Hektor lay on the ground, and the men of Ilion
sought in vain to redeem it from Achilleus.   But Phœbus
Apollo came down to guard it, and he spread over it his
golden shield to keep away all unseemly things.[119] At last
the king Priam mounted his chariot, for he said, 'Surely
he will not scorn the prayer of a father when he begs the
body of his son.'   Then Zeus sent Hermes to guide the
old man to the tent of Achilleus, so that none others of
the Achaians might see him.   Then he stood before the
man who had slain his son, and he kissed his hands and
said, 'Hear my prayer, Achilleus.   Thy father is an old
man like me, but he hopes one day to see thee come
back with great glory from Ilion.   My sons are dead,

and none had braver sons in Troy than I ; and Hektor, the flower and **pride** of all, has been smitten by thy spear. Fear the gods, Achilleus, and pity me for the remem brance of thy father, for none has ever dared like me to kiss the hand of the **man who** has slain his son.' So Priam **wept** for his dear child Hektor, and the **tears** flowed down the cheeks of Achilleus **as** he thought of his father Peleus and his friend Patroklos, and the cry of their mourning went up together.[120]

So the body of Hektor was borne back to Ilion, and a great sacrifice was done to the gods beneath the earth, that Hektor might be welcomed in the kingdom of Hades and Persephonê. But the time drew nigh that the doom of Achilleus must be accomplished, and the spear of Phœbus Apollo [121] pierced his heart as they fought **near** the Skaian gates of Ilion. In the dust lay the body of Achilleus, while the Achaians fought the whole day long around it, till a mighty storm burst forth from the heaven.[122] Then they carried it away to the ships, and placed it **on** a couch, and washed it in pure water. And once **more** from her coral caves beneath the sea rose the silver-footed Thetis, and the cry of the nymphs who followed her filled the air, so that the Achaians who heard it trembled, and would have fled to the ships ; but Nestor, the wise chief of the Pylians, said, ' Flee not, ye Argives, for those **who** come to mourn for the dead Achilleus.' So Thetis stood weeping by the body of her child, and the nymphs wrapped it in shining robes. Many days and nights they wept and watched around it, until at last they raised a great pile of wood on the sea-shore, and the flame went up to heaven. Then they gathered up the ashes, **and placed** them, with the ashes of Patroklos, in a golden **urn** which Hephaistos wrought and gave to Dio- nysos ; and over it they raised a great cairn on the shore

of the sea of Hellê, that men might see it afar off as they
sailed on the broad waters.

———o———

SARPÊDON.

WHEN Bellerophôn departed for the land of
the setting sun, he left in Lykia a beautiful
child named Laodameia, who became the
mother of Sarpêdon. And when the Achaians
came against the city of Priam to avenge the wrongs
and woes of Helen, Sarpêdon took down his spear and
shield from the wall, and girded his sword upon his thigh,
and went forth to do battle for the brave Hektor against
the hosts of Agamemnon. Sadly he left the home where
he had lived joyously with his wife and children; and
there was mourning and sorrow in the house of Sarpêdon,
for they thought that they had looked on him for the
last time.

Then among the Trojan warriors fought Sarpêdon;
and of all none was braver or more stout of heart than
he. When others were faint of spirit, his voice still
cheered them on; and the bright smile on his face
roused them to fight more boldly for their country. If
the hosts of the Trojans fell back in the strife, then
Sarpêdon rebuked Hektor with friendly words, and told
him how he had come from the far Lykian land to fight
for Priam, and had left his children and his wife behind
him. He told him of all his wealth, and how he had
left rich banquets and soft couches to do battle with the
mighty Achaian chieftains.

Many fell beneath his hand; and of these none was
braver or fairer than Tlêpolemos, the son of Herakles,

who had toiled for the mean Eurystheus, and now dwelt
with Hêbê in the halls of Olympos. Boldly he came
towards him, exulting in the strength of his youth, and
he chid Sarpêdon, and taunted him with shrinking back
from the battle.

'Do they call thee a child of Zeus?' he said. 'What
knowest thou of war and battles? My father Herakles
came hither with six ships only, and destroyed the city
of Ilion when Laomedon was king; and dost thou think
to escape my arm?' But Sarpêdon said only, 'Thy
father Herakles destroyed Ilion because the heart of
Laomedon was not pure, and he dealt treacherously
with him by keeping back the reward of his toil; but I
have no need to fear thee, and the day of thy death is
come.'

So Tlêpolemos fell, and long time the Achaians were
sore pressed, for the Trojans strove mightily to seize
their ships. High above the din of battle was heard the
voice of Hektor; and Sarpêdon cheered on his men to
the fight. Then said he to his kinsman Glaukos, 'Let
none be matched with us for brave deeds. Are we not
honoured more than all other men in Lykia; and look
they not on us as on the bright heroes? The lands
which they have given to us are rich with trees and corn;
therefore must we do battle the more valiantly, that in
after time men may say, "Our chieftains are rich and
wealthy, and their garners are full and plenteous; but
they fight for their people, and their name is great
throughout the wide earth."' [123]

Fierce and terrible was the fighting day by day; and
at night the blaze of many fires reddened the sky. But
Patroklos came forth from the tent of Achilleus, and the
face of the battle was changed. Smitten by his spear,
many of the bravest among the Trojan warriors were

slain, and all were filled with fear as Patroklos drew near
them in the fight. Then Sarpêdon said once more,
'Why shrink ye thus, men of Ilion? I will go forth
against him.' And he shouted his war-cry, and ran to
meet Patroklos.

Then from his throne in the dark cloud Zeus looked
down on his child Sarpêdon, and he spake to Hêrê the
queen and said, 'Ah me, must Sarpêdon die, who is the
dearest to me of all the sons of men; or shall I rescue
him from the fight and bear him to his Lykian home?'
Then answered Hêrê, 'The doom of Sarpêdon must be
accomplished; and if thou drawest him away from the
strife, then remember that other gods also have children
among the hosts who fight round Ilion, whom they will
seek to save from death. But if thine heart is grieved
for Sarpêdon, still let him die by the hands of Patroklos,
and, when his body lies dead, send Hypnos and Thanatos
to bear him away to his far-off Lykian land, where his
people shall mourn for him many days and lay him in
the earth and raise a cairn over his sepulchre.' So Zeus
hearkened to the words of Hêrê; but the big drops fell
from the sky, because he was grieved for his child
Sarpêdon.

Then Patroklos fought with Sarpêdon on the Ilian
plain, and thrust his spear into his side, so that the life-
blood gushed out. The darkness of death fell on his
eyes, but his heart failed not for fear, as he cried,
'Glaukos, brave friend and warrior, take thou my place,
and cheer on the Lykians to the battle; and let not the
Achaians have my body, for that were a shame to thee
and to my people.' So died Sarpêdon, the son of Zeus;
and Glaukos was grieved at the heart, for he could not
go to his aid, because his arm was torn with a grievous
wound. Then he prayed to Phœbus Apollo the Lykian-

born,[124] and Phœbus **drew the** black **blood** from the wound, and cheered the soul of Glaukos.

Fierce was the strife over the body of the Lykian king, **until at** length **even** the brave Hektor was driven back, and the Achaians took the bright armour of Sarpêdon. Then from the dark cloud Zeus spake **to** Phœbus Apollo **and** said, 'Hasten now, O Phœbus, and bear the body of my child Sarpêdon to the stream of Simoeis. There bathe it in the pure waters and **anoint** it with ambrosia, and wrap it in shining robes, and then bid Hypnos and Thanatos carry it to the land of his people.'

So Phœbus Apollo bathed **the** body **of** Sarpêdon in the stream; and the round moon rose up from behind the dark eastern hills. No breeze whispered **in the heaven** above, **no sound was** heard upon the earth beneath, as the powers of sleep and death drew near on their noiseless wings. Gently they looked on the face of Sarpêdon, still and cold, but fair beyond the beauty which is given to the sons of men before the toil of life is ended. Then they raised him softly in their arms, and the still air sounded not with the waving of their wings, as they bore him homewards through the silent hours of night.

The first rays of Eôs quivered in the pale sky as they laid the body of Sarpêdon in his own hall. Then was there sorrow and mourning for the great chief of the Lykians; but their tears were stilled as they looked on his face, so passing fair in the happy sleep of death. So they laid him gently in the earth, and raised a great heap of stones above his grave, that in time to come men might tell of the great deeds of the good and brave Sarpêdon.

MEMNÔN.

FROM the burning land of the Ethiopians came Memnôn the fair son of Eôs, to aid the men of Troy against the Achaian chieftains. Like the brave and beautiful Sarpêdon, he was foremost in the strife of battle, and few might withstand the strength of his arm. Smitten by his sword fell Antilochos, the son of the old chieftain of Pylos. Bitter and deep was the grief of Nestor, the sweet-voiced speaker of the Achaians; and deep was the vow by which Achilleus sware that he would avenge the death of Antilochos on the bright Son of the Morning.

Then in the thickest fight Achilleus sought out Memnôn, and he knew him by the height of his glorious form, and his beauty which was beyond the beauty of the sons of men. Long time they strove, but nothing might stand against the might of Achilleus; so the son of Eôs was smitten down, and the heavy sleep of death fell on his eyes.

But Eôs saw her child die, and she came down to the earth and took away his body from the battle-field. In the pure waters of a river she washed away the dark blood, and wrapped it in a glittering robe. Long time she mourned, and her tear-drops fell on the earth whenever the sun rose up in the sky or sank beneath the waters of the sea. Then at last in bitter sorrow she hastened to the home of the undying gods, and fell before the throne of Zeus and said, 'O Zeus, look upon my grief, and give me comfort in my misery, for Achilleus has slain my child, and the bright Memnôn lies pale and cold in death. If ever it hath been a joy to thee to look

upon my face, when the first light of morning quivers in
the sky,—if ever thou hast loved to see my glory spread
its soft and **tender** flush before the path of the bright
sun—then let not my child wander among the dark
shades in the land of Hades and Persephonê. Speak
thou the word, and he shall come up in his brightness
to gladden the heart of the undying gods.' Then Zeus
bowed his head and spake the word; and Eôs wept no
more, but hastened down to the earth; and Memnôn
rose with her to the high Olympos, to feast with the
undying gods in the halls of Zeus.[125]

—*o*—

HEKTOR AND ANDROMACHÊ.

FAR away from the strife of battle, brooding over
the wrongs which he had suffered, lay Achilleus,
the son of Peleus; for Agamemnon had **taken**
away the prize which the Achaians had set
apart for him from the spoils of war. No more was his
war-cry heard in the battle-field; and his spear smote
not down the warriors who came forth to fight **for** Ilion.
Then the other chieftains of the Achaians put forth all
their strength in the battle against the Trojans; but the
strongest and the bravest of all was Diomêdes, the son
of Tydeus. Wherever he came, his enemies fell back
before him, till all trembled at the sound of his voice
and the sight of his glittering spear. One after another
fell the bravest and best of the Trojan warriors, until at
last Helenos spake to Hektor and said, 'Brother, the
Achaians are pressing us hard, and the gods favour not
the Trojans; what then shall we do, if they come not to
our aid in the hour of need? Hasten, then, into the

N

city, and gather the women together, and bid **them** go
to the temple of Athênê and there beseech her with gifts
and prayers that she may help the Trojans against the
fierce Diomêdes and the other chieftains who fight in the
hosts of Agamemnon.' Then Hektor answered and said,
'I will do **thy** bidding, my brother; but, men of Troy,
let not your hearts be cast down while I go to the sacred
Ilion, and bid our matrons pray to the virgin daughter
of Zeus to aid us in our need. It may be that she will
hear our prayer; but if she hearken not, be not dismayed,
for one good omen not even the gods can take away from
men, when they fight for their home and the land in
which they were born.' [126]

So Hektor hastened to the house of Priam. Very
fair it was to look at in the bright sunshine which
streamed into the golden chambers. Then forth from
the rich hall, where the king held banquet with his
chieftains, came forth the lady Hekabê, leading her
child Laodikê to meet her brother. And when Hektor
came near to her, she took him by the hand, and called
him by his name, and spake in a soft and loving voice,
'Wherefore comest thou hither, my son, from the battle-
field? Are the men of Ilion so sore pressed in the
fight that thou seekest the aid of the bright gods?
Tarry yet a little while, and I will bring thee wine to
gladden thy fainting heart.'

But Hektor said, 'Stay me not, my mother, for I
have a great work to do; and if I tarry now by thy
side, my heart may lose its strength, and my arm may
fail me in the strife. But gather together the matrons
of Ilion, and bid them hasten to the shrine of Athênê
and seek her favour by gifts and prayers. I go to the
house of Paris, if so be I may rouse him to go forth
against the enemy. Weak of heart, and mean of soul,

he lies on his golden couch, and heeds not the evils which for his sake we are suffering. Of a truth, less bitter would **be** our sorrow if he were gone from the land of living **men** to the dark kingdom of Hades.'

So Hekabê parted from her child; and with the **Ilion** matrons she hastened to the temple of Athênê. With rich gifts and prayers they besought her aid, and Theâno, the priestess, placed on her knees a beautiful robe [127] which Hekabê had brought; and the smoke of the sacrifice went up to the high heaven, but Athênê hearkened not to their prayer.

Then came Hektor to the house of Paris and found **him in** his golden chamber burnishing his weapons and his armour. Near to him sat the Argive Helen, and her handmaidens plied their tasks around her. Then Hektor spake **in** grief and anger, and said, 'O Paris, idle and heedless thou sittest here, while the Trojan warriors are smitten down in the strife. Wouldst thou deal lightly by others who brought upon their country the evils which we bear for the sake of thee? Rise up and go forth to the battle, that our ancient city be not burnt with fire.'

But Paris answered gently, 'I chide thee not, Hektor, that thou hast rebuked me, for well have I deserved thy reproof. Yet not in anger or in wrath did I forsake the people of my land; but my grief lay heavy upon me, and I sought to give myself up to my tears. But Helen hath prayed me to go forth to the fight; wherefore wait till I have put on my armour, or go thou first, and I will follow thee to the battle.'

But Hektor stood silent and spake no word, until Helen spake **to** him softly and tenderly, and said, 'O Hektor, brave of heart and kind of soul, never hast thou

spoken a hard word to me who deserved all thy wrath.
Ah, would that the dark wave had swallowed me as I
came to Ilion in the ship of Paris from the city of
Menelaos! Then had I been at rest, and thou hadst
not suffered all the evils which have come for my sake
upon the men of Ilion. But tarry here a little while,
and rest by my side; for great and sore is the toil
which thou hast borne for me in the fight against the
hosts of Agamemnon.' But Hektor answered hastily,
'Ask me not, Helen, to tarry with thee now. Thy
words are kind and loving, but I may not heed them.
My people yearn for my coming; wherefore do thou
urge on Paris that he hasten to put on his armour and
meet me before I leave the city. And now I go to my
own home, that I may greet my wife and my child,
before I depart to the battle, for I know not if I shall
return again in peace from the strife of arms.'

Quickly he sped to his house; but the bridal-
chamber was desolate, and he heard not the voice of
Andromachê among the maidens, as they plied their
tasks in the great hall. Then he said, 'Tell me,
maidens, is Andromachê gone to the homes of her
kinsfolk or to the shrine of the pure Athênê, where the
Trojan matrons are seeking by gifts and prayers to
win her favour?' Then one of them answered, 'If
indeed I must tell the truth, she hath not gone to her
kinsfolk nor to the temple of Athênê; but she bade the
nurse bring with her thy child, and she sped, like one
on whom the hand of the gods lies heavy, to the high
tower of Ilion, because she heard that the Trojans were
hard pressed by the fierce Diomêdes and all the chieftains of the Achaians.'

Then Hektor tarried not to listen to more words.
By the way that he had come he hastened again to

the Skaian gates ; and there as she ran to meet him he
saw his wife and the child whom Hektor called Ska-
mandrios but the men of Troy called Astyanax, because
of the great deeds of his father.   There he stood still
and looked gently on his child, but he spake no word ;
and Andromachê took him by the hand, and, looking
gently and fondly into his face, she said, ' Hektor, wilt
thou hearken to my words ?   Sure **I** am that thine own
brave heart will bring thee to thy **ruin** ; and well thou
knowest that thy death brings shame and sorrow to me
and to our child.   Ah, would that with thee I could go
down to the dark land of Hades ! for what hope have I
when thou art gone ?   The fierce Achilleus in one day
slew my father and my seven brethren, when he took
the sacred city of the Kilikians.   Yet did he no wrong
to the body of Eëtion ; but he laid him gently in the
earth and raised a great mound above his grave, and
the nymphs who **dwell upon the** mountains planted
round it the clustering elm-trees.   There, too, was my
mother slain **by Artemis** in the halls of her father.   All
are gone ; but **in** thee, Hektor, I have father and
mother, and husband and brethren.   Hearken then to
my words, and abide with me on the tower, and let thy
hosts stand beside the ancient fig-tree, where they say
that the wall is weakest.   And partly do I believe it,
for why should there the Achaians make their fiercest
onsets, if **some** one of the undying gods had not shown
them that there they may scale the wall, and that thou
heedest not its weâkness ? '

Then Hektor strove to soothe Andromachê and said
gently to her, ' I have cared for all these things already ;
but ask me not to tarry here upon the wall, for never
must the people say that Hektor shrank from the battle-
field.   I must go forth to the fight, not as in the heedless

days of youth, when men seek to win praise and glory, for my name is great already, and they call me the first among the warriors of Ilion. But well I know that we fight in vain ; for the doom is fixed that the sacred Ilion shall fall, and Priam and his people shall be slain. But more than all I grieve for thee, and for the sorrows that shall come upon thee when thou art carried away captive to some far-off land. There, at the bidding of some Argive woman, thou shalt toil and spin and weave ; and all who see thee weeping shall say, " Look at the wife of Hektor, who was the bravest of all the warriors of Ilion," and thy tears will be more bitter when thou hearest them speak my name, for the dark earth will lie heavy above me in the land of Troy, and I shall be far away from thee in the dark kingdom of Hades.'

So he turned to the babe who lay like a fair star in the arms of the nurse, and he stretched forth his arms to take him ; but the child gazed fearfully at the long spear and the brazen helmet and the horse-hair plume which waved proudly above it, and he shrank back with a cry, and nestled in the folds of his nurse's robe. Then Hektor laughed, and took the helmet from his head, and placed it on the ground, and the child feared no more to go to his father. Gently he took him in his arms, and he prayed aloud to Zeus and the undying gods that they would bless his child and make him glorious among his people, that so, in time to come, men might say, ' This man is stronger and braver than Hektor.'

So he gave the child to Andromachê, who received him smiling through her tears. The brave heart of Hektor was moved with the sorrow of his wife, and he laid his hand gently on her and called her by her name, and said, ' Grieve not overmuch, O my wife, for none shall lay Hektor low before the day of his doom is come. That day no man can avoid, be he good or be he evil. So let me go forth to the battle, and I will take heed for the guarding of the city ; and do thou hasten to thy home, and there ply thine own task with thy hand-maidens around thee.'

Then from the ground he took up his burnished helmet ; and in grief and sorrow Andromachê tore herself from his arms, and went slowly towards her home. Many a time she turned back to look upon him ; but scarcely could she see the flashing of his armour, for the tears ran too quickly down her cheeks. So in silence and sadness of heart she entered her bridal-chamber, where she thought not to hear the voice of Hektor again ; and her handmaidens wept when they knew that once more he was gone forth to the fight, for they feared the wrath of Athênê and the strength of the mighty Diomêdes.[128]

------*o*------

THE LOTOS-EATERS.[129]

AMONG the chiefs of the Achaians who fought before the walls of Ilion, there was none who gained for himself a greater glory than Odysseus the son of Laertes. Brave he was in battle, and steadfast in danger ; but most of all did the Achaians seek his aid in counsel, when great things must be weighed and fixed. And so it was that, in every peril where there was need of the wise heart and the ready tongue, all hastened to Odysseus, and men felt that he did more to throw down the kingdom of

Priam than the mightiest chieftains who fought only with sword and spear.[130]

Yet, in the midst of all his toil and all his great exploits in the land of Ilion, the heart of Odysseus was far away in rocky Ithaka, where his wife Penelopê dwelt with his young son Telemachos. Many a time, as the weary years of the war rolled on, he said within himself, 'Ah, when will the strife be ended, and when shall we spread our sails to the breeze, and speed on our way homewards over the wine-faced sea?' At last the doom of Paris was accomplished, and the hosts of Agamemnon gave the city of Ilion to fire and sword. Then Odysseus hastened to gather his men together, that they might go to their home in Ithaka; and they dragged the ships down to the sea from the trenches where they had so long lain idle.[131] But before they sat down to row the ship out to the deep water, Odysseus spake to them and said, 'O friends, think now, each one of you, of his home, of his wife, and of his children. Ten times have summer and winter passed over us since we left them with cheerful hearts, thinking that in but a little time we should come back to them laden with glory and booty. Ten years have they mourned for us at home; and we, who set out for Ilion in the vigour of our manhood, go back now with grey hairs, or bowed down with our weary labour. Yet faint not, O friends, neither be dismayed. Think how they wait and long for you still at home, and as we go from land to land in our voyage to rocky Ithaka, let not weariness weigh down your hearts, or things fair and beautiful lead you to seek for rest, till our ships are moored in the haven which we left ten years ago.'[132]

With shouts of joy they sat down to their long oars;

and when they had rowed the ships out into the open
sea, they spread **the white** sails to the breeze, and
watched the Ilian land as it faded away from their sight
in the far distance. For many a day they went towards
the land of the setting sun, until a mighty wind from the
north drove them to a strange country far out of their
course **to Ithaka.** Fair it was and peaceful beyond all
lands which they had seen. The sun looked down out
of the cloudless heaven on fruits and flowers which
covered the laughing earth. Far away beyond the lotos
plains the blue hills glimmered in a dreamy haze. The
trees bowed their heads in a peaceful slumber; and the
lagging waves sank lazily to sleep upon the sea-shore.
The summer breeze breathed its gentle whisper through
the air, and the birds sang listlessly of their loves from
the waving groves. Then said the men of Odysseus to
one another, 'Would that our wives and our children
were here! Truly Ithaka is but a rough and barren
land, and a sore grief it is to leave this happy shore to
go home, and there find, it may be, that our children
remember us no more.' And Odysseus said within himself, 'Surely some strange spell is on this fair land;
almost might I long to sit down and sleep on the shore
for ever; but Penelopê waits for me in my home, and I
cannot rest till I see her face once more.' Then he bade
three of his men go forth and ask the name of the land
and of the men who lived in it. So they went slowly
from the beach where the waves sang their lulling song
to the sleepy flowers; and they wandered along the
winding stream which came from the glimmering hills
far away, till, deep down in a glen where the sun shed
but half its light, they saw men with fair maidens lying
on the soft grass under **the** shade of the pleasant palm-
trees. Before them was spread a banquet of rich and

rosy fruit, and some were eating, and others lay asleep.
Then the men of Odysseus went up to them, and sat
down by their side, for they feared them not, as men are
wont to fear the people of a strange land. They asked
not their name, for they remembered not the bidding of
Odysseus; but they drank the dark wine and ate of the
rosy fruit which the fair maidens held out to them.
'Eat,' they said, 'O strangers, of the fruit which kills all
pain : surely ye are weary and your hearts are faint with
sorrow, and your eyes are dim as with many tears. Eat
of our fruit and forget your labours ; for all who eat of
it remember no more weary toil and strife and war.' So
they ate of the fruit, and then over their senses stole
softly a strange and wondrous sleep, so that they saw
and heard and spake even while they slumbered. On
their ears fell the echo of a dreamy music, and forms of
maidens, fair as Aphroditê when she rose from the sea
foam, passed before their eyes ; and they said one to
another, 'Here let us sit, and feast, and dream for
ever.'

Long time Odysseus waited on the sea-shore, and less
and less he marvelled that they came not back, for he
felt that over his own heart the strange spell was falling:
and he said, 'Ah, Penelopê, dearer to me than aught
else on the wide earth, the gods envy me thy love ; else
would they not seek to beguile me thus in this strange
land of dreams and slumber.' So he rose up, as one
rises to go forth to battle, and he went quickly on the
path by which his men had gone before him. Presently
he saw them in the deep dell, and the rich fruit of the
lotos was in their hand. Then they called to Odysseus
and said, 'We have come to the land of the Lotos-eaters;
sit thou down with us and eat of their fruit, and forget
all thy cares for ever.' But Odysseus answered not; and

hastening back, he bade the others come with him and bind the three men, and carry them to the ship. ' **Heed** not the people of the land,' he said, ' nor touch their rosy fruit. It were a shame for men who have fought at Ilion to slumber here like swine fattening for the slaughter.'

So they hastened and bound the three men who sat **at** the banquet of the Lotos-eaters; and they heeded not their words as they besought them to taste of the fruit and forget all their misery and trouble. And Odysseus hurried them back to the shore, and made them drag down the ships into the sea and sit down to their long oars. ' Hasten, friends, hasten,' he said, ' from this land of dreams. Hither come the Lotos-eaters, and their soft voices will beguile our hearts if we tarry longer, and they will tempt us to taste of their fruit; and then we shall seek no more to go back again to the land of toiling men.'

Then the dash of their oars broke the calm of the still air, and roused the waters from their slumber, as they toiled on their weary way. Further and further they went; but still the echo as of faint and lulling music fell upon their ear, and they saw fair forms of maidens roaming listlessly along the shore. And when they had rowed the ship further out into the sea, still the drooping palm-trees seemed to beckon them back to slumber, as they bowed their heads over the flowers which slept in the shade beneath them. And a deeper peace rested on the Lotos-land, as the veil of evening fell gently on the plain and the dying sun kissed the far-off hills.[133]

———o———

ODYSSEUS AND POLYPHEMOS.[124]

HEN the blue hills of the Lotos-land had faded away in the far distance, the ships of Odysseus went on merrily with a fresh breeze : and the men thought that they would soon come to rocky Ithaka, where their homes were. But Athênê was angry with Odysseus, and she asked Poseidon, the lord of the sea, to send a great storm and scatter his ships. So the wind arose, and the waters of the sea began to heave and swell, and the sky was black with clouds and rain. Many days and many nights the storm raged fiercely ; and when it was over, Odysseus could only see four or five of all the ships which had sailed with him from Troy. The ships were drenched with the waves which had broken over them, and the men were wet and cold and tired ; and they were glad indeed when they saw an island far away. So they sat down on the benches, and took the great oars and rowed the ships towards the shore ; and as they came near, they saw that the island was very beautiful with cliffs and rocks, and bays for ships to take shelter from the sea. Then they rowed into one of these quiet bays, where the water was always calm, and where there was no need to let down an anchor, or to tie the ship by ropes to the sea-shore, for the ship lay there quite still of itself. At the head of the bay a stream of fresh water trickled down from the cliffs, and ran close to the opening of a large cave, and near the cave some willow trees drooped their branches over the stream which ran down towards the sea.

So they made haste to go on shore ; and when they had landed, they saw fine large plains on which the corn might grow, but no one had taken the trouble to sow the seed ; and sloping hills for the grapes to ripen on the vines, but none were planted on them.[135] And Odysseus marvelled at the people who lived there, because they had no corn and no vines, and he could see no houses, but only sheep and goats feeding on the hill-sides. So he took his bow and arrows, and shot many of the goats, **and** he and his men lay down on the ground and had a merry meal, and drank the rich red wine which they had brought with them from the ship. And when they had finished eating and drinking they fell asleep, and did not wake up till the morning showed its rosy light in the eastern sky.

Then Odysseus said that he would take some of his men and go to see who lived on the island, while the others remained in the ship close to the sea-shore. So they set out, and at last they came to the mouth of a great cave, where many sheep and goats were penned up in large folds ; but they could see no one in the cave or anywhere near it ; and they waited a long while, but no one came. So they lit a fire, and made themselves merry, as they ate the cheese and drank the milk which was stored up round the sides of the cave.

Presently they heard a great noise of heavy feet stamping on the ground, and they were so frightened that they ran inside the cave, and crouched down at the end of it. Nearer and nearer came the Cyclops, and his tread almost made the earth shake. At last in he came, with many dry logs of wood on his back ; and in came all the sheep, which he milked every evening ; but the rams and the goats stayed outside. But if Odysseus and his men were afraid when they saw Polyphemos the Cyclops come in, they were much more afraid when he took up a great stone, which was almost as big as the mouth of the cave,

and set it up against it for a **door**.   Then the men whispered to Odysseus and said, 'Did we not beg and pray
you not to come into the cave? but you would not listen
to us ; and now how are we to get out again ?   Why, two-
and-twenty waggons would not be able to take away that
huge stone from the mouth of the cave.'   But they were
shut in now, and there was no use in thinking of their
folly for coming in.

So there they lay, crouching in the corner of the cave,
and trembling with fear lest Polyphemos should see them.
But the Cyclops went on milking all the sheep, and then
he put the milk into the bowls round the sides of the
cave, and lit the fire to cook his meal.   As the flames
shot up from the burning wood to the roof of the cave,
it showed him the forms of Odysseus and his companions,
where they lay huddled together in the corner ; and he
cried out to them with a loud voice, 'Who are you that
dare to come into the cave of Polyphemos?   Are you
come to rob me of my sheep, or my cheese and milk that
I keep here ?'

Then Odysseus said, ' No ; we are not come to do you
harm : we are Achaians who have been fighting at Troy
to bring back Helen, whom Paris stole away from Sparta,
and we went there with the great king Agamemnon,
whom everybody knows.[136]   We are on our way home
to Ithaka ; but Poseidon sent a great storm, because
Athênê was angry with me ; and almost all our ships
have been sunk in the sea, or broken to pieces on the
rocks.'

When he had finished speaking, Polyphemos frowned
savagely and said, 'I know nothing of Agamemnon, or
Paris, or Helen ;' and he seized two of the men, and
broke their heads against the stones, and cooked them
for his dinner.   That day Polyphemos ate a huge meal,

and drank several bowls full of milk ; and after that he fell fast asleep. Then as he lay there snoring in his heavy sleep, Odysseus thought how easy it would be to plunge the sword into his breast and kill him ; and he was just going to do it, when he thought of the great stone which Polyphemos had placed at the mouth of the cave ; and he knew that if Polyphemos were killed no one else could move away the stone, and so they would all die shut up in that dismal place.

So the hours of the night went wearily on, but neither Odysseus nor his friends could sleep, for they thought of the men whom Polyphemos had eaten, and how they would very likely be eaten up themselves. At last they could tell, from the dim light which came in between the top of the stone and the roof of the cave, that the morning was come ; and soon Polyphemos awoke and milked all the sheep again ; and when he had done this, he went to the end of the cave, and took up two more men and killed and ate them. Then he took down the great stone from the mouth of the cave, and drove all the cattle out to graze on the soft grass on the hills ; and Odysseus began to hope that they might be able to get away before Polyphemos came back. But the Cyclops was not so silly as to let them go, for, as soon as the cattle were gone out, he took up the huge stone again as easily as if it had been a little pebble, and put it up against the mouth of the cave ; and there were Odysseus and his friends shut up again as fast as ever.

Then Odysseus began to think more and more how they were to get away, for if they stayed there they would soon be all killed, if Polyphemos went on eating four of them every day. At last, near the sheep-fold, he saw a club which Polyphemos was going to use as a walking-stick. It was the whole trunk of an olive-tree, fresh and

green, for he had only just cut it and left it to dry, that
he might carry it about when it was fit for use.   There
it lay like the mast of a ship, which twenty men could
hardly have lifted;[137] and Odysseus cut off a bit from
the end, as much as a man could carry, and told the
men to bring it to a very sharp point ; and when they
had done this he hardened it in the fire, and then hid it
away till Polyphemos should come home.   By and by,
when the sun was sinking down, they heard the terrible
tramp of his feet, and felt the earth shake beneath his
tread.   Then the great stone was taken down from the
mouth of the cave, and in he came, driving the sheep
and goats and the rams also before him, for this time he
let nothing stay outside.   So he milked the sheep and the
goats, as he had done the day before ; and then he killed
two more men, and began to eat them for his supper.
Then Odysseus went towards him with a bottle full of
wine, and said, 'Drink this wine, Polyphemos ; it will
make your supper taste much nicer ; I have brought it
to you because I want you to do me some kindness in
return.'   So the Cyclops stretched out his hand to take
the wine, and he drank it off greedily and asked for
more.   'Give me more of this honey-sweet wine,' he
said ; 'surely no grapes on this earth could ever give
such wine as this : tell me your name, for I should like
to do you a kindness for giving me such wine as this.'
Then Odysseus said, 'O Cyclops, I hope you will not
forget to give me what you have promised : my name is
Nobody.'   And Polyphemos said, 'Very well, I shall
eat up Nobody last of all, when I have eaten up all his
companions ; and this is the kindness which I mean to
do for him.'   But by this time he was so stupid with all
that he had been eating and drinking, that he could say

no more, but fell on his back fast asleep ; and his heavy snoring sounded through the whole of the cave.

Then Odysseus cried to his friends, ' Now is the time; come and help me, and **we will** punish this Cyclops for all that he has done.' So he took the piece of the olive-tree, which had been made sharp, and put it into the fire, till it almost burst into **a** flame, and then he and two of his men went and stood over Polyphemos, and pushed the burning wood into his great eye as hard and as far down as they could. **It** was a terrible sight to see; but the Cyclops was so stupid and heavy in sleep that at first he could scarcely stir. Presently he gave a great groan, so that Odysseus and his people started back in a fright, and crouched down at the end of the cave : and then the Cyclops put out his hand and drew the burning wood from his eye, and threw it from him in a rage, and roared out for help to his friends, who lived on the hills round about. His roar was as deep and loud as the roar of twenty lions ; and the other Cyclôpes wondered when they heard him shouting out so loud, and they said, ' **What** can be the matter with Polyphemos ? we never heard him make such a noise before : let us go and see if he wants any help.' So they **went to** the cave, and stood outside the great stone which shut it in, listening to his terrible bellowings ; and when they did not stop they shouted **to** him, and asked him what was the matter. ' Why have you waked us up in the middle of the night with all this noise, when we were sleeping comfortably ? Is any one taking away your sheep and goats, or killing you by craft and force ?' And Polyphemos said, ' Nobody, my friends, is killing me by craft and force.'[138] When the others heard this they were angry, and said, ' Well, then, if nobody is killing you, why do you roar so ? If you are ill, you must

o

bear it as best you can, and ask our father Poseidon to make you well again;' and then they walked off to their beds, and left Polyphemos to make as much noise as he pleased.

It was of no use that he went on shouting. No one came to him any more; and Odysseus laughed because he had tricked him so cunningly by calling himself Nobody. So Polyphemos got up at last, moaning and groaning with the dreadful pain, and groped his way with his hands against the sides of the cave until he came to the door. Then he took down the great stone, and sat with his arms stretched out wide; and he said to himself, 'Now I shall be sure to catch them, for no one can get out without passing me.'

But Odysseus was too clever for him yet; for he went quietly, and fastened the great rams of Polyphemos together with long bands of willow. He tied them together by threes, and under the stomach of the middle one he tied one of his men, until he had fastened them all up safely. Then he went and caught hold of the largest ram of all, and clung on with his hands to the thick wool underneath his stomach; and so they waited in a great fright, lest after all the giant might catch and kill them. At last the pale light of the morning came into the eastern sky, and very soon the sheep and the goats began to go out of the cave. Then Polyphemos passed his hands over the backs of all the sheep as they went by, but he did not feel the willow bands, because their wool was long and thick, and he never thought that any one would be tied up underneath their stomachs. Last of all came the great ram to which Odysseus was clinging; and when Polyphemos passed his hand over his back, he stroked him gently and said, 'Is there something the matter with you too, as there is with your master? You

were always the first to go out of the cave, and now to-
day for the first time you are the last. I am sure that
that horrible Nobody is at the bottom of all this. **Ah,
old ram,** perhaps it is that you are sorry for your master,
whose eye Nobody has put out. I wish you could speak
like a man, and tell me where he is. If I could but
catch him, I would take care that he never got away
again, and then I should have some comfort for all the
evil which Nobody has done to me.' So he sent the ram
on ; and when he had gone a little way from the cave,
Odysseus got up from under the ram, and went and un-
tied all his friends, and very glad they were to be free once
more, although they could not help grieving, when they
thought of the men whom Polyphemos had killed. But
Odysseus told them to make haste and drive as many of
the sheep and goats as they could to the ships. So they
drove them down to the shore and hurried them into
the ships, and began to row away ; and soon they would
have been out of the reach of the Cyclops, if Odysseus
could only have held his tongue. But he was so angry
himself, that he thought he would like to make Polyphemos also still more angry ; so he shouted to him, and
said, ' Cruel Cyclops, did you think that you would not
be punished for eating up my friends? Is this the way
in which you receive strangers who have been tossed
about by many storms upon the sea?'

Then Polyphemos was more furious than ever, and he
broke off a great rock from the mountain, and hurled it
at Odysseus. On it came whizzing through the air, and
fell just in front of **his** ship, and the water was dashed
up all over it ; and there was a great heaving of the sea,
which almost carried **them** back to the land. Then they
began to row again with **all** their might ; but still, when
they had got about twice as far as they were before,

Odysseus could not help shouting out a few more words to Polyphemos. So he said, 'If any one asks you how you lost your eye, remember, mighty Cyclops, to say that you were made blind by Odysseus, the plunderer of cities, the son of Laertes, who lives in Ithaka.'

Terrible indeed was the fury of Polyphemos when he heard this, and he said : 'Now I remember how the wise Têlemos used to tell me that a man would come here named Odysseus, who would put my eye out. But I thought he would have been some great strong man, almost as big as myself; and this is a miserable little wretch, whom I could almost hold in my hand if I caught him. But stay, Odysseus, and I will show you how I thank you for you kindness, and I will ask my father Poseidon to send you a pleasant storm to toss you about upon the dark sea.'

Then Polyphemos took up a bigger rock than ever, and hurled it high into the air with all his might. But this time it fell just behind the ship of Odysseus : up rose the water and drenched Odysseus and all his people, and almost sunk the ship under the sea. But it only sent them further out of the reach of the Cyclops ; and though he hurled more rocks after them, they now fell far behind in the sea, and did them no harm. But even when they had rowed a long way, they could still see Polyphemos standing on the high cliff, and shaking his hands at them in rage and pain. But no one came to help him for all his shouting, because he had told his friends that Nobody was doing him harm.

—*o*—

ODYSSEUS AND KIRKÉ.

WHEN Odysseus got away safely with his ships from the island of the cruel Cyclops Polyphemos, he thought that now he should be able to sail home to Ithaka quietly and happily, and he said, 'Surely now we shall have some rest and peace after all our long wandering and toil.' But he was mistaken, for a great storm came. The waves rose up like mountains, and the ships were driven towards the shore, and all except the ship of Odysseus were dashed upon the rocks, and all the men were drowned. And Odysseus was grieved when he saw it, and he thought that no one could ever have been so unlucky and so miserable as he was.

But there were more troubles to come still. The storm was over, and the soft breeze was carrying them gently over a bright sea, when they saw an island far away. And Odysseus said, 'Let us go and rest on this island, and perhaps we may find some one there who may be kinder to us than Polyphemos was.' So they sailed into a little bay where the trees and flowers grew down to the very beach; and on the side of the hill which rose up gently from the water they saw a splendid house in a large and beautiful garden. And Odysseus sent a great many of his men to go and see who lived in it, and ask for something to eat and drink. So three-and-twenty men set out with Eurylochos at their head, and when they came near the house they thought that they had never seen so grand a place before. All round it there were marble pillars, and on the stones were carved beautiful flowers, and figures of men and beasts. Before the front of the house there were great wolves and fierce-looking lions lying down upon the ground; but when the men came near they did not tear them in pieces, or growl and roar at them, but they went gently up to the sailors and fawned on them just as a dog would do. And inside the house they saw a lady sitting on a golden throne, and weaving bright-coloured threads to make a splendid robe. And as she wove she sang with a low soft voice the song which made the fierce beasts before her door so tame and gentle.

Now the sailors of Odysseus felt so weak and tired after their long voyage, that they thought they could have nothing happier than to stay in the house of the lady Kirkê, who sang so sweetly as she sat on her golden throne. So they knocked at the door, and the lady Kirkê herself came out and spoke to them kindly, and asked them to come in. Then, as fast as they could, the three-and-twenty men hurried into the great hall, without thinking what the lady Kirkê might be able to do to them. But Eurylochos would not go in, for he remembered the strange things which he had seen, and he said: 'I am afraid to trust myself with the lady Kirkê, for if she can make even wolves and lions as gentle as a dog, how can I tell what she may do to me and my companions?' So he stayed outside, while the three-and-twenty sailors sat down at the long tables full of good things to eat and drink which were spread out in the great hall of Kirkê's palace. But they did not know that she had mixed strange things in all the food and in all the wine, and that if they tasted any of it, she would be able to do to them whatever she liked. And when Kirkê asked them to take whatever they would like to have, they began to eat and drink as though they had never had a meal before. So they went on eating until they could eat no longer, and then Kirkê touched each of them gently with the long thin staff which she held in her hand, and said to them, 'You have eaten so much that you are little better than swine. Swine therefore shall **ye** become, and fatten like them in a sty.'

Scarcely had she said the **word** when they began to be changed. They looked at their hands and feet, and they saw that they were turning into the cloven hoofs of swine; and **as** they touched their faces or their bodies they **felt that** they were becoming covered with bristles; and when they tried to speak, they found that they could do nothing but grunt. Then Kirkê said, 'Away with **you**;' and **away** they went each to his own sty, and began to eat the acorns and the barley meal which were placed in their troughs. But although they had been turned into pigs, they still remembered what they had been, and grunted lamentably when they thought of all the trouble which they had brought on themselves by their greed.[139]

For a long time Eurylochos waited on the marble steps which led up to the house of Kirkê, hoping that the three-and-twenty men would soon come out again. But **they did** not come, and Eurylochos could not tell what had happened; and now the sun was sinking down towards the sea. So he ran down quickly to the beach, where the ship of Odysseus was fastened by the stern-cable to the land; and when **he** saw Odysseus he could not speak, because he felt so wretched. But after they had asked him many times why the tears were running down **his** cheeks, he told them how they had gone to the house of Kirkê, and how all the men had gone into her palace and never come out again, while he stayed outside, because he was afraid of the magic arts of the wise and beautiful lady Kirkê.

Then Odysseus was very angry, and he hung his silver-studded sword on his shoulder, and took his bow and arrows to go and kill the lady Kirkê; and he told Eurylochos to show him the way. But Eurylochos was afraid, and he said, 'Do not ask me to go with you; you do not know how terrible and treacherous is the lady Kirkê. She tames the wolves and lions, and she sings with a sweet and gentle voice, which will make you do anything that she wishes.' But Odysseus spoke angrily to Eurylochos, and said, 'Stay here if you like, and eat and drink and enjoy yourself; but I must go and see if I can set my men free from the power of the lady Kirkê.'

So he left the ship and began to mount the hill which led to her palace; and perhaps Odysseus might have been turned into a hog, if there had been no one to tell him of his danger. But on the road he met a beautiful youth with a golden rod in his hand: and this was Hermes, the messenger of Zeus, who had come from Olympos to save Odysseus from the wiles of Kirkê. And Hermes kissed his hand and said, 'Whither are you going, Odysseus, up this rocky path? Do you not know what has happened to the sailors who went up with Eurylochos? They have all been turned into swine and are shut up in Kirkê's sties: and if you go on by yourself, you will be changed as they have been. But I will give you something, so that you need not be afraid of Kirkê.[110] Take this root and carry it with you into her palace; and when she strikes you with her golden staff she will not be able to turn you into a hog as she has turned the others.' Then Hermes tore up from the earth a black root, called

Môly, and gave **it to Odysseus** ; and Odysseus thanked **Hermes, and went on to the** palace of Kirkê. And as he mounted the **marble** steps, **the** wolves and lions came and fawned gently upon him, and he heard the song which Kirkê sang as she wove the bright-coloured threads **for** her beautiful robe ; and Odysseus said, 'Can any one **who** sings so sweetly be so wicked and cruel?' But when he reached the door and called out to be let in, the lady Kirkê left her golden throne and opened the door for Odysseus ; and she brought him in and placed him on a seat studded with silver nails and put a footstool under his feet. Then she brought him meat and wine, and when Odysseus had eaten and drunk as much as he wished, she struck him with her staff, and said, 'Now be turned into a hog, as your **sailors** have been turned before you, and be off to the sty which is ready for you.'

Then Odysseus took his mighty sword which **hung** across his shoulder, and his eyes shone like flaming **fire** as he looked at the lady Kirkê ; and he spake in a **loud** and terrible voice, and said to her, 'Wicked and **cruel** woman! where are all my men **who** came up here with Eurylochos? Unless you show me where they are, I will kill you with this two-handed sword which **I** have in my hands.' And Kirkê started back when she saw that she had no power over Odysseus, and she said, 'I am sure that Hermes **must** have given Odysseus something to guard against my spell, or else **he** must have been turned into a hog when I struck him with **my** golden wand.' She was terribly frightened, for **she** could not tell what Odysseus might do to her; **but** she saw that there was no **help** for it. So she showed him the way to the sties, and **there** the sailors were. Although they were now swine, there was just enough to show Odysseus what they had been and who they were.   He was terribly grieved, but he could hardly help laughing as he saw their bodies covered with bristles, and their long snouts and hoofs. But when he asked them how they came to be in such a state, they could only shake their heads and grunt pitiably.

Then Odysseus was more angry than ever, and he turned fiercely to the lady Kirkê, and said, 'I will certainly kill you, unless you immediately turn all these pigs into men again.'   And Kirkê knew from the tone of his voice that she had no chance of escaping ; so she struck them each with her long wand, and they became men again as they had been before.   After this Kirkê pretended to love Odysseus, and she said, 'Come and stay with me for a year.   Look at my beautiful house, and see the wolves and lions standing tamely on the marble steps. Stay and be happy here ; I know how to charm all your cares away.'

But Odysseus said, 'Lady, I thank you ; but I may not stay, for I long to reach my home.   Ten years we were at Troy, and we have now been many years on our road home ; and my wife Penelopê has almost ceased to hope that I shall ever come back again ; and if I stay away longer, I am sure that she will die.'   Then Kirkê let him go ; but first she told him that there were some dangerous places for him to pass before he could reach his home, and how he must take great care as he passed by the island of the Seirens.   So Odysseus thanked Kirkê ; and he went on board as quickly as he could with all his men, and rowed out into the deep sea ; and then they set the sails to go to the rugged island called Ithaka where the lady Penelopê was living.

———o———

ODYSSEUS AND THE SEIRENS.

HEN Odysseus and his men had left the island of the lady Kirkê, a fresh breeze carried them merrily for several days over the sea. But after that the wind sank **down, and** there was a calm. The sails flapped against the mast, and they **had** to take them down and to row the ship on with their long oars. The sun was shining hot and fierce, and the men were very tired. There was not even a ripple upon the sea, and not a breath of air to cool their burning faces. And Odysseus remembered how the lady Kirkê had told him that he would have to pass near the Seirens' island where the sea was always calm, and how she said that he must take care not to listen to the Seirens' song, if he did not wish his ship to be dashed to pieces on the rocks. For, all day long, the Seirens lay on the sea-shore, or swam about in the calm water, singing so sweetly that no one who heard them could ever pass on without going to them : and whoever went to them was killed upon the rocks, for the Seirens were very beautiful and cruel, and they sang their soft enticing songs, to draw the sailors into the shallow water, that their ships might be broken **on the** terrible reefs which lay hidden beneath the calm sea. And when Kirkê told Odysseus of the Seirens' rocks, she said that he must fill his sailors' ears with wax, that they might not hear the song and be drawn in upon those terrible reefs.

So, as the sun shone down fiercely on their heads, Odysseus thought that they must be coming near to the island of the Seirens ; and he took a large lump of wax and pressed it in his fingers till the hot sun made it soft

and sticky.   Then he called the men and said that now
he must fill their ears with wax, and so they would not
hear the song of the beautiful and cruel Seirens.   But
Odysseus was a very strange man, and liked to hear
and see everything ; so he said that he must hear the
song himself, and that they must tie him to the mast for
fear he should leap into the sea to swim to the Seirens'
land.

Then he filled the sailors' ears with wax so that they
could hear nothing ; and they took a large rope and
put it two or three times round the arms and waist of
Odysseus; and then they sat down again on their benches,
and began to row the ship on as quickly as they could.
Presently through the breathless air, and over the still
and sleeping sea, there came a sound so sweet and
soothing that Odysseus thought that he could no longer
be living on the earth.   Softer and sweeter it swelled
upon the ear, and it seemed to speak to Odysseus of rest
and peace, although he could hear no words : and he
felt as if he could give up everything if only he might
hear those sweet sounds for ever.   So he made signs to
the sailors to row on quicker ; but presently the song
rose in the sultry air, more sweet and gentle and enticing ;
and it seemed to say, ' O tired and weary sailors, why do
you toil so hard to row your ship under this fierce hot
sun ?   Come to us, and sit among these cool rocks :
come and rest,—come and rest.'   But he did not yet
hear the words, for they were still too far from the
Seirens' rocks.   Still, nearer and nearer the sailors rowed ;
and now he heard the words of their song, and he knew
that they were speaking to himself, for they said, ' O
Odysseus, man of many toils and long wanderings, great
glory of the Achaians, come to us and listen to our song.
Every one who passes over the sea near our island stays

to hear it, and forgets all his labour and all his trouble, and then goes away peaceful and happy. Come and rest, Odysseus, come and rest. We know all the great deeds which you have done at Troy, and how you have been tossed by many storms, and suffered many sorrows sailing on the wide sea. But here the sea is always calm, and the sun cannot scorch you in the cool and pleasant caves where you shall hear us sing.'

Then Odysseus cried out to the sailors, 'Let me go, let me go, they are calling me; do you not hear?' And he struggled with all his might to break the cords that bound him; but when they saw him trying to get free, they went and tied stronger cords round his arms and waist, and rowed on quicker than ever. And still Odysseus prayed them to set him free, that he might leap into the sea and swim to the Seirens' caves. 'I cannot stay,' he said; 'they are calling me by my name; their song rises sweeter and clearer than ever; let us go, let us go.' And again he heard them singing, 'O man of many toils, we are waiting for you and will sing you to sleep, and charm all your cares away for ever.' But quicker and quicker the sailors rowed on, till at last they had passed the island. And the Seirens saw that Odysseus was going away; but yet again they sang, 'Come back, Odysseus, come back and rest in our cool green caves, O man of many griefs and wanderings.' But the sound of their sweet song was now faint before it reached the ship of Odysseus, and he could only just hear them say, 'Will you leave us, will you leave us? Ah, Odysseus, you do not know what you are losing. Come to our cool green caves; we are waiting,—we are waiting.'

But the power of the Seirens' song grew weaker as the ship went further away; and Odysseus began to think how foolish and silly he had been. He could not hear any more the words of the song, as they called him by his name; but still he half wished to go back to the Seirens' land, while yet he heard the sound of their singing, as it came faint and weak through the hot and breathless air. Soon it was all ended. The sky was still; the waves were all asleep; the clouds looked down drowsily on the water; and Odysseus thought that he could die, he was so tired and spent with struggling.

So when the sailors saw that Odysseus did not struggle any more, they went and set him free, and took the wax out of their ears. And Odysseus said, 'O friends, it is better not to hear the Seirens' song; for if but two or three of us had heard it, we should have gone to them, and our ship would have been sunk in their green caves.'

And they said, 'It is indeed better not to hear it. You were so busy listening to their song that you could not see what we saw. All the way as we passed by the island, logs of wood and bits of masts were floating on the water : and these must have been pieces from ships which have been broken on the rocks, because the sailors heard the Seirens' song.' [141]

———o———

THE CATTLE OF HÉLIOS.

FAR away down the gentle stream of Ocean,[142] Odysseus had journeyed to the dark kingdom of Hades and Persephonê, where the ghosts of men wander after their days on earth are ended. There he talked with Agamemnon and the wise seer Teiresias, with Minos and with Herakles. There he had listened to the words of Achilleus in the meadows of asphodel, and told him of the brave deeds and the great name of his son Neoptolemos. There the shade of Herakles spake to him, but Herakles himself was in the home of Zeus and lay in the arms of Hêbê, quaffing the dark wine **at the** banquets of the gods. And the shade told him of the former days, how all his life long Herakles toiled for a hard master who was weaker than himself, but Zeus gave him the power. Then Odysseus tarried no more **in** the shadowy land, for he feared lest Persephonê **the** queen might place before him the Gorgon's head which no mortal man may see and live. So he went back to his ship, and his men took their oars and rowed it down the stream of Ocean till they came to the wide sea; and then they spread the white sails, and hastened to the island of Aiaia, where Eôs dwells and where Hêlios rises to greet the early morning.

From her home which the wolves and the lions guarded, the lady Kirkê saw the ship of Odysseus, as she sat on her golden throne, weaving the bright threads in her loom. And straightway she rose, and bade her handmaidens bring bread and wine to the sea-shore for Odysseus and his men. Long time they feasted on the smooth beach, until they fell asleep for very weariness; but Kirkê took Odysseus to her own home, and bade him sit down by her side while she told him of all the things which should befall him on his way to Ithaka. She told him of the Seirens fair and false, and of their sweet song by which they tempt the weary seamen as they sail on the white and burning sea. She told him of the wandering rocks, from which no ship ever escaped but the Divine Argo, when Iason led the warriors to search for the golden fleece.[143] She told him of the monstrous Skylla with her twelve shapeless feet, and her six necks, long and lean, from which six dreadful heads peer out over the dark water, each with a triple row of spear-like teeth, as she seizes on every living thing which the waves of the sea cast within her reach. She told him of Charybdis, the deathless monster, who thrice each day hurls **forth** the water from her boiling pool, and thrice each day sucks it back. She warned him of the Thrinakian land where the cattle of Hêlios[144] feed in **their** sunny pastures. There each evening as the sun goes down, and each morning as he rises from the eastern sea, the two fair maidens, Phaethousa and Lampetiê, come forth to tend them. These children of Hêlios their mother Neaira, tender and loving as the light of early day, placed far off in the Thrinakian land to tend their father's herds. 'Wherefore go not near that island,' said the lady Kirkê, 'for no mortal man shall escape the wrath of Hêlios if any hurt befall his cattle. If thy comrades stretch forth a hand against them, thy ship shall be sunk in the deep sea, and if ever thou mayest reach thy home, thou shalt return to it a lonely man, mourning for all the friends whom thou hast lost.'

Even as she spake, the light of Eôs tinged the far-off sky; and Kirkê bade Odysseus farewell, as he went back to the ship. So they sailed away from the home of the wise goddess, and they passed by the Seirens' land, where Odysseus alone heard the sweet sound of their singing as it rose clear and soft through the hot and breathless air. Thence they came to the secret caves of Skylla; and her six heads, stretched out above the boiling waters, seized, each, one of the men of Odysseus, and he heard their last shriek for help as they were sucked down her gaping jaws. But they went not near the whirlpool of Charybdis, for Odysseus feared the warning of Kirkê.

The sun was sinking down in the sky as the ship of Odysseus drew near towards the beautiful island of Hêlios. The long line of light danced merrily on the rippling sea, and the soft breeze fanned their cheeks with its gentle breathing. Then spake Odysseus and said, 'Listen, friends, to my words. Before we left her home, the lady Kirkê talked with me, and told me of all the things which should come to pass as we journeyed home to Ithaka. She told me of the Seirens, of Skylla and Charybdis; and all things have come to pass as she said. But most of all she warned me not to set foot on the island of Hêlios, for there his cattle are tended by the bright maidens Phaethousa and Lampetiê. Each day Hêlios looks down upon them, as he journeys through the high heaven; and no mortal man may lay his hand on them and live. Wherefore hearken to me, and turn the ship away so that we may not come to this land. Well I know that ye are weary and sick with toil, but better is it to reach our home wearied and hungry, than to perish in distant lands for evil deeds.' Then was Eurylochos filled with anger, for he had forgotten how he alone would not enter the halls of Kirkê when all his comrades were turned into swine, and how he had himself warned Odysseus against her wiles. So he spake out boldly, and said, 'O Odysseus, hard of heart, and cruel in soul, thou faintest not in thy limbs, neither is thy body tired out with toil. Surely thou must be framed of hard iron, that thou seekest to turn us away from this fair and happy land. Our hearts are faint, our bodies tremble for weariness, and sleep lies heavy on our eyelids. Here on the smooth beach we may rest in peace, and cheer our souls with food and wine: and when the sun is risen, we will go forth again on our long wanderings over the wide sea. But now will we not go, for

P

who can sail safely while the night sits on her dark
throne in the sky? for then dangers hang over mortal
men, and the sudden whirlwind may come and sink us
all beneath the tossing waters.'

So spake Eurylochos, and all the men shouted with
loud voices to go to the Thrinakian land. When
Odysseus saw that it was vain to hinder them, he said,
'Swear then to me, all of you, a solemn oath that ye
will touch not one of the sacred herds who feed in the
pastures of Hêlios, but that ye will eat only of the bread
and drink the wine which the lady Kirkê gave to us.'
Then they sware, all of them; and the ship came to
land in a beautiful bay, where a soft stream of pure
water trickled down from a high rock, and deep caves
gave shelter from the dew of night. Then they made
their meal on the beach, and mourned [145] over their
six comrades whom the monstrous Skylla had swallowed with her greedy jaws, until sleep came down upon
their eyelids. But when the stars were going down
in the sky, and before Eôs spread her soft light through
the heaven, Zeus sent forth a great wind to scourge
the waters of the sea, and a dark cloud came down
and hid all things from their sight. So, when the sun
was risen, they knew that they could not leave the
island of Hêlios; and they dragged their ship up on
the beach to a cave where the nymphs dance, and
where their seats are carved in the living rock. Then
Odysseus warned them once more : 'Friends, hurt not
the cattle in this land, for they are the flocks of the
great god Hêlios, who sees and hears all things.'

All that day the storm raged on; and at night it
ceased not from its fury. Day by day they looked
in vain to see the waters go down, until the moon had
gone through all her changes. Then the food and the

wine which the lady Kirkê gave to them was all spent,
and they knew not how they might now live. All this
time none had touched the sacred cattle; and even now
they sought to catch birds and fishes, so that they
might not hurt the herds of Hêlios. Wearied in body,
and faint of heart, Odysseus wandered over the island,
praying to the undying gods that they would show him
some way of escaping; and when he had gone a long
way from his comrades, he bathed his hands in a clear
stream, **and** prayed to all the gods, and they sent
down a sweet sleep on his eyelids; and he slept
there on the soft grass, forgetting his cares and
sorrows.

But while Odysseus was far away, Eurylochos
gathered his comrades around him, and began **to**
tempt them with evil words. 'O friends,' he said,
'long have ye toiled and suffered: listen now to my
words. There is no kind of death which is not dreadful
to weak and mortal men; but of all deaths there **is**
none so horrible as to waste away by slow gnawing
hunger. Wherefore let us seize the fairest of the cattle
of Hêlios, and make a great sacrifice to the undying
gods who dwell in the wide heaven; and when we reach
our home in Ithaka, we will build a temple to Hêlios
Hyperîon, and we will place in it rich and costly
offerings, and the fat of rams and goats shall go up
day by day to heaven upon his altar. But if he will, in
his anger, destroy a ship with all its men for the sake
of horned cattle, then rather would I sink by one
plunge in the sea than waste away here in pain and
hunger.'

Then with loud voices all his comrades cried out
that the words of Eurylochos were good, and they
hastened to seize the fairest cattle of Hêlios. Soon

they came back, for the herds fed near at hand, fearing
no hurt and dreading not the approach of men.   So they
made ready the sacrifice, and sprinkled soft oak leaves
over the victims, for they had no white barley in their
ship.   Then they prayed to the gods, and smote the
cattle, and flaying off the skin, placed the limbs in order,
and poured the water over the entrails ; for they had no
wine to sprinkle over the sacrifice while it was being
roasted by fire.   And when the sacrifice was done, they
sat down and feasted richly.

But Odysseus had waked up from his sleep ; and as
he drew near to the bay where the ship was drawn up on
the shore, the savour of the fat filled his nostrils.   And
he smote his hands upon his breast, and groaned aloud
and said, 'Father Zeus, and ye happy gods who know
not death, of a truth ye have weighed me down by a
cruel sleep ; and my comrades have plotted a woful
deed while I was far away.'

Then swiftly the bright maiden Lampetiê sped away
to her father Hêlios, and the folds of her glistening
robe streamed behind her as she rose to the throne of
Hyperion.   Then she said, 'Father Hêlios, the men of
Odysseus have laid hands on the fairest of thy cattle,
and the savour of their fat has come up to the high
heaven.'   Then was Hêlios full of wrath, and he cried
aloud and said, 'O Zeus, and all ye the undying gods,
avenge me of Odysseus and his comrades, for they have
slain my cattle whom I exulted to see as I rose up into
the starry sky and whensoever I came down again to
the earth from the high heaven.   Avenge me of Odysseus ; for if ye will not hearken to my prayer, I will go
down to the land of King Hades and shine only among
the dead.'

Then spake Zeus out of the dark cloud and said,

'O Hêlios, take not away thy bright light from the heaven, and forsake not the children of men who till the earth beneath ; and I will send forth my hot thunder-bolts, and the ship of Odysseus shall be sunk in the deep sea.'

Woful was the sight as Odysseus drew nigh to the ship and to his comrades who stood round the burnt-offering. With fierce and angry words they reviled each other, and they looked with a terrible fear on the victims which they had slain ; for the hides crept and quivered as though still the life were in them, and the flesh moaned as with the moan of cattle, while the red flame curled up round it. For six days they feasted on the shore, and on the seventh day the wind went down and the sea was still.

Then they dragged the ship down to the water, and sailed away from the Thrinakian land. But when they had gone far, so that they could see only the heaven above and the wide sea around them, then the dark cloud came down again, and Zeus bade the whirlwind smite the ship of Odysseus. High rose the angry waves, and the fierce lightnings flashed from the thick cloud. Louder and louder shrieked the storm, till the ropes of the mast and sails snapped like slender twigs, and the mast fell with a mighty crash and smote down the helmsman, so that he sank dead beneath the weight. Then the ship lay helpless on the waters, and the waves burst over her in their fury until all the men were swept off into the sea and Odysseus only was left. The west wind carried the battered wreck at random over the waters ; and when its fury was stilled, the south wind came and drove Odysseus, as he clung to the mast, near to the whirlpool of Charybdis and the caves of the greedy Skylla. For nine days and

nights he lay tossed on the stormy water, till his
limbs were numbed with cold, and he felt that he
must die.   But on the tenth day he was cast upon
the shore, and so he reached the island where dwelt
the lady Kalypso.

———?———

ODYSSEUS AND KALYPSO.

THE lady Kalypso sat in her cave weaving the
bright threads with a golden shuttle, when
she saw a man thrown up by the waves on
the sea-shore.   So she rose in haste, and
when she came to the beach, Odysseus lay before her
stunned on the rocks, with his limbs numbed and
stiffened with the cold.   Gently she raised him in her
arms and carried him to her home ; and there she
tended him by night and by day, while Odysseus yet
knew not that he had been saved from the stormy sea.

When he awoke from his long sleep, he saw before
him a fair woman who looked on him with eyes full of
tenderness and love; and Odysseus half thought at first
that he was again with the wise and beautiful Kirkê;
but soon he saw that the face of Kalypso was fairer and
the light of her eye more soft and tender.   At last he
spoke in a faint and low voice, 'Lady, I thank thee for
all thy care and gentleness ; and now tell me, I pray thee,
thy name and the name of the land in which thou dost
dwell.'   Then Kalypso answered (and her voice was
sweet as the sweetest music), 'O stranger, the gods call
me Kalypso, and I dwell alone in this fair island which
is called Ogygia.   But thou art faint and weak ; tell me
not now of thy sorrows, but rest here in my cave till thy

strength comes back to thee again, and then thou shalt tell me the tale of thy sufferings.' So she put before him bread to eat and a goblet of dark wine, and Odysseus feasted with Kalypso in the cave. And as he looked around he saw that a great fire was burning upon the hearth, and the sweet scent of cedar wood and incense rose up from it.

So day by day Kalypso tended Odysseus in his weariness, and day by day she spoke to him more gently and lovingly. She asked him not again of his sufferings, or whence he came or whither he was going; she cared not for aught else, if only he might abide with her in her lonely home: [146] and she feared to ask him of his toil and woe, lest he should seek to go to some other land. But the heart of Odysseus was far away in his own country, and he yearned to depart to Ithaka and be with his wife Penelopê and see his son Telemachos once more. Long time he hid his sorrows in his breast, for Kalypso spake only of her love, and how that he should remain with her always in her glittering cave. But at last Odysseus fell down at her knee and besought her with tears, and said, 'Lady, I thank thee for thy love and care; and now, I pray thee, let me go away in peace to my own home. My name is Odysseus, and my father Laertes is chieftain in the land of Ithaka. Ten years we fought at Troy, and for many years since the city of Priam fell have I wandered over the dark sea, because the mighty Athênê was angry with me. At her bidding Poseidon, the lord of the waters, sent a great storm and scattered my ships, and we were carried to distant lands and to savage people, to the land of the Lotos-eaters, the Cyclôpes, and the Læstrygonians, till at last all our ships were shattered save one only, in which I sailed with the men that remained to me. But when we came

to the island of Thrinakia, my comrades slew the fairest
of the cattle of Hêlios, and offered sacrifice with them to
the gods, and feasted for many days. Then Hêlios besought Zeus in his anger, and a great whirlwind seized
my ship, and all my men were dashed into the sea, and
I only remain alive of all the great host which I led to
Troy from Ithaka. Pity me, lady, for my great sorrow,
and send me to my home; for year by year my wife
Penelopê looks for my coming and wastes away in a
secret grief, and if I go not back soon she will die.'
But Kalypso said, 'Ah, Odysseus, what dost thou ask?
I cannot send thee to Ithaka, for here I dwell alone,
and have neither ships nor men. Yet wherefore dost
thou so yearn to go to barren and rocky Ithaka? What
dost thou lack here of all that thy soul may lust after?
Here thou canst share my riches, and here thou hast my
love. Think not more of Penelopê: long since she has
forgotten thee, and it may be that now her love is given
to another.' But Odysseus spake quickly and said,
'Lady, thou knowest not what thou sayest; sure I am
that Penelopê has not forgotten me, and that she loves
me still as in the ancient days. Ah, lady, thou art of
no mortal race, and thou knowest not the love of men
and women.' Then a look of anger passed over the
gentle face of Kalypso, as she answered, 'Dost thou
chide me, stranger, and wilt thou not give me thy love?
Urge me not in thy folly, for the anger of the gods is
terrible. Yet think not of my wrath, O man of many
toils and sorrows; rest with me in my home, where no
grief may vex thee, and I will charm thy cares away by
the sound of my sweet singing. I can tell thee of the
feasts of the gods in high Olympos, of Hêbê and Harmonia and the laughter-loving Aphroditê. Rest, rest,
Odysseus. What is thy home to thee, when my arm is

round thee and my voice falls gently on thine ear?
Think not now of toil and labour : rest, rest.'

Then she sang with a low sweet voice, and the touch
of her hand as it rested on his head brought down a
deep sleep on his eyelids.   At her bidding the happy
dreams came and stood beside his couch,[147] and whispered to him of new joys and the delights of more than
mortal love.   So she laid her spell upon Odysseus, and
he feared to speak more of his home in Ithaka.   Twelve
moons passed through their changes, and still he abode
in the cave of Kalypso, listening to her sweet songs and
soothed by her gentle love ; but often, when the thought
of his home came back upon his mind, he hastened to
the sea-shore, and wept with bitter tears for his great
misery, and yearned for the day when he might go to
rocky Ithaka.

But, for all her great anger, Athênê loved Odysseus
still, and she went to Zeus and told him of his hard lot,—
how Kalypso kept him by her evil spells in the island of
Ogygia.   Then Zeus called Hermes, the slayer of Argos
with the hundred eyes, and bade him go to the lady
Kalypso and command her to send Odysseus to his
home.   So Hermes bound his golden sandals on his feet,
and took in his hand the staff with which he brings sleep
on the eyes of men or rouses them from their rest.   Then
from the high Olympos he flew down to the earth beneath,
and skimmed the waves of the sea like a bird, until he
came to the island of Kalypso.   Quickly from the shore
he hastened to her cave.   The sun shone brightly from
the high heaven ; the trees cast their cool shade on the
rock.   The sea-birds rested with folded wings on the
branches.   Round the stems of the pine and the cypress
the vine clung lovingly, and its long clusters of rich
grapes hung before the opening of the cave, while four

fountains gave forth their pure streams to water the soft
meadows where the violet and the rose looked up into
the blue sky.

As Hermes stood before the cave, he heard the sweet
singing of Kalypso, while she plied her task with the
golden shuttle.   In the cave the fire was burning upon
the hearth, and the sweet smell of cedar and incense
filled the air.   But Hermes saw not Odysseus as he
entered in, for he was far away weeping on the sea-shore.
Then Kalypso rose in haste, for she knew his face, and
said, 'Wherefore comest thou thus to me with thy golden
wand?   If thou bringest to me a charge from Zeus, tell
me his will, that I may do it.'   Then before him she
placed the food of the gods and poured out for him the
nectar wine ; and when Hermes had feasted merrily, he
spake and said, 'I come from the great Zeus, who bids
thee send away Odysseus that he may go to his home in
Ithaka.   Long time has he fought at Troy, and grievous
sorrows have fallen upon him since he left the land of
Priam ; and it is not the will of Zeus that he should die
here far away from his own people.'

And Kalypso trembled as she heard his words, and
she said, 'O Hermes, hard· of heart are the gods of
Olympos, who grudge to us the love of mortal men.
So when the rosy-fingered Eôs [148] loved Orion, then
Artemis slew him with her unerring darts in Ortygia ;
and when Iasion was beloved of Dêmêtêr, he was smitten
by the thunderbolts of Zeus.   And now ye grudge me
the love of Odysseus whom I saved from the stormy
water, as he lay stunned and bruised on the sea-shore.
I have cherished him in my home, and I thought to
make him immortal as myself and free from the doom of
the sons of men.   But the will of Zeus must be obeyed,
and I will not withstand it.   If Odysseus seeks to go

away from my land, let him **go ; but** I cannot give him help, for I have neither ships nor men.' But Hermes only said, '**See** thou despise not the bidding of Zeus, lest he be wroth with thee in time to come ;' and then he rose on his golden sandals to the halls of Olympos.

Then Kalypso hastened to the sea-shore, and there she saw Odysseus weeping for his grievous sorrow that he might not return to his home. Gently she went towards him, and she laid her hand on his arm and said, '**Weep** not, Odysseus. I have given thee my love, and I have sought for thine ; but if thou carest **not** to give **it, I will aid thee to** build a raft, and thou shalt go hence in peace, with plenty of food and wine ; and I will send a soft and gentle breeze which shall take thee to thine own land, since so the gods will who are mightier than I.'

But Odysseus was full of fear when he heard these words, for he thought that Kalypso was speaking craftily, and he said, 'Lady, dost thou seek to entrap me by guile, when thou biddest me cross the wide sea on a raft, where even the great ships may not pass? Even at thy bidding I may not go, unless thou wilt swear that no **harm** shall come to me for following thy counsel.' Then Kalypso smiled, and laid her hand gently upon him and called him by his name ; and she sware by the waters of the Styx, and the broad earth, and the high heaven above, that she sought not to hurt him by her words ; and she led him back to her cave and spread a rich banquet before him. Then as they feasted together she said, 'Wilt thou go away, Odysseus? If thus thy heart is fixed, farewell now and in the time to come. But if thou couldst know the sorrows which await thee before thou mayest see thy home, sure I am that thou wouldst not forsake me. Ah, Odysseus, I can make thee undying as myself, and thy wife Penelopê is not fairer than I. The daughters of men cannot vie in strength and beauty with the deathless children of the gods.' But Odysseus said, 'Be not angry, lady. Well I know that my wife Penelopê cannot be matched with thee for thy glorious beauty, for she is but a mortal woman, and thou canst not die or grow old. But even thus would I return to her and to my home; for my heart is wasted away while I yearn to see Ithaka once more. And if sorrows and storms await me still, I am ready to bear them. Many woes have I suffered in the years that are past; let these be added to their number.'

So, when Eôs spread her rosy fingers in the sky, Kalypso arose and put a bright robe on him, and a golden girdle round his waist; and she placed a sharp axe in his hand, wherewith he cut down the wood for the raft, and Kalypso helped him to build it. When four days were past the raft was ready, and Kalypso parted from Odysseus on the sea-shore; and as he went away from the land, she looked on him long with a tender and loving gaze, and sent a soft and gentle breeze to carry him on his way. Then she went back slowly to her lonely cave.

But Poseidon was filled with wrath as he saw the raft of Odysseus coming near to the Phæakian shore; and he stirred up a great storm, so that the heaven was black with clouds and rain. Sorely was Odysseus tossed on the heaving sea, until his raft was shattered, and once again he was plunged in the raging waters. But from her green cave beneath the sea Inô the daughter of Kadmos heard his cry for help, and she rose up to comfort him under the wrath of King Poseidon. So Odysseus was gladdened by her words, and knew that now he should one day come to Ithaka; and he battled more stoutly with the angry sea, until, weary with pain and cold and hunger, he lay numbed and stiff on the Phæakian shore. There, as he slept amidst the bushes that grew high up on the beach, Athênê went to the house of King Alkinoös, and spake to his child Nausikaâ, the fairest and purest of all the daughters of men ; and Athênê brought her down to the sea-shore, that so she might save Odysseus, who had known so great grief in his long wanderings after the fall of Troy.

———*o*———

ODYSSEUS AND NAUSIKAÂ.

ERRY was the laughter of the maidens as they played on the sea-shore with Nausikaâ, the daughter of Alkinoös. They had gone down to the beach to wash their clothes ;[149] and now they were playing after their work was done. They were just going back to the city, when one of them threw the ball, with which they were playing, at another of the girls ; but the ball missed her, and rolled down into a deep and narrow place, and they gave a great cry which woke up Odysseus, who was lying cold and almost dead among the rocks. And he opened his eyes, and said to himself, 'Did I not hear the sound of voices like the voices of merry girls ? I must go and see if they can help me, and lead me to some one who will give me food and shelter.' So he crept out from among the rocks where he had been lying, and came to the place where the girls were. When they saw Odysseus with his clothes all torn, and his hair matted and twisted over his face, the others were frightened, and began to scream ; but Nausikaâ was a good and brave girl, and she told them not to be so silly; but to help the poor stranger if they could. And Odysseus came, and knelt down to her, and said, 'Lady, you see how very miserable I am. The storm has broken my raft to pieces; and for many hours I have had to swim in the sea, till I was cold and faint ; and then the waves tossed me among the rocks, where I lay bruised and stunned, until I heard your voices. But tell me now where I am, and if there is any one here who can help me and give me something to eat and drink and then send me home to Ithaka.'

And Nausikaâ said, 'Do not be afraid, O stranger, whoever you are. You shall have all that you can want. My name is Nausikaâ, and I am the daughter of Alkinoös, the king of the Phæakians, who live in this happy island. Come with me, for I am sure that he and my mother Arêtê will be good and kind to you ; and when you are well and strong again, you shall go on home to Ithaka ;' and as she spoke, she looked so gentle and good, that Odysseus thought he had never seen any one half so beautiful before ; and he followed her gladly, as she showed him the way to the house of Alkinoös.

Never had Odysseus seen any dwelling so splendid. The house stood in a glorious garden, where there were all manner of fruits and flowers, and where the fruits and flowers lasted all the year round. There were no trees to be seen there without leaves, nor any whose leaves were yellow or withered, for there was no winter there and no autumn ; but the soft west wind and the gentle sun ripened the fruit on some of the trees while others were coming into blossom ; and even on the same tree you might see some of the fruit ripe, and some only just hardening from the bud. All the year round the purple grapes shone amongst the broad vine leaves, and the apples and pomegranates made a splendid show among the dark green olives which were mixed up with them. And in the garden there were two fountains, one of which sent its clear cool water to refresh the trees and plants and flowers; and from the other they brought water to the house of Alkinoös.

But if Odysseus wondered to see such splendid gardens, he wondered much more when he looked at the house of Alkinoös. The walls were covered with plates of brass, and on the top was a cornice of gold and purple. The doors and seats were of gold and silver, and there were figures of dogs, all of gold, which Hephaistos made and gave to guard the house of Alkinoös.[150] Round the rooms were hung tapestries which the women wove with bright threads of gold and silver and all other colours: and on them were embroidered the feasts of the Phæakians, as they sat eating and drinking at the tables loaded with all good things. And round the large court there were figures of young men, all made of gold, which held burning torches in their hands at night, to give light in the palace of Alkinoös.

So Odysseus went through the great hall, wondering how Alkinoös could have got all those riches; and when he came up to the golden throne on which the king was sitting with his wife Arêtê, he fell on his knees before them, and told them of his great toils and sorrows, and prayed **them to** give him a ship to take him home to Ithaka.

Then Alkinoös took him kindly by the hand, and set him on a seat, and told the servants to bring him everything that he wanted. So they feasted together, and the minstrels sang a beautiful song, which was all about the war of the Achaians at Troy. And when Odysseus heard the song, the tears came into his eyes, for he thought of all his **brave** friends whom he had lost. So Alkinoös told the minstrel to stop, because his song gave Odysseus pain, and he said, 'What is it that grieves thee, O stranger? Tell me who thou art, and all that thou hast seen and suffered.'

Then Odysseus told him his name, and the story of his great deeds at Troy, and of his toils and wanderings since he left the city of Priam. He told him of the Cyclops Polyphemos and the lady Kirkê, of the sweet-singing Seirens, of Skylla and Charybdis, and Kalypso, and how at last he was thrown on the Phæakian shore where he met the beautiful Nausikaâ and her merry companions as they were playing on the beach.

And then Odysseus said again, 'Let me go; I am weary of wandering about so long, and I want to rest in my own home.' But Alkinoös said, 'Stay with us, for surely you can never live in a more beautiful place than this. Here the sun is always shining, and the fruits always ripe; and you see how rich we are with gold and silver things, and how we have everything that we want. Stay with us, and you shall have Nausikaâ for your wife, and by and by you shall be king of the Phæakians over whom I rule.' But Odysseus thanked Alkinoös, and he said, 'You are very kind and good to me: and I seek not to leave you because my home is richer and more beautiful than yours, for Ithaka is a rocky and barren island, where only the sheep and goats can feed, and where we have very few fruits and flowers; and I am not fit to be the husband of your child Nausikaâ. She is indeed very beautiful and good; but I am now grow-ing old, and I have had hard toils and long wanderings: and besides, my wife Penelopê is waiting for me at home, and almost thinks that I shall never come back again; and I am longing to see my son Telemachos, who was only a little child when I went away to Troy. Let me then go home, and I shall never forget how kind you have all been to me in this beautiful island of the Phæakians.'

Then Alkinoös ordered a large ship to be got ready, and fifty men to row Odysseus across to Ithaka. And he gave him rich presents, and Arêtê and the good and beautiful Nausikaâ brought him splendid dresses to carry to Penelopê.

Then Odysseus went down to the sea-shore; and as they sailed away he looked back many times to the splendid home of Alkinoös, and felt very sorry that he had to leave such kind friends. But he said, 'I shall soon see Penelopê and Telemachos, and that will comfort me for all my sorrows, and all my toils by sea and land, since I left Troy to come back to Ithaka.'

——o——

THE VENGEANCE OF ODYSSEUS.

 FAIR breeze filled the sail of the Phæakian ship in which Odysseus lay asleep as in the dreamless slumber of the dead. The wild music of the waves rose on the air as the bark sped on its glistening pathway; but their murmur reached not the ear of the wanderer, for the spell of Athênê was upon him, and all his cares and griefs were for a little while forgotten.

The dawn light was stealing across the eastern sky when the good ship rode into the haven of the sea-god Phorkys, and rested without anchor or cable beneath the rocks which keep off the breath of the harsh winds. At the head of the little bay a broad-leaved olive-tree spread

Q

its branches in front of a cave where the sea-nymphs wove their beautiful purple robes.   Gently the sailors raised **Odysseus** in their arms; gently they bore him from the ship, and placed him on the land with the gifts which Alkinoös and Arêtê and Nausikaâ had given to him when he set off to go to Ithaka.   So the Phæakians went away, and Odysseus rested once more in his own land.   But when he awoke from his sleep, he knew not where he was, for Athênê had spread a mist on land and sea.   The haven, the rocks, the trees, the pathways wore a strange look in the dim and gloomy light; but while Odysseus yet pondered where he should stow away the gifts lest thieves should find them, there stood before him a glorious form, and he heard a voice which said, ' Dost thou not know me, Odysseus?   I am Pallas Athênê, who have stood by thy side to guard thee in all thy **wanderings and deliver** thee from **all** thy **enemies.** And now that thou standest again **on** thine own land of Ithaka, I have come **to thee once more, to bid thee** make ready for the great vengeance, and to bear with patience all that may befall thee until the hour be come.'   But Odysseus could scarcely believe that he was in Ithaka, even though it was Athênê who spake to him, until she scattered the mist and showed him the fair haven with its broad spreading olive-trees, and the home of the sea-nymphs, and the old hill of Neritos with its wooded sides.

Then they placed the gifts of the Phæakians in the cave hard by the stream of living waters which flowed through it to the sea, and Athênê touched him with a staff, and all the beauty of his form was gone.   His face became seamed with wrinkles, his flashing eyes grew dim, and the golden locks vanished from his shoulders.   His glistening raiment turned to noisome rags, as Athênê put a beggar's wallet on his shoulder and placed a walking staff in his hand, and showed him the path which led to the house of the swineherd Eumaios.

So Odysseus went his way; but when he entered the courtyard of Eumaios in his tattered raiment, the dogs flew at him with loud barkings, until the swineherd drove them away, and led the stranger into his dwelling, where he placed a shaggy goatskin for him to lie on. 'Thou hast welcomed me kindly,' said Odysseus; 'the gods grant thee in return thy heart's desire.' Then Eumaios answered sadly, 'My friend, I may not despise a stranger though he be even poorer and meaner than myself, for it is Zeus who sends to us the poor man and the beggar Little indeed have I to give; for so it is with bondmen when the young chiefs lord it in the land. But he is far away who loved me well and gave me all my substance. I would that the whole kindred of Helen had been uprooted from the earth, for it was for her sake that my master went to fight with the Trojans at Ilion.'

Then Eumaios placed meat and wine before him. 'It is but a homely meal,' he said, 'and a poor draught; but the chiefs who throng about my master's wife eat all the fat of the land. A brave life they have of it, for rich were the treasures [151] which my master left in his house when he went to take vengeance for the wrongs of Helen.' 'Tell me thy master's name, friend,' said the stranger. 'If he was indeed so rich and great, I may perhaps be able to tell you something about him, for I have been a wanderer in many lands.' 'Why, what would be the use?' answered the swineherd. 'Many a vagabond comes here with trumped-up tales to my master's wife, who listens to them greedily, hoping against hope. No; he must long ago have died; but we love Odysseus still, and we call him our friend though he is very far away.' 'Nay, but thou art wrong this time,' said the stranger, 'for I do know Odysseus, and I swear to thee that the sun shall not finish his journey through the heavens before thy lord returns.' But Eumaios shook his head. 'I have nothing to give you for your news. Sure I am that Odysseus will not come back. Say no more about him, for my heart is pained when any make me call to mind the friend whom I have lost. But what is you name, friend, and whence do you come?'

Then Odysseus was afraid to reveal himself; so he told him a long story how he had come from Crete, and been made a slave in Egypt, how after many years Phoinix had led him to the purple land, how Pheidon the chief of the Thesprotians had showed him the treasures of Odysseus, and how at last he had fallen into the hands of robbers, who had clothed him in beggarly rags and left him on the shore of Ithaka. But still Eumaios would not believe. 'I cannot trust your tale, my friend, when you tell me that Odysseus has sojourned in the Thesprotian land. I have had enough of such news since an Æolian came and told me that he had seen him in Crete with Idomeneus mending the ships which had been hurt by a storm, and that he would come again to his home before that summer was ended. Many a year has passed since; and if I welcome you still, it is not for your false tidings about my master.' 'Well,' said Odysseus, 'I will make a covenant with you. If he returns this year, you shall clothe me in sound garments and send me home to Doulichion; if he does not, bid thy men hurl me from the cliffs, that beggars may learn not to tell lies.' 'Nay, how can I do that,' said Eumaios, 'when you have eaten bread in my house? Would Zeus ever hear my prayer again? Tell me no more false tales, and let us talk together as friends.'

Meanwhile Telemachos was far away in Sparta, whither he had gone to seek his father Odysseus, if haply he might find him ; and one night as he lay sleepless on his couch, Athênê stood before him and warned him to hasten home. 'The suitors are eating up thy substance, and they lie in wait that they may slay thee before the ship reaches Ithaka ; but the gods who guard **thee** will deliver thee from them, and when thou comest to the land, go straightway to the house of Eumaios.'

Then in the morning Telemachos bade farewell to Menelaos, and the fair-haired Helen placed in his hands a beautiful robe which her own fingers had wrought. 'Take it,' she said, 'as a memorial of Helen, and **give** it to thy bride when thy marriage day has come.' So they set off from Sparta, and came to Pylos ; and there, as Telemachos offered sacrifice, the wise seer Theokly-menos stood by his side, and asked him of his name and race, and when he knew that he was the son of Odysseus, he besought Telemachos to take him with him to the ship, for he had slain a man in Argos and he was flying from the avenger of blood. So Theoklymenos the seer came with Telemachos to Ithaka.

Then again Odysseus made trial of the friendship of Eumaios, and when the meal was over, he said, 'To-**morrow, early** in the morning, **I must go** to the house of Odysseus. Therefore let some one guide me thither. It may be that Penelopê will listen to my tidings, and that the suitors will give alms **to** the old man. For I can serve well, my friends, and none can light a fire and heap on wood, or hand the winecup, more deftly than myself.' But Eumaios was angry, and said sharply, 'Why not tarry here? You annoy neither **me** nor my friends, and when Odysseus comes home, be sure he will give you coat and cloak and all else that you may need.' And the beggar said, 'God reward thee, good friend, for succouring the stranger,' and he asked him if the father and mother of Odysseus were yet alive. Then Eumaios told him how his mother had pined away and died after Odysseus went to Ilion, and how Laertes lingered on in a wretched and squalid old age.

But the ship of Telemachos had now reached the land, and he sent some of his men to tell Penelopê that her son was come back, while he himself went to the house of Eumaios. Glad indeed was the swine-herd to see him, for he had not thought to look upon his face again. And Telemachos said, ' Is my mother yet in her home, or has she wedded another, and is the bridal couch of Odysseus covered with the webs of spiders ? ' Nay, she is still in her home,' said Eumaios ; ' but night and day she sheds bitter tears in her grievous sorrow.' Then Telemachos spied the beggar ; and when he learnt his story from Eumaios, he was troubled. 'What can we do with him? Shall I give him a cloak and a sword and send him away? I am afraid to take him to my father's house, for the suitors may flout and jeer him.' Then the beggar put in his word: ' Truly these suitors meet us at every turn. How comes it all about? Do you yield to them of your own free will, or do the people hate you, or have you a quarrel with your kinsfolk ? If these withered arms of mine had but the strength of my youth, soon should some of these suitors smart for their mis-deeds ; and if their numbers were too great for me to deal with, better so to die than see them thus devour the land.' ' Nay, friend, your guesses are wrong,' said Telemachos. ' The people do not hate me, and I have no féud with my kindred ; but these suitors have swarmed in upon us like bees from all the country round about.'

Presently Eumaios rose **up** to go with tidings to Penelopê; and when he was gone a glorious form stood before the door, but the eyes only of Odysseus saw **her,** and he knew that it was Pallas Athênê. 'The time is come,' she said; 'show thyself to Telemachos and make ready with him for the great vengeance.' Then Athênê passed her golden staff over his body, and straightway his tattered raiment became a white and glistening robe. Once more the hue of youth came back to his cheek and the golden locks flowed down over his shoulders, so that Telemachos marvelled and **said, '** Who **art** thou, stranger, that thou lookest like one of the bright gods? But now thy garment was torn, and thy hands shook with age.' 'Nay, I am no god,' answered the man of many toils and sorrows; 'I am thy father.' Then Odysseus kissed his son, and the tears ran down his cheek; but Telemachos would not believe. 'Men change not thus,' he said, 'from age to youth, from squalor and weakness to strength and splendour.' 'It is the work of Athênê,' said the stranger, 'who can make all things fresh and fair; and if I be not Odysseus, none other will **ever** come to Ithaka.' Then Telemachos put his arms around his father and wept, and the cry of their weeping went up together; and Odysseus said, 'The time for vengeance draws nigh. How many are these suitors?' 'They may be told by scores,' said Telemachos; 'and what are two against so many?' 'They are enough,' answered Odysseus, 'if only Zeus and Athênê be on their side.'

Then Telemachos went to the house of Odysseus where **the** suitors were greatly cast down because their

messengers had not been able to kill him. And Penelopê came forth from her chamber, beautiful as Artemis
and Aphroditê, and she kissed her son, who told her
how he had journeyed to Sparta, seeking in vain for his
father.   But Theoklymenos, the seer, put in a word and
said, 'Odysseus is now in Ithaka, and is making ready
for the day of the great vengeance.'

Presently Eumaios went back to his house, and there
he found the beggar, for Odysseus had laid aside his
glistening robe and the glory of youth had faded away
again from his face. So they went to the city together, and
sate by the beautiful fountain whither the people came to
draw water ; and Melanthios the goatherd, as he drove
the flock for the suitors, spied them out and reviled
them.   'Thieves love thieves, they say : where hast
thou found this vagabond, friend swineherd?' and he
pushed Odysseus with his heel.   Then Odysseus was
wroth, and would have slain him, but he restrained
himself, and Eumaios prayed aloud to the nymphs that
they would bring his master home.   And Melanthios
said, 'Pray on, as thou wilt ; but Telemachos shall soon
lie low, for Odysseus shall see Ithaka again no more.'
Then he drove the goats onwards to the house of
Odysseus, and Eumaios and the beggar followed him ;
and as they communed by the way, the swineherd bade
him go first into the house, lest any finding him without
might jeer or hurt him.   But the beggar would not.
'Many a hard buffet have I had by land and by sea,'
he said, 'and I am not soon cast down.'   Soon they
stood before the door, and a dog worn with age strove
to rise and welcome him ; but his strength was gone,
and Odysseus wept when he saw his hound Argos in
such evil plight.   Then, turning to Eumaios, he said,
'The hound is comely in shape. Was he swift and

strong in his youth?' 'Never anything escaped him in
the chase; but there are none to care for him now.' It
mattered not, for the twenty long years had come to an
end; and when Argos had once more seen his master,
he sank down upon the straw and died.[152]

Then Odysseus passed into his house, and he stood
a beggar in his own hall, and asked an alms from
Antinoös. 'Give,' said he, 'for thou lookest like a
king, and I will spread abroad thy name through the
wide earth. For I too was rich once, and had a
glorious home, and often I succoured the wanderer;
but Zeus took away all my wealth, and drove me forth
to Cyprus and to Egypt.' But Antinoös thrust him
aside. 'What pest is this?' he said. 'Stand off,
old man, or thou shalt go again to an Egypt and a
Cyprus which shall not be much to thy liking.' Then
Antinoös struck him on the back; but Odysseus stood
firm as a rock, and he shook his head for the vengeance
that was coming. But the others were angry and said,
'Thou hast done an evil deed, if indeed there be a god
in heaven; nay, often in the guise of strangers the gods
themselves go through the earth, watching the evil and
the good.'[153]

When the tidings were brought to Penelopê, she said
to Eumaios, 'Go call me this stranger hither, for he may
have something to tell me of Odysseus.' But the beggar
would not go then. 'Tell her,' he said, 'that I know
her husband well, and that I have shared his troubles;
but I cannot talk with her before the sun goes down.
At eventide she shall see me.'

Then as Odysseus sate in the hall, there came up to
him the beggar Arnaios, whom the suitors called Iros
because he was their messenger, and he said, 'Get up,
old man, and go, for the chiefs have bidden me to cast

thee out ; yet I would rather see thee depart of thy own
will.' But Odysseus said, 'Nay, friend, there is room
enough here for both of us. You are a beggar like me,
and let us pray the gods to help us ; but lay not thine
hand upon me, lest I be angry and smite thee ; for if I
do, thou wilt not, I take it, care to come again to the
house of Odysseus, the son of Laertes.' But Iros looked
 cornfully at him, and said, 'Hear how the vagabond
talks, just like an old furnace woman. Come now, and
gird up thyself, and let us see which is the stronger.'
Then Antinoös, who had heard them quarrelling, smiled
pleasantly and called to the other suitors : 'See here,
the stranger and Iros are challenging each other. Let
us bring them together and look on.' But Iros shrank
back in fear as the beggar arose, and only one feeble
blow had he given, when Odysseus dashed him to the
ground. Then all the suitors held up their hands and
almost died with laughter, as the stranger dragged Iros
from the hall and said, 'Meddle not more with other
men's matters, lest a worse thing befall thee.' Then
Odysseus gathered up his tattered garment and went
and sat down again upon the threshold, while the
suitors praised him with loud cheers for his exploit,
and Amphinomos held out to him a goblet of rosy
wine : 'Drink, stranger, and mayest thou have good
luck in time to come, for now thy lot is hard and
gloomy enough.' The kindly words stirred the beggar's
heart, and he said, 'Hear my counsel, Amphinomos,
and trust me who have borne many griefs and sorrows
and wandered in many lands since Zeus drove me from
my home. Depart from these evil men who are wasting
another's substance and heed not the woes that are
coming, when Odysseus shall once more stand in his
father's house.' But Amphinomos would not hear, for

so had Athênê doomed that he should fall on the day of the great vengeance.

So, laughing at the beggar as he sat quietly on the threshold, the suitors feasted at the banquet table of Odysseus, till the stars looked forth in the sky. But when they were gone away to sleep, Odysseus bade Telemachos gather up their arms and place them in the inner chamber. And they carried in the spears and shields and helmets, while Athênê went before with a golden lamp in her hand to light the way. And Telemachos said, 'Surely some one of the blessed gods must be here, my father, for walls, beams, and pillars all gleam as though they were full of eyes of blazing fire.' But Odysseus bade him be silent and sleep, and Telemachos went his way, and Odysseus tarried to take counsel with Athênê for the work of the coming vengeance.

Then, as he sat alone in the hall, Penelopê came forth from her chamber, to hear what the stranger might tell her of Odysseus. But before she spake, Melantho reviled him as her father Melanthios had reviled him by the fountain ; and Odysseus said, 'Dost thou scorn me because my garments are torn and my **face** is seamed **with** age and sorrow? Well, I too have been young **and** strong. See then that the change come not on thee when Odysseus returns to his home.' Then Penelopê asked him straightly, 'Who art thou, stranger, and whence hast thou come?" And the beggar said, 'Ask me not, for I have had grievous troubles, and the thought of all my woes will force the tears into my eyes, so that ye may think that I am mad with misery.' But Penelopê urged him : 'Listen to me, old man. My beauty faded away when Odysseus left me to go to Ilion, and my life has been full of woe since the suitors came thronging round me, because my husband, as they said,

lived no more upon the earth. So I prayed them to let
me weave a shroud for Laertes, and every night I undid
the web which I had woven in the daytime. Thus three
years passed away, but in the fourth the suitors found
out my trick, and I know not how to avoid longer the
marriage which I hate. Wherefore tell me who thou
art, for thou didst not spring forth a full-grown man
from a tree or a stone.' Then Odysseus recounted to
her the tale which he had told to the swineherd Eumaios,
and the eyes of Penelopê were filled with tears as the
stranger spoke of the exploits of Odysseus. 'Good
friend,' she said, 'thy kindly words fall soothingly on my
ear. Here shalt thou sojourn, and I will give thee a robe
which I had meant for him who will come back again to
me no more.' But Odysseus would not take it, and he
strove to comfort her, till at the last he sware to her that
before the year's end her husband should stand before her.

And now at the bidding of Penelopê his old nurse
Eurykleia came with water to wash his feet, and looking
hard at him she said, 'Many a stranger has come to this
house, but never one so like in form and voice to my
child Odysseus;' and the stranger answered smiling,
'Most folk who have seen us both have marked the
likeness.' So she knelt down to wash his feet; but
Odysseus turned himself as much as he could from the
fire, for he feared that she might see the mark of the
wound which the boar's tusk had made long ago when
he went to Parnassos.[154] But he strove in vain. For
presently she saw the scar, and she let go his feet, and
the water was spilt upon the ground, as she cried out,
'It is Odysseus: and I knew him not until I saw the
print of the deadly wound which Autolykos healed
by his wondrous power.' Then Odysseus bade her be
silent, for Athênê had dulled the ear of Penelopê that

she might not hear; and he would **not that any** should know that the chieftain had come back to his home.

Soon all were gone, and Odysseus alone remained in the hall through the still hours of night. But when the morning came, the suitors again feasted at the banquet board, and many a time they reviled the beggar and Telemachos, until Penelopê brought forth the bow which Iphitos the son of Eurytos had given to Odysseus. Then she stood before the chiefs and said, 'Whoever of you can bend this bow, that man shall be my husband, and with him I will leave the home which I have loved, and which I shall still see in my dreams.' But when Antinoös saw it, his heart failed him, for he knew that none had ever bent the bow save Odysseus only, and he warned the suitors that it would sorely tax their strength. Then Telemachos would have made trial of the bow, but his father suffered him not.[155] So Leiôdes took it in his hand, and tried in vain to stretch it, till at last he threw it down in a rage and said, 'Penelopê must find some other husband; for I am not the man.' But Antinoös reviled him for his faintheartedness, and he bade Melanthios bring fat to anoint the bow and make it supple; yet even thus they strove in vain to stretch it.

Then Odysseus went out into the courtyard, whither the cowherd and the swineherd had gone before him; and he said to them, 'Friends, are ye minded to aid Odysseus if he should suddenly come to his home, or will ye take part with the men who devour his substance?' And they sware both of them that they would fight for their master to the death. Then Odysseus said, 'I am that man who after grievous woes has come back **in** the twentieth year to his own land; and if ye doubt, see here is the scar of the wound where the boar's tusk pierced my flesh, when I went to Parnassos in the days of my youth.' When they saw the scar, they threw their arms round Odysseus, and they kissed him on his head and his shoulders and wept, until he said, 'Stay, friends, lest any see us and tell the suitors in the house. And now hearken to me. These men will not let me take the bow ; so do thou, Eumaios, place it in my hands, and let Philoitios bar the gates of the court-yard.' But within the hall Eurymachos groaned with vexation because he could not stretch the bow ; and he said, 'It is not that I care for Penelopê, for there are many Achaian women as fair as she ; but that we are all so weak in comparison of Odysseus.' Then the beggar besought them that he too might try, and see whether the strength of his youth still remained to him, or whether his long wanderings had taken away the force of his arm. But Antinoös said, 'Old man, wine hath done thee harm ; still it is well to drink yet more rather than to strive with men who are thy betters.' Then said Penelopê, 'What dost thou fear, Antinoös? Vex not thyself with the thought that the beggar will lead me away as his bride, even if he should be able to stretch the bow of Odysseus.' 'Nay, lady,' he answered, 'it is not that ; but I dread lest the Achaians should say, "The suitors could not stretch the bow, but there came a wandering beggar, who did what they strove to do in vain." '

Then the swineherd took up the bow, but the suitors bade him lay it down again, until at last Telemachos told Eumaios to bear it to Odysseus ; and as the swineherd placed it in the beggar's hands, Eurykleia shut the doors of the hall and made them fast with the tackling of a ship. Then, as Odysseus raised the bow, the thunder pealed in the heaven, and his heart rejoiced because Zeus had given him a sign of his great victory. Presently the arrow sped from the string, and Antinoös lay dead upon the floor. Then the others spoke in great wrath and said, 'The vultures shall tear thy flesh this day, because thou hast slain the greatest chief in Ithaka.' But they knew not, as they spake thus, that the day of the great vengeance was come; and the voice of Odysseus was heard above the uproar, as he said, 'Wretches, did ye fancy that I should never stand again in my own hall? Ye have wasted my substance, ye have sought to steal my wife from me, ye have feared neither gods nor men; and this is the day of your doom.' The cheeks of the suitors turned ghastly pale through fear; but Eurymachos alone took courage and told Odysseus that Antinoös only had done the mischief, because he wished to slay Telemachos and become king in Ithaka in the stead of Odysseus. 'Spare then the rest, for they are thy people, and we will pay thee a large ransom.' But Odysseus looked sternly at him and said, 'Not this house full of silver and gold shall stay my hand in the day of my great vengeance.'

Then Eurymachos drew his sword and bade his comrades fight bravely for their lives; but again the clang of the bow was heard, and Eurymachos was stretched lifeless on the earth. So they fell, one after the other, until the floor of the hall was slippery with blood. But presently the arrows in the quiver of Odysseus were all spent, and laying his bow against the wall, he raised a great shield on his shoulder and placed a helmet on his head, and took two spears in his hand. Then Agelâos called to Melanthios, 'Go up to the stair door and shout to the people, that they may break into the hall and save us.' But Melanthios said, 'It cannot be; for it is near the gate of the hall, and one man may guard it against a hundred. But I will bring you arms, for I know that Odysseus and his son have stowed them away in the inner chamber.' Hastily he ran thither and brought forth shields and spears and helmets, and the heart of Odysseus

failed him for fear as he saw the suitors donning their
armour and brandishing the lances. 'Who has done
this?' he asked; and Telemachos answered, 'It is my
fault, my father. I left the door ajar; but Eumaios shall
go and see whether some of the women have given this
help to the suitors, or whether, as I think, it be Melanthios.' So Eumaios and the cowherd placed themselves
on one side of the chamber door, and when Melanthios
came forth with more arms for the chieftains, they caught
him, and binding him with stout cords they hoisted him
up to the beams and left him dangling in the air. 'Keep
guard there, Melanthios, all night long in thy airy ham-
mock, and when the golden Morning comes back from
the stream of Ocean you will not fail to see her.'

But in the hall the troop of suitors stood facing
Odysseus and Telemachos in deadly rage; and presently Athênê stood before them in the likeness of
Mentor. Then all besought her help; and the suitors
threatened her and said, 'Be not led astray, Mentor,
by the words of Odysseus; for if you side with him,
we will leave you neither house nor lands, wife nor
children, when we have taken vengeance for the evil
deeds of the son of Laertes.' But the wrath of Athênê
was kindled more fiercely, and she said, 'Where is thy
strength, Odysseus? Many a year the Trojans fell
beneath the stroke of thy sword; and by thy wisdom it
was that the Achaians stormed the walls of breezy
Ilion. And now dost thou stand trembling in thine
own hall?' Then the form of Mentor vanished; and
they saw a swallow fly away above the roof-tree. In
great fear the suitors took council together, and six
of them stood forth and hurled their spears at Odysseus and Telemachos. But all missed their mark except
Amphimedon and Ktesippos, and these wounded Telemachos on the wrist and Eumaios on the shoulder.

But once again Athênê came, and this time she held aloft her awful Ægis before the eyes of the suitors, and the hearts of all fainted for fear, so that they huddled together like cattle which have heard the lion's roar, and like cattle were they slain, and the floor of the hall was floated with blood.

So was the slaughter ended, and the house of Odysseus was hushed in a stillness more fearful than the din of battle, for the work of the great vengeance was accomplished.

But Penelopê lay on her couch in a **sweet** slumber which Athênê had sent to soothe her grief, and she heard not the footsteps of Eurykleia as she hastened joyously into the chamber. 'Rise up, dear child, rise up. Thy heart's desire is come. Odysseus stands once more in **his** own home, the suitors are dead, and none are left to vex thee.' But Penelopê could not believe for joy and fear, even when Eurykleia told her of the mark of the boar's bite which Autolykos and his sons **had** healed. 'Let us go, dear nurse,' she said, 'and see the bodies of the chieftains and the man **who** has slain them.' So she went down into the hall, and sate down opposite to Odysseus, but she spake no word, and Odysseus also sat silent. And Telemachos said to his **mother, '** Hast thou no welcome for my father who has borne so many griefs since Zeus took him from his home twenty long years ago?'

And Penelopê said, 'My child, I cannot speak, for my heart is as a stone within me; yet if it be indeed Odysseus, there are secret signs by which we shall know each other.' But when she bade Eurykleia make ready the couch which lay outside the bridal chamber, **Odysseus** asked hastily, 'Who has moved the couch **which I** wrought with my own **hands,** when I made the

R

chamber round the olive-tree which stood in the courtyard? Scarcely could a mortal man move it, for it was heavy with gold and ivory and silver, and on it I spread a bull's hide gleaming with a purple dye.'

Then Penelopê wept for joy, as she sprang into his arms; for now she knew that it was indeed Odysseus who had come back in the twentieth year. Long time they wept in each other's arms; but the keen-eyed Athênê kept back the bright and glistening horses of the morning, that the day might not return too soon.

Then the fair Eurynomê anointed Odysseus, and clothed him in a royal robe; and Athênê brought back all his ancient beauty as when he went forth in his youth to Ilion. So they sate together in the light of the blazing torches, and Penelopê heard from Odysseus the story of his griefs and wanderings, and she told him of her own sorrows, while he was far away at Ilion avenging the wrongs and woes of Helen. But for all his deep joy and his calm peace, Odysseus knew that here was not the place of his rest.

'The time must come,' he said, 'when I must go to the land where there is no sea; but the seer who told me of the things that are to be, said that my last hour should be full of light, and that I should leave my people happy.'

And Penelopê said, 'Yet may we rejoice, my husband, that the hateful chiefs are gone who darkened thy house and devoured thy substance, and that once again I hold thee in my arms. Twenty years has Zeus grudged to me this deep happiness; but never has my heart swerved from thee, nor could aught stay thee from coming again to gladden my heart as in the morning of our life and joy.'

TALES OF THEBES.

LAÏOS.

ON the throne of Kadmos, in the great city of Thebes, sat Laïos, the son of Labdakos. He had passed through many and sore troubles since his father died, for Amphion and Zethos, the sons of Antiopê, had driven him from his kingdom, and for a long time Laïos dwelt in a strange land. But now he trusted to live in peace with his wife Iokastê, the daughter of Menoikeus, and to die happily in a good old age. Still, although all things seemed to go well with him, he could not forget the words which Phœbus Apollo spake when he sent to Delphi to ask what should befall him in the after days; and so it came to pass that, while others rejoiced to hear the merry laughter of children in their homes, Laïos trembled when he heard the tidings that a son had been born to him. For the warning was that he should be slain by his own child.[156]

Many days he spent in sadness and gloom, and he spake no word of love or tenderness to Iokastê, nor did he look on the child as he lay helpless in his cradle. At last he bade his servants take the child and leave him on the rugged heights of Kithairôn. So Iokastê sat in silence, although her heart was breaking with grief, for she knew that it was vain to plead for the life of her babe; and presently the servants set forth from the house of Laïos to go to the mountain where his flocks were feeding. There, in a hollow cleft, they placed the child, and, as they went away, they said, ' If the nymphs

see him not as they wander along the rough hill-side,
Laïos will have no need to fear the warnings of Apollo.'

So once more there was seeming peace in the king's
house at Thebes ; and the grief of Iokastê was soothed
as the months passed by, for she said, ' It is better that
my child should sleep the sleep of death than that he
should live to slay his father.'

But the danger had not passed away, for the babe was
in the house of Polybos, who ruled at Corinth.   Once
had the sun gone down beneath the sea, and once had
the light of Eôs tinged the eastern sky, when a shepherd
who tended his flocks on the cool hill-side saw the babe
wrapped in his white shroud.   Then his heart was
touched with pity, and he said, ' I will take him to my
master's house ; for if his parents will it not that the
child should live, it will profit nothing to take him back
to Thebes, and he cannot do harm to any one in the
Corinthian land.'

So Meropê, the wife of Polybos, received the babe
with great gladness, for she had no child ; and she called
his name Œdipus, because his feet were swollen with the
linen bands which were bound about them when they
took him away from the house of Laïos.   Many times
the year went round, and Œdipus grew up with fair and
ruddy countenance, and all men loved him.   No cloud
dimmed the brightness of his childhood and his youth,
for Polybos and Meropê looked on him with a happy
pride, and thought how the love of Œdipus should cheer
them in the days of weakness and old age.   So the fame
of the young man was spread abroad, for he was foremost
in every sport and game, and none returned from the
chase more laden with booty.   But one day it came to
pass that there was a feast in the house of Polybos, and
one of the guests, whom Œdipus had beaten in the foot-

race, spake out in his anger and said that he was not in very truth the child of Meropê.

The feast went on with mirth and song; but there was a dark cloud on the face of Œdipus, for the words of the stranger had sunk deep in his heart, and he sate still and silent till the banquet was ended. When the morning was come, he went to Meropê and said, 'Tell me the truth, my mother; am I not indeed thy son?' Then she cast her arms around him and said, 'Who hath beguiled thee thus, Œdipus? Can any know better than I that thou art my child indeed? and never was a son more dear to his parents than thou art to us.' But, although he asked no more questions, yet after a while the doubt came back, and he said within himself, 'None can be more tender and loving than Meropê, but she did not tell me plainly that I really am her son.' So in the darkness of the night he went sadly from the home where he had lived without care or trouble till the misery of this doubt came upon him. Once more he passed along the heathy sides of Kithairôn, not knowing that there he had been cast forth to die; and he journeyed on to the shrine of Phœbus Apollo at Delphi. There, as he stood before the holy place, a voice came to him which said, 'Thy doom is that thou shalt slay thy father.'

Then Œdipus was bowed down with the weight of his fear and sorrow; and he resolved within himself that he would never go back to Corinth, that so he might not become the slayer of Polybos. So he went away from Delphi, heavy and displeased, and he journeyed on in moody silence, with his heart full of bitter thoughts. He cared not whither the road might lead him, and it chanced that as he came near to the meeting of the roads which go to Daulis and to Thebes, he heard suddenly the voice of one who bade him turn aside from the path while his chariot passed **by.** Then Œdipus started like **one** awaking from a dream, and looking up he saw **an old man** sitting in the chariot. An angry flush was on his face, as he charged his servant to thrust aside the stranger who dared to stand in his path. So the servant lifted up his whip to strike Œdipus; and Œdipus said, ' Who **are** ye that ye should **smite** me? **and why** should I **yield** to thee, old man, because **thou** ridest in a fine chariot and seekest to turn others aside from the road which is open for all men?' But when the driver of the chariot sought again to **strike** him, Œdipus smote him with the full strength of **his** arm, so that he sank down from his seat. Then the face of the old man grew pale with fury, and he leaned forth to strike down Œdipus with the dagger which was in his hand. But he smote him not, for Œdipus turned aside the blow, and he struck the **old** man on his temples, and left him lying dead by the **side of the** chariot.

So he journeyed onwards; but as **he** drew near **to** the great city of Kadmos he saw mothers sitting with their children by the wayside, and the air was filled with their wailing. Their faces were pale as though from **a** deadly plague, and their limbs quivered as if from **mortal** fear; and Œdipus said, ' Children of Kadmos, what evil has befallen you, that ye have fled from your homes and are sunk down thus on the hard earth?' Then they told him how on a high cliff near the city of Thebes a horrible monster, with a maiden's face and a lion's body, sate looking on the plain below, and how the breath of the Sphinx poisoned the pure air of the heaven and filled **their** dwellings with a noisome pestilence. And they **said,** ' Help us, stranger, if thou canst, **for** if help come not **soon,** the city and people of Kadmos will be destroyed; ·for like a black cloud in the sky the Sphinx rests on the cliff, and none can drive her away unless he first answer the riddle with which she baffles the wisest of the land. Every day she utters her dark speech, and devours all who seek to answer it and fail.' Then said Œdipus, 'What may the riddle be?' And they answered, 'This much only does the Sphinx say, "On the earth is a two-footed living thing which has four feet and three and only one voice. Alone of all creatures it changes in its form, and moves most slowly when it uses all its feet." Now, therefore, stranger, if thou canst answer the riddle, thou wilt win a mighty prize; for Laïos, our king, has been slain, we know not by whom, and the elders have spoken the word that he who slays the Sphinx shall have Iokastê for his wife and sit on the throne of Kadmos.'

Then, with a cheerful heart, Œdipus went onwards, until he drew near to the cliff on which the Sphinx was sitting. With a steady gaze he looked on her stern unpitying face, and said to her, 'What is thy riddle?' and all who heard trembled as she spake to Œdipus. Then he thought within himself for a while, and at last he looked up and said, 'Listen, O Sphinx : the creature of whom thou hast asked me is man. In the days of his helpless childhood he crawls on his four feet; in his old age a staff is his third foot, and his movement is slowest when he crawls on four feet.'

The paleness of death came over the face of the Sphinx, and every limb quivered with fear, until, as Œdipus drew nearer, she flung herself with a wild roar from the cliff. Presently the men of Thebes trampled on her ghastly carcass; and they led Œdipus[157] in triumph to the elders of the city, shouting 'Io Paian' for the mighty deed which he had done. Then was the

feast spread in the great banquet-hall, and the minstrels
sang his praise, and besought strength and wealth for
him and for the people. So Iokastê became the wife
of Œdipus,[158] and all men said, 'Since the days of
Kadmos, the son of Telephassa, no king hath ruled us
so wisely and justly;' and the name of the gloomy Laïos
was forgotten.

——o——

ŒDIPUS.

FOR many years Œdipus reigned gloriously in
Thebes, and the fame of his wisdom was
spread abroad in the countries round about.
He looked on his sons and daughters as they
grew up in health and strength; and it seemed to him
as though trouble and sorrow could scarcely vex him
more. But the terrible Erînys, who takes vengeance
for blood, had not forgotten the day when Laïos fell
smitten by the wayside; and, at the bidding of Zeus,
Phœbus Apollo sent a plague upon the Theban land.
The people died like sheep in the city and in the field,
and the pestilence was more grievous than in the days
when the Sphinx uttered her dark riddle from the cliff.
At last the elders of the city came to Œdipus and said,
'O king, thou didst save the city and the people long
ago, when we were sore pressed by a horrible monster;
save us now, if thou canst, by thy great wisdom.' But
Œdipus said, 'Friends, the plague which is slaying us
now comes from no monster, but from Zeus who dwells
on Olympos; and my wisdom therefore cannot avail to
take it away. But I have sent Kreon my brother to

the shrine of Phœbus Apollo at Delphi to ask him wherefore these evils have come upon us.'

But the coming of Kreon brought strife only and anguish to the city, and the fearful Erinys who wanders through the air waved her dark wings over the house of Œdipus; for Phœbus had told him that there was no **hope for the** land until they cast forth the man whose hands were polluted with blood. Then said Œdipus, 'This were an easy task if we only knew on whom lies the bloodguiltiness;[159] but I know neither the man nor the deed for which this doom is laid upon him.' And Kreon answered, 'O king, it is for Laïos, who was slain as he was journeying into the Phokian land.'

Then everywhere through the city and in the field went the messengers of Œdipus, charging all to bring forth the murderer, and threatening grievous pains to any who should hide or shelter him. But none stood forth to own his guilt or to charge it on another; and in his sore strait Œdipus sent for the blind seer Teiresias, who knew the speech of birds and the hidden things of earth and heaven. But when he was led before the king, Œdipus saw that the heart of the wise prophet was troubled, and he said gently, 'Teiresias, thou understandest things that are hidden from other men; tell me now, I beseech thee, on whose hands is the stain from the blood of Laïos. Let me but know this, and the pestilence will straightway cease from the land.' But Teiresias answered hastily, 'Ask me not, O king, ask me not. Let me go again to my home, and let us bear each his own burden.' So Teiresias kept silence, and many times Œdipus prayed him to speak, until his wrath was roused, and he spake unseemly words to the prophet, and said, 'If thou answerest not my question, it must be because thine own hands are polluted with the blood of

Laïos.' Then from the countenance of the prophet flashed unutterable scorn, as he said slowly, so that none might hear but Œdipus, 'O king, thou hast sealed **thine** own doom. On thine hand lies his blood, not on mine. Dost thou not remember the words which Phœbus spake to thee at Delphi, when thou hadst gone thither from the house of Polybos?' But, in his rage and madness, Œdipus took no heed of prudence and wisdom, and he cried with a loud voice, and said, ' Hearken, O people, to the words of Teiresias ; hath he not spoken well when he said that Laïos was smitten by my hand?' Then there rose wild cries and shoutings, and bitter words **were** spoken against the seer, who had dared to revile the king ; but as he turned to go, Teiresias said only, ' It is easy to cry aloud, it is harder to judge and to find out the truth ; search ye it out well before ye say that I have spoken falsely.'

So once more a terrible doubt filled the mind of Œdipus. In the day his thoughts vexed him, and evil dreams stood before him in the dark hours of night ; and daily the plague pressed more heavily on the people, until at length he asked Iokastê of the time when Laïos had been slain, and what tidings were brought of the deed. And she said, ' One only lives to tell the tale, and he said that, at a place where three ways met, robbers fell on the king and slew him ; and the deed was done not long before thy coming to Thebes.' Then a strange fear came over Œdipus ; as he remembered the old man whom he had smitten in his chariot, and he told her of all the things which befell him as he journeyed to Thebes from Delphi. ' But in thy words is hope,' he said ; ' for if Laïos fell by a band of thieves, then am I guiltless of **his blood.** Yet hasten now, and bring hither the man

who saw the deed, for I will not close my eyes in sleep
until this secret is made known.'

But while one went for the man, there came a messenger from Corinth with tidings that Polybos the king
was dead ; and Œdipus lifted up his hands and said, ' I
thank thee, O Zeus ; for the words of Phœbus Apollo,
that I should slay my father, can never be accomplished.'
But the messenger answered hastily, 'Thy thanks are
wasted, O king, for the blood of Polybos runs not in thy
veins. I found thee on the rugged heights of Kithairôn,
and saved thee from the doom which was prepared for
thee. So from the house of Polybos there is for thee
neither hope nor fear.' Then the heart of Œdipus beat
wildly with a horrible dread, and he said, ' O thou that
dwellest at Delphi, have thy words in very deed been
accomplished, and I knew it not ? ' Presently the hope,
which the words of Iokastê had waked up in him, was
taken away ; for the old man who had seen the deed
said now that one only had slain the king, and the tokens
remained sure that the hands of Œdipus were polluted
with his father's blood.

Then was there woe unspeakable in the city of
Kadmos, and the hearts of all the people were bowed
down with grief for all the miseries which had burst
like a flood on the house of Labdakos, and a great cry
went up to heaven. For the lady Iokastê lay dead, and
Œdipus had done a fearful deed when he saw her
stretched cold and lifeless before him. With his own
hands he tore out his eyes and hurled them away ; for
he said, ' It is not fit that the eyes which have seen such
things should ever look upon the sun again.'

From that day forth the terrible Erînys who hovers in
the air, and the awful Atê,[160] who visits the sins of the
fathers upon the children, abode by day and by night in

the house of Œdipus. His sons strove together in their vain and silly pride, and each sought to be king in his father's place, till at last they cast Œdipus forth, and he wandered in wretchedness and misery from the land of the Kadmeians. His grievous sorrow had quenched his love for his people, and he said, in bitterness of spirit, that his body should not be buried in the Theban land. So his child Antigonê led him onwards, and sought to cheer him in his fierce agony. But the dark cloud rested ever on his countenance, until, one day, he said to Antigonê, 'My child, I think that the end of my long suffering is nigh at hand ; for there came to me last night a vision of a dream which said, " Man of many troubles, thou shalt lie down to rest in the grove of the Eumenides, and for the land in which thy body shall lie there shall be wealth in peace and victory in war."' So he went on with a good heart, journeying towards rocky Athens, and as he passed through a wood where the waters of a little stream murmured pleasantly in the still summer air, he sat down on a seat carved in the living rock, while Antigonê stood by his side. But presently a rough voice bade him rise and depart. 'Stranger, dost thou not dread the wrath of the mighty beings whose very name we fear to utter? In this grove of the Eumenides no mortal man may rest or tarry.' But Œdipus said gently, 'Yet move me not, I pray thee, for I am not as other men, and the visions of Zeus have told me that this shall be the place of my rest. Go then to Theseus who rules at Athens, and bid him come to one who has suffered much and who will do great things for him and for his people.' So Theseus came at the bidding of Œdipus ; and there were signs in the heaven above and on the earth beneath, that the end was nigh at hand, for the ground shook beneath their feet, and the thunder was heard in the cloudless sky. Then **Œdipus** bade Antigonê farewell, and said, 'Weep not, my **child**; I am going to my home, and I rejoice to lay down the **burden** of my woe.' And to Theseus he said, 'Follow me, O friend, for the blind shall guide thee this day. The dreams which Zeus sends have shown me the place where I must sleep after the fever of my life is ended; and so long as thou revealest not my resting-place to men, thy people shall prosper and wax mighty in peace and in war.' But even while he yet spake, there came a voice which said, 'Œdipus, why tarriest thou?' and the sound of the thunder echoed again through the cloudless sky. Then he spake the parting words to Theseus, and besought him to guard his child Antigonê; and he said, 'Here must thou stay until thou seest that the things are accomplished of which the vision hath fore-warned **me**. Follow me not further.' So Œdipus de-parted alone, and Theseus knew presently that Zeus had fulfilled his word.[161]

From that day forth, the city of Athênê grew mighty in the earth, and no enemy prevailed against it. For to no one did Theseus show the place where Œdipus rested in the hidden dells of Kolonos, save to the man who should rule at Athens after him. Thus only the king knew where lay the secret spell which made the city of Erechtheus mightier than the city of Kadmos; and the men of Thebes sought in vain to find the grave of Œdipus where the Kephîsos flows by the sacred grove of the Eumenides.

HERE was strife between Eteokles and Polyneikes, when they had driven forth their
father from the city of Kadmos; for Œdipus
had laid on them a heavy curse for their cruel
deed, and the awful Erínys heard it, and she sware with
an oath that there should be no peace for the men of
Thebes until the whole house of Laïos should be utterly
destroyed. At first the brothers agreed that each should
be king in his turn, and that the power should pass
daily from the one to the other; but soon there grew
up jealousy between them and hatred, and bitter words
were spoken, until at last Eteokles rose up against his
brother and thrust him out of the city.

So Polyneikes went away in rage and sorrow, and
took the road which goes to Argos; and as he came
near to it, he met a stranger by the wayside, and they
talked together, until there arose a quarrel between
them. But while they were fighting, Adrastos the king
passed by, and he saw that on the shield of Polyneikes
was a boar, and a lion on the shield of the other
stranger, whose name was Tydeus; and he said within
himself, 'Long ago Phœbus forewarned me that my
daughters must be married to a lion and a boar; surely
these must be they of whom he spake.' And he went
up to them and parted them in their battle, and said,
'Come with me, friends. I am Adrastos, and I rule in
this city of Argos. There are better things in store for
you than vain strife and hard blows.' So, when Argeia
became the wife of Polyneikes, and Dêipylê was given
to Tydeus who came from the rugged mountains of

Ætolia, Adrastos sware **to** avenge the wrongs **of** both the strangers, **and** to place them again on the thrones of their fathers.

Then throughout the land of Argos the messengers went to and fro to summon the chieftains to the war; **but** when they met in council at Argos, Amphiaraos rose up and said, 'Friends, ye are going to your death, **for to** me are shown many things which are hidden from your eyes; and I see the eagles gathered which shall **tear** the flesh from your bones, if ye go against the city and people of Kadmos.' But none hearkened to his warnings, and they dragged Amphiaraos to the war against his will.

So round the walls of Thebes camped the army of the great Argive chieftains; and within the city was fear and trembling, until Teiresias the wise seer spake and said, 'Thebans, the victory shall be yours, and your enemies shall perish utterly, if ye offer a great sacrifice to Arês.' Then Menoikeus the son of Kreon answered, 'What can a man give better than his life?' and he went forth and slew himself without the city.[162] Then the Argives battered more fiercely against the gates, and put ladders to climb the walls; but the thunderbolt fell from heaven, and smote many of them, and the Thebans hurled mighty stones from the wall and crushed the foremost of their warriors. Still the battle raged fiercely, until Eteokles went forth and said, 'Men of Argos, ye are fighting in a vain quarrel; for ye have no cause to hate the men of Thebes. Bring forth Polyneikes my brother, that we may fight together, and so shall the strife be ended, and ye shall go back to your homes in peace.'

Then the awful Erinys, as she hovered unseen in the **air, waved her** dark wings over the brothers when they

S

came forth to meet each other.   On their faces was the
blackness of hatred strong as death; but no word was
spoken as they drew each his sword, and the mortal
strife began.   Then the Erînys gave to their arms an
unearthly strength, and presently the bodies of the two
brothers were stretched dead upon the plain.   But the
men of Argos and of Thebes said that there was no
victory where none lived to claim it, and again they
fought, until Tydeus the Ætolian fell with a deadly
wound, and a mighty crowd of enemies pressed hard to
slay Amphiaraos.   Then he rose up in his chariot, and,
lifting up his hands to the broad heaven, he said, 'O
Zeus, the hour is come; and the things of which thou
didst show me the tokens have been accomplished.
Yet save me from the sword of men, if the doom is that
I must die.'   So his prayer was heard, and the earth
clave asunder, and the chariot of Amphiaraos was seen
no more; and the place where it sank down became
holy ground, for the flocks and herds would not touch
the grass which grew soft and green upon it,[163] and the
birds lighted not near the pillars of his temple.

Then a mighty terror fell on the men of Argos, when
they knew that Amphiaraos had been taken from the
land of living men; and the chieftains fled away each
to his own home.   With the swiftness of the wind as it
sweeps over the waters, Adrastos rode on his horse
Areiôn over hill and vale and along the sea-shore;
and as they saw his blood-stained raiment streaming
on the breeze, the people of the land knew that
Zeus had accomplished the doom of the chiefs who
went to place Polyneikes on the throne of his father
Œdipus.

ANTIGONÊ.

WHEN the army of the Argives was scattered and the two sons of Œdipus had slain each other, Kreon became king in Thebes, and he sent messengers through the city, who said, 'Hearken, ye people, to the words of the king. Eteokles has fallen in a righteous quarrel, and a great sacrifice shall be done to the gods who dwell beneath the earth, that they may welcome him when he comes before them; but the body of Polyneikes shall be cast forth to the beasts of the field and the fowls of the air; and the man who dares to lay it in the ground, or so much as to sprinkle earth upon it, shall be stoned to death before the people of the city.'

So the body of Polyneikes was cast forth on a mound of earth, and guards were placed there to see that none should bury it or sprinkle earth upon it. But Antigonê spake to Ismênê, her sister, and besought her help that the fitting things might be done for the body of their brother; but Ismênê said, 'What good can come from despising the words of those who rule in the city? Hath anything prospered in the house of Laïos since the plague came to search out the pollution of blood? and how shall it profit to bring another woe on the woes that are past?' And Antigonê answered, 'Be it even as thou wilt, my sister; thou knowest, it may be, what it is best for thee to do. I speak not for any love which Polyneikes showed to us or to our father. But there are other laws besides the laws of gentleness and pity; and justice, which lives for ever, cries out that the offerings must be given for those who wander on the banks of the Stygian stream.' [164]

So the maiden went forth, and when the shades of night covered the earth, she scraped away the sand until the body of Polyneikes sank down into the shallow grave. But the men who were placed to guard the body woke up from their sleep, and seized the maiden, and carried her in the morning before the king. And Kreon said, 'Thou hast sealed thine own doom, Antigonê, for the word which I have spoken may not be recalled, and this day thou shalt die.' But the maiden answered, 'Do with me as thou wilt; I have obeyed a law which is higher and stronger than thy word.' So they carried the maiden to a hollow rock, and there they placed her with a loaf of bread and a flask of water.

But dark signs were seen again in the heavens, and the seer Teiresias came before Kreon, and said,[165] 'Take good heed, O king, what thou doest. The wrath of the awful Erînys is coming again upon the city, and few hours shall pass before thou shalt atone with the life of one whom thou dost love for the death of the maiden Antigonê. I have heard the strange voices of birds, which told me of fresh woes for this hapless land; and I have listened to the sounds which tell of strife and war. The fire burns not on the altar of sacrifice, and the flesh of the victim wastes away in the smouldering cinders; for the gods who dwell beneath the earth are wroth with thee, and thou hast done to them a grievous wrong while thy thought was how thou mightest do hurt to Polyneikes.' Then Kreon said, 'The evil may be yet undone. The traitor's body shall be buried, and we will bring forth Antigonê from the cave where they have left her to die.'

Hastily and in much fear they went to save the

maiden; but when they entered the cave, the body of Antigonê lay before them stiff and cold in death, and by her side sat Haimon, the son of the king; but when Kreon bade him rise and go home, he said, 'It is too late; the joy of my life is gone; what have I to live for now?' Then he plunged a dagger into his heart, and in the home of Hades and Persephonê he won again the love which Kreon had denied to him in the land of living men.

So the years went on, but the days of Kreon passed in gloom and sorrow, for the light which had risen for a little while in the house of Laïos was quenched at the death of Haimon; and there came rumours of war from Argos, for the sons of the chieftains who had fought for Polyneikes were grown up to manhood, and they had vowed a vow to avenge the blood of their fathers. Once more Kreon sent for the blind prophet; but Teiresias would not come, for he said, 'There is no hope, and the undying gods fight against the children of Kadmos.' So the hearts of the Thebans were bowed down with fear, and Kreon fled away in terror when the army of the Argives drew nigh to the walls of the city. Thus was the house of Laïos rooted utterly out of the land, and the vengeance of the awful Erînys was accomplished.

ERIPHYLÊ.

HEN the first war of the seven chiefs against Thebes was ended, the men of Argos, with the help of the men of Athens, took from the Thebans the dead bodies of their comrades and burnt them with fire, and then went back to their own land. But the words of Amphiaraos were yet to be accomplished, which he spake to Alkmaion his son when he departed for the war.

Now the wisdom of the far-seeing gods had rested on Amphiaraos, for he was sprung from the seer Melampous, who knew the speech of birds. And thus it was that, when Adrastos besought his aid against the men of Thebes, Amphiaraos forewarned him of the evils which should come upon them. 'The Atê of Zeus presses sore upon Polyneikes,' he said, 'for the curse of a father has a mighty power. Wherefore I go not to the war.' Then was there great fear, and the chieftains took counsel hurriedly in the hall of Adrastos, for of all the warriors of the land none had so great fame as the wise seer Amphiaraos. His spear had wounded the great boar of Kalydon which was slain by the beautiful Atalantê, and his wisdom had guided the chiefs who sailed in the ship Argo to fetch away the golden fleece. But Amphiaraos dwelt with his wife Eriphylê, and in an evil hour he had sworn to Adrastos her brother that, if ever there rose up strife between them, he would follow the bidding of Eriphylê. So the chieftain of Argos went to his sister, and said, 'Our task is vain, if Amphiaraos goes not forth with us to the war. Wherefore I have brought thee a rich gift, that thou mayest persuade him to go. Lo! here is the necklace which Hephaistos wrought and Kadmos gave to his wife Harmonia when he had come to Thebes from the far-off Eastern land.' The lustre of gold and gems dazzled the eyes of Eriphylê, and her heart was corrupted by the bribe, so that she said, 'Fear not, my brother. It shall be even as thou wilt.' So her word was spoken, and Amphiaraos bade farewell to his home and to his children; but to Alkmaion his eldest-born he said, 'The treachery of thy mother sends me forth to an **evil war; if I come** not back, avenge me **of** her.'

Then Alkmaion remembered his father's words when **the remnant of** the host of the Argives returned faint of heart from the seven-gated walls of Thebes, and when they told him how Zeus had opened the earth and taken **to** himself his child Amphiaraos. So Eriphylê died, and the awful Erînys, who hovers in the air, came down to **take** vengeance for the deed. Unheard by others, the **waving of her** dark wings **and the hiss of** her poisoned **breath fell loud and harsh on** the ear of Alkmaion, and **gave him neither** peace **by day nor** sleep **by night. In** madness **of** spirit he wandered **through the** land, **driven** by her merciless scourge, **till he** came to the **shrine of** Phœbus Apollo **at** Delphi. **There** the priestess **bade** him offer the necklace which Adrastos gave to Eriphylê, and told him that, if he would have rest from the scourge **of** Erînys, **he must find a spot which the sun** had not yet **seen when he** avenged **his father. In sorrow of heart** Alkmaion wandered **from Delphi, over** mountain **and** through valley, seeking **in vain for the** place **of which the** priestess **had spoken, until** he **came to** the shores of the mighty Achelôos, **where it** flows **slowly out** into the sea. There the slime, **borne** down **by** the waters, rises **higher and** higher as **the years** roll round, **and** makes **new land, gaping** and desolate, where the **lank** and coarse **grass sweeps** in a wild tangle **over** the ground. Here, **as** he sank **down in** utter weariness, Alkmaion heard a voice which said, '**This is the place of** thy rest, for **here** the blood which thou hast **shed** cannot taint **the** air; and here, when **ten years have** passed away, thy hands shall again be pure, and thou **shalt** return and lead thy kinsfolk **to** avenge **the** blood **of** their fathers against the **men of** Thebes.' [156]

Even so it came to pass; and when the Epigonoi [107] made ready for the war, Alkmaion went forth from his hiding-place, and led them from Argos against the city of Kadmos. But the undying gods cared no more to shield Kreon, and all things came to pass according to the words of the seer Teiresias, and the chiefs of Argos burst through the seven gates and smote the men of Thebes, and made Thersandros, the son of Polyneikes, king in the stead of Kreon, the son of Menoikeus.

MISCELLANEOUS TALES.

ATYS AND ADRASTOS.

EN years had Crœsus reigned in Sardes, and all things had prospered to his hand. His garners were laden with grain, his folds were full of sheep, his houses were stored with gold and silver and all precious things. Among all kings there **was** none richer than Crœsus, and none more mighty. No sound of war or strife was heard in all his land, for he ruled his people gently, so that even the men whom he had conquered hated him not ;[168] and Crœsus thought, in the gladness of his **heart,** that of all men he was happiest.

Now about this time Solon the Athenian came into the Lydian land, for he had left his own country, because he had given his people good laws, and he willed not that they should be broken. **So he** made his countrymen swear an oath that they would use his laws for ten years, and then he went away that he might not be compelled to alter them himself. So he came to Sardes, and Crœsus welcomed him gladly, giving him rich banquets and gifts of all good things. When he had been there three days, Crœsus bade his servants lead Solon through all the houses where his treasures were stored up ; and when he had seen them all, Crœsus spake to him and said, ' I have heard of thy wisdom, O Athenian stranger, and how thou hast given good laws to thy people, and that thou art going now through many lands, to see the cities and ponder on the ways and the life of men. Tell me, then, hast thou ever known a man whom thou wouldst

call happy in all things?' This question Crœsus asked,
thinking surely that he would be named as the happiest
of all men; but Solon flattered him not, and named
Tellos the Athenian. Then Crœsus turned sharply on
him, and asked him why he named Tellos; and Solon
answered, 'Because Tellos lived when things went well
with the city, and his own children were good and fair,
and he saw their children springing up and prospering
steadily; and also because after such a life he died very
gloriously, for there was a battle between the men of
Athens and Eleusis, and he came to the aid of the Athenians, and having put the enemy to flight died nobly, and
the people buried him on the ground where he fell,[169] and
honoured him greatly.'

Then Crœsus thought within himself, 'Surely after
Tellos he must think me the happiest;' so he asked
Solon. But Solon named Kleobis and Biton, and said,
'These men lived in Argos, rich in goods and strong in
body; and it chanced that there was a feast held in
honour of Hêrê, but the oxen were not at hand to take
their mother to the temple. So they placed her in the
chariot, and drew it thither over forty and five furlongs;
and the people at the feast marvelled at their strength,
and held their mother happy that she had such children.
Then she stood up before the shrine of Hêrê, and prayed
the goddess to give to her children the happiest thing
which mortal man may have. So the young men lay
down there in the temple, for they were weary, and fell
asleep and died; and thus Hêrê showed that death is
better than life, and that there can be no better gift for
man than to die happily.'

But Crœsus was angry and sore displeased, and said,
'So then, O Athenian, thou holdest my happiness in so
little account that thou hast not even thought me equal

to men of low estate?' Then Solon answered, 'O Crœsus, dost thou ask me, who know that the gods are full of jealousy, about the happiness of man? In a long life there is much to be seen and suffered from which man would willingly turn aside; and in his threescore years and ten, there is not one single day which brings not with it some change or turn of things, so that man in all his life on earth has no sure abiding. And now, O king, thou art rich and wealthy, and all things thus far have prospered to thy hand, but happy I may not call thee until I learn that thy life has been happily ended; for the rich man is not wealthier than he who has only whereby he may live, unless he keeps all his wealth until the hour of his death. Many a rich man is very wretched, and many in humble estate have good fortune. So, then, in the case of all we must wait till they die; for the sum of human happiness is when a man is fair in person and sound of mind and limb, when no sickness vexes him and no evil chance annoys him, and when his children grow up fair and strong; but all these things together never fell to the lot of any man, and he who has had most of them and goes down to the grave yet having them best deserves the name of happy. But everywhere we must look to the end; for the stateliest tree is often torn up by the roots, while yet it stands forth in the fulness of its beauty.'

Thus spake Solon; but his words displeased the king, because he had thought little of his wealth and treasures, and bade him wait till the end should come.

So Solon departed; and after he was gone, as Crœsus lay asleep in the night, there came a dream which stood over him and warned him that Atys his son should be smitten by a spear and die. Now Atys was the pride of his father's heart, and Crœsus rejoiced to see his child

braver and stronger than all his fellows, and going forth
boldly to the chase, and coming back laden with booty.
Another son he had, but he spoke not, for he was dumb;
and it was a grief of mind to Crœsus that the fate should
be upon the bright and fair Atys. But when he arose in the
morning, he said nothing of the dream; only he took all
the swords and spears that hung in the men's chambers,
and put them where none might fall down and hurt his
son; and then he made for him a marriage-feast, and
gave him a fair bride, that Atys might forget his sturdy
pastimes in the joys of love.

But before the marriage-feast was ended, there came
a man in great sorrow, and besought Crœsus to cleanse
him from guilt, for his hands were stained with murder.[170]
So Crœsus cleansed the stranger, and then asked him
whence he came and whom he had slain. And the man
said, 'I am Adrastos the son of Midas, and I slew my
brother unwittingly; so my father drove me forth, and I
have neither home nor money.' Then Crœsus spake to
him kindly and bade him be comforted, saying, 'Thou
hast come to the house of a friend where thou shalt want
for nothing; and the lighter that thou canst bear this mishap, by so much it will be to thee a gain.'

Not long after these things there came men of the
Mysians to Crœsus, who said, 'O king, we are sore
vexed by a mighty boar which lurks in the clefts and
dells of Olympos, and destroys our harvests, and hurts
and slays all those who go forth against him. Help us,
then, and let thy son Atys and thy chosen youths go
forth with us that we may smite this monster.' But
Crœsus answered them hastily, 'Think not of my son,
for I cannot send him with you; he has married a wife,
and his heart is fixed on his love. But I will send chosen
men of the Lydians with all my dogs, and I will charge

them to put forth all their strength, that so ye may destroy this wild beast from the land.'

But Atys heard why the Mysians had come; and even while his father was yet speaking, he came hastily into the room, and said, ' Father, in times past it was my pride to go forth to the battle and the chase, and it was a delight to thee, also, that I came back laden with riches and glory; and now thou keepest me away from both, but wherefore I know not. Hast thou seen in me either cowardice or faintness of heart? or dost thou think that I can show myself now to my comrades who praised me once for my bravery and my strength? Nay, with what eyes will my bride look upon me, if I pass my life as a woman, and touch neither sword nor spear? Let me go forth to the hunt, or show me in calm and plain speech that it is better for me to stay at home.'

Then Crœsus looked sadly on the face of Atys, as he stood in all his beauty before him, and he said, ' My child, I charge thee not with faintness of heart, and it may be that I see in thee no fault at all; but there came one night a dream which stood over me in my sleep, and said that thou shouldst be smitten by a spear and die; therefore have I brought thee a bride, and held for thee the marriage-feast, if by any means I may save thee from the doom which hangs over thee : and, indeed, thou art my only child, for I look not on thy brother as on a living son, for the fountain of his speech is closed.'

But Atys said, ' My father, none can blame thee for thy care and forethought, when such a dream hath visited thee; but thou hast not read its meaning right, for a boar hath neither hands nor spear, and it cannot smite in the way of which the dream forewarned thee. If indeed the dream had said that I was to die by a tooth, then were there some reason in thy words; but it talked

only of a spear-point. Let me go, then, for we have not
now to fight with men.' Then Crœsus said, 'I will not
gainsay thy words, my son; only I pray the gods may
prove them true.' And so saying, he sent for Adrastos
the Phrygian, and charged him to guard his son. And
he said, 'I welcomed thee, Adrastos, when thou wast
grieving for a mischance, for which I reproach thee not;
I cleansed thee from thy guilt, I have fed thee at my
table; and now I ask of thee a requital for my kindness,
and sure I am that thou wilt not think it a hard one.
Go forth with my son to this chase; thieves may fall
upon him by the way; be then at hand to guard him, if
such a mishap overtake him. Go, then, and win honour
for thyself also. Thou art young still, and thy limbs are
stout and strong. It is not meet that a son should fall
behind his father.'

Then said Adrastos, 'O king, I had not thought to
go forth to the chase again; for it is not seemly that such
a man as I should mingle with those who are gay and
happy, nor have I the will to do so. But to thee I owe
a great debt, and therefore will I go forth and guard thy
son with all care. So, then, be not cast down; my own
pledge I give thee, that thy son shall come back to thee
in health and strength even as he leaves thee.'

From the gates of Sardes the huntsmen went forth in
gladness of heart; and the sound of song and laughter
rose into the still morning air. At their head rode the
brave and fair Atys, and the Phrygian Adrastos was by
his side. Merrily in the sunshine glanced the spears of
all the train, as they rode gaily on towards the brushwood thickets which clothe the sides of the Mysian
Olympos. Soon they tracked the boar in his hiding-
place, and chased him through thicket and marsh and
plain, until at last he turned round to bay, and there was

a fierce fight, while each man pressed forward that he might slay the boar and win the glory himself. There, in the throng, Adrastos launched his spear at the boar and smote Atys the brave and fair; and the vision of the dream was accomplished.

In haste and grief the messenger sped back to Sardes to tell the king how Adrastos had slain his son. Then the mind of Crœsus was maddened with rage and sorrow; and his grief was the more bitter because his son had been slain by the man whom he had cleansed from the guilt of murder, so that in his agony he called on Zeus the purifier to witness all the evil which the stranger had done to him, and on him who guards the hearth, because unwittingly he had welcomed to his board the murderer of his child, and on him who hears the oaths of friends,[171] because the man who swore to guard his son had smitten him with his spear.

But even while he yet prayed, the Lydians came bearing the body of Atys, and laid it down at the feet of Crœsus. Then with outstretched arms Adrastos drew nigh, and, kneeling down before him, besought the king to smite him for his evil deed; and he wrung his hands in agony and said, 'O Crœsus, I came to thee with the guilt of murder, and thou didst cleanse me; I went forth to guard thy son, and my spear hath slain him. Slay me now, for life is hateful to me for all this misery.' Then, even in the bitterness of his grief and agony, the heart of Crœsus was moved with pity for Adrastos, and he said, 'O friend, I seek not more atonement, now that thou hast judged thyself to be worthy of death : and I know now that thou art not the cause of this sorrow to me, saving only that thy hand hath done the deed against thy will; but it comes from that god who forewarned me of the end that was coming.'

T

So Crœsus buried the brave and fair Atys; and Adrastos the Phrygian lingered weeping till all were gone, and then he slew himself upon the grave.

And Crœsus called to mind the words of Solon, and he knew now that they were true.[172]

---o---

THE VENGEANCE OF APOLLO.[173]

N the cool evening time King Darius walked in his royal garden, and the noblest of the Persians were around him. Then came there a messenger from the western land in haste and said, 'O king, the men of Athens with the sons of Javan have taken the city of Sardes, and the temple of the great goddess Kybêbê has been burnt.' And King Darius answered quickly and said, 'What sayest thou, O messenger, that men of whom I have never heard the name have come with my slaves against the land of the great king?' Then he bade them bring a bow and arrows; and while one went for them, the Persians stood round him in silence, for they feared to say aught while the king was angry. So when he took the bow, he fitted an arrow to it and shot it up into the sky, and prayed, saying, 'O Zeus that dwellest in the high heavens, suffer me to be avenged upon the men of Athens. The sons of Javan are my slaves, and sorely shall they be smitten for the deeds which they have done.' Then he gave command, and each day, when the banquet was spread in the gilded hall and the king sat down to meat, there stood forth one who said with a loud voice, 'O king, forget not the men of Athens.'

But Zeus hearkened not to the prayer of the great

king, for the ships were made ready, and his chieftains
and warriors hastened away to the Athenian land and
fought in Marathon. But they fared not well in the
battle, for the men of Athens strove mightily for their
country, and the bright heroes came back to aid their
kinsfolk. Then were there seen wonderful forms taller
and more glorious than the sons of men ; and the mighty
Echetlaios with his great ploughshare smote down the
chiefest of the Medes. So in great fear the Persians
fled to the sea-shore, while the men of Athens slew them
on the land and in the water as they struggled to reach
the ships. And when the fight was over, they spoiled
the Persians who lay dead on the sea-shore and took
rich plunder, for scattered about they found embroidered
turbans, and bright swords and daggers, and golden bits
and bridles, and silken robes and jewels.

Thus sped the hosts of King Darius ; and the messenger came again in haste, as he sat on his golden throne
in Susa, while the nobles of Persia did obeisance before
him. Then the king said, 'Speak, O man, hast thou
brought good tidings that my slaves have chastised the
people of the strange city?' And the messenger
answered, saying, 'O king, the men of Athens have
slain thy mighty men with the sword, and burned thy
ships ; and few have come back of all the great army
which thou didst send against them.'

Great and fierce was the wrath of King Darius when
he heard the tidings, and he hastened to make ready
ships and men and horses, that he might go forth himself against the men of Athens. Then in every city of
the Persian land was heard the din as of men who have
a great work to do ; and the armourers wrought spears
and swords and shields, and in the harbours they built
countless ships to sail over the dark sea. But Zeus

hearkened not yet to the prayer of the king ; so Darius
died, and Xerxes his son sat upon his throne, and the
chief men of the Persians were gathered round him.
Then the king spake and said, ' Be ready, O Persians,
every one of you, for I will go forth with all my great
power, and make slaves of the men of Athens ; and so
may the gods do to me, and more also, if I burn not the
temples of their gods with fire, and bring not hither the
golden treasures which lie in the house of Phœbus
Apollo at Delphi.'

Then, with all his great hosts, King Xerxes set forth
from Susa, and his satraps and warriors and slaves
followed him, with a great multitude of every nation and
people ; and they crossed over from the land of Asia by
a bridge which was built over the sea of Hellê. Thus
they journeyed on in pomp and glory, and King Xerxes
thought that they had done great things when his host
slew Leonidas and three hundred men of Sparta who
guarded the passes of Thermopylæ. So his heart was
filled with pride, and he chose out the bravest of his
warriors, and charged the men of Thessaly to lead them
to Delphi and the temple of Phœbus Apollo.

Then was there great fear and terror in Delphi, for a
messenger came and said, ' The hosts of King Xerxes
are coming to slay the men of this land and take away
the treasures which lie in the house of King Apollo.' So
the Delphians went in great sorrow to the temple, and
bowed their heads to the earth and prayed, saying,
'Child of the light, who dwellest here in thy holy temple,
thieves and robbers are coming against us, and they are
purposed to take away thy sacred treasures ; tell us, then,
what we shall do, for at thy bidding we are ready to bury
them deep in the earth till the storm of war be overpast.'
Then came there a voice from the inmost shrine, but it

was not the voice of the priestess, for Phœbus Apollo himself came down to speak his will, and said, ' Move them not, men of Delphi. I will guard my holy place, and none shall lay hand on my sacred things.'

So they went away in gladness of heart, and made ready for the coming of the Persians ; and all the men of Delphi left the city, saving only sixty men and the prophet Akêratos, and these sat down before the steps of the temple. In silence they waited till the Persians should come, and they marvelled at the great stillness on the earth and in the heaven. There was not a cloud in the sky, and the two peaks of Parnassos glistened in the blazing sunshine. Not a breath lifted the green leaves of the sacred laurels, not a bird sang in the breathless air. Presently, as he turned round to look, the prophet saw the sacred weapons of Phœbus, which no mortal man might touch, lying on the temple steps ; and he said to the sixty men who tarried with him, ' Lo, now will Phœbus fight for his holy temple, for his own hand hath made ready the weapons for the battle.'

Soon in the deep valley and along the bank of the Kastalian stream were seen the hosts of the Persians, as they came on with their long spears flashing in the bright sunshine. Far away the men of Delphi saw the blaze of their burnished armour, and heard the tramp of their warhorses. Onward they came, and they said one to another, ' The gods have fought for us, and the prize is won already. See, yonder is the home of Phœbus, and none remain of the men of Delphi to do battle for his holy temple.'

Still the sun shone without a cloud in the sky, and no breeze broke the stillness of the laurel groves. Still glistened the sacred arms as they lay on the steps of the temple, and the opened doors showed the golden treasures which were stored up within. There lay the throne of Midas, and the golden lion of Crœsus. There lay the mighty mixing bowl, all of pure gold, which at the bidding of Crœsus was wrought by the Samian Theodoros. There lay all the rich gifts which the men of Hellas had offered up to win the favour of the lord Apollo.

Then the leaders of the Persians stretched forth their hands, as though all these things were given up to them by the god who had forsaken his people; but even as they came near to his holy ground, the lightning flashed forth, and the crash of the thunder was heard in the blue heaven, and the dark cloud fell on the peaks of Parnassos. Then, like the roar of a raging torrent, burst forth the mighty wind. Down from the steeps of the Delphian hill thundered the huge rocks, and trees uptorn from their roots were hurled on the hosts of the barbarians. Louder and fiercer grew the din; and cries and shoutings were heard from the Alean chapel, for the virgin Athênê fought against the men of Xerxes. Smitten by the fiery lightnings, they fell on the quaking earth, when suddenly there was heard a sound more fierce and terrible, and two cliffs were hurled down from the mountain-top. Underneath this huge mass the mightiest of the Persians lay still in the sleep of death; and all who yet lived fled with quaking hearts and trembling steps from the great wrath of the lord Apollo.

So fought the god for his holy temple; and when from their hiding places the men of Delphi saw that the Persians fled, then from caves and thickets they poured forth to slay them; and they smote them as sheep are slain before the altar of sacrifice, for even the bravest of their warriors lifted not their arm against them. Long time they followed after them in hot haste; and among them were seen two giant forms, clothed in bright armour, smiting down the hosts of the **enemy.** Then they knew that Phylakos and Autonoös, the **heroes of** the place, had come forth to aid them, and they smote the Persians more fiercely till the going down of the **sun.**

So the fight was ended ; and the stars came forth in **the** cloudless sky, and the laurel groves were stirred **by** the soft evening breeze. With songs of high thanks-giving the men of Delphi drew near to the temple, and they saw that Phœbus had placed again within his shrine **the sacred** arms which no mortal **man** may handle. Then was there rich spoil gathered, and the holy place of Apollo shone with gifts of gold and silver, which the men of Delphi offered in gladness of heart for all the great things which he had done for them. And in every house of the Delphians were seen robes and turbans rich **with** gold and silver and embroidery. On their walls hung spears and shields and swords and daggers, which the Persians bore when they came to Delphi.

So in after days they told **their** children the wondrous tale how Phœbus Apollo smote down the hosts of Xerxes; and they showed them the spoils which they took by the aid of the bright heroes, and the two rocks, lying **on** the holy ground before his shrine, which Phœbus tore **from** the peaks of Parnassos in the day of his great vengeance.

THE STORY OF ARÍON.

LONG time ago, in the great city of Corinth, there lived a man whose name was Aríon, and he made beautiful music on a golden harp, which all the people flocked to listen to. Men and women, boys and girls, all came to hear Aríon play and sing ; and when his songs were ended they gave him money, and Aríon became a rich man. When he had lived for a long time in the house of Periandros, who was called the tyrant [174] of Corinth, he thought that he would like to see some new places which he had never seen before. So he went into a ship and asked the sailors to take him to Sicily and Italy ; and they sailed over the blue sea a long way for many days and weeks, and came to many towns, where Aríon played and sang and got more money, till at last he came to Taras. There. he stayed a long time, because it was a rich and beautiful city, and all the people who came to hear him gave him plenty of money.

By and by Aríon thought that he had enough, and he began to wish to see Corinth and his friend Periandros once more. So he went down to the beach, and said that he wanted a ship to take him back to Corinth, and that he would only go with Corinthians, because he thought the men of Corinth better than the men of any other place. Just then there was drawn up on the beach a ship which had come from Corinth, and the sailors told him that they were Corinthians, and would take him home again. So Aríon promised to go with them, and he sent down his harp and all his boxes full of fine clothes and gold and silver, to be put on board the ship.

And when the sailors saw the boxes, and felt how heavy they were, they said to each other, 'What a rich man he must be! would it not be pleasant to have only a little of all this money which has been given to Arion for playing on a harp?'

Then on the next day Arion came down to the shore, and went into the ship. It was a beautiful day; there was scarcely a cloud in the sky, and there was a fresh breeze just strong enough to fill the sails and move the ship gently through the water. The waves danced and shone like gold in the bright sunshine, while the ship tossed up the white foam as she sailed merrily on towards Corinth. So they went on many days, and Arion sat at the head of the ship to see how it cut through the water; and as they passed one place after another, he thought that they would soon reach Corinth. But the sailors in the ship were wicked men. They had seen the large boxes full of money which Arion had brought with him into the ship, and now they made up their mind to kill him and take his gold and silver. So one day while he was sitting at the bow of the ship, and looking down on the dark blue sea, three or four of the sailors came up to him and said that they were going to kill him. Now Arion knew that they said this because they wanted his money; so he promised to give them all that he had if they would spare his life. But they would not. Then he asked them to let him play once more on his harp, and sing one of the songs which he loved the best, and he said that when it was finished he would leap into the sea. When they had given him leave to do this, Arion put on a beautiful dress, and took his harp in his hand, and stood up on the deck of the ship to sing. And as he sang, the sailors began to feel sorry that they were going to kill him, because they would have no more of

his sweet music when he was dead.   But when they
thought of all the gold and silver which Aríon was taking
to Corinth, they made up their minds that they would
not let him live ; and Aríon took one last look at the
bright and sunny sky, and then he leaped into the sea,
and the sailors saw him no more.

So the ship sailed on merrily over the dark water, just
as though it were not carrying so many wicked men to
Corinth.   But Aríon was not drowned in the sea, for a
great fish called a dolphin was swimming by the ship
when Aríon leaped over ; and it caught him on its back
and swam away with him towards Corinth much faster
than the ship could sail in which the wicked sailors were.
On and on the great fish swam, cutting through the foam
of the sea which was tossed up over Aríon ; and by and
by he saw at a distance the high cliffs and peaks which
he knew were the cliffs and peaks above Corinth.   So
presently the fish came close to the shore and left
Aríon on the beach, and swam away again into the
deep sea.

Aríon was cold and tired with being so long in the
water, and he could hardly crawl up into the city as far
as the house where Periandros the tyrant lived.   At last
he reached the house, and was taken into the great hall
where Periandros was sitting.   And when he saw Aríon,
Periandros rose up, and came to meet him, and said,
'Why, Aríon, what is all this?   Your clothes are dripping
with water ; I thought you were coming to Corinth from
Sicily in a ship, but you look more as if you had been in
the sea than in a ship : did you swim here through the
water?'   Then Aríon told him all the story ; how he
had left Taras in a ship with Corinthian men whom he
had hired to bring him home, and how they had tried
to kill him that they might take his money, and how the

dolphin had brought him to the shore when they made him leap from the ship into the sea. But Periandros did not believe the story, and he said to Arîon, 'You cannot make me think that this strange tale is true : who **ever** swam on a dolphin's back before?'[175] So he told his servants to give Arîon all that he wanted, but not to let him go until the ship in which he had left Taras came to Corinth.

Two days afterwards, Arîon was standing by the side of Periandros, and looking out over the sea : and presently he saw the white sails of a ship which was sailing into the harbour with a gentle breeze from the west. As it came nearer and nearer, Arîon thought that it looked very like his own ship, until at last he was able to see from the colours on its prow that it was the very ship in which he had been sailing. Then he said to Periandros, 'See, they are come at last, and now go and send for these sailors, and see whether I have not told you the truth.' So Periandros sent down fifty soldiers with **swords** and spears and shields, to bring up all the sailors from the ship.

Now the ship was sailing in merrily towards the shore, **and** the soft west wind filled out its white sails as it cut through the water. And as they looked on the beautiful land to which they were coming, they thought of all the things which they should be able to buy with Arîon's gold and silver ; and how they would do nothing but eat and drink and be merry, as soon as they got out of the ship. So when they came to the beach, they let down the sails, and lowered the masts, and threw out ropes from the stern to fasten the ship to the shore. But they never thought that the fifty soldiers whose spears and shields were shining gaily in the sunshine had been sent on purpose to take them ; and they could not make out why it was that, as soon as they came out from the ship upon the dry land, the soldiers said that they must all go as quickly as **they** could to the house of Periandros. Ten of the soldiers stayed behind to guard the ship, while the rest led the sailors to the palace. When they were brought before him, Periandros spoke to them kindly, and asked them from what place they had come ; **and the** sailors said that they had come from Italy, from the great city of Taras. Then Periandros said, 'If **you** have come from Italy, perhaps you can tell me something about my friend Arion. A long time ago he left Corinth, and said that he was going to Sicily and Italy ; and I cannot think why he should be away so long, for if the people have given him as much money for his music as they did here, he must now be a very rich man.' Then the sailors said, 'Yes, we can tell you all about Arion. We left him quite safe at Taras, where every one wanted to hear him sing; but he said that he should not come to Corinth, until they had given him more gold and silver and made him a richer man.' Just as they were telling this lie, **the door of** the room was opened, and Arion himself walked in ; and Periandros **turned** round to the sailors, and said, 'See, here is the man whom you left quite safe and well at Taras. How dare you tell me so great a lie? Now I know that Arion has told me the truth, and that you wished to kill him, and made him leap into the sea ; but the dolphin caught him as he fell, and brought him here on its back. And now listen to me. Of all Arion's gold and silver you shall have none ; everything that was his you shall give back to him; and I shall take away your ship, and everything in it which belongs to you, because you wished to rob and kill Arion.' Then the soldiers came, and turned these wicked sailors into the street, and drove them on, calling to the people to come and see the men who had sought to murder Arion. And all came out of their houses, and hooted at the sailors as they passed by, until they were ready to sink down with fear and shame.

So Periandros took their ship, and gave back to Arion all his gold and silver, and—what he loved better than his riches—his golden harp. And every one came to hear the wonderful tale of Arion and the dolphin ; and Arion made a large statue out of stone to look like a man on a dolphin's back, and placed it on Cape Tainaron, that the people might never forget how the dolphin saved Arion when he was made to leap into the sea.

----o----

THE BATTLE OF THE FROGS AND THE MICE.[176]

THIRSTY mouse, who had just escaped from a weasel, was drinking from a pool of water, when a croaking frog saw him, and said, 'Stranger, whence hast thou come to our shore, and who is thy father ? Tell me the truth, and deceive me not, for if thou deservest it, I will lead thee to my house and give thee rich and beautiful gifts. My name is Puffcheek, and I rule over the frogs who dwell in this lake, and I see that thou too art an excellent prince and a brave warrior. So make haste, and tell me to what race thou dost belong.'

Then the mouse answered him and said, 'Friend, why dost thou ask me of my race ? It is known to all the gods, and to men, and to all the birds of heaven. My name is Crumbfilcher, and I am the son of the great-hearted Breadgnawer, and my mother is Lickmill, the daughter of king Hamnibbler. I was born in a hovel, and fed on figs and nuts and on all manner of good things. But how can we be friends? We are not at all like each other. You frogs live in the water; we feed on whatever is eaten by man. No dainty escapes my eye, whether it be bread, or cake, or ham, or new-made cheese, or rich dishes prepared for feasts. As to war, I have never dreaded its din, but, going straight into it, have taken my place among the foremost warriors.[177] Nor do I fear men, although they have large bodies; for at night I can bite a finger or nibble a heel without waking the sleeper from his pleasant slumber. But there are two things which I dread greatly—a mouse-trap and a hawk; but worse than these are the weasels, for they can catch us in our holes. What then am I to do? for I cannot eat the cabbages, radishes, and pumpkins, which furnish food to the race of frogs.'

Then Puffcheek answered with a smile, ' My friend, thou art dainty enough, but we have fine things to show on the dry land and in the marsh, for the son of Kronos has given us the power to dwell on land or in the water as it may please us. If thou wouldest see these things, it is soon done. Get on my back and hold on well, so that thou mayest reach my house with a cheerful heart.' So he turned his back to the mouse, who sprang lightly on it and put his arms round his soft neck. Much pleased he was at first to swim on the back of Puffcheek, while the haven was near; but when he got out into midwater, he began to weep and to curse his useless sorrow. He tore his hair, and drew his feet tightly round the frog's stomach. His heart beat wildly, and he wished himself well on shore, as he uttered a pitiful cry and spread out his tail on the water, moving it about like an oar. Then

in the bitterness of his grief he said, 'Surely it was not
thus the bull carried the beautiful Europa on his back
over the sea to Crete ; surely——' But before he could
say more, a snake, of which frogs and mice alike are afraid,
lifted up his head straight above the water. Down dived
Puffcheek, when he saw the snake, never thinking that
he had left the mouse to die. The frog was safe at the
bottom of the marsh, but the mouse fell on his back and
screamed terribly. Many times he sank and many times
he came up again, kicking hard ; but there was no hope.
The hair on his skin was soaked with wet and weighed
him down, and with his last breath he cried, 'Puffcheek,
thou shalt not escape for thy treachery. On the land **I**
could have beaten thee in boxing, wrestling, or running ;
but thou hast beguiled me into the water, where I
can do nothing. The eye of justice sees thee, and
thou shalt pay a fearful penalty to the great army of
the mice.'

So the Crumbfilcher died ; but Lickplatter saw him as
he sat on the soft bank, and uttering a sharp cry, went to
tell the mice. Then was there great wrath among them,
and messengers were sent to bid all come in the morning
to the house of Breadgnawer, the father of the luckless
Crumbfilcher, whose body could not even be buried, because it was floating in the middle of the pond. So they
came at dawn, and then Breadgnawer, rising in grief and
rage, said, ' Friends, I may be the only one whom the
frogs have sorely injured ; but we all live but a poor life,
and I am in sad plight, for I have lost three sons. The
first was slain by a hateful weasel who caught him outside his hole. The next one cruel men brought to his
death by a newfangled device of wood, which they call a
trap ; and now my darling Crumbfilcher has been choked

in the waters.   Come and let us arm ourselves for the war
and go forth to do battle.'

So they put on each his armour.   For greaves around
their legs they used the beans on which they fed at night,
and their breastplates they made cunningly out of the
skin of a dead weasel.   For spears they carried skewers,
and the shell of a nut for a helmet.   So they stood in
battle array, and the frogs, when they heard of it, rose
from the water and summoned a council in a corner of
the pond.   As they wondered what might be the cause
of these things, there came a messenger from the mice,
who declared war against them and said, 'Ye frogs, the
mice bid you arm yourselves and come forth to the battle,
for they have seen Crumbfilcher, whom your king Puffcheek drowned, floating dead on the water.'   Then the
valiant frogs feared exceedingly, and blamed the deed of
Puffcheek; but the king said, 'Friends, I did not kill the
mouse **or see him** die; of course he **was** drowned while
he amused himself in the pond by trying to swim like a
frog, and the wretches now bring a charge against me
who am wholly guiltless.   But come, let us take counsel
how we may destroy these mice ; and this, I think, is the
best plan.   Let us arm ourselves and take our stand where
the bank is steepest, and when they come charging against
us, let us seize their helmets and drag them down into
the pond.   Thus we shall drown them all and set up a
trophy for our victory.'   So they put on each his armour.
They covered their legs with mallow leaves, and carried
radish leaves for shields, and rushes for spears, and snail-
shells for helmets.   Thus they stood in array on the
high bank, brandishing their spears and shouting for
the battle.

But Zeus summoned the gods to the starry heaven, and,
pointing to the hosts of the frogs and mice, mighty as the

armies of the Kentaurs or the giants, he asked who would aid each side as it might be hard pressed in the strife; and **he** said to Athênê, 'Daughter, thou wilt go surely to the aid of the mice, for they are always running about thy shrine, and delight in the fat and the morsels which they pick from the sacrifices.'

But Athênê said to the son of Kronos, 'Father, I go not to help the mice, for they have done me grievous mischief, spoiling the garlands and the lamps for the sake of the oil. Nay, I have greater cause for anger, for they have eaten out the robe which I wove from fine thread, and made holes in it; and the man who mended it charges a high price, and, worse still, I borrowed the stuff of which I wove it, and now I cannot pay it back. Yet neither will I aid the frogs, for they are not in their right senses. A little while ago, I came back tired from war and wanting sleep; but they never let me close my eyes with their clatter, and I lay sleepless with a headache till the cock crew in the morning. But, O ye gods, let us aid neither side, lest we be wounded with their swords or spears, for they are sharp and strong, even against gods; but let us take our sport by watching the strife in safety out of heaven.' [178]

Then the gods did as Athênê bade them, and went all into one place; and the gnats, with their great trumpets, gave the signal for the battle, and Zeus thundered out of the sky because of the woes that were coming. Mighty were the deeds which were done on both sides, and the earth and the pond were reddened with the blood of the slain. So, as the fight went on, Crumbstealer slew Garliceater before he came to land; **and** Mudwalker, seeing it, threw at him a clod of earth, and, hitting him on the forehead, almost blinded him. Then, **in** his fury, Crumbstealer seized a great stone, and crushed the leg of the frog, so that he fell on his back in the dust. Then Breadgnawer wounded Puffcheek in the foot, and made him limp into the water.

But among the mice was a young hero, with whom none could be matched for boldness and strength, and his name was Bitstealer. On the bank of the pond he stood alone, and vowed a vow to destroy the whole race of the frogs. And the vow would have been accomplished, for his might was great indeed, had not the son of Kronos pitied the frogs in their misery, and charged Pallas Athênê and Arês to drive Bitstealer from the battle. But Arês made answer and said, 'O Zeus, neither Athênê nor Arês alone can save the frogs from death. Let us all go and help them;[179] and do thou, son of Kronos, wield thy mighty weapon with which thou didst slay the Titans, and Kapaneus, and Enkelados, and the wild race of the giants, for thus only can the bravest of them be slain.' So spake Arês; and Zeus hurled his scathing thunderbolts, and the lightnings flashed from the sky, and Olympos shook with the earthquake. The frogs and mice heard and trembled; but the mice ceased not yet from the battle, and strove only the more to slay their enemies, until Zeus, in his pity, sent a new army to aid the frogs.

Suddenly they came on the mice, with mailed backs and crooked claws, with limping gait, with mouths like shears, and skins like potsherds. Their backs were hard and horny, their arms were long and lean, and their eyes were in their breasts. They had eight feet and two heads, and no hands. Men call them crabs. With their mouths they bit the tails and feet and hands of the mice, and broke their spears, and great terror came on all the mice, so that they turned and fled. Thus the battle was ended, and the sun went down.[180]

:

THE TREASURES OF RHAMPSINITOS.

HERE was once a king of Egypt who was called Rhampsinitos. He was very rich and very greedy. He tried to get as much money as he could from his people; but the more that he had, the more he wanted. His house was full of gold and silver; and his servants every day brought him more, until he was puzzled to know where he should put it. For a long time he thought how he might hide it, for he could hardly rest by day or sleep by night for fear that thieves might come and take away some of his riches. At last he sent for a mason and told him to build a great and strong room, which should have no windows and only a single door, fastened with huge iron bars and with strong bolts and locks. So the room was built in a corner of the palace, and the outer wall faced the road-way. When the house was finished, Rhampsinitos carried all his silver and gold secretly into it; and the whole room was filled with his riches. There were jars full of gold round the walls, and others which were full of diamonds, and pearls, and rubies, and jaspers; and in the middle of the room there was a great heap of coins, which shone so bright that they almost made that dismal place look cheerful. Then King Rhampsinitos thought himself a happier man, and he went to sleep more soundly, because he fancied that now no one would be able to steal his money.

Not long after this the old mason who had built the treasure-house fell ill, and he called his two sons to his bedside, and said to them, 'I am so weak and ill that I know I shall soon die · but I do not wish to leave you

without telling you the secret of the house where king
Rhampsinitos has hoarded up his money. I have little
to give you myself, for the king tried to make me work
hard and to give me as little as he could for all my
trouble. But I know a way in which you may get money
when you are in need of it. The king does not know
that I have placed a mark on one of the stones in the
wall of his treasure-house on the side which faces the
road. This stone can be easily taken out and put
back again by two men, or even by one, and his money
can be taken without moving the bolts or touching the
locks.'

Soon after he had told them this secret the old mason
died; and not long afterwards his two sons began to
think about the treasures of king Rhampsinitos, for the
money which the old mason left them was soon wasted
in eating and drinking with their friends. But they did
not care, for they knew that when they wanted it they
could get plenty of money from the treasures of king
Rhampsinitos. So one night, when the moon was shining
high up in the sky, they went very softly to the house
where the money was hid; and after looking about for a
little while, they found the stone, and they put it aside,
and went into the room. They were afraid to stay there
long; but they filled their clothes with as much gold and
silver as they could carry, and when they had put back
the stone carefully, they went home and showed their
mother all the money which they had stolen from the
king. The next night they went again; and for many
nights they kept on going, till at last king Rhampsinitos
began to think that some of the heaps of money were
smaller than they used to be; and every day when he
went into the treasure house, he looked at the heaps, and
rubbed his eyes, and looked at them again, for he could

not make out how it was that they seemed to grow smaller and smaller. And he said, 'This is very odd: what can it be that takes away my money? The locks of the treasure-house are not touched, and the bolts and bars have not been moved; and still my heaps of gold and silver seem every day to become smaller than they were.' Then he thought that perhaps it might be his own fancy, until he put a heap of coins on purpose in one part of the room: and very soon these were taken away. Then he knew that some thief had found out a way to come in without unlocking the door. But king Rhampsinitos did not care much about it, for he said, 'I think I know how to catch the thief who comes to steal my money.' So he got a large trap which was big enough to hold a man's leg, and put it in the treasure-house.

In a day or two after this, the sons of the old mason came again, and the younger one went in first, and presently stepped into the trap. His leg was terribly hurt, but he did not scream or make any noise, because he was afraid that king Rhampsinitos might hear him. Then he called to his brother who was standing outside, and showed him how he was caught in the trap, and that he could not get his leg out of it; and he said, ' Make haste, brother, and cut off my head, and carry it away. You must do this; for if you do not, the king will come and see who I am, and then he will have your head cut off as well as mine.'

His brother was very sorry, but there seemed to be no help for it. So he cut off his head and took it home with him; and when king Rhampsinitos came in the morning to look at his gold and silver, he started back and held up his hands in great wonder; for he saw that **two** men had come in and that one had carried away the dead man's head, and he knew that there was some one else still alive who might come and rob him of his money. Then he thought of a way to find him out, and he told his servants to take the body out of the trap and hang it up on a wall, and ordered the soldiers to watch, and if they saw any one crying or weeping near it, to take him and bring him before the king.

Now when the mason's elder son got home, he was obliged to tell his mother that his brother had been caught in the trap, and that he had cut off his head and brought it away with him ; and his mother was very sorry and very angry too, and she said that he must go and get the body and bury it along with the head. And she was still more angry when in the morning the soldiers hung the body of her son high up on the wall ; and she called her elder son, and said to him that she would go and tell king Rhampsinitos all that had been done, unless he went and brought his brother's body to her. At first her son was greatly troubled and could not think what to do ; but presently he started up from his seat, and went out, and got five or six asses, and on their backs he placed large leather sacks full of wine, which he had bought with the money of king Rhampsinitos. Then he drove the asses by the wall on which his brother's body was hung up ; and when he came near the soldiers who were guarding it, he loosened the string which was round the mouth of two or three of the sacks, and the wine began to trickle down upon the ground. Then he cried out with a loud voice for all the guards to hear, and tore his hair, and ran about the road as if he did not know which sack to tie up first. Quickly the soldiers came up, and there was such a pushing as was never seen before. Instead of helping him to tie up the leather bottles, they ran for cups to catch up the wine

as it streamed out on the ground, and they drank it up
as fast as their cups were filled. Then the mason's son
began to scold them, and pretended to be dreadfully
angry ; but the soldiers tried to coax and soothe him,
until at last he drove his asses off the road, and began
to put the sacks right again.

Then the guards came round him, and began to talk
and laugh with him ; and by and by he gave them one
of the bottles of wine to drink. But they said that they
would not drink it unless he drank some of it with them.
So they poured the wine out into the cups, and they
drank and made merry together. Then he gave them
another bottle, and another and another, till all the
soldiers fell down on the ground fast asleep. They had
been so long drinking and laughing together, that it was
now night, and it was so dark that nobody could see
what he was doing. Then the mason's son went softly
to the wall and took down his brother's body which was
hanging on it, and afterwards he went to all the soldiers
one by one, and shaved off the whiskers and beard from
one side of their faces ; and then he returned home to
his mother and gave her the body of his brother.

When the morning came, the soldiers woke up from
their heavy sleep. They felt very dull and stupid, but
when they looked at the wall they saw that there was no
dead body hanging on it ; and when they looked at each
other, they knew what a trick the mason's son had played
them. They were dreadfully angry and terribly afraid ;
but there was no help except to go and tell the king.
As they went, a crowd of people gathered round them,
and every one shouted with laughter to see the soldiers
who had half their whiskers and beards shaved off. But
when king Rhampsinitos heard what the mason's son
had done, he was quite furious, and he said ; 'What can

I do to find out the man who has done these very wicked and very clever things?'

So he sent a herald all through the country, and told him to say with a loud voice that the king would not punish the man who had stolen his money, but would give him his daughter for a wife, if he would only tell him how he had got into his treasure-house. Then the son of the old mason came and told Rhampsinitos all the story, and the king looked at him earnestly, and said : ' I believe that the Egyptians are cleverer than all other men ; but you are cleverer than all the Egyptians.'

NOTES.

Note 1, *page* 4.

This tale is in the Homeric hymn combined with the myth of the Pythian Apollo. It is obvious that we have in this hymn two poems, not one; and, indeed, no attempt has been made to cement the two together. The second hymn, which narrates his wanderings, follows abruptly, at the 180th line, the close of the first, which guarantees his permanent abode in Delos. See Mure's Critical History of the Language and Literature of Ancient Greece, vol. ii. p. 327. It may be remarked that the way in which Lêtô addresses the island of Delos is an instance of the degree in which things inanimate were invested with life, though not with human personality. So in the Hesiodic Theogony (129, &c.), the poet speaks of the 'long hills,' as springing from the union of Ouranos and Gaia, without losing the consciousness that he is speaking of hills, not of persons. The amount of direct personification in Greek mythology is by no means so extensive as has sometimes been supposed. Compare Grote, History of Greece, vol. i. p. 2, with Max Müller, Comparative Mythology, Chips from a German Workshop, ii. 66.

Note 2, *page* 5.

Here, as with the island of Delos in the tale of the Delian Apollo, Telphûsa, although she can feel and express anger, is not the nymph of the fountain, but the fountain itself.

Note 3, *page* 6.

As with the myth of Endymiôn, the cattle of the sun receive more than one local habitation. In the adventures of Odysseus they are localised in the island of Thrinakia. See Tale LII.

Note 4, *page* 9.

It might perhaps be rash to infer the later date of this legend merely from the high moral tone with which it concludes. The greater antiquity of the Delian legend would be proved by the fact that it speaks of the earlier festival at Delos as still in its glory. But these words of exhortation to the Cretan priests show conclusively the object for which the oracles were set up; and the length of time during which they retained their influence is a sufficient guarantee that, on the whole, that purpose was faithfully kept in view.

A friendly critic in the Home and Foreign Review (April 1863) objects that the legend is thus made the vehicle of a moral teaching which it does not even 'adumbrate.' The charge of Apollo to his priests was, in his judgment, confined to taking care of his temple, and not suffering its credit or revenue to decline. This is, doubtless, in part the meaning of the command: but the question is whether the keeping up the credit of the temple does not in itself involve a higher morality. The point of paramount importance is to ascertain (if this be possible) on what foundation the authority of the Delphic oracle in particular was raised. It exercised for many centuries an enormous influence, and it acquired an almost exceptional reputation for truthfulness. It is impossible to believe that the people so trusted it on any other ground than that, in whatever degree, the oracle maintained the general principles of fair dealing, honesty, and justice. If its power had rested wholly or mainly on ambiguous or equivocal answers (which, however, were returned chiefly to political inquirers), the reputation of the oracle would not long have been maintained.

But the words of the command leave, after all, little room for doubt. The priests were to abstain 'from every vain word or deed, and from the wanton insolence which is the custom or usage of mortal men.' It is hard indeed to think that the expression—

$$\mathring{\eta}\acute{\epsilon}\ \tau\iota\ \tau\eta\mathring{\upsilon}\sigma\iota o\nu\ \mathring{\epsilon}\pi o s\ \mathring{\epsilon}\sigma\sigma\epsilon\tau\alpha\iota\ \mathring{\eta}\acute{\epsilon}\ \tau\iota\ \mathring{\epsilon}\rho\gamma o\nu,$$

means only that they were to 'play no tricks with the strangers.' It enjoins a definite course of speech and action—a course which is emphatically contrasted with the ordinary conduct of mankind. There is nothing unfair in saying, that the 'vain word or deed' of the Homeric hymn may be explained by like expressions which are common to the writers of the Old Testament.

Note [5], *page* **10.**

The expression, δσσε δέ οἱ πυρὶ λαμπετόωντι ἐΐκτην, belongs, in Iliad i. 104, to Agamemnon. But it may be pardonable to take any legitimate opportunity of impressing on the mind of a child the forms of thought or of expression with which one day he must become familiar in the reading of Homer. The words applied to Apollo himself, ὁ δ' ἤϊε νυκτὶ ἐοικώς, appear scarcely to harmonize with the idea of his youth, which has been made to stand out most prominently in the tale.

Note [6], *page* 10.

The drawing of the bow may serve to familiarise a child with one of the many minute descriptions which the Homeric poets delight to give and to repeat, of what we should consider the most ordinary acts and the least calling for special detail—

> **νευρὴν** μὲν μαζῷ πέλασεν, τόξῳ δὲ σίδηρον ·
> αὐτὰρ ἐπεὶ δὴ κυκλοτερὲς μέγα τόξον ἔτεινεν,
> λίγξε βιός, νευρὴ δὲ μέγ' ἴαχεν, ἆλτο δ' ὀϊστὸς
> ὀξυβελής, καθ' ὅμιλον ἐπιπτέσθαι μενεαίνων.

Note [7], *page* **12.**

This popular notion is mentioned by Pausanias, to whom the sight of the stone was a sufficient proof of the truth of the history.

ἡ δὲ πλησίον μὲν πέτρα καὶ κρημνός ἐστιν, οὐδὲν παρόντι σχῆμα παρεχόμενος γυναικός, οὔτε ἄλλως οὔτε πενθούσης · εἰ δέ γε πορρωτέρω γένοιο, δεδακρυμένην δόξεις ὁρᾶν καὶ κατηφῆ γυναῖκα.—lib. xxi. 5.

Like most other legends, the tale of Niobê is told with a great variety of detail, chiefly in her genealogy and the number of her children. To the poets the myth furnished matter rather of illustration than narration, as to Sophocles, Electra 150, Antigonê 822, in which latter passage he places the scene of her woes on the Lydian hill; whereas the mount Sipylos, on which she wept herself to death, is in Iliad xxiv. 616, near the banks of the Achelôos. As if to show still further the many forms in which a myth may be treated, so long as its main characteristics are preserved, the Homeric poet makes Achilleus use the tale of Niobê to induce him to feast in the midst of his sorrow for Hektor.

Note [8], *page* 13.

In mythical speech Daphnê, Eôs, and Iolê expressed the same idea. All these were said to come back in the evening to greet the sun who had journeyed companionless through the hot hours of the day. In the Odyssey v. 390, &c., Eôs closes, as well as ushers in, the day.

In this legend, as I have related it, Daphnê is not changed bodily into a plant; and more than one reviewer has fastened on this version a charge of needlessly thrusting in a purely modern sentiment. By one writer it is spoken of as a piece of Euemerism; by another it is denounced as degrading the myth from a genuine to an artificial state. The Greek legend, it is insisted, knew no such poetical subterfuge, and simply changed Daphnê into a laurel and Narkissos into a flower.

The charge of introducing modern sentiment, whether in translating Greek poetry or relating Greek legends, is one which, if established, involves a complete condemnation of the tale so told or the poem so translated. But in the instance of Daphnê, the reviewers have curiously inverted the real history of the legend. There is no need to lay any stress on the many versions under which a large proportion of these myths have been handed down. A glance at the article 'Daphnê' in Dr. Smith's Dictionary of Greek and Roman Biography and Mythology would have shown that the legend of the actual metamorphosis was not a favourite one with the Greek mythographers. The version that when Daphnê was being chased by Apollo, Gê opened the earth to receive her and created the laurel tree to console Apollo, is on this point conclusive; but if any doubt still remained on the comparatively modern introduction of the metamorphosis, it would be set at rest by the evidence furnished in the Vedic poems, which exhibit the myth in its original form as part of the common speech of the people. In them Indra himself slays Dahanâ, as the Sun-light kills the dawn. The myth, like that of Kephalos and Prokris, is thus resolved into its earliest elements. All later versions arose from a forgetfulness of its real origin, and from that tendency to localise myths which ran through the whole of Greek mythology.

'If we translate, or rather transliterate, *Dahanâ* into Greek, Daphnê stands before us, and her whole history is intelligible. Daphnê is "young and beautiful—Apollo loves her—she flies before him, and dies as he embraces her **with** his brilliant rays." Or, as another poet of the Veda (x. 189) expresses it, "The dawn comes near to him; she expires as soon as he begins to breathe—the mighty one irradiates the sky." Any one who has eyes to see and a heart to feel with **nature** like the poets of old, may still see Daphnê **and Apollo, the dawn** rushing and trembling through the **sky,** and fading away at the sudden approach of the bright **sun.** The metamorphosis of Daphnê into a laurel tree is a continuation of the myth **of** peculiarly Greek growth. Daphnê, in Greek, meant no longer the dawn, but it had become the name of the laurel. Hence the tree Daphnê was considered sacred to the lover of Daphnê, and Daphnê herself **was fabled to** have **been changed into a** tree when praying to her mother to protect her from **the violence of Apollo.'**— Max Müller, *Essay on Comparative Mythology, Chips from a German Workshop*, ii. **93.**

Note [9], page 15.

Virgil (Georgic iv. 323, &c.) seems to reject the idea of immortality here attributed to Aristaios by Pindar (Pyth. ix. 3).

Note [10], page 15.

Professor Max Müller (Essay on Comparative Mythology) regards this legend as a specimen of genuine mythological allegory, which, expressed in modern language, would be equivalent to saying, 'The town of Kyrênê in Thessaly sent a colony to Libya under the auspices of Apollo.' With this myth he mentions many more in which the mere substitution of a more matter-of-fact verb at once divests a tale of its miraculous appearance. If the present tale shows to how late a time such mythological expressions were prevalent, the whole class to which it belongs is valuable as determining the extent to which actual allegory entered into Greek mythology. Here, under strictly personal forms, an event is described which Mr Grote (History of Greece, vol. iv. p. 39) attributes to the middle of the seventh century B.C., 'so far as can be made out under much contradiction of statement.' The complete human personality of Kyrênê may be contrasted with the opposite way in which Pindar (Olymp. vii. 100, &c.) treats the legend of Rhodes. But the difference may be accounted for by the weaker personality of Hêlios as compared with that of Phœbus Apollo. The mythical idea of Hêlios still survived so far as to confine him to the local habitation of the sun. Phœbus, though still the lord of light, becomes a separate being, who may roam at will through the world. Hence there was not the same necessity to allegorise Rhodos, who, as wedded to Hêlios, still remains nothing more than an island.

> Βλάστεν ἐξ ἁλὸς ὑγρᾶς
> νᾶσος · ἔχει τέ μιν ὀ-
> ξειᾶν ὁ γενέθλιος ἀκτίνων πατήρ.

And, if the poet goes on to speak of her children, his expressions refer almost wholly to geographical divisions of the island.

Note [11], *page* 15.

Shelley's translation of this hymn is a marvel of power and beauty. It is also on the whole a remarkably faithful version ; and the vein of sly humour running through the poem is admirably preserved.

The analysis of this hymn seems to furnish a sufficient explanation of the comic air with which certain portions of the narrative are invested. Hermes is the wind, or air in motion, and the remembrance of the old myth, although not fully retained, was by no means wholly effaced. Under these conditions it was impossible that the result should be any other than what it is. Like the fire, which at its first kindling steps out with the strength of a horse from its prison, the wind may freshen to a gale before it be an hour old, and sweep before it the mighty clouds big with the rain that is to refresh the earth. Where it cannot throw down, it can penetrate. It pries unseen into holes and crannies, it sweeps round dark corners, it plunges into glens and caves ; and when the folk come out to see the mischief it has done, they hear its mocking laugh as it hastens on its way. These few phrases lay bare the whole framework of the Homeric legend, and account for the not ill-natured slyness and love of practical jokes which enter into the character of Hermes. The burlesque into which the adventures of Herakles easily pass arose from no intention of disparaging the hero's greatness; and Mr. Grote would appear to be mistaken when he says (Hist. of Greece, vol. i. p. 82) that the hymnographer concludes the song to Hermes ' with frankness unusual in speaking of a god.' Nor can we determine, from the mere existence of this comic element, the particular use for which these hymns were composed. Colone Mure (Crit. Hist. Gr. Lit. vol. ii. p. 317) has little hesitation in concluding 'from the discreditable and even ludicrous light in which the character and conduct of the deities are often exhibited in their text,' that many 'even of the earlier more genial among them' were composed, not for recitation in any religious solemnities, but 'for familiar occasions of festive conviviality, where the adventures of the popular objects of worship were made, like all other subjects, to contribute their share to the common fund of mirthful entertainment.' That they may have been so used, it is impossible to deny; but an equally strong argument against such exclusive use might be drawn from those graver passages, even in the Hymn to Hermes, which are scarcely surpassed for beauty and dignity even in the Lay of Dêmêtêr. Colonel Mure has summed up all the reasons against assigning the authorship of these hymns to the poets of the Iliad or the Odyssey; and these reasons are conclusive. Yet if the composition of the greater epics belongs to an age much earlier than that to which it is generally assigned, these hymns may well have been written at a time which, in the belief of Herodotos or Thucydides, was the age of Homer. But the question now raised is whether these are not older than the Iliad and Odyssey in the form in which we have them. See Mr. F. A. Paley's Introduction, Homer, Iliad, i.–xii.

These hymns, as Colonel Mure has well remarked, are epical lays, complete in themselves; and among their number he reckons the lay of Demodokos, recited in the Odyssey, as being 'in all essential respects an epic hymn to Vulcan.' His remark seems to militate against his own theory of the complete unity of the Odyssey.

Note [12], page 17.

Dr. Mommsen (Hist. of Rome, vol. i. p. 18) believes that 'the enigmatical Hellenic story of the stealing of the cattle of Hêlios' by Hermes 'is beyond doubt connected with the Roman legend about Cacus.' It is also connected with that of Herakles and Echidna in the Scythian tale; but the solution of the enigma is in all the same.

Note [13], page 17.

Mr. Grote, in his short analysis of this hymn, says of this incident that Hermes 'stole the cattle of Apollo in Pieria, dragging them

backwards to his cave in Arcadia ' (Hist. of Greece, vol. i. p. 80).
This is no necessary inference from the passage in the hymn (75, 76),
although Livy (i. 7) has accepted this clumsy addition in the story
of Cacus. The poet means apparently that he so varied the track
of the cattle that no one could know whence they had come or
whither they were going ; and so Shelley has understood it.

> ' Backward and forward drove he them astray,
>> So that the tracks which seemed before were aft.'   (xiii.)

This would accurately describe the action of wind, while the
other device would not.

Note 14, page 17.

The Hymn to Hermes (111) ascribes to him the gift of fire, thus
asserting more and less than Shelley in his translation—

> ' Mercury first found out for human weal
>> Tinder-box, matches, fire-arms, flint and steel.'   (xviii.)

The list should be brought down to the mere item of tinder-wood.
Mr. Kelly would refer this legend to the Sanskrit *chark*, in which
the fire is churned. See his 'Curiosities of Indo-European Folk-
lore.'

Note 15, page 17.

Hymn, 130. This line is unfortunately diluted by Shelley—

> ' His mind became aware
> Of all the joys which in religion are.'   (xxi.)

Note 16, page 18.

The flames fanned by the wind consume the sacrifice ; but the
wind, though hungry, cannot eat of it.

Note 17, page 22.

Hymn, 372-3. This seems by far the keenest piece of satire to
be found in the poem. The passage, in fact, lays down the great
principles of English law, that a criminal charge must be proved by
witnesses, and that prisoners are not to be threatened or coerced into
confession. It is a passage which might come from the poet of a

puople who met in Agora in the age of the Iliad, but could never have come from the Asiatic. It would be well for French justice if it might less frequently be said of the judge—

μηνύειν ἐκέλευεν ἀναγκαίης ὑπο πολλῆς.

Note [18], *page* 25.

The contrast in the tone of this passage (Hymn, 549) with the concluding lines of the Hymn to Apollo is manifest. See Note [4].

Note [19], *page* 25.

The Thriai are beings of the same type with the Graiai and the Gorgons.

Note [20], *page* 25.

Colonel Mure, who with Mr. Grote thinks that the oxen were dragged by their tails, holds that 'it is the supernatural element of the subject which alone gives point and seasoning to an otherwise palpable extravagance' (Crit. Hist. Gr. Lit. vol. ii. p. 339). His explanation apparently fails altogether to account for the character of the hymn. It may be true that 'Hermes, in his capacity of god, is gifted from the first moment of his existence with divine **power** and energy,' but so also is Apollo; and if, 'as a member of the Hellenic pantheon, he is subjected to the natural drawbacks of humanity, and, **by** consequence, at his birth to those of infancy,' so **also,** again, is Apollo. Nor does this help to explain why Hermes should go off to play, sing, and thieve, when but a few hours old. Colonel Mure believes that the 'spirit of the jest' lies in 'the obligation to perform, through the agency of his imbecile human personality, the mighty deeds' by which he seeks 'at once to assert his rank among his fellow-gods;' but he forgot that the real point to be explained is, why Hermes should have to do this rather than Apollo or Dionysos. It is characteristic of Colonel Mure's criticism to pronounce the making of the lyre 'an elegant expedient,' hit on by the poet, for 'accommodating the dispute (between Hermes and Apollo) on terms honourable to each party' (p. 343).

Note [21], *page* 26.

In the beautiful hymn, which contains the myth of the Sorrow of

X

Dêmêtêr, Colonel Mure, in his Critical History of the Language and Literature of Ancient Greece, vol. ii. p. 349, simply sees, 'under poetical disguise, the fundamental doctrine of the Eleusinian mysteries.' Believing that, under this disguise of human adventure, the hymn sets forth the vicissitudes of the natural year, the sowing and reappearance of seed, and the failure of vegetation during the winter, he pronounces the subject to be one 'but little adapted for poetical treatment.'

Mr. Grote, in his History of Greece, vol. i. p. 55, thinks that 'though we now read this hymn as pleasing poetry, to the Eleusinians, for whom it was composed, it was genuine and sacred history. They believed in the visit of Dêmêtêr to Eleusis, and in the mysteries as a revelation from her, as implicitly as they believed in her existence and power as a goddess.'

It is obvious that these two methods of regarding the legend are directly opposed to each other. According to Mr. Grote, the poet was regarding facts of history as conceived by the historic sense of an epical age: while, in Colonel Mure's judgment, he is consciously putting forth under concrete forms certain abstract physical truths. Probably by neither of these methods shall we arrive at the true meaning or the origin of the legend.

That the hymn was composed with a special reference to the mysteries of Eleusis, and that such points of detail as the substitution of barley meal with water and mint for the ordinary wine-cup represent actual ceremonies in those mysteries, cannot of course be denied. But the argument which from this would infer the directly mystical or allegorical character of the hymn would also bring us to the same conclusion with regard to the Hymn to Apollo, in which Colonel Mure discerns no such character. The labour of Lêtô in Delos is as capable of abstract physical interpretation as the stealing away of Persephonê; and, although not so obviously, the same method might be applied to the hymns in honour of Dionysos or Aphroditê.

It is also not less clear that in this hymn the poet is not inventing a myth, but applying it; and even if we could prove that to him it was only a physical allegory, it would not affect the question either of its origin or of its meaning before he came to handle it; and still less could it show that the subject was 'but little adapted for poetical treatment.' The truth is that such subjects appear unpoetical, because (and only in so far as) they come before us simply as generalised abstractions. But such a judgment would condemn perhaps the larger portion of the Greek mythology, and it would fall with the greatest force on those myths which we feel instinctively to be the most beautiful. It is even easier to reduce to such abstract propositions the legends of Endymiôn and Orpheus, of Kephalos and Prokris, than the tale of Dêmêtêr and Persephonê. Yet the beauty of those legends not only is unquestioned, but depends chiefly on this very fact, that they invest with life that which we have come to look upon as mere physical law. But the question of beauty is, perhaps, one on which controversy is useless ; and whether or how far the Hymn to Dêmêtêr appeals to human sympathy, or leaves an impression of deep poetical feeling and power, must be left to the judgment of its readers.

If, however, we believe with Mr. Grote, that this legend was regarded as genuine history, even in the sense in which we must hold the term to apply to an epical age, the hypothesis will not carry us any nearer to the knowledge of **its origin and** growth. We desire to know not whether the poet of the late **Homeric or** Hesiodic age looked on the sorrows of Dêmêtêr as an allegory or a history, but how the tale came into being, and how its local detail and colouring were gradually attached to it. Still we are not more justified in imputing to him a consciousness of allegorising, than in accusing him of the more direct scepticism which was the growth of an age still later. The poet believed in the truth of his words in a sense as real, though it may be not the same, as that in which we maintain the truth of facts which are historical to us. Nor need we hesitate to admit that he believed in the personal visit of Dêmêtêr to Eleusis, and her personal institution of the mysteries there celebrated. But if the very names employed preclude the idea (not of the personality, but) of the localising of these mythical beings, if it is clear that Dêmêtêr and Gaia could not originally have been limited to Eleusis or to Attica, we **have to see** in what sense the tale here told could be attributed to them **with a** strict conviction of its truth.

The question is one which can be answered only by an investigation into the earliest conditions of speech as expressive of the first movements of the human mind. In its earliest stage human language expressed simply the impressions received by the mind from outward things. In the absence of any standard of comparison, in the total want of any data for induction or analogy, it was inevitable that all phenomena should, to the men of those remote ages, appear invested with the same character of personality and conscious agency, and that abstract nouns, which imply previous generalisation, could not possibly exist. Their consciousness of the departure and return of light differed in no respect from the consciousness of their own sinking to sleep and their own awakening. There was, therefore, as much an attribution of personal agency to the lord of life and light who chased away the dark shadows, as there was the sensation of personality in themselves. In the absence of a standard of comparison, the sun felt and laboured not otherwise than men felt and toiled. In the absence of all grounds for analogy, the sun who rose to-day was a different being from the sun who yesterday died in the western waters. The massing of the evening clouds, through which his rays were tossed, was a real death struggle : the calm twilight was his motionless repose after death. The night toiled with the birth of the coming day ; and the new sun sprung into life only to bring death to his parent and to the dawn whom he loved, and after brief toil, not for himself but for men, to die at the return of the night from which he had been born.

The same conviction of a living presence was expressed even in the most minute details. The purple clouds of the morning were the cattle of the sun, whom the dawn sent forth to their pastures ; the glittering dew was the bride, whom unwillingly he slew in his fiery embrace. Modern science may show such convictions to be unreasonable ; but there is still that within us which answers to the mental condition which necessitated such thoughts and language. We do not look on the changes of day and night, of light and darkness, with the passionless equanimity which our philosophy requires; and he who from a mountain summit looks down in solitude on the long shadows as they creep over the earth, while the sun sinks down into the purple mists which deaden and enshroud his splendours, cannot well shake off the feeling that he is looking on the conscious struggle of departing life.

Not only, then, would such a mental state account for, and necessitate the birth of infinite forms of mythical speech, but it would also make them regard the same object in different ways, and with conflicting conceptions. The sun, who drove away the night, might be looked upon as the ever-renewed or never-dying one ; or the night, ever blotting out the glory to which it had given birth, might be regarded as invincible and eternal. The sun might be Endymiôn, gifted with everlasting youth, or Tithonos sunk into an endless old age. Thus one vast class of legends, **and,** among these, of legends even contradictory, can be traced back to the early language on the recurrence of day and night. A class, perhaps not less wide, grew out of the same mythical speech on the recurrence of the seasons, of frost and heat, of winter and summer, if indeed these are not mere amplifications and adaptations of the former class.

To one or other of these classes the manifest allegorical meanings discerned by Colonel Mure would indubitably assign the Hymn to Dêmêtêr. If *we* can extract such meanings from it, it only proves that the legend is the bequest of an earlier age, to whom the departure of summer was the actual stealing her away from the earth who was her mother, and that the poet believed in the human existence **of those** beings or powers which an earlier age could invest with life **without contracting them** to anthropomorphic conditions.

If it be urged that this hypothesis, while it accounts for certain myths or portions of myths, yet fails of explaining all, the fact may be admitted without acknowledging the force of an objection which would preclude the introduction of every science until the conclusions of that science were all demonstrable. That our inability to decipher certain portions of a manuscript is no valid reason for putting aside other portions which we can both read and understand, is Bishop Butler's well-known criterion for the interpretation of the prophetical books of the Old Testament. The same method is strictly applicable to the science **of** comparative mythology. We may not be able to explain every detail in the legends of Herakles and Orpheus, of Endymiôn and Dêmêtêr ; but if we can adequately explain most, or even some of them, while at the same time we exhibit a condition of thought through which the **human** mind must have passed, and of language expressing that thought **and** no other, we may await in full confidence the light which the further progress of the science must throw on myths, or details of myths, which at present we may be unable to interpret.

Thus, **then,** until we arrive at the scepticism or incredulity of later ages, **we** have **to uphold** the perfect sincerity and good faith of those who handed **down the** rich inheritance of mythical speech. They who **first** framed **this speech** spoke truthfully, because to them the **sun and** moon, the clouds and dew, were beings not less *personal* **than** themselves. They who spoke of Hêlios and Selênê, still more of Endymiôn, of Herakles, and of Orpheus, spoke not less truthfully, because to them these were beings not less *human* than themselves.

Nay, the degrees of this human personality serve to show the extent
to which the old mythical speech had retained or lost its meaning.
The poet has still a dim notion that Selênê is the moon, while
Artemis is born and lives in this lower world. Hêlios still surveys
all things on the earth from his throne in the high heaven, while
Orpheus dies on the banks of the Hebros, and Endymiôn sleeps on
the hill of Latmos. Zeus sometimes is the sky under which men
may take their sleep, but more often he dwells on the Thessalian hill,
while Phœbus Apollo has an earthly home in Delos, or Patara, or
Pythô.

Yet more, comparative mythology explains very much, if not all,
of the unattractive or even repulsive details of Greek legend which
led Pindar to lay down as a canon of mythological credibility—

'Εμοὶ δ' ἄπορα γαστρίμαρ-
γον μακάρων τιν' εἰπεῖν· ἀφίσταμαι.   *Olymp.* i. 82.

Mythical speech could take no heed of the after-consequences
which must ensue when the personality of physical phenomena was
translated into anthropomorphism. In the former, the sun kisses
the dew of the morning, and the morning loves the sun ; yet she is
faithless to him, because the dewdrops reflect each a different lover,
who is yet one and the same ; and finally, the sun kills the dew,
because he loves her. But in the words of a later age, Kephalos
loves Prokris, who, after being false to him, again wins his love,
and is then by him unintentionally killed. And when so brought
under anthropomorphic conditions, they must fall under the laws
which affect the mutual relations of mankind ; and if some myths,
or portions of them, still retain their former power and beauty,
others may not less become immoral or repulsive or unnatural.
Yet it is no light thing that we are enabled to acquit a series of
generations of a wilful demoralisation, which it is impossible to
explain by any reference to the mythical ages which preceded, or
the times of more logical speculation and inquiry which followed
them.

Note [22], *page* 26.

Hymn to Dêmêtêr, 12—

τοῦ καὶ ἀπὸ ῥίζης ἑκατὸν κάρα ἐξεπεφύκει,
κηώδει δ' ὀδμῇ πᾶς τ' οὐρανὸς εὐρὺς ὕπερθεν,
γαῖά τε πᾶσ' ἐγέλασσε, καὶ ἀλμυρὸν οἶδμα θαλάσσης.

Colonel Mure (Critical History, &c., ii. p. 353) condemns the

passage as a 'monstrous hyperbole.' Few perhaps will acquiesce
in a judgment which comes not unnaturally from one who shows
himself incapable of entering into the mind and language of a
mythical age. It may be of more interest to remark that, in the
context of the lines above quoted, the personality of Dêmêtêr is
divided, for the marvellous narcissus is placed as a bait for Persephonê by Gaia, the accomplice of King Polydegmôn. In mythical
speech Gaia and Dêmêtêr were one and the same; but in the
hymn the personality of Gaia is far more vague, standing to that
of Dêmêtêr in the relation of Phœbus Apollo or Herakles to Hêlios.
Again, Dêmêtêr is the ruling power, ordering or checking the
growth of things, while Gaia is the personified earth, out of whose
substance they spring—a relation similar to that of Poseidon, the
divine lord of the sea, to Nereus, the dweller in its waters.

Note [23], *page* 27.

This expression comes from a singularly beautiful **fragment of**
Stesichoros :—

> Ἀέλιος δ' Ὑπεριονίδας δέπας ἐσκατέβαινε
> χρύσεον, ὄφρα δί ὠκεανοῖο περάσας
> ἀφίκοιθ' ἱερᾶς ποτὶ βένθεα νυκτὸς ἐρεμνᾶς·
> ποτὶ ματέρα, κουριδίαν τ' ἄλοχον
> παῖδάς τε φίλους· ὁ δ' ἐς ἄλσος ἔβα
> δαφναῖσι κατάσκιον
> ποσσὶ πάϊς Διός.

Unfortunately, **it is** but a fragment. But it clearly describes the
parting of Hêlios, who descends into his golden cup, from the son
of Zeus, who goes away on foot to his thick laurel grove.

Beautiful as it is, the idea evidently does not belong to the earliest stage of mythical speech. We have advanced far beyond the
age which each night saw the sun die, when we come to the image
of a golden cup in which Hêlios visits his home at night, and is
gently carried to the place of his rising in the morning. The
trembling doubt of his reappearance has given way to a well-estab-
lished analogy, which has even produced a theory as to the means
of his transit from the west to the east. Hêlios also is here more
humanised than he is elsewhere; he returns to his wife and children,
even if we hesitate to decide whether the word Ὑπεριονίδας gives
him a parent Hyperion, or whether it is as strictly a synonym as

where Homer speaks of Ἠλέκτωο Ὑπερίων.   The latter is Colonel
Mure's view, and undoubtedly the assigning Hyperion as a father to
Hêlios is a later idea ; but it seems scarcely less certain that the
poet uses the **word as** a patronymic, for he speaks of his mother
as of his wife **and** children.   There is no need to lay a stress on the
patronymic form of the word, as there are more instances than one
of **such** forms, which cannot be so explained ; as Οὐρανίων and
Οὐρανίδης belonging to Οὐρανὸς, Ἐνδυμίων to Ἐνδύμα ; and even
the **long** penultima of the word **is** perhaps scarcely an adequate
reason for believing it to **be a** shortened form of Ὑπεριονίων.
Probably the patronymic form of what was really a mere synonym
gave rise to the myth that Hêlios was the son of Hyperion.

The names of most of the Greek months, which have the same
termination, follow in quantity the analogy of Ἐνδυμίων, Οὐρανίων.
If then Ὑπερίων be **not a shortened** form, it can only be classed
among the many departures from analogy in the formation **of words.**

Note [24], page 30.

The myth of Endymiôn has produced rather an idea **than a tale.**
It has little incident, and scarcely anything which might **entitle it to**
be regarded as epical history ; for the few adventures **ascribed to**
Endymiôn by Pausanias, viii. 1, have manifestly no connexion **with**
the **original** legend.   The visit of Selênê, followed by **an endless**
sleep, is in substance all **that poets** or antiquarians tell us **of ; and**
even this is related **by Pausanias** with so many variations **as to show**
that the myth, from its obvious solar character, **was** too stubborn to
be more than thinly disguised.   If Endymiôn heads an army or
dethrones a king, or if his tomb was shown in Elis, this is the mere
arbitrary and pointless fiction of a later age.   And thus, according
to the standard of judgment to which the epical age adhered, the
myth remains susceptible of any treatment which shall not violate
the essential **character of** the legend in the attributes whether of
Selênê or Endymiôn.   Doubtless Virgil, had he been so minded,
might have given to us on this subject a poem as exquisite as that
in which, with a beauty incomparably beyond that of all his other
works, he has told the tale of Orpheus and Eurydikê.   As it is,
Endymiôn sleeps, whether on the hill or in the cave of Latmos,
and Selênê comes to him : but so obvious is the mythical meaning,
that we seem to see throughout the greeting of the moon to the

dying sun. Looking at it by the light which philology and comparative mythology together have thrown upon it, we may think it incredible that any have held it to be an exoteric method of describing early astronomical researches. But it is scarcely less difficult to acquiesce in the criticism contained in the article on Endymiôn in the Dictionary of Greek and Roman Biography and Mythology, by Dr. Smith. We there read that 'the stories of the fair sleeper Endymiôn, the darling of Selênê, are unquestionably poetical fictions in which sleep is personified. His name and all his attributes confirm this opinion. Endymiôn signifies a being that gently comes **over** one : he is called a king, because he has power over all living creatures ; a shepherd, because (*sic*) he slumbers in the cool caves of Mount Latmos, that is, the mount of oblivion. Nothing can be more beautiful, lastly, than the notion that he is kissed by the soft rays of the moon.'

A method so arbitrary may extract almost any meaning from any myth. If it be meant that the sleep here personified is the sleep of man, the assertion rests on a very questionable, or, at least, a very forced etymology ; **and** the title of king **or** shepherd no more be**longs to the** mythical conception **than** does **his** tomb in Elis. **Yet** more, Endymiôn **is** not spoken of as **a** being who comes **over any** one **else, or as** having power over all living creatures, but as **one** who **cannot shake** off his own sleep, **a** sleep **so** profound that they **who are vexed in heart may well** envy it—

Ζαλωτὸς **μὲν ἐμὶν** ὁ **τὸν** ἄτροπον ὕπνον ἰαύων
'Ἐνδυμίων.　　　　　　　Theokritos, *Eidyll.* **iii.** 49.

Finally, after naming these points which are in no way inherent in the myth, the really essential part of the tale is introduced simply as a beautiful notion, the invention, perhaps, of some later poet.

But the sleep of Endymiôn is the sleep of the sun. He is the child of Aëthlios, nay, as we have seen in the analogous synonym of Hyperion, he is Aëthlios himself, labouring and toiling through his whole life ; and, more strictly still, he is the child of Protogeneia, the early dawn, who, when his fiery course is ended, dives down into the dark sea. The verb, whether as δύω in the later speech of Homer, or as ἐνδύω in the earlier mythical dialect, is expressive only of the downward plunge, and altogether fails of representing the slowly-penetrating and all-pervading power which we mean by sleep. It can hardly be questioned that ἐνδύμα ἡλίου was once the equivalent of ἡλίου δυσμαί, and that originally the sun ἐνέδυ πόντον, where Homer uses only the simple verb. Then from ἐνδύμα came Ἐνδυμίων, in a manner analogous to that of his other epithet Hyperion. The whole idea of Endymiôn, who is inseparable from the material sun, **is** different from that of the separate divinity of Phœbus Apollo, and stands to the latter in the relation of Gaia to Dêmêtêr, of Nereus to Poseidon, with many others which might be named.

Note [25], *page* 32.

The epithet of happy as applied to night may perhaps be thought **fairly** to represent the terms εὐφρόνη, and νὺξ φιλία and ἀμβροσίη of the Greek poets. Probably none of these are mere euphemisms, although the words may express conflicting notions. The last epithet owes its origin to that idea of night as the conqueror of the day, which has already come before us ; but probably even with Homer this idea of its eternity had been modified into **the** notion of sensuous enjoyment, as the nectar and ambrosia which nourished the gods may also lead us to suppose.

Note [26], *page* 33.
See No. LII.

Note [27], *page* 34.

Hic situs est Phaethon, currus auriga paterni,
Quem si non tenuit, magnis tamen excidit ausis.

Ovid. *Met.* ii. 327.

The Roman poet has in this instance kept much more closely than in many others to the spirit of Greek mythology. The personality of Phaethon arose solely from the disintegration of the original solar myth. As long as Phœbus, Phaethon, Lykios, Delios, Endymiôn, were with others simply names for the sun, there could be no separate personification of each. In the measure in which their real meaning was forgotten, the temptation to give to each name its own embodiment became more and more powerful ; and the process served at the same time to account for some phenomena which must in themselves be perplexing. It was natural to think that some one else must be sitting in the chariot and driving the horses of Hêlios, when the sun's light, instead of being beneficent, became hurtful or **deadly.** But Phaethon must still be of kin to Hêlios, and must **share, in** whatever measure, his glorious **attributes.** He may lack the strength, but not the brightness or the spirit of his father ; and that which would be the calm consciousness of power in the parent would become a rash and fiery ambition in the child. Phaethon thus stands to Hêlios in the relation of Patroklos to Achilleus **or of** Telemachos to Odysseus. So analysed, the myth does not lose its interest, but it ceases to be a mystery. In this aspect, it has been worked up into a poem of great power and beauty by Mr. Worsley ; and it is precisely this character which he has given to the bright son of Klymenê :—

> ' Noble in presence, though a cloud of grief
> Hung shadowy dark upon his brows ; all else
> Redundant with warm youth ; his radiant locks
> Fair as a girl's, when stealing shades embrown
> The wavy yellow, and the fine glint of gold,
> Like fire-dust, sparkles in her sun-lit hair ;
> The while, from underneath his brooding brows,
> Flashed eager expectation, mixed with pain
> **And wonder** and delight—a **surging sea,**
> **Phaethon by** the Sun's great portal stood.'
>
> *Poems and Translations.*

Note [28], page 37.

The groundwork of this tale is given in Homer (Iliad, i. 397-406). But the poet mentions no reason for the conspiracy, nor does he speak of any change as resulting from it in the government of Zeus. These additions are perhaps more in accordance with the varying conceptions of Zeus in the tragedies of Æschylus. In the Prometheus Bound he is the merciless taskmaster : elsewhere he is the just and equitable judge. If he spoke of the same being, some cause was necessary to produce the change ; and this passing hint in Homer may supply it. The complicity of Athênê here again calls for notice, as bringing her into direct conflict with the will of Zeus.

Note [29], page 38.

The translation of Semelê from Hades is mentioned by Pindar in the same beautiful ode which paints so forcibly the paradise of the good. Olymp. ii. 40.

Note [30], *page* 41.

The power of transformation at will, exercised by Phœbus Apollo as well as Dionysos, is embodied especially in Proteus, who in the familiar legends of the North appears as 'Farmer Weathersky.'

Note [31], *page* 44.

This **legend** represents Dionysos **in** a character which **bears a** striking contrast to the gravity and majesty attributed to him in the Homeric hymn. There the wine through which the vessel floats, and **the vine** which suddenly enwraps the sail-yards, attest his divinity to those who have made him a prisoner. For **a** further examination of the subject, see Grote, History of Greece, **vol. i.** pp. 38–50, where the later and more corrupt forms of Hellenic belief and worship are traced to Egyptian, Asiatic, and Thracian **influence.** The legend of Pentheus is chiefly valuable as showing, **along with** that of the Thracian Lykurgos, possibly also with that of Orpheus (Virgil, Georg. iv. 522), that the change was **not accom-**plished without a vehement opposition.

Note [32], *page* 44.

The king of the flaming fire. **His daughter** Korônis (who is the same as Danaê or Prokris) is here, like the Sanskrit **Ahalyâ,** represented as **the** daughter of the sun, because, in the words of **Kumârila,** she goes before him at his rising.

Note [33], *page* 45.

The story of Korônis is in all essential points the same as that of the Arcadian Kallisto (Paus. viii. 3 ; Apollod. iii. 8, 2). As in other legends, the real origin of the tale is seen at once in the almost transparent account of Apollodorus.

Note [34], *page* 47.

For the Cyclôpes of Homer, **see** XLIX. The influence of the Iamidai is described **by** Pindar as strictly a moral one :—

τιμῶντες ἀρετάς,
ἐς φανερὰν ὁδὸν ἔρχονται. *Olymp.* vi. 122.

Note [35], *page* 47.

These are, again, the horses which Zeus gave to Peleus, the Harits (χάριτες) of Vedic mythology.

Note [36], *page* 48.

This withholding of the gifts is the drought which follows when the summer sun journeys through an unclouded sky. The incident occurs again in the story of Hesionê, where Laomedon plays the part of Ixion.

Note [37], *page* 52.

Pind. Pyth. ii. 74.

Note [38], *page* 53.

This is one more among the many names which describe the wide-spreading light of the dawn—Europa, Eurydikê, Eurymedê, Euryphassa, &c.

Note [39], *page* 54.

To be tantalised is therefore only a phrase expressive of the disappointment of Orpheus when he turns to embrace Eurydikê, whom he recovers only to lose again. In the restoration of Pelops to life we see simply the power of the Kolchian Medeia, which she can exercise at her will; and thus is dispelled the moral horror which roused the special indignation of Pindar against this tale.

Note [40], *page* 55.

The punishment of Atê, like the strangling of the serpents by the infant Herakles, belongs to an earlier period than that in which the toils of Herakles were catalogued. As in the Iliad, Atê is here simply the spirit of mischief, whether foolish or obstinate (Homer, Il. i. 412, &c.); she assumes a very different form in the hands of Æschylus, as the avenging destiny which broods over a house until the expiation for blood is accomplished. In like manner the force of μοῖρα is intensified in later thought, until finally ἀνάγκη is exalted to absolute omnipotence. Eurip. Alkêstis, 968, &c.

Note [41], *page* 56.

I have not hesitated to introduce into the legend of Herakles the beautiful Apologue of the sophist Prodikos, preserved by Xenophon in his Memorabilia of Socrates, ii. 1, 21, &c. It is conceived in the very spirit of that mythical language which called the idea of Herakles into being, while it goes far towards refuting the groundless calumnies brought against the **Athenian sophists.** In his admirable defence of these public teachers, Mr. Grote (History of Greece, vol. viii. p. 516, &c.) has justly expressed his astonishment that any one can be found who discerns an equivocal meaning in a picture of such **pure and** unselfish virtue. If the Apologue of Prodikos has any **meaning,** it is that the object of virtue is not reputation, but the benefit of others ; not power and influence, **but** the answer of a good conscience.

Note [42], *page* 60.

The numbering of the labours of Herakles was the work of an **age** subsequent to that of the epic poets. The Homeric poetry knows **of** no such catalogue ; but from the idea of Herakles as toiling for others, and not for himself, such legends would be multiplied indefinitely ; **and the** ingenuity of a later time would, as in the epic cycle, be exercised in weaving them into a connected history.

Note [43], *page* 62.

The legend of **Herakles,** like every other legend of Greek mythology, exhibits the peculiar character of the Greek mind. His birth and death, together with the greater number of his labours, are **localised in** various parts of Greece ; but in no other sense can it be **asserted (as in Dr.** Smith's Dictionary of Greek and Roman **Bio**graphy and Mythology, art. 'Herakles,' vol. ii. p. 400 *b*) that the myth was developed on Greek soil. The opinion of Buttmann, **who** looks on Herakles simply as a poetical creation of the Greek **mind,** fails altogether to account for the points of resemblance between the Greek myth and that of other Aryan nations, while that of K. O. Müller, who deduces it from the consciousness of power innate in every man, leaves out of sight the essence of the tale,—the involuntary toil of one who is compelled to labour for a master weaker than himself. With a truer insight into the nature of the legend, Dr. Thirlwall (History of Greece, vol. i. ch. v.) perceived **the** connexion **between** the labours of Herakles and the course of **the sun ; but he** considers that the chief features of his life were borrowed from the Phœnician mythology. More recent research has only extended the ground of Dr. Thirlwall's judgment. The affinity of Greek with Eastern mythology remains; but the idea of borrowed wealth has been displaced by that of a common inheritance.

Note [44], *page* 62.

See page 155.

Note [45], *page* 64.

ἀλλ' ὅτε δὴ τρίτον ἦμαρ ἐϋπλόκαμος τέλεσ' ἠώς.   *Od.* v. 390.

Note [46], *page* 65.

This incident (Hesiod. Theog. 562) does not harmonise well with the Promethean tale as told by Æschylus. Mr. Grote has analysed the whole myth of Promêtheus with great care (History of Greece, part i. ch. iii.) But the main question to be determined is how far the picture given by Æschylus is his own invention, and whether he has 'really relinquished the antique simplicity of the story,' or restored it to its earlier form. As it stands, there can be no doubt that the idea of Æschylus (Prom. 440–507) is fundamentally opposed to the conception of the Hesiodic ages.

Note [47], *page* 66.

Hesiod. Theog. 590–616; Works and Days, 59–104. In the latter poem the office of Athênê is to teach Pandôra how to weave —a task more in accordance with her character than that of simply placing a veil upon her.

In the incident of the cask of evils, I have given the only version which would seem to be at all warranted by the words of Hesiod. It has, however, been contended that the shutting up of Hope within the cask from which the evils had been suffered to escape was a merciful alleviation, and not an aggravation of the misery of men— that the escape of Hope would have left men to utter despair, and that to prevent this Pandôra was commanded immediately to replace the lid—

αἰγιόχου βουλῆσι Διὸς νεφεληγερέτdο.

The genuineness of this line is, however, very doubtful. Plutarch quotes the passage without it; but it may further be remarked that the whole legend represents Zeus as inexorably hostile to men, and as unlikely to interfere at all in their behalf. In Mr. Grote's opinion, the point is one which does not admit of question.

'Pandôra does not (in Hesiod) *bring with her* the cask, as the common version of this story would have us suppose : the cask exists fast closed in the custody of Epimêtheus, or of man himself, and Pandôra commits the fatal treachery of removing the lid. The case is analogous to that of the closed bag of unfavourable winds which Æolus gives into the hands of Odysseus, and which the guilty companions of the latter force open, to the entire ruin of his hopes (Odyss. x. 19–50). The idea of the two casks on the threshold of Zeus, lying ready for dispensation—one full of evils, the other of benefits—is Homeric (Iliad xxiv. 527).

Δοιοὶ γάρ τε πίθοι κατακείαται ἐν Διὸς οὔδει, &c.

Plutarch assimilates to this the πίθος opened by Pandôra. Consolat. ad Apollon. c. vii. p. 105. The explanation here given of the Hesiodic passage relating to Hope is drawn from an able article in the Wiener Jahrbücher, vol. cix. (1845) p. 220, by Ritter ; a review of Schömann's translation of the Promêtheus of Æschylus. The diseases and evils are inoperative so long as they remain shut up in the cask ; the same mischief-making influence which lets them out to their calamitous work takes care that Hope shall still continue a powerless prisoner in the inside.' (History of Greece, part i. ch. iii.)

Note [48], *page* 69.

This is the version of the legend given by Æschylus, who clearly implies (Prom. 110) that the knowledge of fire was imparted to men for the first time by Promêtheus (cf. note 14). Among the many variations of this myth, the only one calling for special attention is that which makes Athênê the accomplice of Promêtheus in the theft of fire, and represents his tortures on Mount Caucasus as a punishment for his unlawful love for the virgin child of Zeus. This version implies that the love was returned ; and the union of Promêtheus and Athênê in this attempt to benefit mankind, against the will of Zeus, may throw some light on the original idea of the goddess, while it places a difficulty in the way of some modern theories.

Note [49], *page* 72.

On the extent to which human sacrifices prevailed in Greece within any historic or semi-historical period, see Grote, Hist. of

Greece, vol. ii. **p.** 170, &c. The origin of the practice may be traced either to **a** perverted notion of human duty, or to such etymological mistakes (whether wilful or not) as led to the institution of the Suttee sacrifice in India. Dictionary of Science, Literature, and Art, s. v. 'Suttee.'

Note ⁵⁰, page 73.

Apollodoros (iii. 8, 1) merely says that Lykaon was with his sons killed by the thunderbolt. Pausanias (viii. **2,** 1), **on** high religious and moral grounds, is firmly convinced **that** he was transformed into a wolf. The story, however, is simply a device to explain the origin and meaning of a name ; but the Greek explanations of mythical names are much more frequently wrong than right. **If the** original force of each word had been thoroughly remembered, the great fabric of their mythology could never have been built up. But the growth of precisely such tales **as those** into which they were expanded was inevitable, as soon as the meaning of the old names was either half understood or altogether forgotten. Under the former class stand Melantho and Melanthios, the children of Dolios **and** enemies of Odysseus. **But** the explanation became utterly **wrong when** the name of Iolê **was referred** to poison, and the epithet of Lykeios, applied to Apollo, was connected, like that of Lykaon, with wolves. Midway between **these two** classes stand **such** names as Odysseus **and** Œdipus, in which a faint link, still perceptible in the **spirit of the** tale, carries us to the old mythical phrase.

But such transformations, few as they are, seem **in** no way to be relics, as Mr. Gladstone contends, of original nature-worship among the Greeks (Homer and the Homeric Age, vol. ii. p. 412). Most of them are to be explained by referring to the language of the oldest Vedic hymns. The bull of Europa is the bull Indra, who is afterwards degraded into the Minotauros and other monsters. On these and on the frequently recurring dragons and serpents, enough has already been said. But there appears to be no attempt in **the** Homeric **poetry to** analyse accurately the characteristics of **beasts, and** to **frame tales** in illustration of them. **The** Battle of **the** Frogs and Mice (LXIII.) is a sharp satire, valuable as showing the estimate of a later age for what is called the supernatural mechanism of Homer ; and the fables of Æsop cannot be held to

Y

prove the existence of such stories during the age in which the Homeric poems were composed. Simonides of Amorgos, in his satirical portraiture of women, shows much the same power of discrimination with Æsop; but he simply uses the main features in brute character to point his sarcasm, without any attempt to depict brute life. The theory which traces all such indications in Greek poetry to an old nature-worship thus becomes utterly untenable. Such a supposition might possibly account for the sacredness of the sun's oxen in Thrinakia, but it cannot account for Hermes stealing them when he is but an hour old. Hence some little uncertainty is also thrown over Mr. Dasent's hypothesis of a primæval belief that 'men under certain conditions could take the shape of animals' (Norse Tales, cxix.) There is no doubt that such a belief prevailed long before the time of Herodotus; but if, as it would seem, there is no trace of it in the Homeric poems, it is at the least possible that the idea, with all its consequences of wehrwolves and loup-garous, may be traced to the same sort of mistake which connected the name of the Lykian sun-god with the destruction of wolves, and so gave rise to the fable of Lykaon. To this origin may perhaps be assigned the involuntary transformations to which so many of the personages in the Norse tales are subjected. But there still remains the genuine Beast epic of the North, which accurately describes the relations of brute animals with one another, and, in Mr. Dasent's words, 'is full of the liveliest traits of nature.' These tales Mr. Dasent traces not to nature-worship, but to 'that deep love of nature and close observation of the habits of animals which is only possible in an early and simple stage of society,' and he refers to similar stories in the Hindu Pantcha Tantra and the Hitopadesa. Hence we have to seek for the common origin of both; but the mere fact of their composition seems to be conclusive against the idea of nature-worship, which, of all forms of thought, would most completely blind the eyes and dull the minds of men to the real characters whether of men or beasts. Had Norsemen really worshipped bulls, bears, and wolves, they would never have written of them with an affectionate familiarity.

Note [51], *page* 75.

Professor Max Müller, in the passage (Comp. Myth. p. 12) where he shows the absurdity of supposing that Greeks sat down deliberately to concoct ridiculous legends, says that **this** myth of Deukalion and **Pyrrha** 'owes its origin to a mere pun on λáος and **λâas.**' (See also Grote, History of Greece, vol. i. p. 134; Pind. Ol. ix. 71.) But Delitzch, in his Commentary on Genesis, asserts **that,** 'according to the legend of the Macusi Indians in South America, the only man who survived the flood repeopled the earth **by** changing stones into men. According to that of the Tamanaks of Orinoko, it was a pair of human beings who cast behind them the fruit of a certain palm, and out of the kernels sprang men and women.' The chief suspicion about American native traditions arises from the possible intermeddling of Christian missionaries, who may have thought it to their interest to make out a correspondence of such legends with those of the Old World, and especially with the records of the Hebrew Scriptures. Hence Burton, in the volume which relates his visit to the Great Salt Lake City, does not hesitate to ascribe the alleged original belief of the North American Indians in a great Spirit, unseen but omnipotent, **to** the Jesuit missionaries, who first instilled the belief into them, and then asserted **that** the Indians had the belief before **their** arrival. But if the idea of such interference be rejected (and it is, very **possibly,** worth little), then the harmony of many of their legends **with those of the** Old **World** increases the marvel, if not the mystery, **which attaches to the diffusion** of Aryan mythology. The legend **on the** subject of women, which Mr. Hind, in his Labrador Explorations, says that he heard from wandering native tribes, presents the closest correspondence with that of Pandôra in Hesiod. If, then, these Labrador Indians did not learn it from Jesuit missionaries (and it seems highly improbable that they should so have learnt it, nor can **we** conceive the motive which could have led the Jesuits to impart this legend rather than others), then we must carry back these tales still further to a common source from which the mythology of the Aryan and the North American Indian may both have taken their rise. The agreement of many negro stories with European traditions still further complicates the problem. Dasent, Popular Tales from the Norse, p. xxxi. &c.

Note [52], *page* 75.

Nothing, it would seem, can be gained by attempts to prove that the legend of Deukalion is derived directly from the account

of the Noachian deluge as given in the Pentateuch.   It is impossible
to deny that essentially the two stories are the same; but so also
are the Babylonian and other legends on the same subject; and if
we resort to the supposition of conscious borrowing in this case, we
must take up the same hypothesis in every other—a labour before
which the stoutest would quail.   Further, we should have to determine first which is the oldest tale of the flood to be found in
what is called profane history; and this is a task for which at
present we appear scarcely to have sufficient materials.   It is of no
slight moment that the Egyptians, with whom the Hebrews are
represented as in earliest and closest intercourse, had no traditions
of a flood (Edinburgh Review, July 1862, p. 100), while the Babylonian and Hellenic tales bear a strong resemblance in many points
to the narrative in Genesis.   But we have no warrant for assuming
any intercourse between Jews and Greeks in or before the Hesiodic
age; and the legend of Deukalion was known to the author of the
Catalogue of Women, a poem which, if not written by Hesiod,
belongs certainly to his age, or to the age immediately succeeding.

> Ἤτοι γὰρ Λοκρὸς Λελέγων ἡγήσατο λαῶν,
> Τούς ῥά ποτε Κρονίδης Ζεύς, ἄφθιτα μήδεα εἰδώς,
> Λεκτοὺς ἐκ γαίης λᾶας πόρε Δευκαλίωνι.

Mr. Grote refers to conflicting accounts of the genealogy of Deukalion, as given by the Scholiast on Homer, on the authority both of
Hesiod and Akousilaos (History of Greece, part i. ch. v.).   It is
seemingly doubtful whether the story of Ogyges is earlier or later
than that of Deukalion.   It has certainly assumed more strictly the
form of a local legend; but Mr. Grote supposes it to refer to
Deukalion's deluge (Ibid. ch. xi. vol. i. p. 266).   As evidence of
an historical flood, these tales have as much and as little value as
the lay of Achilleus for determining the reality of the Trojan war.
In Deukalion's flood those who can reach the top of the hills
escape: the flood of Xisuthrus, in the Babylonian mythology,
spares all the pious (Niebuhr's Lectures on Ancient History, vol. i.
p. 18).   In the Hindu version, the flood is universal; but Manu,
the man, enters the ark with the seven sages, who remain with
him till it is landed on the peak called Naubandhana, so called from
the binding of the ship. (Story of Nala and Damayanti, Milman's
translation.)

The names occurring in the legend of Deukalion are significant. His own name suggests a comparison with that of Polydeukes, the glittering son of Leda. His father is Promêtheus, in whom we recognise (not, according to Mr. Kingsley, in his pleasant tale of the Water Babies, p. 286, the false system of deductive philosophers,) but) the same idea of piercing forethought, which comes out again in Athênê, Asklepios, and Iamos, the children or the kinsfolk of the sun-god Phœbus Apollo. His wife is Pyrrha, the red, a name which to the Greek mythographers expressed the colour of the earth, but which may rather belong to the class of names of which Phoinix, Iolê, Iolaos, Iokastê, are examples. Pyrrha, again, is the daughter of Epimêtheus, the passive receiver of impressions, and so passing into the receptive character of Dêmêtêr and Persephonê. Deukalion is, moreover, the father of Minos, who is connected with a large family of solar legends, running into the mythology of Argos, Megara, Thebes, and Athens.

Note [53], page 75.

In this legend, I must acknowledge my obligation to Mr. Freeman's poem of Poseidon and Athena.

Note [54], page 76.

' The sunbeams are my shafts, with which I kill
    Deceit, that loves the night and fears the day.
All men who do, or even imagine, ill
    Fly me.'   Shelley, *Hymn of Apollo.*

Note [55], page 77.

Sophokles (Œd. Col. 696, 709) seems to assign an equal value to both the gifts.

Note [56], page 78.

Ἀμβρόσιαι δ' ἄρα χαῖταί περρώσαντο ἄνακτος
κρατὸς ἀπ' ἀθανάτοιο.   Homer, *Il.* i. 529.

Note [57], page 79.

The ocean of Greek mythology, with its unbroken calm, has nothing to do with Thalassa, the rough and angry sea.

Note [53], *page* 81.

The poets of the Iliad and Odyssey mention but one Gorgon, and in their descriptions she retains no trace of beauty. It matters little whether the legends which speak of the change in her form are older than those poems or later. Both are equally true to the mythical phraseology from which all such tales were derived. The story which says that from her head sprang the winged horse Pegasos (another form of the Harits, χάριτες, or horses of Indra) is remarkable chiefly because it makes her also the mother of Chrysâôr, which occurs elsewhere simply as an epithet of Apollo (with the golden sword). Hesiod, Works and Days, 769.

Note [59], *page* 82.

Χρυσόπατρος, the child of the golden shower—a fitting name for the son of Danaê, Dahanâ, the Dawn.

Note [60], *page* 82.

The Lament of Danaê, by Simonides of Keos, exists only as a fragment. Mr. Isaac Williams has given a translation of it in his Christian Scholar, p. 181.

Note [61], *page* 83.

The name Polydektes is only another form of Polydegmôn; and it is under both these names that Hades steals away Persephonê (Hymn to Dêmêtêr, 9, 17). We have not far to go for the meaning. It is but the love of the night for the evening. In Homer Eôs ends as well as begins the day (Od. v. 390); and Danaê here represents the beautiful hues of twilight, which the darkness vainly strives to make its own. It is true that Hades wins the love of Persephonê; but Persephonê is the summer, whom the winter, another image of darkness, steals from the mourning earth, her mother. Thus the vain attempt of Polydektes to win the love of Danaê is a mere counterpart to that of Apollo when he seeks to embrace Daphnê.

Note [62], *page* 85.

Mr. Kingsley, in his Heroes, introduces a strong moral element into the tale, when he says that she lost her beauty for sinning 'a sin at which the sun hid his face.' **But** Medusa cannot **in any** sense be either morning, day, or evening; and hence the sun could not be said to see her deeds.

Note [63], *page* 85.

Not the **narrow strait to which** we confine the name, but the broad Hellespontos, **from which the** storm-tossed mariner might **see** the distant cairn on the grave of Achilleus. (Od. xxiv. 82.) See, further, Note [87].

Note [64], *page* 87.

The weapons **of all the** solar heroes—of Meleagros, Theseus, **Achilleus,** Sigurd, **Odysseus,** Rustem, Herakles, Philoktetes, are **all irresistible.**

Note [65], *page* 88.

The idea of age would be directly suggested wnenever the evening was regarded as the lingering survivor mourning for the departed glories of the **day.**

Note [66], *page* 88.

The departure of Perseus to the land of the Graiai may be resolved into the phrase, 'The sun has gone to the land of the twilight.'

Note [67], *page* 91.

This 'invisible cap' is worn by Athênê in Iliad v. 845, and is represented on the shield of Herakles (Asp. Herakl. 222).

Note [68], *page* 91.

It is scarcely necessary to refer to Mr. Kingsley's fine poem, in which he has made the episode of the Dragon as attractive as it can be made in hexameters which are really anapœstic.

Note [69], *page* 92.

The idea of a weighty and solid heaven would seem to be a much later conception than that of Ouranos, Varuna, who, spread over all things, looks down on the earth which he loves. The idea of the **brazen** firmament found no disfavour with Greek astronomers.

Note [70], *page* 93.

The pursuit of the Gorgons is the chase of Darkness after the bright sun, who just escapes its grasp as he enters into the peaceful morning sky, the Hyperborean gardens, where sorrow, strife, and death can never enter.

Note [71], *page* 94.
Note [22].

Note [72], *page* 95.

The celebrated oracle of Zeus Ammon, in the Libyan desert. The name was then referred to the sands by which the temple was surrounded, although it was only a Greek form of the Egyptian Amoun or Amen (Herod. ii. 42).

Note [73], *page* 98.

Diktys is made a fisherman, in the same way that Lykaon is turned into a wolf—to account for the name. The name points more probably to the root of δείκνυμι, and so is connected with the idea of light as revealing the secrets of darkness. Hence the brother of Polydektes would be a fitting friend for Danaê.

Note [74], *page* 101.

Achilleus also presides at games after his victory over Hektor— the reason in both cases being the same.

Note [75], *page* 102.

The man of sorrow comes naturally to Argos, when the bright hero, the sun of the land, has departed from it.

Note [76], *page* 102.

These are simply local legends, to account for certain cities and their buildings. Still the myths adhere to the old idea, for the builders come from Lykia, the land of light, which gives to Phœbus the name Lykêgenês, and they are the Cyclôpes, who sometimes forge the thunderbolts of Zeus beneath the burning mountain, and sometimes, as in the Odyssey, appear as (the mists and black clouds) the monstrous offspring of the sea-god Poseidon. Here, as elsewhere, we cannot infer from the silence of the Homeric poets that the latter is the older myth. Probably both may have come down together.

Note [77], *page* 103.

In the ordinary versions of this legend, Prokris is made to yield, as it would seem, almost immediately to the words of Kephalos, when he appears before her in disguise. The essential part of the tale is the identity of Kephalos under his several forms, while the time during which the change takes place is of little consequence. By lengthening the absence of Kephalos a difficulty is avoided which seems to rob the story of all its interest. Prokris may be inconstant, but the purity of the morning dew cannot be sullied ; and the variation, introduced for this purpose, maintains, rather than departs from, the original idea embodied in the tale.

Note [78], *page* 103.

The example of Nausikaâ, the daughter of the Phæakian king Alkinoös, would of itself show that the washing of linen was no unworthy task for a princess of the house of Erechtheus.

Note [79], *page* 103.

In the Hymn to Dêmêtêr, that goddess is first seen by the daughters of Keleos, king of Eleusis, when they come to draw water from the fountain.

Note [80], *page* 103.

Prokris and Hersê are, in fact, merely different forms of the same name. *Prush* and *prish* in Sanskrit means to sprinkle, chiefly with raindrops, and Bopp connects the word with the Latin *frigere*, and our *frost* ; while Hersê comes from the Sanskrit *vrish*, to sprinkle, and is seen again in the Latin *ros*, and Greek ὁρόσος. See also Max Müller, Comparative Mythology, p. 85.

Note [81], *page* 105.

If Eôs, or the morning, is represented here as the rival of the dew, in other legends, as in Daphnê (IV.), she appears as avoiding, rather than seeking, the love of the sun.

Note [82], *page* 109.

In the versions given by the collectors of mythical tales, Prokris appears before Kephalos disguised as a man, and under that form demands and receives his love. The legend is not found in Homer, or even in later **poets**; and **it is** obvious that this feature, which represents too truly the state of Greek society during the historical ages, must have been introduced into the tale at a very late date. The whole tone of feeling and expression throughout the Homeric poems is utterly alien to a sentiment which sprang up between the heroic age and the earliest period which may claim anything like an historical character.

Note [83], *page* 112.

Professor Müller has remarked (Comparative Mythology, **p.** 86), **that** the Greek myth of Kephalos was localised in Attica. The **first** meeting with Prokris takes place on the eastern promontory of **Hymettos** : a straight line drawn westwards from this **point would** touch the Leukadian cape whence Kephalos sinks to sleep in the sea.

Note [84], *page* 112.

Such expressions may perhaps be regarded as bringing into too great prominence a sentiment pre-eminently Christian. Undoubtedly the introduction of modern sentiment, of whatever kind, in the interpretation of Greek poetry or philosophy, is a danger which has not been avoided as carefully as it ought to be. Mr. Ruskin yields **to** the temptation **when** he says that Homer, **while telling of** the **death of** Polydeukes, still speaks instinctively of the earth as the giver **and sustainer of** life; and Mr. M. Arnold, in the **same** spirit, sees in the most trivial details and repetitions of Homer a uniform 'grand style,' which is the modern requisite for an epic poem. It must be admitted also that in this instance our modern sentiment **attaches** too great **a force to one or** two expressions in Greek poets, **and chiefly to the** beautiful passage of Pindar, **Olymp. ii. 100,** &c. **Yet in this exquisite** ode the poet seems **to rise above other poets** and moralists, not so much in the clearness with which he speaks of immediate retribution after death both to the evil and the good, **as** in the vivid colouring which he throws over the future joyous life **of the righteous.** If others **seldom get** beyond the negative freedom **from** tears **and labour,** he adds **the brightness of** a sun **which** never sets, and golden flowers **on** land **and water** fanned by the breeze which comes from the gentle ocean stream. Compared with this **warm** and glowing life, the shades of Herakles and Achilleus in the Odyssey dwell in a cold and cheerless paradise. But there can be little doubt that the feeling of Pindar is both older and more true. The conviction of immortality would, in the ages of strict mythical speech, be almost unconscious ; and the assumption of a happy immortality would be forced upon them by the necessities of their ordinary language.   It is precisely that conviction which would be weakened, and finally give way before the indifference and scepticism of later ages, and which perhaps we may be permitted to bring out more prominently in legends which clearly belong to the earliest mythological age.   It can scarcely be brought out more forcibly than in the speech of an Indian chieftain to Columbus, if we may only credit its authenticity.   See Washington Irving's Life of Columbus, book vii. ch. v.

Note [85], *page* 112.

In Minos Professor Max Müller recognises the Sanskrit Manu, a mortal Zeus (Lectures on Language, Series II. 457).

Note [86], *page* 115.

Skylla, according to one version, was changed into a fish, Nisos into an eagle.   This is one of the many involuntary transformations which occur in Greek mythology.   See, further, Note [59].

Note [87], *page* 118.

The notion which traced the name of Hellespont to the legend of Phrixos and Hellê is clearly the result of the same localising tendency which we have marked in the myth of Endymiôn, and which may be traced out in very many others.   In this instance it is not so easy to determine what wider fact has been localised.   There can be **no** doubt that if by the Hellespont Homer sometimes means **the** strait known by that name, there are other and more numerous passages in which he applies the name to the open sea.   **In** the former sense he speaks of it as ἀγάῤῥοος, in the latter as πλατὺς and ἀπείρων ; nor could the name πόντος have been given originally to a narrow strait.   But while we admit that the name which first described the whole Egean sea was afterwards limited to the **strait,** we may hesitate to propound or to maintain any theory as **to its** real origin.   If Hellê can be the name of no single person, **it** must in all probability be that of a people, and thus it seems sufficiently clear that the name marks an early position of the Helli, or Selli, and possibly points to some of their early migrations. But from what quarter this migration issued, and to what point it tended, are questions which cannot be answered with certainty. Mr. Gladstone (Homer and the Homeric Age, vol. i. p. 497, &c.) sees in this name, as in that of the river Sellêeis, conclusive proof of the Eastern origin of the Hellenic race, and the evidence of their passage from Asia into Europe. The subject of Hellenic ethnology will probably come out in clearer light at no distant day; but its difficulties will be removed or lessened rather by the patient toil of philological and ethnological research, than by theories which after all may turn out to rest on the accidental resemblance of words which could have had no relation to each other.

Phrixos was held to be the eponymos of Phrygia; the form *Phryxos* may have been adopted to suit the charge brought against him of spoiling the wheat by roasting it. (See Grote, History of Greece, vol. i. p. 170.)

Note [88], *page* 119.

The myth represents Phrixos as having sacrificed the ram to Zeus Phyxios. It is scarcely necessary to apologise for a variation which in no way affects the general character of the tale.

Note [89], *page* 125.

A hand-glass of steel, or other polished metal, sufficed for the needs of Greek and Roman maidens. The Hindoo women carry such mirrors attached by rings to their fingers. They are now of glass; but the fashion probably comes down from an earlier day.

Note [90], *page* 125.

Compare the beautiful description of the death of Alethe in Moore's Epicurean.

Note [91], *page* 125.

This is the legend which, stripped of every marvellous feature, is gravely taken by Herodotus, along with two other legends treated in the same way, as supplying connected causes for the great struggle between the Greeks and Persians in the generation immediately preceding his own. (Tale of the Great Persian War, pp. 3, 267.)

Note [92], *page* 128.

According to the version of Apollodoros (iii. 10, 7), Aithra was

brought by force from Athens to Troizen. The tale is a curious
complication of myths. Having related the story which made
Helen the daughter of Zeus and Nemesis, he goes on to tell how
Theseus stole Helen and brought her to Athens, and how Kastor
and Polydeukes, while Theseus was absent in Hades, took Athens
and brought away thence not only Helen but Aithra. It is easy to
see that they could only have been taken while Theseus was in the
kingdom of the dead.

Note 93, page 131.

'It was not without reason that Theseus was said to have given
rise to the proverb, *Another Herakles*; for not only is there a strong
resemblance between them in many particular features, but it also
seems clear that Theseus was to Attica what Herakles was to the
rest of Greece, and that his career likewise represents the events of
a period which cannot have been exactly measured by any human
life, and probably includes many centuries' (Thirlwall, Hist. of
Greece, vol. i. p. 130). It would have been still more true to say
that his life, like that of Theseus, Bellerophôn, Achilleus, Meleagros, and Odysseus, is but the sun's life of a day or the yearly life
of the seasons.

Note 94, page 135.

The wish to retain as much simplicity as possible for the character of Ariadnê furnished the reason for not adopting that version
which saves the consistency of Theseus by representing him as compelled by Dionysos to give up the daughter of Minos.

Note 95, page 136.

It cannot be necessary to refer to one of the most exquisite lyrical
poems in the English language, in which Shelley sings of the flight
of Arethusa from the heights of Erymanthos to the Ortygian shore,
where love wakens in her when life is ended. Only the constant
reading of the poems in which he dwells on Greek myths will reveal
the astonishing insight which Shelley, by the strength of his personal feeling, obtained into the true character of that mythology.

Note 96, page 138.

Σαφῶς Σιδηρῷ καὶ φέρουσα τοὔνομα. Mr. Grote considers the pun
unworthy of a dignified tragedy. In this instance, possibly, Sophokles may have interpreted the name rightly; it is otherwise with
his pun on the name of Ajax (Aj. 425).

Note [97], *page* 140.

In Homer, Tyrô becomes the wife of Kretheus. Mr. Grote thinks that the present version originated with Sophokles (History of Greece, vol. i. p. 148). As with many other legends, it is possible that several versions may have existed together without any attempt to reconcile their inconsistency.

Note [98], *page* 140.

This, as well as the more common version, is given by Pausanias (ix. 31, 6). However curious may be the reason which he gravely gives for thinking that the flower called the narcissus was known before the death of Narkissos, it is not surprising that his description of the love of Narkissos for his sister implies that modern Greek sentiment which mars the ordinary version of the tale of Kephalos and Prokris.

As in the tale of Daphnê, the rejection of the version which speaks of a metamorphosis involves no intrusion of strictly modern sentiment, although the reasons for rejecting it are not so conclusive as in the myth of Daphnê. But of the many forms in which the tale is told, one only relates the actual change of his body into the flower; another says that he killed himself, and that the plant sprang up from his blood, while the legend preserved by Pausanias states that he melted away into a well; and for his looking into the well more than one reason is given.

Note [99], *page* 141.

The character of this myth as a solar legend was not, and could not have been, present to the mind of Virgil, as he wrote his exquisite lines upon it in the fourth book of the Georgics, the only lines perhaps in which he exhibits true poetical power. But any one who reads them will easily see how his own appreciation of the myth has caused him to give almost every detail of the legend in harmony with its origin. Eurydikê is one of the many names of the dawn, on whose death, when stung by the serpent of night, Orpheus, the sun, descends to seek her in the regions below the earth, and brings her up behind himself in the morning, only to destroy her by his brightness when he turns to look upon her. The name of Orpheus we cannot explain from any similar names in Greek; but, as Professor Max Müller has shown (Essay on Comparative Mythology, p. 127), 'Orpheus is the same word as the Sanskrit Ribhu, or

Arbhu, which, though it is best known as the name of the three Ribhus, was used in the *Veda* as an epithet of Indra, and a name of *the sun*.'

The legend of Orpheus was localised in the country which we commonly mean when we speak of Thrace ; and Virgil sings of his death on the banks of the Hebrus. The name of Thessaly has been substituted, not by the licence which may be permitted in mythological detail, but because the common meaning attached to the word Thrace gives an entirely erroneous conception of the word as it occurs in Homer. We may not, perhaps, be able to determine in which Thrace the legend was first localised ; but it is quite certain that Homer by the term Θρῆϊξ did not mean to describe a man as belonging to the country watered by the Hebrus. When wishing to mark the latter, he uses the form Θρηΐκιος ; and even where he uses this form, there are only one or two instances where it must be taken as limited to this country, as in Iliad, xxiii. 230, where, when the flame of the pyre of Patroklos is extinguished, the winds go homewards, Θρηΐκιον κατὰ πόντον ; and again, when Samos, **Iliad, xii. 12, has the** same epithet. But the term Θρῆϊξ is in Homer strictly an adjective, **equivalent** to τρηχύς. Thamyris the Thracian, who is blinded by the **Muses** at Dorion, in the Pylian dominions of Nestor, is unquestionably a Greek. He is on his road from Oichalia, the abode of the Thessalian Eurytos, and **is** evidently going to take part in a contest of Rhapsodes or reciters of epic poetry. He is a Greek in tongue, which he could not have been if belonging to a country so completely beyond **the** bounds of the Hellenic world as the barbarian Thrace. In short, the inhabitants of all highland districts, whether of Arcadia, Ætolia, Thessaly, or any other, would to Homer be Thracians. In the tale, therefore, Orpheus is placed in some Hellenic Thrace, **as** more in harmony with the spirit of Greek legend. **For a more** complete examination of the subject the reader is referred **to Mr.** Gladstone's ' Homer and the Homeric Age,' vol. i. p. 158, **&c.**

In the legend of Kadmos and Europa the names themselves suggest speculations as to its origin. Niebuhr, while rejecting the existence of any historic Kadmos, receives the names as proof of a Phœnician settlement in Bœotia (Lectures on Ancient History, vol. i. p. 80). But, even if it could be proved that the words are strictly Semitic,

it would be rash to infer from this the fact of such a settlement.
The character of the myth is as clearly solar as is that of the legends
which speak of Endymiôn, or Eôs, or Prokris.

Note [102], *page* 156.

The legend of Bellerophôn exhibits points of resemblance to many
others. (See ' Tale of the Great Persian War,' p. 318, note 2.) It
is plain, however, that in its origin it belongs to the solar myths of
Herakles and Endymiôn and Meleagros. In its general character
(like the legend of Perseus and Andromeda, with a few others) it
approaches more to the spirit of Scandinavian and Teutonic mythology. Bellerophôn must be numbered with the mythic heroes of
the Volsung tale and the Nibelungen Lied, Sigmund, Sigurd, and
Baldr. In all, the original type, although still visible enough, is
more or less overlaid by details and incidents grouped around it by
the peculiar genius of the people amongst whom they have been
handed down. Max Müller, 'Chips from a German Workshop,' ii.
172.

Note [103], *page* 157.

That Homer knew of the death of Meleagros is evident from the
statement in the catalogue, Il. ii. 640. But our ignorance of the
way in which he might have related his death does not justify us in
regarding the versions given by the fabulists as post-Homeric. By
the evidence of language, the incident of the burning brand must
have been known long before the time of Homer, and is a relic of
the genuine solar legend, handed down in the common speech of
the people, yet, like so many other legends, neglected by the epic
poet because it did not suit his purpose to narrate it. It is most
unsafe to argue against the antiquity of a tale from the mere silence
of Homer. A few casual expressions give us hints of factions
amongst the gods—of conflicts between them and the giant Titans :
while an epithet is the chief evidence that even in the Homeric
theology Zeus was not the oldest of the rulers of heaven. But these
incidents involve the whole legend of Promêtheus ; yet of that legend
Homer says nothing. The truth is that the epic poet, naturally
enough, made use of those legends, or parts of legends, which he
found convenient, and amongst their many versions adopted that
which best fitted in with his design. Thus Tlêpolemos (see Tale
No. XLV.) tells of the vengeance which Herakles took upon

Laomedon, **but he** says little of **his** other exploits, and nothing of his loves or of his death.

In the present **tale** I have endeavoured to weave together the Homeric incidents, with what seems to be the older version, into one consistent whole.

Note [104], *page* 164.

Mr. Grote (Hist. of Greece, vol. ii. p. 320, &c.) has brought out very vividly the influence of the great festivals at Olympia and elsewhere in imparting to the various Hellenic tribes something like a national character.

Note [105], *page* 174.

The growth of an historical sense is strikingly shown in the eagerness with which Herodotos adopts the impudent forgeries of the Egyptian priests as the solution of a difficulty in the tale of Troy which he evidently regarded as insuperable. **All his love** for the Trojan legends, all his deep faith in a supernatural order of causation, cannot bring him to think that for ten long years a whole people chose to suffer the miseries of war rather than give up a woman whom they regarded as the cause of all their sufferings. This incredible folly is to him a sufficient justification for accepting the statement that Helen was not at Troy at all, but that she was detained in Egypt by order of the king (Herodotos, ii. 120). It must be noticed that in this instance Herodotos does not refuse to believe on account of any supernatural marvels, although even with regard to these his faith is not altogether uncriticising. **(See** ' Tale of the Persian War,' pp. 268, 276.) His unbelief of **the story here** rests **on the** analysis of human motives, **and he** is proof even against the statement that the Trojan senators wished to give her up, but that **her** great beauty made them abandon their purpose, **as** soon as she **came among them.** (Iliad, iii. 154, &c.) There **can** be no doubt **that so great a** change of sentiment would have been fatal even to **the** preservation of the Trojan legend, if it had not been defended by the safeguard **of** metre until it was committed to writing. The bulk of Vedic prose tradition is indeed greater than that of the Homeric poems; but the former was preserved orally, not only because there has never been a change of feeling regarding its statements, but because it has been specially entrusted to the keeping of a priestly caste. The Sagas of Northern Europe would be more a case in point; but the prose Njala of Iceland would never have survived for Mr. Dasent to edit, had it been handed down orally, and if the sentiment of a later day had come to discern any violent improbability or incongruity in the narrative.

Note [106], *page* 175.

The arrows of Philoktetes and the robe by which Medeia avenges herself on Iason come from Herakles or Hêlios, and are relics of the mythical phrases which described the fiery action of a vertical sun. The idea of the poisoned robe, which was fatal to Herakles himself, was suggested by his death-struggle with the blood-stained clouds of evening.

Note [107], *page* 176.

The variations in the tale of Paris and Œnônê are many in number. Those in which the present story departs from the ordinary version are suggested by Apollodorus and Lykophron ; and perhaps it may be said that there is nothing in Homer inconsistent with them. It is certainly not asserted that Paris had always been so worthless as he shows himself during the time of which the Iliad professes to give the history.

The lament of Œnônê has been versified by Professor Aytoun, in his volume of ' Lays of the Scottish Cavaliers ; ' but the poem of Mr. Tennyson had scarcely left room for another ; and the only justification of the present story is, perhaps, that it gives the whole legend, whereas Mr. Tennyson confines himself to the judgment of Paris and the mourning of Œnônê for his desertion.

Note [108], *page* 177.

χθόνα βάκ-
τροις ἐπικρούσαντας 'Ατρείδας δάκρυ μὴ κατασχεῖν.
Æschylus, *Agamemnon*, 200.

Note [109], *page* 179.
Homer, Iliad, ii. 308-329.

Note [110], *page* 180.

In the great trilogy of Æschylus nothing perhaps is more remarkable than the wonderful power with which he has united legends, not originally connected, into one harmonious whole. In the present tale, I have endeavoured to give some idea of that unity, which is founded quite as much on a profound theological conviction as on his own poetical instincts. Atê with him has lost her ancient character of mischievous folly (Note [49]), and is now the principle of divine vengeance, which, though late, never fails to bring home the sin of the transgressor, and which can never be appeased without a judicial expiation. That this is the one pervading **thought** and belief **in** the **whole** trilogy is plain (if other proof were **wanting),** **from** the fact that the poet has rejected every version which, by representing the sacrifice of Iphigeneia as not really accomplished, would convert the calamities of the house of Agamemnon into mere accidents not referable to a universal **moral law.**

Note [111], *page* 181.

The sign of the snake and the sparrows. Il. 300–331.

Note [112], *page* 182.

These are, in fact, the immortal Harits, who draw the car of Indra up the heaven.

Note [113], *page* 182.

This Dodôna is not the later and more widely known Dodôna of Epeiros. (Gladstone, 'Homer and the Homeric Age,' vol. i. p. 104; Iliad, **xvi.** 233.)

Note [114], *page* 183.

See p. l.

Note [115], *page* 184.

Il. xvii. 438–460.

Note [116], *page* 184.

Il. xviii. 117.

Note [117], *page* 185.

Il. xix. 137.

Note [118], *page* 185.

Il. xix. 409–423.

Note [119], ***page* 186.**

Il. xxiii. 185 ; xxiv. 20.

Note [120], *page* 187.

Il. xxiv. 512.

Note [121], *page* 187.

Il. xxii. 360. This passage furnishes conclusive evidence that the poets of the Iliad were well acquainted with many mythical tales which it formed no part of their object to recount.

Note [122], *page* 187.

Od. xxiv. 42.   Ζεὺς λαίλαπι παῦσεν.

Note [123], *page* 189.

The motives are so given, Homer, Iliad, xii. 310–328. It may be remarked that they attribute the wealth and power of the kings or chiefs to the voluntary action of the people. The Lykia of Homer was not, however, the birthplace of the great Lykian confederacy of later times. But see Freeman's ‘History of Federal Government,’ vol. i. p. 216, note 5.

Note [124], *page* 191.

The character of Apollo, as the lord of light, first won for him the names of Δήλιος and Λυκηγενής, and then localised him in Delos and Lykia. It is the same with Endymiôn and his Latmian cave, with Pyrrha the wife of Deukalion, and a host of others.

Note [125], *page* 193.

The name of Tithonos, the father of Memnôn, must have retained something of its mythical force for the Greek, when he spoke of Eôs as leaving his couch in the morning to bring back daylight to men. If, even when they thus spoke, they had lost the consciousness that Tithonos and Titan were the same, and that both were names for the sun, yet it is absurd to suppose that they thought or spoke of Eôs, the morning, as leaving the couch of a Trojan prince who was the son of Laomedon, and a brother of Priam. But, as Professor Max Müller has remarked (Comp. Mythology), because ‘Tithonos was a prince of Troy, his son, the Ethiopian Memnôn, had to take part in the Trojan war.’ His mythical character is again shown by the tears of ‘morning dew’ which his mother sheds on his death.

Note [126], *page* 194.

See the sentiment of Hektor (Iliad, xii. 243), adopted in no sceptical spirit by Epameinondas. It is curious to remark the totally different interpretations given by the same men of the same omens, if only their own circumstances are changed. A notable instance is furnished by Nikias and his soothsayers, in the case of the eclipse which sealed the death-warrant of the Athenian army before Syra-cuse. See Grote, History of Greece, vol. vii. p. 433.

Note [127], *page* 195.

On the light which this statement has been supposed to throw on the art of sculpture in the Homeric ages, see Thirlwall, History of Greece, vol. i. ch. vi. p. 233, &c.

Note [128], *page* 199.

This incident in the great epic of Homer brings out with special prominence the notions then held on the problem of man's free will and the Divine foreknowledge, or rather predestination. Hektor anticipates the destruction of Priam and his people as an absolute certainty, yet that knowledge does not interfere with his active energy, or with prayers for the aid of Athênê. He knows that present effort is his duty ; the issue he is content to leave with a power over which mortal man has no control. He can look forward to the time when his wife and child shall dwell as slaves in another land ; but the foreboding does not prevent him from doing all he can to defend them now. He gives in immediate action the only solution of the mysterious problem ; and this portion of the Iliad is therefore invested with a deeper pathos and a more genuine human feeling than any other.

Note [129], *page* 199.

The tales here selected from the Odyssey may perhaps impress upon the reader's mind its general character as a poem, of the sub-stantial unity of which there can be but little question. They profess to do no more than to represent faithfully those parts of the Odyssey from which they are taken ; nor will they be found to exhibit any departure from the original narrative in more than one or two unimportant points of detail. But special care has been taken not to fasten upon the poet any didactic aim further than his words may clearly justify us in so doing. This notion of secondary motives has found acceptance not only with Christian writers, but with Latin poets of the Augustan age. While the former have seen in the Odyssey an allegory setting forth the passage of the soul through the probation of life, and in the longing of Odysseus for Ithaka discover the yearning of his soul to reach its home in heaven, a writer like Horace will extract from the same poems a keen and systematic satire on vices which could not exist in an epical age,

and a complete philosophy which may vie with that of Chrysippos
or Krantor. By placing the line in which Horace expresses this
conviction on the title-page of his ' Homeric Studies,' Mr. Gladstone
affirms the substantial truth of the view taken by the Latin satirist.
But while it cannot be denied that moral lessons may be drawn from
any poem which treats of human deeds and human sufferings, we
shall have to note one or two instances in which the imputation of
such moral aim is contradicted by the express words of the epic
poet. In whatever way we may decide the question of the composition of the Homeric poems, there is no doubt that they were
written at a time when philosophical analysis was impracticable,
and when such didactic aims, even if they existed, would never
have been perceived by an audience such as that which alone must
have been gathered round the Homeric rhapsodists. Nor can the
ingenuity with which Mr. Gladstone and other writers have drawn
out such meanings overthrow the plain facts urged against such a
course by Mr. Grote, ' History of Greece,' vol. ii. p. 276, &c.

Note [130], *page* 200.

This is the conception of Odysseus as given by Homer. It cannot be denied that the proximity of wisdom to craft is betrayed
even in the Iliad, and that Odysseus can boast of having assassi-
nated a man with the most mean and cowardly stealthiness, without,
it would seem, the faintest idea of the greatness of his treachery.
But, on the whole, he exercises that legitimate influence, gained by
power of thought and readiness of words, which was the guarantee
of future Hellenic development, as its absence amongst Eastern
nations gave the assurance of their hopeless bondage. But the
character of Odysseus suffered during each succeeding generation,
and, along with that of most of the Homeric heroes, underwent a
miserable degradation, even in the hands of the best tragedians of
Greece. (See more particularly Gladstone's ' Homer and the
Homeric Age,' vol. iii. 590, &c.) It must, however, be admitted
that in Mr. Gladstone's eyes the contrast is heightened by his exag-
gerated estimate of the Homeric Achilleus and Helen, if not of
Odysseus and others.

Note [131], *page* 200.

Homer, Iliad, ii. 151–154. There is probably nothing in the
mythology of Northern Europe which answers to the Nostoi or
return of the heroes from Ilion. But the kinsfolk of Gunnar carry

on the strife in their own land. As soon as Brynhild or Helen is placed in another country, a foreign expedition is the result ; and the necessity of return would naturally furnish a subject of almost inexhaustible richness for an age in which all such tales were received as so much veritable history.

Note [132], *page* 200.

It would be absurd to depreciate the deep and honest love which during his whole absence Odysseus feels and expresses for his home, and which grows altogether more intense as that absence is prolonged. But a protest must be entered when it is asserted that by this deep human love the poet intended to signify the yearning of the soul for its home in heaven, and the course of the Christian warrior battling with fleshly temptations in his heavenward journey. The poet **had no** such didactic or theological aim ; and certainly Odysseus, **although** exhibiting a marvellous power of self-restraint **at all times** when such restraint was necessary, is no pattern of strict asceticism. This is evident not only in his determination to listen **to** the Seirens' **song** while he takes measures to counteract its dangers, and in his indulgence of his appetite when Hermes has provided him with a safeguard against all evil consequences, but still more in the conditions of his sojourn with Kirkê and Kalypso, even while he went forth daily to weep on the sea-shore overcome by his inexpressible yearning for his home.

Note [133], *page* 203.

The choric song in Mr. Tennyson's 'Lotos-eaters' gives a vivid picture of the feelings of men who have shared in the Lotos-eaters' feast. It is, however, a philosophical analysis ; and the single expression of Homer (βούλοντο νόστου λάθεσθαι) does not immediately suggest speculations on the end and purpose of human life, although it may leave room for them. In this episode the self-restraint of Odysseus is conspicuous ; but he was conscious of a great and pressing danger, and conscious also that he had no charm or antidote against it ; and at all such times his self-control and determined energy never failed him. Had Hermes been present now with some preservative, doubtless Odysseus would have been as curious to taste the fruit of the lotos, as he was ready to feast with Kirkê or listen to the Seirens' song.

Note [134], *page* 204.

See p. lii.

Note [135], *page* 205.

ἐν δὲ λιμὴν εὔορμος, ἵν' οὐ χρεὼ πείσματός ἐστιν,
οὔτ' εὐνὰς βαλέειν οὔτε πρυμνήσι ἀνάψαι.   *Odyssey*, ix. 137.

The charge brought against the epic and tragic poets of Greece,
that they fail of apprehending the features of natural scenery, and
that their descriptions express merely sensuous impressions, is, it
must be admitted, not without weight, although by writers like Mr.
Ruskin it has been pushed too far. Yet the description of the
Cyclop's island, of the Seirens' rocks, of the sea-shore in Phæakia,
with others, may be held in some measure to rebut this charge ; and
one or two quotations are here given, to show that the details of
which they speak are not a translator's invention.

Note [136], *page* 206.

A more decided picture is given (Odyssey, ix. 140, 141) of the fountain by the cave at the head of the harbour, and the poplar-trees
clustered round it.

Note [137], *page* 208.

It should, perhaps, be stated that the Cyclop's ingorance of
Agamemnon and the Achaian heroes is rather implied than expressed. Odysseus believes that the name of Agamemnon would at
least secure him from harm, and Polyphemos replies that he would
not spare him for any dread even of the wrath of Zeus himself.
(Odyssey, ix. 278, &c.)

Note [138], *page* 209.

The actual comparison which the poet here makes of the intended
club of Polyphemos is to the mast of a twenty-oared ship. But it
is more curious to note the special number of waggons, namely,
two-and-twenty, which he says would be wanted in order to move
the stone which the hands of the giant placed with ease against the
mouth of the cave. In an elaborate discussion (Studies on Homer,
vol. iii. p. 425, &c.), Mr. Gladstone maintains that the sense of
number in Homer was very vague and imperfect. It is scarcely
necessary to specify examples to prove the universal tendency to
use round numbers in order to leave the impression of magnitude
or multiplicity. The catalogue alone in the second book of the
Iliad, would yield an indefinite number of examples. But such

instances scarcely explain the two-and-twenty waggons, which is
not a round number. And, **however** readily we may admit the
indistinct notion of number **shown** by Homer, we cannot forget
that the existence of words for specific numbers in hundreds, and
even in thousands, is a sufficient proof that at least before his time
the process of enumeration, of which they are the result, had **been**
gone through. **The** vague and imperfect sense of the poet **can**
hardly then be considered a condition imposed on him by necessity.

Note [139], page 215.

The impression, on reading of the deception of Polyphemos by
the name Οὖτις, **would** naturally be that the poet intended a pun.
This natural **view has not** been allowed to **pass** unquestioned, and
the opinion **has** been advanced, that, if a pun **be** intended, it **lies**
probably in **the** contrast of οὖτις as a mere play of sound against
μῆτις, from which Odysseus has his common epithet of πολύμητις,
'the man of much counsel.' The illustration seems far-fetched,
and the notion itself of little force. There is, however, one line
which appears decisive as to the meaning of the poet. When the
other Cyclôpes are asking Polyphemos what ails him, they put the
question in the usual form—

ἦ μή τις σ' αὐτὸν κτείνει δόλῳ ἠὲ βίηφιν ;

Odyssey, ix. 406.

Now, if the poet had purposed to contrast οὖτις with μῆτις, 'counsel,' the reply of Polyphemos must have been conveyed in a corresponding form ; **whereas,** instead of δόλῳ ἠδὲ βίηφιν, his answer is—

ὦ φίλοι οὖτίς με κτείνει δόλῳ ΟΤΔΕ βίηφιν.

The negative is clumsy, as making Polyphemos state an untruth ;
but in no other way would the idea of the nonentity of Odysseus
have been impressed on the giants outside the cave, and the use of
ἠδὲ would have invested οὖτις with as much substance as Odysseus
himself.

Note [140], page 216.

The tale of Kirkê and her magic art appears to tell decisively
against any special didactic aim in the Odyssey. We may admit
the temptation to regard the friends of Odysseus as victims of
gluttony, and Odysseus himself as saved by his power of self-control. But the words are ambiguous, and we may take them in a
sense which is not warranted by the poem. Whenever a present

or future hurt may be avoided, or an advantage gained, his self-restraint is never wanting; but, failing this, he nowhere shows himself unwilling to gratify either his appetites or his passions. In the same way the three-and-twenty men may be considered gluttons; but their transformation is attributed directly to the drugs mingled with the food.

ἀνέμισγε δὲ σίτῳ

φάρμακα λύγρα.   *Odyssey*, **x. 235.**

And for Odysseus himself no restraint is even necessary. From Hermes he receives the antidote, φάρμακον ἐσθλόν, by the help of which he may at once indulge his appetite and defy the arts of Kirkê.

Note [141], *page* 222.

The last paragraph of this tale is the only one of which the narrative in the Odyssey does not contain the substance. It may perhaps be held to give the story a moral aim which we have seen that the poet did not intend directly to convey. But the incident does not violate the general character of the tale; and there can, of course, be no reason why from it we may not draw the warning to avoid temptation not less than to resist it, if only we are careful not to think that, to the poet, the Seirens were the embodiment of sin, and the people of Odysseus the sons of men journeying through a world of temptation. The fact that Odysseus resolves to hear everything himself, while his companions are rendered proof against their song, sufficiently overthrows any such supposition.

Note [142], *page* 222.

The Ocean of Homer is not a sea, but a river, to which the poet gives the epithet applied to inland streams. With its deep yet gentle current it surrounds the earth, while it feeds the great seas which communicate with its mouths in the far East. No storms trouble the smooth flow of its waters, no tide raises or depresses its level; and the names by which the poet expresses its unbroken calm stand out in marked contrast with the words of evil omen which speak of the dangers of the sea (Thalassa). For the Homeric geography see Gladstone's 'Homer and the Homeric Age,' voL iii. section 3.

Note [143], *page* 223.

The passage of the Argo broke the spell, and the Symplêgades thenceforth remained firmly fixed in the sea.

Note [144], page 224.

In the legend of the Pythian Apollo, these cattle have their local habitation near the Lakonian **Helos**. Their pastures had once been in the blue fields of heaven.

Note [145], page 226.

Homer, Odyss. xii. 308. Here, as elsewhere, the appetite of hunger and thirst is satiated before, as it would seem, they call to mind the loss of their comrades. Modern sentiment might question the sincerity of a grief which seldom, perhaps never, diminished the natural desire for food and drink. It may, however, be compared with Odysseus' yearning for his home, while yet he at least endures the love **of Kirkê and** Kalypso.

Note [146], page 231.

Though attended by their handmaidens, Kirkê and Kalypso have none whom they call husbands. This difference in their condition **from that** of most of the gods may depend on a further distinction in the mythical ideas respecting them. They live, it would seem, **even** without the society of their kindred gods, unless when some **special cause brings a** messenger from Zeus.

Note [147], page 233.

In the Iliad the Dream has a real personality, with good **and evil** dispositions. The hurtful Dream is sent by Zeus to the tent of Agamemnon (Il. ii. 9, &c.); nor is the Dream apparently less personal, or less capable of discrimination, which visits the couch of Xerxes after he has dismissed the great council of the Persians (Herodotos, vii. 12). Mr. Grote (History of Greece, vol. v. p. 14) has remarked that in this instance Herodotos betrays the weakened conviction of a later age by using the neuter ὄνειρον in place of the masculine ὄνειρος; but the latter is certainly used in the tale of Atys and Adrastos (Herod. i. 34).

Note [148], page 234.

It is not easy to think with Professor Newman (Reply to Mr. M. Arnold on Translating Homer), that this epithet has a reference to **the** Eastern custom **of** tinging the eyes and fingers with henna. The custom may **be** as old as Homer, and may not have been unknown to the poet; but the whole notion of Eôs is so inseparably connected with the idea of morning or evening light, that such an explanation of the epithet becomes at the least superfluous. On such a supposition it is very difficult to understand why the epithet should be limited to Eôs only.

Note [149], *page* 237.

The washing of the clothes is no unimportant incident in the story of Odysseus and Nausikaâ. It is a formal thing in asking leave for which Nausikaâ gives more than one weighty reason ; and the process itself is described with the same minuteness of detail. The whole furnishes not the least pleasing element in the picture, which Mr. Gladstone has drawn out, in colours perhaps too glowing, of the state of society in the Homeric age.

Note [150], *page* 239.

The description of the palace of Alkinoös adheres closely to the Homeric detail, which leaves on the mind an impression not less of elegance than of magnificence. Much caution is needed in inferring from such descriptions the state of the arts in the Homeric age. The poetical picture may be substantially true, when taken in detail : yet the combination may be the result of the poet's sense of beauty, and power of expressing it. We may refer to the remarks of Bishop Thirlwall on the subject, ' History of Greece,' vol. i. ch. vi.

Note [151], *page* 243.

The riches of Odysseus answer to the treasures of Tantalos and Ixion. In Teutonic story they are the treasures which the Niflungs hide away during the winter.

Note [152], *page* 249.

This hound reappears in the legend of Kephalos and Prokris, as well as in that of Tantalos. It is the glistening hound which stands by the side of Artemis, or guards Zeus in the Dictæan cave.

Note [153], *page* 249.

The thought recalls the passage in the epistle to the Hebrews xiii. 2, ' Be not forgetful to entertain strangers, for thereby some have entertained angels unawares.'

Note [154], *page* 252.

Odysseus, like Œdipus, retains the mark left by an early struggle. The story is one of the many forms of the battle which the newly born sun has to fight with the powers of darkness. These appear sometimes as serpents which try to throttle Herakles; sometimes as the boar which seeks to rend Odysseus; sometimes, as with Œdipus, it is a mark left by the bonds in which he was swathed when, like Telephos or Paris, he was exposed on the hill-side. The boar's tusk reappears in the myth of Adonis, to whom the encounter proves fatal, because in this tale it represents the dark power at eventide, not in the morning, and thus answers to the thorn which pierces the beautiful maiden of old Teutonic legend, or which causes the death of Isfendiyar in the Persian epic. (Max Müller, Comparative Mythology, Chips from a German Workshop, ii. 108.)

Note [155], page 253.

In the same way even Patroklos cannot wield the spear of Achilleus, and Hermes cannot have all the wisdom of Phœbus, nor can any save Œdipus read the dark sayings of the Sphinx.

Note [156], page 263.
Introduction, p. xxvii.

Note [157], page 267.

The victory of Œdipus over the Sphinx is but the slaying of the serpent Fafnir or the Pythian dragon, by one who to the strength and beauty of Sigurd or Phœbus adds the wisdom of Promêtheus and Medeia. There can be no doubt that the riddle of the feet is a late insertion. It is one of the enigmas in which a rude people take delight; and a different riddle might be introduced in all the versions of the tale. It mattered not what the dark saying might be, as long as it was a dark saying, like the inarticulate growl of the thunder.

Note [158], page 268.

As long as this incident retained any part of the meaning still seen in the myth which tells us how Iolê at the last came back to Herakles, here the tale of Œdipus doubtless ended. When translated into the ordinary relations of life, the unwitting marriage of a son with his mother might well give rise to such a tragedy as that which Sophokles has immortalised.

Note [159], page 269.
See note 170.

Note [160], *page* 271.

See note 110.

Note [161], *page* 273.

So ends the tale of the long toil and sorrows of Œdipus. The last scene exhibits a manifest return to the spirit of the solar myth. His beauty is utterly marred, and his disguise is as complete as that of Odysseus when he first trod the soil of Ithaka after his return from Troy. Still there is about him more than human power. He must not die the common death of all men, for no disease or corruption can touch the body of the brilliant sun; and so the poet says, with instinctive truthfulness, that his departure forms no matter for weeping—

οὐ στενακτὸς οὐδὲ σὺν νόσοις
ἀλγεινὸς ἐξεπέμπετ', ἀλλ' εἴ τις βροτῶν
θαυμαστός.   Soph. *Œd. Col.* 1667.

And not less truly does he associate the very sorrows of Œdipus with the long struggle of the sun against the clouds who are arrayed against him. It is a life-long toil, and his trials come—

αἱ μὲν ἀπ' ἀελίου δυσμᾶν,
αἱ δ' ἀνατέλλοντος,
αἱ δ' ἀνὰ μέσσαν ἀκτῖν',
αἱ δὲ νυχιᾶν ἀπὸ ῥιπᾶν.   *Œd. Tyr.* 1248.

Note [162], *page* 275.

A counterpart to this act is found in the Roman tales of the self-devotion of Curtius and the Decii.

Note [163], *page* 276.

Paus. ix. 8, 2. The same tokens were alleged as proof of the burial-place of many a mediæval saint. See also Grote, History of Greece, vol. i. p. 374.

Note [164], *page* 277.

The reason which Antigonê gives as determining her conduct is eminently characteristic. If her husband die, she may marry again; if she lose one child, she may have another; but when her parents are dead she cannot hope for more brothers. Herodotos represents the wife of Intaphernes as choosing to save her brother and abandon her husband and children to death (iii. 119). Now, that the tone of thought **in both** these stories is precisely the **same,** all must admit ; but Mr. Grote apparently takes this coincidence as conclusively proving that Sophokles was the companion of Herodotos. He refuses to determine ' which **of** the two obtained the thought **from** the other,' but thinks that **'the** comparison of Herodot. iii. **119** with Soph. **Antig.** 905, proves a community of thought . . . hardly explicable **in** any other way' (History of Greece, vol. viii. p. 443). But this only starts a fresh difficulty, for it implies that either Herodotos **or** Sophokles originated this thought, which, as Mr. **Grote asserts, 'is** certainly not a little far-fetched,' **and, as we might** safely add, is **to** all appearance decidedly non-Hellenic. It is possible that Herodotos may have brought the Persian legend into closer **harmony** with Western forms of expression ; but we lose ourselves in an inextricable labyrinth when we say that it was borrowed directly by the one from the other. The bear and the hyæna have no tails. The Norseman and the negro not only say that they lost them long ago, but they account for the fact in the same way—"that both owe their loss to the superior cunning of another animal" (Dasent, Tales from the Norse, Introd. li.) The cases **are** almost parallel. In each case we have fragments of primeval thought which have floated at random down the stream **of time.**

Note [165], *page* 278. 6
Soph. Antig. 1000.

Note [166], *page* 281. 79

The rising of land from alluvial deposit at the mouth of the Acheloôs was a fact of sufficient importance to demand and receive its own local legend. Thucydides was somewhat prone to believe in epônymi—that is, he had no objection to say that Italy was named after Italos, king of the Sikels ; but when he has to speak of mythical heroes, he generally lays the burden of responsibility on popular tradition : λέγεται δε καὶ ᾽Αλκμαίωνι, κ. τ. λ. (ii. 102), or else he reduces the tale to his own standard of credibility. See Grote, Hist. of Greece, i. 547.

Note [167], *page* 282. ○

The sons of the seven chieftains who had attacked Thebes in the former **war,** Appollod. iii. 72 ; Grote, Hist. of Greece, vol. i. p. 378.

Note [168], *page* 285. 3

It would seem that the Asiatic Greeks scarcely regarded their subjection by Crœsus as a conquest. The real oppression which followed the victories of Cyrus called forth a vehement but unsuccessful resistance.

Note [169], *page* 286. 4

Thucydides (ii. 34) mentions this as a rare honour granted for their unmatched valour to those who fell at Marathon.

Note [170], *page* 288. 6

In the Homeric age, murder or homicide, although furnishing a legitimate cause for revenge to the kinsfolk of the slain or murdered man, was in no other respect an offence against society, and involved no necessity for a religious expiation. At least, nothing of the kind is mentioned in the Iliad or Odyssey; and Mr. Grote (History of Greece, vol. i. p. 34), from the statement of Herodotos that the ceremonial of expiation was the same among the Greeks and Lydians, infers that the former borrowed it from the latter. It seems as easy to account for the change by the gradual expansion of thought and feeling on the subject. As long as murder was a matter for pecuniary compensation, there was nothing like a public prosecution for the crime; but the institution of the latter would seem to involve a notion of religious impurity, as well as the idea of an offence against society.

Note [171], *page* 291.

The many offices and attributes here assigned to Zeus seem all to unite in one person. It may be said that in the language of the mythical ages there was more than one Zeus. The Zeus who reckons up the number of his earthly loves is certainly not the Being of strict truth and justice to whom Achilleus instinctively addresses his prayer. But this distinction scarcely applies to the time of Herodotos.

Note [172], *page* 292. 0

As in the legend of the Vengeance of Apollo (p. 118), the actors in this tale are mortal men; but it illustrates, more forcibly perhaps than any other, the belief of the Greeks in the ordering of human affairs by the gods. In fact, their whole religious philosophy may be said to be embodied in the beautiful story of the life of Crœsus. It brings out prominently the change which has exalted the Moirai or Fates into powers which neither Zeus nor Apollo are able to withstand. It exhibits, not less vividly than the Book of Job (ch. xiv. &c.), the changes and chances of all mortal life ; the jealousy of the gods against excessive riches and excessive happiness ; the retribution which visits the sins of the fathers upon the children, **and which** may close in darkness and woe the most brilliant and prosperous career. It shows also the old belief of the conditions essential to happiness, **the** extent **to** which material good fortune **and natural** advantages **were** held requisite to constitute a happy **life. The conviction** must have been both **wide and deep, as** the philosophy even of a later day sufficiently attests ; but the very completeness in which it exhibits this scheme of belief removes the tale from the province of history to that of legend or fiction. 'The more valuable,' says Mr. Grote (History of Greece, vol. iii. p. 207), 'this narrative appears in its illustrative character, the less can we presume to treat it as a history.' Nay, even with regard to the whole life of Crœsus, Mr. Grote thinks that ' the religious element must be viewed as giving the form—the historical element as giving the **matter only,** and not the whole matter, of the story,' and that 'these **two** elements will be found conjoined, more **or** less, throughout **most** of the history of Herodotos ' (vol. iv. p. 266). It is curious to remark how Aristotle attempts to meet the difficulties involved **in** the Herodotean belief, and how far he still remains under the influence of the old philosophy. The definition of happiness, which precedes his analysis of human virtue, will, and action, cannot **dis**pense with a certain amount of material prosperity (*ἱκανῶς κεχορηγημένον τοῖς ἐκτὸς ἀγαθοῖς*), and that not for a part, but during the whole of life (*οὐ τὸν τύχοντα χρόνον ἀλλὰ τέλειον βίον.*—Eth. Nic. i. 10, 15). Thus the great ethical teacher, scarcely less than the historian and poet (Sophokles, Œd. Tyr. 1528), has to reserve his judgment in the case of each man until his part has been played out on the stage of life.

Note [172], *page* 292. ⊙

This tale simply brings together some incidents which are necessarily separated in the history of Herodotos (v. 101–105, vi. 113–120, viii. 32–39). The expedition of the Persians to Delphi is involved in great obscurity (see General History of Greece, p. 195) ; but the legend brings out in wonderful clearness the mingled action of gods, heroes, and men.

It may **be as** well to mention that the name Javan was that by

which the Greeks were commonly known to the Persians, because
it has been objected that in the tale 'Darius talks of the sons of
Javan, as if he had been acquainted with Genesis.' The words of
the Scholiast were scarcely needed to tell us that the nations of the
East did not speak of the Greeks by their Hellenic name.

Πάντας τοὺς Ἕλληνας Ἰάονας οἱ βάρβαροι ἐκάλουν.

Æschylus puts into the mouth of Atossa a familiar name when he
makes her say of her son—

Ἰαόνων γῆν οἴχεται.

This recognition of the Ionian, to the exclusion of other portions
of the Hellenic race, is in itself, as Niebuhr has noticed, a remarkable circumstance, which points apparently to important historical
facts. In his judgment it proves that the Ionians must have inhabited
the countries bordering the eastern shores of the Egean in very
ancient times, 'which cannot be well reconciled with the ordinary
notions of the Ionian settlements in Asia Minor.' Lectures on
Ancient History, vol. i. p. 226.

Note [174], *page* 298. 6

Although the several tyrannies of Greece arose in very different
ways, and were upheld by very different means, yet they all had one
feature in common, the suppression, namely, of a free constitution,
and the usurpation of a power to which there was no title of hereditary descent. This to the Greek furnished the justification for his
implacable hatred of them, and for the employment of any means
whatsoever for their forcible suppression. The hereditary βασιλεύς,
whether king or chieftain, met with respect if not reverence; and
even the abuse of his power was scarcely a sufficient plea for his
deposition. But for the tyrant there was no road to the affection of
those who ought to have been his fellow-citizens; and therefore there
could be for him no sense of safety. He might rule with the greatest
gentleness, his care might raise his people to a high degree of
material prosperity; but not the most righteous use of an unlawfully
gotten power could plead on behalf of a man who had trampled on
the laws and freedom of his country.

Note [175], *page* 301. 299

Herodotos specially notes the incredulity of Periandros:
Περίανδρον δὲ ὑπὸ ἀπιστίης Ἀρίονα μὲν ἐν φυλακῇ ἔχειν οὐδαμῇ
μετιέντα, ἀνακῶς δὲ ἔχειν τῶν πορθμέων (i. 24).

The incipient rationalism, combined with a strong faith, of Herodotos himself, is well brought out by Mr. Grote, History of Greece, vol. i. p. 527, &c.

The legend of Herodotos makes the dolphin land Arion at Tainaron, not Corinth. The variation may be pardoned as giving the tale more interest for children. Herodotos speaks of the statue as existing in his own day. The statue localised the legend.

Note 176, page 303.

The question of the date of this poem has been examined by Colonel Mure (Crit. Hist. Gr. Lit. vol. ii. p. 360). He regards the poem itself as 'conceived in a very happy spirit of mixed Homeric and Aristophanic satire against the absurdities of the popular religion.' Yet it is, after all, simply the inevitable extension of a principle which is seen at work in the Iliad and the Odyssey. In those poems, it is true, some of the gods and heroes are saved from the indignity of sarcasm ; and the reasons why they should be so preserved are plain. But the transition to the temper of actual satire becomes natural, when we look to the singular passage in which Hêrê, Poseidon, and Athênê are represented as absurdly foiled by a mere giant in their attempt to bind the father of gods and men (Il. i. 400). It may well be doubted whether even the lay of Demodokos would furnish a more powerful stimulus to the sarcasm of a later age than this passage which Mr. Gladstone has unaccountably ignored in his description of the attributes and character of the spotless Athênê.

Professor Max Müller quotes (Hist. of Sanskrit Literature, p. 494) a hymn in the 7th Mandala, which, under form of a panegyric of the frogs, 'is clearly a satire on the priests.' 'It is curious to observe,' he adds, 'that the same animal should have been chosen by the Vedic satirist to represent the priests which by the earliest satirist of Greece was selected as the representative of the Homeric heroes.'

Note 177, page 304.

It seems almost profane to point out the sarcasm which attacks the words of Hektor in what is perhaps the most beautiful passage of the Iliad—

μάθον ἔμμεναι ἐσθλὸς
αἰεὶ καὶ πρώτοισι μετὰ Τρώεσσι μάχεσθαι.

Note [178], *page* 307.

A privilege which, before the final struggle between Achilleus and his enemies, Zeus reserves to himself, that he may gladden his heart with the sight of the battle (Il. xix. 23).

Note [179], *page* 308.

A reference to the mission of all the gods, **by Zeus, to take** part in the final conflict before Ilion.

Note [180], *page* 308.

The names of the frog and mouse warriors are scarcely more transparent than those of many heroes and minor characters in the **Iliad** and Odyssey. Eurykleia and Melantho tell their tale as clearly as Psicharpax and Troxartes ; but these names of the latter poem are, in Colonel Mure's words, 'the more interesting to the modern reader from the light they throw on many petty details of social life in the age from which the poem has been transmitted' (Crit. Hist. Gr. Lit. vol. ii. p. 359).

PRINTED BY BALLANTYNE, HANSON AND CO
EDINBURGH AND LONDON